Gender and Diversity Representation in Mass Media

Gülşah Sarı
Bolu Abant Izzet Baysal University, Turkey

A volume in the Advances in Media, Entertainment, and the Arts (AMEA) Book Series

Published in the United States of America by
IGI Global
Information Science Reference (an imprint of IGI Global)
701 E. Chocolate Avenue
Hershey PA, USA 17033
Tel: 717-533-8845
Fax: 717-533-8661
E-mail: cust@igi-global.com
Web site: http://www.igi-global.com

Copyright © 2020 by IGI Global. All rights reserved. No part of this publication may be reproduced, stored or distributed in any form or by any means, electronic or mechanical, including photocopying, without written permission from the publisher.
Product or company names used in this set are for identification purposes only. Inclusion of the names of the products or companies does not indicate a claim of ownership by IGI Global of the trademark or registered trademark.

Library of Congress Cataloging-in-Publication Data

Names: Sari, Gulsah, 1984- editor.
Title: Gender and diversity representation in mass media / Gulsah Sari, editor.
Description: Hershey : Information Science Reference, [2020] | Summary: ""This book examines social gender representations in the content of mass media in various cultures"--Provided by publisher"-- Provided by publisher.
Identifiers: LCCN 2019016829 | ISBN 9781799801283 (hardcover) | ISBN 9781799801290 (paperback) | ISBN 9781799801306 (ebook)
Subjects: LCSH: Gender identity in mass media. | Mass media and minorities. | Mass media and ethnic relations. | Mass media and race relations.
Classification: LCC P96.G44 G45 2020 | DDC 302.23081--dc23
LC record available at https://lccn.loc.gov/2019016829

This book is published in the IGI Global book series Advances in Media, Entertainment, and the Arts (AMEA) (ISSN: 2475-6814; eISSN: 2475-6830)

British Cataloguing in Publication Data
A Cataloguing in Publication record for this book is available from the British Library.

All work contributed to this book is new, previously-unpublished material.
The views expressed in this book are those of the authors, but not necessarily of the publisher.

For electronic access to this publication, please contact: eresources@igi-global.com.

Advances in Media, Entertainment, and the Arts (AMEA) Book Series

Giuseppe Amoruso
Politecnico di Milano, Italy

ISSN:2475-6814
EISSN:2475-6830

MISSION

Throughout time, technical and artistic cultures have integrated creative expression and innovation into industrial and craft processes. Art, entertainment and the media have provided means for societal self-expression and for economic and technical growth through creative processes.

The **Advances in Media, Entertainment, and the Arts (AMEA)** book series aims to explore current academic research in the field of artistic and design methodologies, applied arts, music, film, television, and news industries, as well as popular culture. Encompassing titles which focus on the latest research surrounding different design areas, services and strategies for communication and social innovation, cultural heritage, digital and print media, journalism, data visualization, gaming, design representation, television and film, as well as both the fine applied and performing arts, the AMEA book series is ideally suited for researchers, students, cultural theorists, and media professionals.

COVERAGE

- Applied Arts
- Arts & Design
- Gaming
- Design Tools
- Traditional Arts
- Blogging & Journalism
- New Media Art
- Print Media
- Computer aided design and 3D Modelling
- Digital Heritage

IGI Global is currently accepting manuscripts for publication within this series. To submit a proposal for a volume in this series, please contact our Acquisition Editors at Acquisitions@igi-global.com or visit: http://www.igi-global.com/publish/.

The Advances in Media, Entertainment, and the Arts (AMEA) Book Series (ISSN 2475-6814) is published by IGI Global, 701 E. Chocolate Avenue, Hershey, PA 17033-1240, USA, www.igi-global.com. This series is composed of titles available for purchase individually; each title is edited to be contextually exclusive from any other title within the series. For pricing and ordering information please visit http://www.igi-global.com/book-series/advances-media-entertainment-arts/102257. Postmaster: Send all address changes to above address. Copyright © 2020 IGI Global. All rights, including translation in other languages reserved by the publisher. No part of this series may be reproduced or used in any form or by any means – graphics, electronic, or mechanical, including photocopying, recording, taping, or information and retrieval systems – without written permission from the publisher, except for non commercial, educational use, including classroom teaching purposes. The views expressed in this series are those of the authors, but not necessarily of IGI Global.

Titles in this Series

For a list of additional titles in this series, please visit:
[go here and find specific BS URL: http://www.igi-global.com/book-series/]

Handbook of Research on Consumption, Media, and Popular Culture in the Global Age
Ozlen Ozgen (Atilim University, Turkey)
Information Science Reference • copyright 2019 • 454pp • H/C (ISBN: 9781522584919)
• US $295.00 (our price)

Understanding Rivalry and Its Influence on Sports Fans
Cody T. Havard (The University of Memphis, USA)
Information Science Reference • copyright 2019 • 307pp • H/C (ISBN: 9781522581253)
• US $175.00 (our price)

Handbook of Research on Transmedia Storytelling and Narrative Strategies
Recep Yılmaz (Ondokuz Mayıs University, Turkey) M. Nur Erdem (Ondokuz Mayıs University, Turkey) and Filiz Resuloğlu (Kocaeli University, Turkey)
Information Science Reference • copyright 2019 • 599pp • H/C (ISBN: 9781522553571)
• US $245.00 (our price)

Enhancing Art, Culture, and Design With Technological Integration
Mehdi Khosrow-Pour, D.B.A. (Information Resources Management Association, USA)
Information Science Reference • copyright 2018 • 301pp • H/C (ISBN: 9781522550235)
• US $185.00 (our price)

Handbook of Research on Form and Morphogenesis in Modern Architectural Contexts
Domenico D'Uva (Politecnico di Milano, Italy)
Information Science Reference • copyright 2018 • 493pp • H/C (ISBN: 9781522539933)
• US $265.00 (our price)

Promoting Global Competencies Through Media Literacy
Melda N. Yildiz (New York Institute of Technology, USA) Steven S. Funk (Montana State University – Billings, USA) and Belinha S. De Abreu (National Telemedia Council, USA)
Information Science Reference • copyright 2018 • 300pp • H/C (ISBN: 9781522530824)
• US $195.00 (our price)

For an entire list of titles in this series, please visit:
[go here and find specific BS URL: http://www.igi-global.com/book-series/]

701 East Chocolate Avenue, Hershey, PA 17033, USA
Tel: 717-533-8845 x100 • Fax: 717-533-8661
E-Mail: cust@igi-global.com • www.igi-global.com

Editorial Advisory Board

Ebru Gülbuğ Erol, *Istanbul University, Turkey*
Birgül Koçak Oksev, *Bartın University, Turkey*
Gizem Parlayandemir, *Istanbul University, Turkey*
Alev Fatoş Parsa, *Ege University, Turkey*

Table of Contents

Foreword xvii

Preface xviii

Acknowledgment xxi

Section 1
Gender and Diversity Representation in Media Studies

Chapter 1
Overview of Gender With Examples From Turkish Media 1
    Gülşah Sarı, Bolu Abant Izzet Baysal University, Turkey

Chapter 2
Social Gender Representation in the Context of the Representation Problem
in the Media 17
    Özge Gürsoy Atar, Beykent University, Turkey

Chapter 3
The Politico-Poetic Representation of Turkish Women in *Türk Kadını*
Magazine (1966–1974) 35
    Fatma Fulya Tepe, Istanbul Aydın University, Turkey

Chapter 4
Inter-Family Communication Languages via the Discourse in Women's Roles
in Turkish TV Series 59
    Şebnem Gürsoy Ulusoy, Istanbul Gelişim University, Turkey

Chapter 5
A Feminist Reading of an Oriental Tale: "Crystal Manor and Diamond
Ship" 77
    Derya Çetin, Bolu Abant Izzet Baysal University, Turkey
    Mevlüde Deveci, Fırat University, Turkey

Chapter 6
Gender Representations in Cartoons: *Niloya* and *Biz Ikimiz* 90
    Arzu Karasaç Gezen, Bolu Abant Izzet Baysal University, Turkey

Chapter 7
A Rebellion Against the Metallization of the Female Body: "Dove Beyond Figures" 121
    Rengim Sine Nazlı, Bolu Abant Izzet Baysal University, Turkey

Chapter 8
Gender Representation in SMS Jokes 140
    Yasmeen Sultana, Sindh Madressatul Islam University, Pakistan
    Naima Saeed, University of Karachi, Pakistan
    Tansif Ur Rehman, University of Karachi, Pakistan

Section 2
Gender and Diversity Representation in Film Studies

Chapter 9
Man, Masculinity, and Violence in Turkish Cinema After 2000: The Case of Kenan Imirzalioglu 157
    Gökhan Gültekin, Sivas Cumhuriyet University, Turkey

Chapter 10
Rehabilitating Hegemonic Masculinity With the Bodies of Aging Action Heroes 178
    Kelvin Ke, Shelton College International, Singapore

Chapter 11
Gender Construction in Transmedial Narration: Star Wars Transmedia and Fandom 197
    Işıl Tombul, Independent Researcher, Turkey

Chapter 12
Overview of the Gay Characters in the New Cinema of Turkey 218
    Özgür İpek, Sivas Cumhuriyet University, Turkey

Chapter 13
Thinking About the Concept of Social Gender With a Film: The Analysis of the Film *Tersine Dünya* With Judith Butler's Concept of Subject – Discussing the Fact of Social Gender That Is Presented in the Narrative of the Film 228
    Berceste Gülçin Özdemir, İstanbul University, Turkey

Chapter 14
Presentation of Female Character Subjectification in Iranian Cinema..............248
    Dilek Ulusal, Kırıkkale University, Turkey

Chapter 15
Gender in the Honky Tonk as a Space of Representation: The Film *Dutturu Dunya*......260
    Meltem Yılmaz Bilecen, Sivas Cumhuriyet University, Turkey

Chapter 16
Gender Is Political: Evaluation of Gender in *Susuz Yaz* (*Dry Summer*) and *Yilanlarin Öcü* (*Revenge of the Snakes*) Films......275
    Pelin Erdal Aytekin, Aydın Adnan Menderes University, Turkey

Chapter 17
A Feminist Film: *Caramel* 295
    İkbal Bozkurt Avcı, Fırat Universtiy, Turkey
    Derya Çetin, Bolu Abant Izzet Baysal University, Turkey

Compilation of References 308

About the Contributors 332

Index 336

Detailed Table of Contents

Foreword xvii

Preface xviii

Acknowledgment xxi

Section 1
Gender and Diversity Representation in Media Studies

Chapter 1
Overview of Gender With Examples From Turkish Media 1
    Gülşah Sarı, Bolu Abant Izzet Baysal University, Turkey

In this study, the representation of gender in the media was examined. Examples of the media representations in the media has been presented as an introduction to the book. Gender development takes place in news, series, advertisements and the prevailing gender in cinema. After the theory part which includes academic studies and differences from sex. It was supported by examples from the media. In the study, women, men and homosexual representations in the Turkish media have been examined. At the end of the study, women have been depicted in the media in a disadvantaged and secondary position. Especially the news that the word "woman" in the news is reinforcing the disadvantageous position of women. In series and advertisements, women are either a carrier of an object or traditional role in the face of a man's perspective. In addition, men reinforce their dominant position in the society as well, while homosexuals are also disadvantaged like other women and continue their positions in the media.

Chapter 2
Social Gender Representation in the Context of the Representation Problem in the Media 17
    Özge Gürsoy Atar, Beykent University, Turkey

Women's television programs appear as an indispensable broadcasting component of the morning television broadcasting series. Three women's programs, which were broadcasted in 2018, were analyzed in the study of how women participate in these television programs and the presentation of gender roles. First, the issue of social representation in the context of the problem of representation in the media was discussed. Later on, feminism and women's programs in the media were examined and the situation in the media was determined. In the application part of the study, numerical data were evaluated, and discourse analysis was conducted within the framework of the women's programs examined.

Chapter 3
The Politico-Poetic Representation of Turkish Women in *Türk Kadını* Magazine (1966–1974) 35
    Fatma Fulya Tepe, Istanbul Aydın University, Turkey

This chapter aims to explore the ways women are represented in the context of 20th century Turkey by analyzing four poems, namely "Türk Kadını" (Turkish Woman), "Anadolu Kadını" (Anatolian Woman), "Kadın–Ana" (Woman-Mother), and "Ayşe," published in the *Türk Kadını* magazine in the 1960s. Purposive sampling was used in the selection of the poems, which were later interpreted with the strategies of descriptive content analysis. In these poems, the Turkish woman is being represented and celebrated in at least the following four ways: (1) by being celebrated for combining heroism, goodness, and naturalness; (2) by having her struggle with primitive conditions of life celebrated as yet another form of heroism; (3) by being celebrated as a creative mother of the nation, charged with finding solutions to the problems of the country; (4) by being celebrated as a hardworking daughter of the nation to whom the country owes recognition and support.

Chapter 4
Inter-Family Communication Languages via the Discourse in Women's Roles in Turkish TV Series 59
    Şebnem Gürsoy Ulusoy, Istanbul Gelişim University, Turkey

Modernization and urbanization have changed many phenomena. One of these changes is the representation of mother and women. It is seen that the modernization and urbanization and motherhood concept of women have changed. Maternity representations have recently changed in Turkish series. Within the scope of the study, the language of the woman in the family as a mother and her place in the family were examined. It is also an important issue whether urban culture changes the representations of motherhood. In this sense, social media, urbanization, modernization, and the changes in women's representations are all interrelated.

Chapter 5
A Feminist Reading of an Oriental Tale: "Crystal Manor and Diamond Ship" 77
    Derya Çetin, Bolu Abant Izzet Baysal University, Turkey
    Mevlüde Deveci, Fırat University, Turkey

Tales, which have an important place in the process of socialization, contain various ideological constructions like other narratives. This study aims to analyses an important tale of Turkey's tale corpus named "Crystal Manor and Diamond Ship" by the terms of feminist critics. This tale is considered among the tales of Anatolian field and is similar to some western tales such as Rapunzel. However, in terms of subject positions, which are one of the focal points of feminist criticism, the main female character, unlike most fairy tales, seems to be planning and implementing the actions that advance the plot, rather than waiting for a man to rescue her.

Chapter 6
Gender Representations in Cartoons: *Niloya* and *Biz Ikimiz* 90
    Arzu Karasaç Gezen, Bolu Abant Izzet Baysal University, Turkey

The concept of gender refers to the roles, learned behaviors and expectations determined by the society for women and men, apart from the biological differences between women and men. These expectations differ from society to society and even within different sections of the same society; based on such distinctions as rural/urban, class and ethnicity, etc., they may vary depending on the distinctions. It is important how these roles are offered in terms of shaping the children's views on gender roles at very young ages. The aim of this study is to analyze the cartoons within the frame of rural and urban life in terms of gender representations. In this study, 30 episodes of cartoons were analyzed by using the content analysis technique. The study strives to reveal how male and female characters are represented within the context of gender. The findings have shown that despite the existence of egalitarian representations in terms of gender, the contents emphasizing inequality are more dominant.

Chapter 7
A Rebellion Against the Metallization of the Female Body: "Dove Beyond Figures" 121
    Rengim Sine Nazlı, Bolu Abant Izzet Baysal University, Turkey

Media is used as an important tool in the uniformization of the female body metallized on the axis of consumption culture. Ads are of special importance in order for these bodies, which are standardized by media bodies, to reach every segment of the society. The beauty measures of each period are introduced with these films as the main determinant for women to be happy. Moreover, these measures, which are a means of domination, can cause illnesses in which women sometimes lose their lives. In such an environment, Unilever's Dove, a personal care brand, launched a campaign called mark *Beyond Figures*. It continued to act with this approach in advertising films. In this study, it is aimed to determine how women analyze advertising films beyond the figures. The interviews that will be evaluated in the context of coding, criterion will be examined by reception analysis.

Chapter 8
Gender Representation in SMS Jokes 140
    Yasmeen Sultana, Sindh Madressatul Islam University, Pakistan
    Naima Saeed, University of Karachi, Pakistan
    Tansif Ur Rehman, University of Karachi, Pakistan

This research aims to investigate how language is used in a new mode of communication such as SMS jokes portraying different roles of human gender. A distinct form of ideology is constructed in SMS jokes by using certain expressions which criticize the roles of both the genders in a humorous way which helps in reinforcing the already existing stereotypes about them. The study adopted the qualitative research method and purposive sampling technique was used for the selection of SMS jokes. Through this sampling technique, 30 different gender-biased SMS jokes were selected which were received on the cell phone numbers of researchers. It is believed that only the female gender becomes the target of ridiculous humor, but this study proves that the attitudes associated with both male and female are humiliating. The findings of research reveal that jokes play a pivotal role in constructing the overall image of both the genders. The language which is used in portrayal of both male and female gender is highly subjective, derogatory, abusive, and prejudiced.

Section 2
Gender and Diversity Representation in Film Studies

Chapter 9
Man, Masculinity, and Violence in Turkish Cinema After 2000: The Case of
Kenan Imirzalioglu 157
    Gökhan Gültekin, Sivas Cumhuriyet University, Turkey

The purpose of this study is to trace the relationship between male, masculinity, and violence in Turkish films after 2000. For this purpose, action, adventure, political, and drama films featuring Kenan İmirzalıoğlu, the pioneering anti-hero of male violence in popular Turkish films between 2000-2010 were focused. Thus, the sample of the study was composed of *Deli Yürek: Bumerang Cehennemi* (2001),

Yazı Tura (2004), *Kabadayı* (2007), and *Ejder Kapanı* (2010) films. In all of these films Yusuf, Cevher, Devran, and Celal acted by İmirzalıoğlu use intense violence in the name of honor, power, and virility. Starting from such observation, the study has endeavored to make an interpretation on appearance of the relationship among man, masculinity, and violence based on the type, orientation, perspective and purpose of violence in the films, included the sample since the 2000s. In pursuit of such meaning first, it will be useful to mention the relationship among violence, man, and masculinity.

Chapter 10
Rehabilitating Hegemonic Masculinity With the Bodies of Aging Action Heroes 178
Kelvin Ke, Shelton College International, Singapore

The aging action hero has become an important figure in post-millennial action cinema. Its significance can be seen in how aging heroes can be seen in such franchises like *The Expendables* (2009 – 2013), *Taken* (2008 – 2014), *The Fast and the Furious* (2001 – 2017), *Mission Impossible* (1995 – 2018), and *James Bond* (2006 – 2015). In the following chapter, it is argued that the aging action hero and the aging male body is significant because they provide an opportunity to rehabilitate the tropes of hegemonic masculinity and the indestructible male body by emphasizing the benefits of the aging male body and where male toxicity is replaced by wisdom and maturity; egocentricity is replaced by allocentrism. As a result, the presence of the aging hero shows the dynamism of action cinema in offering different and alternative visions of heroism and heroes.

Chapter 11
Gender Construction in Transmedial Narration: Star Wars Transmedia and Fandom 197
Işıl Tombul, Independent Researcher, Turkey

Transmedia is a narrative that allows a message to meet with the user in different media. With media convergence, a story has become available in different media, and this has also led to the expansion of the market. *Star Wars* has an important transmedia and a wide fandom. Because the film is on the concept of power, the construction of power shows itself in this area with masculine symbolism. In the post-Disney period, the female characters are prominent, but the films protect the masculine narrative. The aim of this study is to examine the construction of gender in the transmedial narrative in *Star Wars* films together with the discussions in fandom. For this purpose, gender construction in the transmedial narrative are analyzed by case study.

Chapter 12
Overview of the Gay Characters in the New Cinema of Turkey 218
Özgür İpek, Sivas Cumhuriyet University, Turkey

Similar to the worldwide perceptions, gay characters in Turkish cinema are mostly perceived and used as elements of humor and comedy. They are also used as standards for measuring the masculinity of other male characters in some Turkish movies. And what about Today? What are the differences between the past and now? It is possible to say that Turkish cinema in 2000s involve more visible sexual identities apart from heteronormative understanding. This study will focus on the reflections and portrayals of only gay characters in New Turkish cinema.

Chapter 13
Thinking About the Concept of Social Gender With a Film: The Analysis of the Film *Tersine Dünya* With Judith Butler's Concept of Subject – Discussing the Fact of Social Gender That Is Presented in the Narrative of the Film..........228
Berceste Gülçin Özdemir, İstanbul University, Turkey

The concept of social gender is an interdisciplinary matter of debate and is still questioned today. Making sense of this concept is understood by the ongoing codes in the social order. However, the fact that men are still positioned as dominating women in the contrast of the public sphere/private sphere prevents the making sense of the concept of gender. This study questions the concept of social gender through the female characters and male characters presented in the film *Tersine Dünya* (1993) within the framework of Judith Butler's thoughts regarding the notion of the subject. The thoughts of feminist film theorists also bring the strategies of representation of female characters up for discussion. Butler's thoughts and the discourses of feminist film theorists will enable both making sense of social gender and a more concrete understanding of the concept of the subject. The possibility of deconstruction of patriarchal codes by using classical narrative cinema conventions is also brought up for discussion in the examined film.

Chapter 14
Presentation of Female Character Subjectification in Iranian Cinema..............248
Dilek Ulusal, Kırıkkale University, Turkey

Cinema is a social practice where myths about femininity and masculinity are produced, reproduced, and represented. Within this context, in cinema which produces feminine myths and forms female representations by reproducing them, feminist narratives are incontrovertible. In this study, female characters in political woman theme film *Ten*, directed in 2002 by Abbas Kiarostami who is recognized as one of the most successful directors of Modern Iranian Cinema, are examined in terms of feminist film theory. As a result of the study, it was observed that the director Kiarostami uplifted the identity of women by the narrative of the female characters he placed in the subject position of the film and tried to overthrow the established perception towards the women who were qualified as "the other" in Iranian society, through cinema.

Chapter 15
Gender in the Honky Tonk as a Space of Representation: The Film *Dutturu Dunya* 260
    Meltem Yılmaz Bilecen, Sivas Cumhuriyet University, Turkey

This study was prepared to investigate the gender roles in honky tonk organization, which has an important place in the bureaucratic structure of Ankara and can be considered as the place of representation against the representations of space, specifically in the film *Dutturu Dunya*. The film *Dutturu Dunya* was shot at a time when the new realism movement started in Turkish Cinema and found personality with Zeki Ökten. In the film, Ulus, Bakanlıklar mounted for the representation of the space and Hıdırlıktepe which is an extension of the representation space and described as the slum area are used as the main place. In the study, the gender roles are explained based on space fiction and dialogue of the film. It was seen as a result of the analysis that unlike the common opinion, not only the body and labor of woman working in honky tonk but also body and labor and labor exploitation of men were realized. The matter distinguishing male and female workers is that honky tonk is a place where woman goes astray but man somehow earns his living.

Chapter 16
Gender Is Political: Evaluation of Gender in *Susuz Yaz* (*Dry Summer*) and *Yilanlarin Öcü* (*Revenge of the Snakes*) Films 275
    Pelin Erdal Aytekin, Aydın Adnan Menderes University, Turkey

Studies on women identity in the context of gender yields significant results, especially when considering the practice of cinema. Mainstream cinema is an essential area of indicators for handling women's identity. *Susuz Yaz* and *Yılanların Öcü* films are two important films in which Metin Erksan dealt with the concept of property within his filmography. These two films, which address the concept of property through the ownership of land and water, also represented the social existence of women's identity with the rural lifestyle in particular, making the social structure in which women are perceived as property visible. In this context, the study evaluates the image of the woman in cinema on the concepts of body, property and rights. The method approach shaped its roots from the foundations of sociology, communication and cultural theories. The subject was presented by analyzing it within the perspective of interpretive social science. It was concluded that the debate on whose property the land and water are also raised the discussion of the property of women's identity.

Chapter 17
A Feminist Film: *Caramel* 295
İkbal Bozkurt Avcı, Fırat Universtiy, Turkey
Derya Çetin, Bolu Abant Izzet Baysal University, Turkey

Feminist film theory evaluates films by some concepts such as subject positions, narrative closures, and fetishism. This theory suggests that the catharsis of popular films is in the service of the male audience. However, many feminist films centered on women are also made, which are outside the mainstream cinema and reach a considerable amount of viewers. This study aims to evaluate *Caramel* (Nadine Labaki, 2007) by the concepts of feminist film theory. The film expresses a country dominated by taboos through these five women.

Compilation of References 308

About the Contributors 332

Index 336

Foreword

This book, which makes evaluations through different approaches on gender, makes an important contribution towards the maintenance of discussability of the gender concept in Turkey. In depth studies on gender presentation in various media tools confirm the academic success of this book. Considering the political, economic and cultural indicators of the Turkish media that are constantly changing, it is inevitable that the book makes important determinations about the subject. Especially women's programs, which have a high rate of watching in the daytime zones of mainstream channels, have striking results in terms of women's representation in Turkish society. On the other hand, tales, which are effective in conceptualizing the world from the beginning of the socialization process with the ways of thinking and acting contained in the narrative structure, are especially effective on the fiction of girls' lives. In this respect, the chapter on the phenomenon of fairy tales examines the connection between the tale and gender representation in detail. On a journey from television to new media, from cinema to branding, resulting of unisex bodies in unisex production process, while increasing the profit margins of brands, eliminates the visual boundaries between women and men and breaks the known rules and makes room for the existence of the third gender. In this respect, the book has chapters which can be seen as a critical manifest that must be read through the body.

    This book, which consists of 17 chapters with the collaboration of many academicians, is a valuable study on gender that is conducted in the field of communication sciences. This study, which approaches the concept of gender through different countries, different cultures and different media tools, includes highly valuable and useful research on the subject and presents different perspectives that exhibits compromising attitude on gender representation. All the academicians who contributed to the field deserve a medal, notably, Assistant Professor, Gülşah Sarı.

Yasemin Kılınçarslan
Uşak University, Turkey

Preface

When it comes to the representation of gender and diversity in the mass media, which is the title of this book, it is obvious that the gender and diversity concepts should be addressed in the first place. When gender is considered, it can be defined as the structuring of the roles, ideas and expectations of women and men in society differently from biological sex. What we call diversity, on the other hand, refers to differences between people. These are not only differences of gender, but also of age, ethnicity, race, class, sexual orientation. Within this context, the representation of gender and diversity in the mass media is about how the differences between the roles, expectations, beliefs, ethnicity, class, age and sexual orientations of men and women are represented in the media. This book is an attempt to explain both gender roles and the diversity among people through representations in the media. Today, in many universities of the world, the subject of gender and diversity is being taught as a topic, discussed in various conferences and examined by several studies in the literature. This book is intended to be a reference book with both contemporary examples it presents and its chapters addressing various domains of the media.

This book consists of two parts as media studies and film studies. The first part addresses the debates on female body, language, discourse, gender and gender roles via written and visual media tools, while the second part gives place to texts that concentrate on masculinity, crime, homosexuality, gender roles and women's identity. When the issues opened to debate based on these two parts are considered together, the general concept of the book emerges and the theme addressed is evaluated comprehensively.

In the book's first chapter entitled "Overview of Gender With Examples From Turkish Media", the concept of gender in the media is examined through the examples presented from the Turkish media. In this chapter, which is an introductory chapter of the book, representations of genders in the mass media is presented and analyzed through current examples.

Preface

In the second chapter entitled "Social Gender Representation in the Context of the Representation Problem in the Media", the social representation problem is discussed in the context of the representation problem in the media, programs whose target audience is women are examined and the situation in the media is identified.

In the book's third chapter entitled "The Politico-Poetic Representation of Turkish Women in *Türk Kadını* Magazine (1966–1974)", four poems entitled Turkish Woman (Anatolian Woman), Anatolian Woman (Anatolian Woman), Woman-Mother (Woman-Mother) are examined and it is aimed to explore the representation ways of women within the context of 20th century Turkey.

In the fourth chapter entitled "Inter-Family Communication Languages via the Discourse in Women's Roles in Turkish TV Series", the language and place of woman in the family are examined. In this chapter, where women on the axis of modernization and urbanization is addressed, whether urban culture has changed the representation of motherhood is also discussed.

In the book's fifth chapter entitled "A Feminist Reading of an Oriental Tale: 'Crystal Manor and Diamond Ship'", gender representations in the fairy tales, one of the most important tools that subtly incises gender to the subconscious is examined within the scope of feminist criticism.

In the sixth chapter entitled "Gender Representations in Cartoons: *Niloya* and *Biz İkimiz*", the cartoons *Niloya* and *Biz İkimiz* are analyzed as to social gender representations within the framework of urban and rural lives.

In the book's seventh chapter entitled "A Female Rebellion of the Body: Dove Beyond Figures", the homogenization of the woman body as a consequence of various pressures as well as the body's commodification is addressed, and whether what the brands are doing is a rebellion or a marketing strategy is questioned through in-depth interviews.

In the eighth chapter entitled "Gender Representation in SMS Jokes", how SMS jokes, which demonstrate different gender roles of the language, are used in a new form of communication is examined.

In the book's ninth chapter entitled "Man, Masculinity, and Violence in Turkish Cinema After 2000: The Case of Kenan Imirzalioglu", the relationship between the male, masculinity and violence in Turkish movies after 2000 is shown. For this purpose, action, adventure, political and drama films featuring Kenan Imirzaliogu, who is he leading hero of male violence, are emphasized.

In the tenth chapter entitled "Rehabilitating Hegemonic Masculinity With the Bodies of Aging Action Heroes", different and alternative perspectives of the importance of the aging action hero and aging male body, the existence of the aging hero, the dynamism of action cinema, heroism and heroes are presented.

Preface

In the book's eleventh chapter entitled "Gender Construction in Star Wars Transmedia and Fandom", gender construction in the narrative structure of Star Wars films is scrutinized.

In the twelfth chapter entitled "Overview of the Gay Male Characters in New Cinema of Turkey", the ways we come across gay characters in the world cinema and in the Turkish cinema is elaborated, and finally which gay characters were created and shown in what ways in the Turkish cinema of the 2000s is analyzed.

In the thirteenth chapter entitled "Thinking About The Concept of Social Gender With a Film: The Analysis of the Film *Tersine Dünya* With Judith Butler's Concept of Subject – Discussing the Fact of Social Gender That Is Presented in the Narrative of the Film", the concept of gender is questioned via the female characters and male characters presented in the movie *Reverse World* (1993) within the framework of Judith Butler's views on the subject.

In the book's fourteenth chapter entitled "Presentation of Female Character Subjectification in Iranian Cinema", the female characters of the 2002-made political and female-themed film "Ten" directed by Abbas Kiarostami, who is accepted as one of the most successful directors of Modern Iranian Cinema, is examined in terms of the feminist film theory.

In the fifteenth chapter entitled "Gender in the Honky Tonk as a Space of Representation: The Film *Dutturu Dunya*", the gender roles in honky tonks, which have an important place in the bureaucratic structure of Ankara and which can be considered the representation venue against the representations of the venue in the movie *Dutturu Dunya*, are analyzed.

In the sixteenth chapter entitled "Gender is Political: Evaluation of Gender in *Susuz Yaz* (*Dry Summer*) and *Yilanlarin Ocu* (*Revenge of the Snakes*) Films", the woman perception in cinema is evaluated as regards to the concepts of body, property and rights.

Finally, "A Feminist Film: Caramel" which is a 2007-made feminist film directed by Nadine Labaki, is evaluated based on the feminist film theory concepts.

In conclusion, this book is very important in terms of offering detailed interdisciplinary data for professionals, researchers, experts and students interested in gender, and of shedding light on the studies to be conducted in this area.

Acknowledgment

As an editor, I owe a great debt of gratitude to my dear academics who wrote chapters for this book. This book will shed light on researchers, students and academics interested in the field thanks to the contributions of valuable authors. I would also like to express my gratitude to the academics of the editorial advisory board who provided full support in the constitution of the book.

I am grateful to my parents Ayşegül and Ramazan Dümen who supported me throughout my education life and career. I am very grateful to my beloved husband, Ramazan Sarı, who has given countenance to the development of the book and is a source of my motivation.

Finally, I would like to thank the IGI Global publishing house for giving me the chance to publish my second edited book.

Gülşah Sarı
Bolu Abant Izzet Baysal University, Turkey

Section 1
Gender and Diversity Representation in Media Studies

Chapter 1
Overview of Gender With Examples From Turkish Media

Gülşah Sarı
https://orcid.org/0000-0001-6590-6530
Bolu Abant Izzet Baysal University, Turkey

ABSTRACT

In this study, the representation of gender in the media was examined. Examples of the media representations in the media has been presented as an introduction to the book. Gender development takes place in news, series, advertisements and the prevailing gender in cinema. After the theory part which includes academic studies and differences from sex. It was supported by examples from the media. In the study, women, men and homosexual representations in the Turkish media have been examined. At the end of the study, women have been depicted in the media in a disadvantaged and secondary position. Especially the news that the word "woman" in the news is reinforcing the disadvantageous position of women. In series and advertisements, women are either a carrier of an object or traditional role in the face of a man's perspective. In addition, men reinforce their dominant position in the society as well, while homosexuals are also disadvantaged like other women and continue their positions in the media.

INTRODUCTION

Sex and gender concepts seem like simple and understandable depictors of some of the most basic features of humankind. People use these words and accept the structures which they bear on daily basis without making effort (Pryzgoda ve Chrisler, 2000: 553). It puts emphasis on the expected roles from males and females and the description of womanhood and manhood. In a UK study, 137 women and men are asked to write down what they think when they see the word gender. In this study, 43.4% of the participants stated that when they saw this word, they thnk of men and women. 11.7% reported that they thought of both male and female as male and female. When we look at the other participants, 9.6% have reported gender or gender roles; 5,8% have reported equality and women's rights; 5.8% have reported masculinity and femininity; 4.4% have reported as female. (Pryzgoda ve Chrisler, 2000: 559-560). From this study, it can be said that people mostly perceive gender and sex as similar.

This study will examine gender representation in the Turkish media over the gender issue. When examining gender in the media, it will be correct to look at both production and content.

THE CONCEPT OF GENDER

Ann Oakley, who introduced the concept of gender to sociology, defines gender as a socially unequal division between masculinity and femininity. (Marshall, 2005: 98). In contrast to the biologically determined sex, social gender is a cultural issue, which is constructed in different ways by different cultures (Fay, 2001: 86). Sex is often used by sociologists to describe the anatomical and physiological differences that cause the body to be defined as male or female. Gender is related to social and cultural differences between males and females and does not have to be a consequence of the sex of the individual. (Giddens, 2012: 505). The first studies on gender are about womanhood. In fact, Giddens (2012: 509) states that, thinking of the feminists' concerns about women's social incapacity, it is not surprising that initial gender-based research has almost focused on women and femininity.

From the historical point of view of the concept of gender, strong women's movements emerged in the first quarter of the twentieth century in socialist parties in Germany, USA and other countries. These movements, although some arrangements in the field of child care and work done, couldn't survive for a long time. It was seen that these policies were marginalized by the freezing of socialism in the West. The concept of social role was introduced in the 1930s. The concepts of "gender role" female role "and "male role" were frequently used in the 1940s. (Connell, 1998: 55-56). Connell (1998: 57) argues that similar studies by three academicians (Mead, Parsons and Beauvoir) helped to take a contemporary form of gender, in the mid-twentieth century. These three academians' Works have tried to unify gender roles and the analysis of work sharing which has been understood in the scope of gender roles (p. 58).

Günindi Ersöz (2016: 22) points out that gender has a contribution to feminist thought, and it is important to point out that social discrimination among the sexes can be tackled only through cultural change.

Men and women learn their roles in social life in the context of their own cultures. The society engrains in gender roles by the names they give from their infancy, the toys they buy, the design of the rooms and the color of their clothes. For example, the names of predators such as "Sahin" and "Kartal" are given to boys; the names that emphasize the beauty and the kindness of the person in terms of tone and intonation such as "Narin", "Ceylan", and "Meltem" are given to women. (Günindi Ersöz, 2016: 25). Female and male infants learn the sex roles expected from them by their family, school, social environment, work life and through mass media. For example, men are expected to "be the head of family" and "earn money and make a living for the family" ; women are expected to "be mother" and "be a wife who is loyal to her husband".

One of the ways to understand the origin of gender differences is the studies on the socialization of gender, which is the learning of gender roles by means of mediators such as family and media. Such an approach distinguishes between sex and gender -the infant binds first, and then develops the second later. One of the ways to understand the origin of gender differences is the studies on the socialization of gender, which is the learning of gender roles by means of mediators such as family and media. Such an approach distinguishes between sex and gender -the infant binds first, and then develops the second later. Gender differences are not determined biologically, they are produced culturally. According to this view, the reason for gender inequalities is the socialization of men and women according to different roles (Giddens, 2012: 506).

Children's toys, picture books and television programs for children all tend to emphasize the differences between the qualities of women and men. Although the situation is changing, most of the children's books, television programs and film men are generally more prominent than women. While male actors play more effective, adventurous roles, women are described as more inactive, expectant, and engaged in domestic work (Weitzman 1972; Zam- muner 1987; Davies 1991 as cited in Giddens, 2012: 507).

This study will examine gender representation in Turkish media over the gender issue. When examining gender in the media, it will be correct to look at both production and content.

GENDER RANGE IN TURKISH MEDIA SECTOR

Another aspect that needs to be considered when looking at gender representations in the media is how much female employment is in the media. Because women are in the position of producer as much as they are media consumers. As it is known that the ratio of women and men working in the media sector is uneven, the distribution is unequal on the part of women. This unequal distribution in the media sector would be useful to explain, with examples from Turkey.

According to the statistics of Turkish Statistical Institute (TurkStat) 2018 data, when one look at the ratio of the women working in publishing department of newspapers and magazines in Turkey between the years of 2005 and 2017, it can be seen that the number of the men working is 9552 but the number of women is 3390 in 2005. In the same year, the number of male personnel is 10286 and the number of female personnel is 5700. The ratio of male employees in the newspapers is 74% while the rate of women is only 26%. When the ratio of male employees is 65%, the ratio of female employees is 35%. In 2017, when it is looked at the ratio of gender, it can be seen that male employees are 10708 and female employees are 4862. The ratio of male employees is 69% while the ratio of female employees is 31%. From 2005 to 2017, female employment increased by only 5%. According to 2017 data of the journal employees, there are 14407 male employees while the number of female employees is 11178. The ratio of male employees is 57% while the proportion of female employees is 43%. Over the past 12 years, the proportion of female employees in magazines has increased by 8% and approached the number of male employees. Considering the senior management positions of the sector, the proportion of men in the gender distribution is overwhelming. For example, when the number of editors working in the newspaper is 666 in 2005, the number of women is 87. In terms of proportionality, 89% is male and 11% is female. Considering the employment of the same staff in journals, the number of men is 544 and the number of women is 128. On average, 81% is male and 19% is female. Although the rates of editor-in-chief in 2005 are higher in favor of women, the rates of men in the two media sectors are overwhelming. In 2017 data, the number of editors in the newspaper is 588 for men and 122 for women. Proportionally 83% is male and 17% is female. In the last 12 years, editor-in-chief ratios have increased by only 6% in favor of women. In 2017, the number of the male magazine employees is 1124 and the women are 395. On average, 74% male and 26% female. Although the proportion of women has increased by 7% in the last 12 years, the proportion of men is still much higher than that of women (Tuik Gov, n.d.).

As it can be understood from the data of TurkStat, it is a fact that the number of the women working in media or in the position of manager is way fewer than men. According to Ersöz (2016: 74), the fact that women cannot take part in decision-making mechanisms is because they prevent them by putting invisible barriers. Günindi Ersöz states that this situation is a "glass ceiling" syndrome and explains that the woman cannot get the promotion she wanted although she waited for a significant promotion after rising up to a certain point as manager (p. 74).

Gender related theoretical information and gender discrimination in the media after gender discrimination will be examined in the study. In the study, advertisements, films, magazine advertisements, news, television series will be included.

GENDER IN MEDIA

It is a well-known fact that the status of femininity in the media works and the unequal positions of women are reproduced through the media (Binark and Gencel Bek, 2010: 158). Media reinforces gender roles. In movies, TV series, television advertisements, television and newspaper news, the gender roles expected from women and men; and the women's disadvantageous positions are seen. According to Binark and Gencel Bek (2010: 158), women's changes in their lives as a result of their participation in business life are not shown in the media texts.

In this study, individual media contents are given as examples.

Gender in News

There is a dominant male dominance both in written and visual media. When the employment rate and executive positions in the media are in favor of men, the representations in the media are shaped according to these ratios. Women couldn't get rid of their position as object in every kind of media contents. According to Kuruoğlu (2006: 242-243), it is underlined that the issue of women is not taken into consideration in news selections, and that the status quo is promised to men instead of women. Woman is imprisoned in a special area or is represented as mother-wife or represented as a "sexual onject" to make people think of some desires or urges. (p. 243).

Both in television news and printed press the women who are both the subject of the news and who make the news are displayed as disadvantage. First of all, it is necessary to give an example from the news about the women reporters. In a 12.12.2003 dated news of Hurriyet it is seen that a male colleague of a female journalist made news when her underwear was seen while she was taking a photograph. In addition to this the photo of the woman reporter at the time of the incident was also included in the report. Hurriyet's news is as follows:

"The Ambassador of the Republic of Russia, Ambassador Aleksandar Chernyshev received a lot of attention from the participants. Members of the press also competed for the opinion of Chernishev on Iraq and Cyprus. Meanwhile, the news reporter of a private television channel Burcu Gokyuzuoglu, who leaned over to ask for a question to Chernyshev, fell victim to her low-waist trousers. Black-colored G-string lingerie appearing reporter warned by the attendees." (Hürriyet News, n.d.)

In television and newspaper news, women are often exhibited in a disadvantaged position. In another news article of Hürriyet newspaper dated 22.02.2019, there is a traffic accident news. It can be seen that the gender is highlighted because the person having the accident is a woman. The title of the news "woman driver spreaded terror!" it is seen that the word "woman" is used in a negative way both in mass and printed media (The Hürriyet, 2019). For example, it can be seen that women are sometimes the subject of the news with the negative expressions such as "unfortunate woman", "woman driver", "woman murder" and " women's walk". Habertürk 's news dated 05 May 2019 is shown below (figure 1).

In the news of which title is "Bust to a massage salloon; 11 people were taken into custody, 6 of them women", although only 6 women were taken into custody, it can be seen that in the image used for the news only women are visible, but not any men.

A report from the Turkish national press on the Gunes's report dated 09.03.2019 reveals an example of negative headings regarding the word woman mentioned above. In the news of which title is "Unfortunate woman beaten at work" it is reported that she (who is considered to be a male because his gender is not emphasized) has been beaten by an unidentified person. The woman's name and surname in the news were given only by the initials within the framework of the ethical rules but a photo of the woman's face is used (Güneş, 2019).

Figure 1.
Source: *(Haber Turk, 2019)*

An example of the news about the murders of women can be given from Hurriyet newspaper. News of the newspaper dated 03.04.2019 "Secret of the mystery murder in the hotel room was solved" was used. While the name, surname and photograph of the woman who is the victim of murder is openly shown only the name not the surname of the man who murdered her is openly shown. Although it is not related to the news, it is mentioned that she is a divorced mother (Yildirim, 2019).

Like women the other disadvantaged people in the media are homosexuals. Homosexual representations in the media are another issue to be examined. It is seen that homosexuals are associated with crime and prostitution in the news (Binark & Gencel Bek, 2010: 180). It is seen that the murder of a gay was given in 04.10.2007 dated Haberturk news from the national press in Turkey. In the news which was given with the title of "Homosexual murder in Nisantasi" it can be understood that gays are being otherized just by looking at the heading. News continues as follows:

According to information obtained, the event occurred in Şişli Tesvikiye District Mansion Mansion Hacı Emin Street in the basement of an apartment building. Mehmet M. (33), who was claimed to be a homosexual and a DJ in bars, was found naked in his home with his throat cut. Mehmet M. who was killed by people or persons who entered the house in the morning, and his laptop and mobile phone was also stolen. The roommate of Mehmet M., who was claimed to be a gay man, reported the situation to the police after seeing him covered with blood. (Haber Turk, 2007)

In the above news, although there is nothing to do with the subject, homosexuality is emphasized. However, his name is also included in the news. In the section of Correct Behaviour Rules of Journalists in the Manifesto of Rights and Duties of Turkey Journalist Community, there is sexual orientation and sexual identity part. In this section, it is said that "*no one can be defined by gender identity or sexual orientation unless it is directly the element of the news*" (Turkey Journalists' Society, 2019). In the news above, the sexual identity of the murdered person was not directly related to the news, but was included in the news and the headline.

Gender in Ads

The presentation of women and men are prepared to reinforce the gender roles. Although their gender roles we can see women as sexual object in the commercials. In recent years a working, free woman image has emerged. "The most basic individual characteristics of the human being as a woman or a man are regulated in accordance with the norms of masculinity and femininity as a strategic effort in advertising." (Batı & Baygül, 2006: 54).

Dumanlı (2011: 135) states that the women who are represented as sexual objects are turned into spectacle objects in the advertisement, and that the body has become a commodity which is bought and sold together with the product, and that the body is used to transmit sexual messages in pieces to the opposite side. It can be said that the female body is transformed into an object of desire by introducing the product to the sexual discourse in the advertisements where the women are included. (Apak and Kasap, 2014: 825). Binark and Gencel Bek (2010: 164) stated that the display of the woman's body in the media and the presenting to the men turned into an appetizer satisfying the sexual desires of the man, and by giving an example of Algida advertisements, it is stated that the women are actually shown as flavoring by tasting the food. Batı and Baygül (2006: 52) likewise stated that the reason for such advertisements is to attract the attention of the audience to the product which is advertised and promoted, and to encourage the men and women to be visibly well-groomed.

Advertising is the content that women are reinforced through the media the role of women as motherhood and housewife. These representations are frequently encountered in cleaning and food advertisements. In the advertisements of these products, women are usually at home responsible for the housework. For example, in the advertisement of "Knorr Cesni" in Turkey the lady of the house is cooking in the kitchen. The husband comes from work, takes his child in his arms and tells her that some guests will come in the evening. In addition to taking care of house and children, now she has to host two famous gourmets of Turkey at home. The gourmets enjoy the dishes of the Knorr brand. The woman is shown only at the kitchen and dining table. She is a housewife, her husband works outside and only shows interest in children when he comes home. Another type of product using housewife character is detergent commercials. In a detergent commercial belongs to "Peros" is in the bathroom. The advertisement starts with an external voice *"number one detergent choice in the world's number one washing machines"*. The lady of the house interrupts this and says *"sorry whose preference?"*. The external voice repeats *"the washing machines"*. The lady of the house laughs and *"So this machine knows the stains that our boy made? Even this machine bore him and gave birth to him. I know how those stains are removed. I'm a mother. My choice is Peros. Listen to my word."*. finally, the external voice says *"the preference of the hearts not the machines"* and the advertisement finishes. The mother in the commercial approves that it is the duty of women to do the cleaning at home and to choose the detergent.

We also see women as businesswomen in commercials. The women who are portrayed as highly successful women in their work, either alone or married, report that their success is supported by a man. Examples can be shown from the advertisements. For example, in the commercial of "Supradyn" in Turkey famous actress Gulse Birsel stars. Gülse Birsel plays a very busy businesswoman in the commercial. She plays a super woman who keeps everything in mind in spite of her busy work (which is sometimes an employee's birthday), who takes care of the details and focuses on a lot of things at once. "Supradyn" food supplement gives energy to her. It is shown in this advertisement that the woman can continue her work life and this intense tempo only by taking food supplements.

Women who are businesswomen but who are also interested in their homes and spouses, who have the support of her husband behind her success, also have advertisements. Famous actress Beren Saat and her husband Kenan Dogulu's –a singer- Arcelik commercial can be shown. In this commercial, Beren Saat portrays a famous actress, primarily in a movie set, then in her garden and in the kitchen. Then, her husband visits Beren during shooting and supports her. In this advertisement it can be seen that to be successful a woman needs the support of her husband.

Looking at male representations in commercials, the traditional male roles were the work life and the head of the family were still in progress. For example in "Knorr Cesni" advertisement mentioned above a male with working-co-father roles was represented. In recent years, the age of marriage delay, the number of people living independently from the family (the same applies to men and women) some commercials are produced for those who live alone. Especially the men living alone should do their own household work. These men's representations in today's advertisements stand out. For example in the Finish washing liquid commercial which has been made in 2019, Feyyaz Duman who is the star of a famous TV star in Turkey, is star of the ads. In ads, Feyyaz Duman is a man who lives alone in his house and does the housework. He uses Finish because of the advice of his mother. In this advertisement, although the male may seem responsible for work outside of the traditional roles, the lower message of the advertisement is shown as a male he must learn what detergent to use from a woman. Therefore, even though the man goes out of his traditional roles, he cannot know the brand choice of the domestic product and only a woman knows who has a traditional role.

Gender in TV Series

Television series are the channels in which gender roles are reinforced. In the series, women are either represented as mothers or spouses, but they are represented as women who are working, or women who have problems in their marriage, or as marginal women who are excluded from traditional roles (women working in the night club, prostitute etc.).

As a mother and wife, women are a good mother who is a good wife who is attached to their home and husband. They don't work outside, care for children, take care of the household. Reyhan who is the main character of "Bir Aile Hikayesi" series in Fox TV is the mother of three children and a housewife. She usually spends her days at home and takes care of children. Her husband, Cem, works outside the office and earns his family's money.

It is not seen in the series that working women are successful in every field like men. In the series men are portrayed as successful in every field. For example, a good husband, a good father, a successful employee. However, when there are women working in the field, it is seen that there is a fault either at home or business life. For example "Arzu" who is a character in "Ufak Tefek Cinayetler" which was on Star TV between 2017 and 2018 is the mother of two children and housewife. She spends the most of her day cooking and devoted herself to her children and husband. After being cheated on by her husband, she gets divorced. She goes into working life, rises in her job and becomes a successful manager. However, with her success in business, she starts to neglect her house and her children sot they feel uncomfortable with this situation. If this character was a man, he probably wouldn't have any problems and wouldn't have been complained about things like work, home, family. In addition to the mother, spouse, working woman typing, there are female typologies that can be called marginal women. For example, the woman in the night club, the woman who is singing or a prostitute, the society excludes these women and doesn't allow them to establish family in the series. Yıldız character from the famous series in Show TV "Cukur" can be shown as an example. Yıldız, who continued her living by singing in the pavilion, is in love with Cumali Koçovalı in his neighborhood. But these two lovers cannot meet each other. Because Cumali's mother was raised and still lives in a highly authoritarian and patriarchal family. According to her, Yildiz is not a suitable bride and she makes her son get married his son to a girl who, according to her own choice, works in a more acceptable job than Yildiz (the message tried to be given is being the daughter of a mafia leader is better than singing in the nightclub). Another similar example is "Kadın" series which is the most popular Tuesday series in Fox TV. Although it is thought that the prevailing gender patterns against women are destroyed, or that the screenwriter is a woman, it does not lead to the destruction of the prevailing stereotypes. Because even though she is a woman director, a producer, a producing company belong to a man and this becomes an obstacle for her. Ceyda character sings in the night club and makes a living. The men who Ceyda has relationship are either married and don't want to leave their wives or the men trying to get advantage from her. Ceyda is not allowed to establish a family in the series. Therefore, it is seen that the dominant ideas in the society are reinforced through the series.

The first season (2015-2016) of "Eskiya Dunyaya Hukumdar Olmaz" series in ATV shows the impact of patriarchal society on women. the head of the family is Hızır Cakırbeyli in the series "Cakırbeyli's" which is a Black Sea region series. Hızır has a wife, a daughter and a boy. He's with a woman other than his marriage, and he has a son from that relationship. His wife (Meryem) asks for a divorce when she finds out, but the family rejects it. Especially the mother-in-law of Meryem said that divorce is not in the traditions so she has to get used to it. It is seen that the women in the series are not working and at home. It is seen that they do not participate in decision making mechanisms but men are influential.

When we look at the representations of homosexual characters in the series, it is seen that they are represented by either they are excluded by society or their parents. An example is Ilhan character from "Ufak Tefek Cinayetler" the series mentioned above. Ilhan is a feminine person with his homosexual clothing, bedroom design and style. Ilhan is portrayed as an element of laughter to the audience with his humor, funny jokes and speaking style. Another example is Selim character from "Cukur" series. Selim is one of the sons of Koçovalı is an homosexual. However, because his family does not know this, he is married to a woman and has children. Gay identity is known only by his wife. His wife doesn't want Selim, but she cannot leave him because the family does not allow the divorce. The family makes a living from weapon smuggling and exacting tribute from pavilions. Selim is the weakest man in this family. He could not protect his brother during a conflict and caused his death. He is portrayed as an excluded and unpopular character in the family.

In the above-mentioned examples, it can be said that the unequal situation prevailing in the society in terms of gender is enhanced by the series.

Gender in Cinema

Cinema is an art in which a variety of references are made about sexes. "Cinema is a cultural practice where women and femininity and men and masculinity, in short, myths on sexual differences are produced, reproduced and represented" (Smelik, 2008: 1). The film narrative gives a variety of messages in a scenario and shooting techniques. A particular event can be shown in many different ways with the shooting angles. "Films propose a number of theses through representative elements that have been selected and combined to form a particular form of design, rather than reflecting a situation, suggesting a certain position or perspective to the audience" (Ryan and Kellner, 2010: 16). In the film, a woman can be brought to the position of the object of the male view by various techniques. For example, the female body can be divided into pieces and become fetish objects. Smelik (2008: 6) likewise says the following:

"In the case of fetishism, the classic cinema replaces the missing penis with a fetish form, ie a hyper-polished object. Femininizing a woman into a fetish prevents her from attending to the 'lack' of attention and transforms her from a dangerous personality

into a perfect object of beauty. The use of fetishism in cinema contributes to the objectification of the female, and therefore the 'woman' cannot be represented as the phallic norm."

Laura Mulvey's *"Visual Pleasure and Narrative Cinema"* is an article about the presentation of women in popular cinema and a cult work. Mulvey states that because the popular cinema is a product, the show itself is shaped as a product and hence the female figure on the screen as a product. (Mulvey, 1993. As cited in Kırel, 2018: 225). It is noteworthy that in many examples of Hollywood cinema, women are represented as a product.[1] In the period called Yeşilçam of Turkish cinema, women were introduced to the audience by introducing them into certain patterns. We used to come across with women who are loyal to their husband and home and also coquette women in Yesilcam. For the woman who came out of traditional patterns, the happy ending was not seen. The most prominent example of this is Ömer Lürfi Akad's 1968 production of Vesikalı Yarim. Sabiha who works in the nightclub is not allowed to build a family.

It is observed that there is no change in the position of women in today's popular Turkish cinema. Today, where women have alternatives to stereotypical roles in Yeşilçam Cinema, they are told to the audience through independent cinema. For example, Zeki Demirkubuz's films Kader (2006), Masumiyet (1997), Yeşim Ustaoğlu's film Pandora's Box (2008) are examples of films against traditional women's roles.

Representation of homosexuals in Turkish Cinema takes place in a popular cinema as a crime element, prostitution, a person infecting the disease or as an element of laughter. It would be more accurate to explain these two representative popular films from two examples. Ayta Sozeri who plays Behiye character in Aile Arasında movie of Ozak Acıktan in 2017 is the trans actress of the film. Sözeri, a transgender person in real life, became the element of humor by his jokes in the film and the rhetoric against him. Another example of the homosexual representations of popular Turkish cinema is the film called Güneşi Gördüm, which was produced by Mahsun Kırmızıgül in 2009. Kadri who is gay hero of the film, was forced to emigrate from the east of Turkey to Istanbul with his family. Because they are a patriarchal family, very important characteristics are attributed to being a man. However, Kadri, one of the members of the family, casts a shadow on this situation. Yüksel (2016: 142) summarizes Kadri's transformation as follows:

Kadri's sex work after articulation of the trans-community gains a sexist content that reinforces the dominant gender norms. The film excludes the transgender subjectivity of sex workers who enjoy sex work in accordance with their own choices by including the transgender image directed towards sex work for compulsory reasons, and the ability of transgender individuals to do any other work than sex work.

In the dialogue between Kadri and his friend they Express there is discrimination towards them and they are not free. This idea is supported in the scene in which Kadri's brother kils him on a bridge and it is seen that the individual who isn't acting according to the expectation of society in terms of gender roles doesn't have the right to live.

FUTURE RESEARCH AND DIRECTIONS

In this study, an overview of the concept of gender is tried to be shown with examples from Turkish media. In other parts of the book, the status of representation in the media will be examined in detail. As a matter of fact, there are shortcomings in the field of male representations and homosexual representations. It is recommended to overcome the deficiencies in these areas especially in future studies.

CONCLUSION

In this study, it has been tried to look at the gender issues in news, advertisements, series and cinema with examples from Turkish media. The study has tried to give various examples of gender in the media. An in-depth analysis of gender representations in the media will take place in other parts of the book. This chapter is an introduction to the book on gender representation in the media.

As can be seen from the examples, the popular culture product (arrays, advertisements, popular films) are depicted in the women's disadvantageous and secondary position in the news. Especially the news that the word woman is reinforcing the disadvantageous position of women. In series and advertisements, women are either a carrier of an object or traditional role in the face of a man's look. It is noteworthy that there is no change in media contents from past to present. This is primarily due to the fact that there are men at peak points in the ownership structure in the media. This situation is detailed in the section on gender distribution in the Turkish media sector. The highly unequal distribution among women is also reflected in production processes. For this reason, the fact that the producers of these contents are women prevent the critique of gender inequality from being carried to the media.

Women's content producers also seem to be the spokesperson of the prevailing ideology. A revolt against gender inequality is now expressed in cinema through independent cinema. However, they cannot announce their voices enough because they cannot achieve success at the box office as popular films or they do not have the chance to be seen in the hall as popular films.

REFERENCES

Apak, K. H., & Kasap, F. (2014). Türk Televizyonlarındaki Gıda Reklamlarında Kadın ve Erkek İmgesi Üzerine Bir İnceleme. *Journal of International Social Research, 7*(34), 814–832.

Batı, U., & Baygül, Ş. B. (2006). Reklamlarda İdeal Kadın Bedeninin Sunumuna İlişkin Bir İçerik Analizi. *Journal of Communication Studies, 2*, 49–73.

Binark, M., & Gencel Bek, M. (2010). *Eleştirel Medya Okuryazarlığı: Kuramsal Yaklaşımlar ve Uygulamalar*. İstanbul, Turkey: Kalkedon Yayınevi.

Connell, R. W. (1998). *Toplumsal Cinsiyet ve İktidar: Toplum, Kişi ve Cinsel Politika* (C. Soydemir, Trans.). İstanbul, Turkey: Ayrıntı Yayınevi.

Dumanlı, D. (2011). Reklamlarda Toplumsal Cinsiyet Kavramı ve Kadın İmgesinin Kullanımı; Bir İçerik Analizi. *Yalova Üniversitesi Sosyal Bilimler Dergisi, 1*(2), 132–149.

Fay, B. (2001). *Çağdaş Sosyal Bilimler Felsefesi* (İ. Türkmen, Trans.). İstanbul, Turkey: Ayrıntı Yayınevi.

Gazetesi, G. (2019). Tarihli haberi. Retrieved from http://www.gunes.com/yasam/talihsiz-kadin-is-yerinde-dayak-yedi-961789

Giddens, A. (2012). *Sosyoloji, (Prep. Cemal Güzel)*. İstanbul, Turkey: Kırmızı Yayınevi.

Güneş. (2019). *Unfortunate Woman Beaten at Work*. Retrieved from http://www.gunes.com/yasam/talihsiz-kadin-is-yerinde-dayak-yedi-961789

Günindi Ersöz, A. (2016). *Toplumsal Cinsiyet Sosyolojisi*. Ankara, Turkey: Anı Yayınevi.

Haber Turk. (2007). *Homosexual Murder in Nisantasi*. Retrieved from https://www.haberturk.com/yasam/haber/38804-nisantasinda-escinsel-cinayeti

Haber Turk. (2019). *The Massage Parlor Raid: 6 Women, 11 Detainees*. Retrieved from https://www.haberturk.com/masaj-salonuna-baskin-6-si-kadin-11-gozalti-2452057#

Haberturk.com. (n.d.). Retrieved from https://www.haberturk.com/masaj-salonuna-baskin-6-si-kadin-11-gozalti-2452057# Date

haberturk.com. (2007). *Tarihli haberi*. Retrieved from https://www.haberturk.com/yasam/haber/38804-nisantasinda-escinsel-cinayeti

Hürriyet. (2019). *The Female Driver Scattered the Horrors!* Retrieved from http://www.hurriyet.com.tr/gundem/kadin-surucu-dehset-sacti-tekme-tokat-saldirdi-41126752

Hürriyet Gazetesi. (2003). Retrieved from http://www.hurriyet.com.tr/gundem/muhabirin-is-kazasi-189230

Hürriyet Gazetesi. (2019). *Tarihli haberi.* Retrieved from http://www.hurriyet.com.tr/gundem/otel-odasindaki-sir-cinayet-cozuldu-41171221

Hürriyet News. (n.d.). *Reporter's Work Accident.* Retrieved from http://www.hurriyet.com.tr/gundem/muhabirin-is-kazasi-189230

Kırel, S. (2018). *Kültürel Çalışmalar ve Sinema.* İstanbul, Turkey: İthaki Yayınevi.

Kuruoğlu, H. (2006). Türkiye'de Televizyon Haber Bültenlerinde Haber Öznesi Olarak Kadın", In D. İmançer (Ed.), *Medya ve Kadın* (pp. 237–271). Ankara, Turkey: Ebabil Yayınevi.

Marshall, G. (2005). *Sosyoloji Sözlüğü* (O. Akınhay, & D. Kömürcü, Trans.). Ankara, Turkey: Bilim Sanat Yayınevi.

Pryzgoda, J., & Chrisler, J. C. (2000). Definitions of Gender and Sex: The subtleties of meaning. *Sex Roles, 43*(7-8), 553–569. doi:10.1023/A:1007123617636

Ryan, M., & Kellner, D. (2010). *Politik Kamera* (E. Özsayar, Trans.). İstanbul, Turkey: Ayrıntı Yayınevi.

Smelik, A. (2008). *Feminist Sinema ve Film Teorisi: Ve Ayna Çatladı* (D. Koç, Trans.). İstanbul, Turkey: Agora Yayınevi.

tgc.org. (2019). Retrieved from https://www.tgc.org.tr/bildirgeler/t%C3%BCrkiye-gazetecilik-hak-ve-sorumluluk-bildirgesi.html

Tuik Gov. (n.d.). *Turkiye Istatistik Kurumu.* Retrieved from http://www.tuik.gov.tr/PreTablo.do?alt_id=1068

tuik.gov. (2019). Retrieved from http://www.tuik.gov.tr/PreTablo.do?alt_id=1068

Turkey Journalists' Society. (2019). *Turkey Journalists' Rights and Responsibilities Statement.* Retrieved from https://www.tgc.org.tr/bildirgeler/t%C3%BCrkiye-gazetecilik-hak-ve-sorumluluk-bildirgesi.html

Yildirim, T. (2019). *Secret of the Mystery of the Hotel Room Solved.* Retrieved from http://www.hurriyet.com.tr/gundem/otel-odasindaki-sir-cinayet-cozuldu-41171221

Yüksel, E. (2016). Güneşi Gördüm ve Teslimiyet Filmlerinde Trans Kimliklerin Mekânsal Örgütlenmesi ve Sınırlılıkları. *Feminist Eleştiri, 7*(2), 138–148.

ADDITIONAL READING

Bolak Boratav, H., Okman Fişek, G., & Eslen Ziya, H. (2017). *Erkekliğin Türkiye Halleri*. İstanbul: İstanbul Bilgi Üniversitesi Yayınları.

Büker, S., & Topçu, Y. G. (2010). *Sinema: Tarih, Kuram, Eleştiri*. İstanbul: Kırmızı Kedi Yayınevi.

Butler, J. (2008). *Cinsiyet Belası: Feminizm ve Kimliğin Altüst Edilmesi* (B. Ertür, Trans.). İstanbul: Metis Yayınevi.

Donovan, J. (2014). *Feminist Teori* (A. Bora, M. A. Gevrek, & F. Sayılan, Trans.). İstanbul: İletişim Yayınevi.

İnceoğlu, Y., & Kar, A. (2010). *Dişilik, Güzellik ve Şiddet Sarmalında Kadın ve Bedeni*. İstanbul: Ayrıntı Yayınevi.

KEY TERMS AND DEFINITIONS

Feminism: It is the name given to the movement that suggests that women should be equal to men both in social (education, work, family life and political life).

Fetishism: The situation of an individual in which he/she uses the objects of the opposite sex and shows the sexual urges he/she feels.

Gender: It is the whole of the roles that society expects from women and men other than biological sex.

Sex: It is a concept referring to the innate biological characteristics of the individual in the context of masculinity and femininity.

Transgender: All sexual orientations other than heterosexuality.

ENDNOTE

[1] For more information see. Serpil Kırel (2018), Kültürel Çalışmalar ve Sinema, İstanbul: İthaki.

Chapter 2

Social Gender Representation in the Context of the Representation Problem in the Media

Özge Gürsoy Atar
Beykent University, Turkey

ABSTRACT

Women's television programs appear as an indispensable broadcasting component of the morning television broadcasting series. Three women's programs, which were broadcasted in 2018, were analyzed in the study of how women participate in these television programs and the presentation of gender roles. First, the issue of social representation in the context of the problem of representation in the media was discussed. Later on, feminism and women's programs in the media were examined and the situation in the media was determined. In the application part of the study, numerical data were evaluated, and discourse analysis was conducted within the framework of the women's programs examined.

INTRODUCTION

With the launch of Magic Box in 1990, the first private television broadcasting began illegally in Turkey. The problems experienced by women became an important material for the producers of programs and started to be used as an important material. These "women's programs", which focus on women and their problems, became a fact of popularity in the 1990s. However, after the events and speeches in

DOI: 10.4018/978-1-7998-0128-3.ch002

Copyright © 2020, IGI Global. Copying or distributing in print or electronic forms without written permission of IGI Global is prohibited.

these programs, many violent incidents occurred. As a result of this situation, the necessity of examining women's programs has emerged. Various researches have been done in the fields of communication.

In the study, firstly the concepts of representation and ideology in the media were analyzed, then gender was analyzed in the context of social gender and literature review was made. Since the historical and social processes cannot be ignored in the evaluation of the existing in the media, the current situation will be revealed by looking at women's programs in Turkish television broadcasting. The study, which will evaluate the existing situation in the media, will refer to the programs of social gender, Turkish women, feminism, representation of women in the media and women's television programs in Turkish television broadcasting and analyze the content of the programs within the framework of all these. While evaluating all of these, the study is based on the view that femininity and masculinity are cultural and socially constructed. Critical discourse analysis method was used in the study and it aimed to show that gender patriarchalism is a cultural/historical phenomenon that can be eliminated.

"In qualitative research, qualification refers to the amount of data collected, not the number of subjects, as in quantitative data. Qualification is achieved when a large amount of data is collected and saturation is achieved". In this study, this method was used by using the feature of analyzing the *"narrative analysis"*, which is one of the qualitative research methods, and the related sequence of events with multiple meanings i.e. historical, archaeological, linguistic, political, scientific and sociological. All the collected data will be compared and multiple processes, reasons, and features in the evidence will be determined. These relations will be taken into consideration from the beginning of the study as qualitative research will allow us to search for patterns and relations from the beginning of the project. In short, the analysis was not spread to a separate final stage of this research, but to the whole. As a result of the inductive nature of qualitative research, an inductive evaluation was carried out.

In the study, the programs Kind but Firm with Müge Anlı, With Esra Erol, and Chasing the Truth with Serap Ezgü were followed between 24 December 2018 and 28 December 2018. The analysis will be made on the tables created by looking at "how women are represented" and "gender discourse". The reasons for examining these programs are that these programs are watched by women and women appear in them. Criminal events that happen to women are dramatized and processed in programs.

The aim of this study is to recognize the repetitive patriarchal discourse in the media and to draw attention to the construction of gender through mass media. As a result, the study aims to discuss the general problems and solutions.

BACKGROUND

Social Gender Representation in the Context of Representation Problem in the Media

There are different approaches to the concept of representation. Van Dijk defines ideology as the "form of social cognition" among the members of any social group. However, he underlines the fact that this definition of ideology does not only mean beliefs about attitudes but also emphasizes the "socio-cognitive nature" of beliefs. Barthes states that ideology is "dominant thoughts" (Hall, 1994: 204).

It seems important to focus on the issue of representation in the media because the existence of representations that can(not) be represented in the media is still problematic. The reason why representation is considered as a problem arises from the fact that the media mostly includes representation of dominant discourses and this situation is seen as a problematic situation especially in social gender representations. As stated by Hall, the concept of representation emphasizes "the process of constructing and communicating meaning, in other words, emphasizes the sense-making process" (Çelenk, 2005: 81).

According to Fiske (2003: 2018), the connotational values and myths shared by members of a culture are included. At the center of this process are the semantic values and myths shared by the members of a culture. At the center of this process are the semantic values and myths shared by the members of a culture. The only way to disseminate and maintain them is to use them frequently in communication. Every time an indicator is used, the lives of the second user level connotation that exist in both the culture and the user are strengthened. Thus, a triangular relationship model arises.

As Ünsal Oskay (2005: 2) states, when a man tells a woman "but you are a woman", he demonstrates how the patriarchal structure that has survived to the present day from the past and what is the dominant culture of society, which infer the inequality in the entire history of mankind to the present as a natural phenomenon.

Feminism in the Media

The existence of feminism, a concept of the 20th century, depends on the ideas of equality and freedom produced by the French Revolution and the struggles arising from them. As Kaplan emphasizes, the transformation in thought structures requires certain social changes. The advancement of industry, science and technology, the dissolving of feudalism, the concentration of the population in certain centers, and the large-scale entrance of women to working life have caused the change of traditional ties and mindsets (Kaplan, 1999: 6).

The concept of feminism has changed since the movement of women's liberation in the 1960s. However, it is possible to say that the changes experienced in the last thirty years have a great effect on the formation of the concept of feminism. Firstly, "the conceptual level feminism" has expanded considerably, including the younger generation, and secondly, the feminist movement has begun to evolve in itself through criticism from the inside. The societies in which feminism was formed were also transformed. In this context, it is possible to say that the concept of feminism has become a complex term. Feminism criticizes certain forms of defining and suppressing women in certain social circles, despite the different definitions of feminism and the different practices that occur in any culture or across cultures (Kırca- Schroeder, 2007: 13-14).

According to Imançer (2010), feminism is the view that opposes the discrimination of women and men and that defends the political, economic and social equality between the sexes and it will be a one-dimensional analysis to consider feminism as only female-male inequality. In fact, the problem of women is a complex phenomenon in which economic, political, ideological and psychological aspects are intertwined.

In the early 20th century, many themes that developed since the Middle Ages had stuck the minds of Western feminists: the rebellion, resistance and innovative initiative of countless queens, princesses, bourgeoisie, peasants, workers, public, women writers, artists, and scientists demonstrated the courage to lift the barriers that stood in economic, military, religious, artistic and scientific life for centuries and took root as a result of their struggle to gain ground (Michel, 1984: 68-69).

According to Bell Hooks (2002:1), feminism is "a movement that aims to end sexism, sexist exploitation and oppression". Bell Hooks indicates that this definition is not hostile to men and that she draws attention to the essence of the issue with the concept of sexism. She points out that in order to understand feminism, human beings should be able to understand sexism.

Hooks stated that feminism was expressed in books in journals and media in a different way, that feminism was portrayed as a male hostility, and that when it is understood correctly by everybody then many mistakes will change. According to Hooks, feminism contains the hope of liberation from the slavery of patriarchy for men. Even if women and men are not always equal, everyone will want to live in a world that no one dominates. Racism, class elitism, and imperialism must also end because feminism alone cannot be much more effective. This view is based on "personalism" which is the philosophy that directed the struggle of the feminists of the International Women's Council for the development of women's rights. According to the feminists of the period between the World Wars, personalism "should result in every same person refusing to distinguish between men and women, as well as to discriminate between people of different classes and races" (Michel, 1984: 73-74).

In the private sphere, feminist women have refused to build a wall between private life and public life, ideological advocacy and daily practice, thus leading to a decline in the rates of marriage and childbirth by playing an innovative role. In this period, as it was claimed, "western women did not want to throw themselves into marriage as they did in their mothers' period". In the field of culture, women began to pursue sexism in images, the way they were presented in literature, in mass media, in advertisements, and in images. According to Michell (1984: 89-92), despite the censorship of men during the reorganization of feminism, women's magazines had to publish good feminist writings to compete with feminist publications. However, the fear environment emitted by intellectual men about freedom of expression and refusal of censorship leads to the inability of women to dare to oppose porn publications and advertisements that have caused them to lose self-respect.

WOMEN'S PROGRAMS

The programs for women first started in 1939 on the radio as "Home Time" and then by the name "Home" without giving an identity to the woman except "the mother of the house". These programs continued until the 1970s under the name of "For the House" containing issues such as child care, education, health, and family relations. Between 1974-80, "Women's World" on TRT-1 and "Women and Family" programs on TRT-2 were broadcasted. While identifying their goals in their respective activities, these programs define women as "one of the basic elements that will realize the happy future of society". In line with this idea, in addition to being "wives and mothers within the family", women are also stated to be "citizens in the world and citizens in the society". However, in these programs, women cannot go beyond a determined identity within the family. In the 1980s, instead of the programs that target the family in the identity of women, "programs addressing adults in general" were introduced. These are programs such as "Günaydın, Günün İçinden, Öğle Üzeri, and Öğleden Sonra", which were broadcasted in compliance with the daily housework programs of housewives (Saktanber, 1995: 216-217).

A competition program named "do you know your spouse?" in the early 1970s attracts attention and this program is observed to be more women-oriented (Serim, 2006: 54). The television program "the Women of 1900s", prepared in 1971 under the direction of Musa Öğün, was discontinued from broadcasting (Serim, 2006: 68). During the period of General Directorate of İsmail Cem in 1974-75, the issue of divorce was not broadcasted in the program named "Forum" (Serim, 2006: 82). Özden Cankaya states that the first women's program called "the Woman and the House" was broadcasted in 1972 and this program mostly targeted urban women

(Cankaya, 2003: 127). Although programs for women and women in the family have been introduced since 1968, a special program for women named "Hanımlar Sizin İçin" was broadcasted for the first time in 1984. When this program was first broadcasted, it became an indispensable part of the morning broadcasting of TV programs with the increase of broadcasting hours (Saktanber, 1995: 2018). After that, the program was broadcasted for a total of 117 episodes under the name "Çalışan Kadınlar Sizin İçin" and in the program, on the one hand, women were recommended to adapt themselves to modern life and on the other hand conventionality was praised. Cankaya (2003: 232) indicates that in this program, discourses that are in accord with women's traditional role were included such as "the wife enters her husband's house alive but gets out dead", "if your marriage goes bad, give birth to a child", and "the educated woman becomes a witch". The state monopoly was broken by the first satellite Turkish television broadcasting in 1990 with Magic Box (Star 1), which was established by the partnership of Kemal Uzan, the owner of Rumeli Holding, with his son Cem Uzan and the then prime minister of Turkey Turgut Özal's son Ahmet Özal (Serim, 2007: 230-232). Thus, women's programs started out of TRT format.

With its current name, the Star TV got different names in fifteen years and was launched on October 6, 1990, and after the evening news on the first day by Gülgün Feyman, the weather forecast was presented by a blond woman named Hülya Ugur. The lady used to finish her words by saying "no matter what the weather is like, let your mood be nice". In 1991, the Turkey Beauty Contest was broadcasted for the first time. Later, on 31 May, the World's Best Model contest was broadcasted on TRT and the Magic Box "pinned TRT down" by broadcasting an erotic film named "I married a Center Spread Beauty" (Serim, 2007: 250-254).

During this period, another TV channel that started broadcasting by breaking the TRT law is Show TV. In order to compete with Interstar, Show TV started broadcasting under the name Show Time and it was seen that the channel managers who were not satisfied with soft eroticism marked a new era on TV screens by broadcasting "Tutti Frutti". Women appeared in the contest exhibited their bodies with music and the contest was presented as an advanced television concept. Turkey's beauty queen of 1991, Defne Samyeli reported the news on Show TV and just before summer, a matchmaking contest named Saklambaç started to be broadcasted. Nurseli Idız presented the show and in the show, three women and three men in the studio were asked questions in separate rooms without seeing each other and some of them became couples according to the answers they liked. Saklambaç (hide-and-seek) was the most watched program on Saturday nights. This program was a format taken from the US and UK televisions as an exact imitation (Serim, 2007: 275-278). (It is possible to indicate that today's marriage programs are the localized format of this program). In 1993, the program "Sıcağı Sıcağına" was one of the copy programs of a "Reality Show". However, in this program, negativity and pain were carried to the screens by showing women who ran away from their husbands' beatings and living on the streets with their children, homeless elderly people, and women animal lovers who shed tears for animals. These programs were broadcasted under the category "reality", people were disgusted about them but on the other hand, could not help watching and the hidden purpose of these programs was to get more advertisements with a high rating. Such programs spread to all TV channels between 1992 and 1995 (Serim, 2007: 278-279).

"Gelinim Olur Musun? – Would you become my bride?" was an important program broadcasted on Show TV in 2004. The program, which attracted women's interest, received a very high rating, and in the afternoon, the entire broadcast was devoted to this program. The last part of this program, which was a women-oriented format of the surveillance programs and which had previously been broadcasted as "Biri Bizi Gözetliyor – The Big Brother is Watching", reached very high ratings. However, the mother-in-law Semra, who did not want her son to marry the girl he wanted, and her son Ata started to appear in morning programs. The continuation programs of the program "Gelinim Olur Musun? – Would you become my bride?" lasted for months in which women gathered in the studio in the morning or participated by phone and accused Semra with criticisms or even with insults. The channel later launched a new similar program called a "Bir Prens Aranıyor – Prince Wanted" and after the increasing numbers of these programs and increasing reactions from the community, RTÜK (The Turkish Supreme Board of Radio and Television) interfered the process. But RTÜK was accused of censorship (Serim, 294-295). Esra Ceyhan, who made a program for women for almost 10 years on ATV, transferred her program to TV 8 due to a decrease of the ratings of her program "A'dan Z'ye – A to Z". In the same period, the talk show program "Yalnız Değilsin – You are not Alone", which was presented by Ayşenur Yazıcı, started. Just like the other talk shows in other channels, in this program, women gathered in a studio who had suffered from severe beatings, co-wives, and similar problems and they mentioned their troubles for hours, they were listened and it was claimed that their problems were solved. However, during the program that was released on May 4, 2009, the mother of a child, who had gone into a coma as a result of being beaten by his/her stepmother, was told that her child died. Then the mother felt faint, poured a few drops of tears and the program was finished.

On 14 May 2005, a woman was shot by her own son after criticizing her husband in the program "Kadının Sesi – The Voice of the Woman" (started by Yasemin Bozkurt in 2003 and continued 5 days a week) and she became paralyzed. After this incident and other death incidents, the program was finished. Later on, surveillance and marriage programs were broadcasted such as "Sahte Gelin – the Fake Bride" and "Gönüllerde İkinci Bahar – the Seconds Spring in the Hearts". "In some private channels, a broadcasting concept that was carried out every weekday in order to solve the social problems of women marked the history of Turkish television. In these live broadcast programs, there were no class consciousnesses, and the women appeared in them were mostly from the lower part of the society, they were deceived by men, they had to live with co-wives, or they were abandoned, beaten or insulted, they were crying and were telling their husbands on the phone things like 'I cheated on you'…" In April 2005, Yasemin Bozkurt presented the program called "Kadının Sesi – the Voice of the Woman". Before the program, a man named Kenan Alp had killed his wife Tjien Alp, whom he had married by bride exchange, by stabbing. The family of the bride told the homicide of their daughter in the program on 14 April 2005. The father of the groom went live and after swearing mutually, both parties threatened each other and Yasemin Bozkurt apparently calmed the threats "you will pay for it!" They calmed down just for that moment because, on May 13, the father of the bride killed his son-in-law. This was not the only incident. In another incident, the woman with a headscarf, who ran away from the beating of her husband, was convinced to remove her headscarf, appear on the live TV program and then go back to her hometown. However, after getting out the bus, her husband killed her after saying "you put us to shame by showing up on television". As a result of this and other events, the program "Kadının Sesi – the Voice of the Woman" was removed. Similar important women's programs were "Ayşe Özgün Sizinle – Ayşe Özgün is with you", "Dobra Dobra – Frankly", and "Yaşama Dair – About Life" (Serim, 2007: 316-338).

A matchmaking contest named Saklambaç started to be broadcasted on Show TV. Nurseli İdiz presented the show and in the show, three women and three men in the studio were asked questions in separate rooms without seeing each other and some of them became couples according to the answers they liked. Saklambaç (hide-and-seek) was the most watched program on Saturday nights. This program was a format taken from the US and UK televisions as an exact imitation and was adapted to Turkish televisions without any change (Serim, 2007: 275-278). This program, called "Saklambaç – Hide and Seek" started to be watched less over time and was removed due to a lower rating. Nearly 10 years after Saklambaç, a new program called "İzdivaç – Marriage" was launched on Turkish televisions. In these 10 years, as mentioned above, the surveillance programs started to be used for marriage, and then they were banned. The marriage programs started for the first time in Turkey on Flash TV by Esra Erol. It is possible to indicate that the program of Saklambaç, which is more localized and which can be called as an example of Turkish customs, is in a way similar to arranged marriage. In time, localized and legitimized marriage program participants were introduced to marry each other. If both sides liked each other, they got to know each other for a while to marry, the relationship was "legitimized" through engagement in society and the relationship resulted in live marriage on TV. First, the woman or man participating in the program told that he/she wanted to marry, explained his/her own features and what kind of a person he/she was looking for. If somebody liked a person on the program, he/she applied and appeared on live broadcasts. The candidate sometimes wants to come by a phone call or sometimes directly appears live in the studio but again just like in the first format, there was a cover, men and women were asking questions to know each other. As a result, the parties decided whether to open the cover or not and talked in front of the people in the studio. After that, they and the people in the studio decided whether there was "electric" between them or not. As a result, they decided whether to continue their relationship or not. Since this format was watched too much, other private channels also broadcasted similar programs. However, the fact that these programs became too much of an issue and numerous scandals (fraud, married people joining the program, etc.) caused RTÜK to ban them. Esra Erol, who presented this program format for the first time and made these programs to become widespread, continued publications by converting the contents of her program to another format which was famous in the same period. In 2018, "Tatlı Sert – Kind and Firm" started to be broadcasted in a format similar to those mentioned above. In this program, losses are sought, the perpetrators of unknown murders are sought. In particular, women's murders, violence against women, and women's search for their children are dramatized.

These women's programs, which are broadcasted on most of the private television channels in the morning and evening with different names, are reproduced as popular cultural products. Although the formats obviously change in certain ratios over time, the content continues with transformation.

Women's issues in the Women's Reality Show programs are publicized and massified. These programs have very heavy content and women suffering from beatings, insults, co-wives and abandoned women are generally included in these programs (Özgür, 2017: 15).

THE RESEARCH METHOD

When the production of meaning within mass communication is desired to be understood as concrete, it does not work for textual content or audience analysis; instead it is necessary to conduct an in-depth content analysis (Ang and Radway as cited in: Jensen, 2005: 131). Therefore, this content will be analyzed in-depth content. Therefore, in this study, in-depth content analysis and discourse analysis will be carried out.

The population of this study consists of women's programs broadcasted in the daytime. The programs taken as a sample were Müge Anli – Tatlı Sert (ATV), Esra Erol (ATV) and Serap Ezgü – Gerçeğin Peşinde (TV 8). The reasons for the inclusion of these three programs are that they are/were long-standing programs that were/have been preferred by television viewers. The programs were followed-up between December 24, 2018 and December 28, 2018. The records of these programs are available on websites. For this reason, an examination was made on the internet for one week.

The Purpose of the Research

This study aimed to find out how women are included in the media in women's programs.

The Hypotheses of the Research

1. Television programs include women, victims or mothers and wives.
2. Male dominant discourse is maintained by women.

FINDINGS AND THE ANALYSIS OF THE FINDINGS

The most talked topic in Esra Erol was the relationship between women and men. We see that the child is in second place and marriage issues are discussed in the third place. There are two experts in Esra Erol's program. A lawyer and a marriage counselor inform the guests. Marriages, family relations, and children are observed to be in the first place. In this context, the issues in which women are included are in these frameworks.

Figure 1. Main topics spoken in "Esra Erol'da" television program

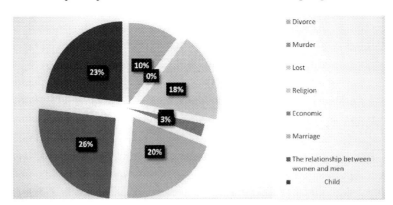

Figure 2. Main topics spoken in "Müge Anli Ile Tatli Sert" television program

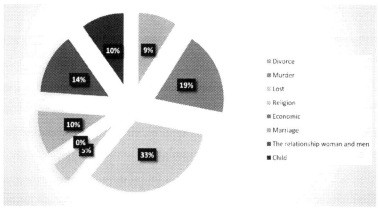

We can see that the topic of missing people is mentioned in the first place. In this program, the second issue is murder and the third is the relationship between men and women. It is possible to conclude that within the context of murder and loss, family relations are determinative and in this context, the results of the disappearances and murders are revealed. In this program, we see that women have repeated their adjectives such as victim, spouse, and sorrowful mother.

The first subject in the "Gerçeğin Peşinde – Chasing the Truth" program is the issue of missing persons. The marriage issue is in second place. We also see that child, murder and male-female relations share the third place. Issues such as religion and economics are rarely discussed in all three programs.

Figure 3. Main topics spoken in "Serap Ezgü İle Gerçeğin Peşinde" television program

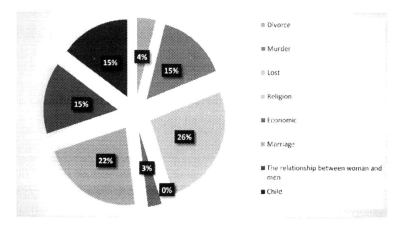

Table 1. Prominent women's discourses in "Esra Erol'da" television program

27 Aralık 2018	"Why does a woman leave her home?"
24 Aralık 2018	"My son, you are a man."
25 Aralık 2018	"What I wanted to be most was a mother"

Table 2. Prominent Women's Discourses in "Müge Anlı ile Tatlı Sert" Television Program

27 Aralık 2018	"What happened to the unlucky mother and daughter?"
27 Aralık 2018	"Were they executed in the family?"
26 Aralık 2018	"How can a mother leave two daughters if she claims that the man is a drug user?"

Table 3. Prominent women's discourses in "Serap Ezgü İle Gerçeğin Peşinde" television program

28 Aralık 2018	"You are two sorrowful mothers"
26 Aralık 2018	"Why is Mother Aisha anxious for her daughter?"
25 Aralık 2018	"What's a woman doing on the street at 6:00 a.m.?"
25 Aralık 2018	"You should think of your daughter as a mother."

When we look at all of the above tables, we see that "motherhood" is loaded on women as an adjective rather than a biological condition. The above-mentioned and prominent discourses in all of the programs are about "what women should do, when and how". When sentences such as "you are the man, my son", "what is a woman doing on the street at 6:00 a.m.?" are formed in television programs, as in the discourses above, the facts that how the patriarchal structure that has survived to the present day, and the dominant culture of the society, which reveals inequality as a natural phenomenon in the history of the whole humans which we live to date, are also revealed.

In the "Müge Anlı ile Tatlı Sert" television program dated 28 December 2018, a hashtag was used for the person who was accused of murder and sentenced to 18 years: #kadıncinayetlerindeindirimolmasın (no deduction of sentence for murdering women). With this hashtag and verbally by Müge Anlı, the female killings were pointed out with the deduction of sentences for different reasons.

On 26 December 2018, a woman named Hatice was mentioned due to the fact that she was claimed to run away because "she had been exposed to violence from her husband". Her daughter claimed that she did not experience violence. However,

Social Gender Representation in the Context of the Representation Problem in the Media

the woman and her mother stated that they were subjected to violence. Müge Anlı, on the other hand, said that "I am not involved in the relationship between husband and wife. Is the new guy a good guy?" In fact, in these discourses, it is seen in the lower texts that "if the woman ran away from home, she went to another person". We hear that many words and subjects are dropped. "How can a mother leave two daughters if you claim the man to be a drug user?" Here, we see that there is a continuous emphasis that the woman is a "mother". The relevant subtitles were as follows: "we have found Belma Tilki, the mother of two children". The woman connected by phone said, "I could not stand the beatings".

In the program "Serap Ezgü Gerçeğin Peşinde" on December 25, 2018, paternal grandfather and grandmother who wanted to see their grandson attended the program. In response, the mother also attended and claimed that she was subjected to violence. The husband named Barış also called and said: "what is a woman doing at 6:00 a.m. in the morning on the street?"

The issue of kidnapping of a 16-year-old girl was discussed in the program "Serap Ezgü Gerçeğin Peşinde" on 27 December 2018. The issue was whether the girl fled to her own free will or not. The claim "Kardelen ran away in order to get married" is given exclusively in television.

On 28 December 2018, after the murder of a woman named Miyase Bedir, the bride was alleged to have had a relationship with another person and they had therefore killed her. When we look at the content of all programs based on "women", we see that the main headings are shaped as follows:

1. Missing women
2. Women who have an affair outside marriage
3. Motherhood of women

We see that the word "mother" is used as an adjective before the names of women on many subjects.

In the program of Esra Erol on December 24, 2018, a family with missing children are looking for their children. The father explains why his children had left home: "Boy, you are a man. Who is going to tell you what?" Even though the word "woman" is not mentioned in the speech of the father who addresses his son who ran away from his hometown after his relationship with a woman 19 years older than him was learned, it proves the position of women in society and the fact that they are more accused than men when they experience something.

In the program "Esra Erol'da", we often see kidnapped children of women by their husbands. On December 26, Meltem said "I just wanted to be a mother in life. I have been a mother and a father of my children. I have work and insurance. I look after my children". Meltem, whose child had been kidnapped by her father, was an employee and a woman earning her money. But she is still a victim. However, we see that the statements against women are generally in the direction of protecting the woman and protecting the child and mother in the child-mother relationship. On 25 December 2018, the father was asked why he did not kidnap the boy but only the girl. He answered, "A girl may suffer from being hurt because her mother is living with a man". Then he was warned by the presenter and the guest lawyer in the program: "it is not a boy or girl issue; children are inseparable".

On 26 December 2018, in the program "Esra Erol'da" in response to a sentence of a father-in-law "she will find a husband and marry him immediately", Esra Erol said his sentence was absolutely wrong.

On December 27, 2018, Esra Erol asks "Why would a woman leave her house?" After this, guests are invited to the studio and the viewers in the studio made conversations about marriage. Here, in fact, a woman will not leave the house without reason is expressed.

On December 28, 2018, Esra Erol said: "we are saving lives here; we are rescuing relationships". On the same date, a man who committed violence to his wife appeared in the broadcast in order to make peace with his wife. He said, "If I do not make peace with my wife, I would like to receive help from the expert here". The woman connected to the broadcast and said "we married by escaping without the approval of our families. I had no place to go. I waited for him to recover". The lawyer and the presenter told the woman "many women think that they can correct their husbands. But that cycle does not change". After that, Esra Erol made the following statement:

"I would like to make an announcement to women here: do not ignore the 'once'. It is not loving. People who love do not hurt his/her loved one. He would not understand even if I insulted him."

In Esra Erol's program, we see that the most popular topics are missing people and events in marriage and family relations. Those who want to be a mother and have no children are also included in the program. In the program, an IVF specialist is treating the families who want children. The results are announced on a live broadcast.

When all the programs are considered, we see that attention is mostly drawn to the fact that women are first "mothers". The citations that gender stereotypes have imposed on women are repeated with the discourses included in the programs. But the program presenters were consciously expressed that they did not want the guests to make statements such as "you are a woman", "you should stay with your husband at all times", etc. and intervened in such situations. The programs reveal as a whole that women cannot get rid of their attributes of "victim, mother, poor and helpless".

Butler (2004, p. 142) stated that the situation of discourse is not the same as what is said or can be said, but stated that being addressed deprives the person from the beginning. It is a form of violence when the person is imposed on a series of things. In this context, we see that even the words used to address women contain violence.

Even though discriminatory discourse towards women is tried to be avoided in the programs, the fact that women are included in these programs shows that the position of women in society should be questioned.

FUTURE RESEARCH DIRECTIONS

In the study, content analysis of the programs was made. In order to further deepen the research, it is suggested that the participants in the program are reached for future studies by asking them why they choose this path. Part of the study can also be carried out in the place the program was produced in order to create a different perspective. It is also possible to carry out viewer research and question the reason why these programs are monitored and what the viewer perceives from these programs.

The following question should be examined in future researches: 'does the fact that women appear in these programs with attributes like helpless, altruistic and so on. reflect the reality of society, or are the women who come to these programs selected especially in such a way that they reinforce the belief "women are like this"?'

CONCLUSION

Within the scope of content analysis, the subjects in the programs and the percentages of the topics in the programs were examined within the scope of content analysis. Within the framework of the discourse analysis, the expressions that were discussed and prominent in the programs were examined. The most prominent topics in the sample programs were: loss, male-female relationship, child and marriage. The problems experienced in all of the programs have been tried to be solved. Losses were sought, problems in marriages were tried to be solved. In these processes, lawyers and experts were present as guides in the programs. The reasons for women's participation in these three programs respectively: 1- victim 2- wife 3- mother. Discourse against women is generally about "protecting" the woman and "protecting the mother and child" within the child-mother relationship.

Most of the private television channels broadcast in the morning and evening with different names. These women's programs are reproduced as popular cultural products. Although the formats change in certain ratios as seen over time, the content continues with transformation. As in all mass culture products, the intention seems to be including women's problems in these programs and eliminating or changing these problems, but this is not the main goal. The continuation of more existing judgments, the continuation of traditional discourses, repetition, and strengthening of them are in question. In these programs, the fact that women are shown as "victims of honor killings", "sexual objects", "bad women", "good spouses" and so on and therefore the channels try to achieve high ratings make women an "instrument" for the channels to make more money.

In women's programs, we see that it proceeds from the basis of identification. But, as Butler put it, here too, identification is based on a difference that she tries to overcome. The woman viewer who thinks that "I am not the identified person" is tried to be attracted for the screen. Women's individual sadness and distress, and the inability to reach their children are often included in the work for the female audiences to establish identity. Although it is emphasized that women's education is important and economic freedom should be in the programs, no real solutions are offered for these issues. The discourses created and continued in women's programs are in concordance with the traditions and moral structure of the society and provide their continuity.

We can see that the basic features of these programs are that the human characteristics and identity of women are not emphasized whatever the position of the woman. Women's 'altruistic mother, a good wife, and good housewife' identities are highlighted. In general, the programs are based on family. It is emphasized that the foundation of society is family and the place of women is in the family. On the other hand, when we look at the content of the programs, it is seen that the woman is aimed to raise awareness and adapt to the public sphere. Women are in a position whose awareness is tried to be raised in child care, education, health, and family relations. Thus, for the adoption of the behaviors approved and corrected by the society, the same contents are repeated in different time periods with different guests but within the same boundaries, and women's models suitable for the social structure are drawn.

The thing that ties us morally, as Butler has stated, is the way others address us because we cannot avoid it and pretend not to understand it. The addressing of others is beyond our will. The abolishment of sexist rhetoric and the adjectives attached to women will be realized with the awareness that women will create.

REFERENCES

Belsey, A., & Chadwick, R. (1998). Kod ve Etik. In A. Basley, & R. Chadwick (Eds.), *Medya ve Gazetecilikte Etik Sorunlar*. Ayrıntı Yayınları, Birinci Basım.

Butler, Ju. (2004). *Kırılgan Hayat Yasın ve Şiddet Gücü*. İstanbul, Turkey: Metis Yayınları.

Cankaya, Ö. (2003). *Bir Kitle İletişim Kurumunun Tarihi: TRT 1927-2000*. İstanbul, Turkey: Yapı Kredi Yayınları.

Çelenk, S. (2005). *Televizyon, Temsil, Kültür*. Ankara, Turkey: Ütopya Yayınevi.

Hooks, B. (2002). *Feminizm Herkes İçindir*. İstanbul, Turkey: Çitlenbik Yayınları.

Jensen, K. B. (2005). Sosyal Kaynak Olarak Haberler: Danimarka Televizyon Haberleri Hakkında Nitel Ampirik Bir Çalışma. In *Medya ve İzleyici Bitmeyen Tartışma*. Ankara, Turkey: Vadi Yayınları.

Michel, A. (1984). Feminizm. Yeni Yüzyıl Kitaplığı, Pres Universitaires De France Yayınları.

Oskay, Ü. (2005). *İletişimin ABC'si*. İstanbul, Turkey: Der Yayınları.

Özgür, Ö. (2017). *Yayınlanan Kadın Programlarında Toplumsal Cinsiyet Rollerinin Sunumu*. Uluslararası Hakemli İletişim ve Edebiyat Araştırmaları Dergisi.

Saktanber, A. (1995). Türkiye'de Medyada Kadın: Serbest, Müsait Kadın veya İyi Eş, Fedakar Anne. In Ş. Tekeli (Ed.), *Kadın Bakış Açısından Kadınlar*. İstanbul, Turkey: İletişim Yayınları.

Schroeder, K. (2007). *Popüler Feminizm, Türkiye ve Britanya'da Kadın Dergileri*. İstanbul, Turkey: Bağlam Yayınları.

Serim, Ö. (2007). *Türk Televizyon Tarihi 1952-2006*. İstanbul, Turkey: Epsilon Yayınevi.

Türkoğlu, N. (2007). *İletişim Bilimlerinden Kültürel Çalışmalara Toplumsal İletişim Tanımlar*. İstanbul, Turkey: Kalemus Yayınları.

Zografu, L. (n.d.). *Lokantamızda Prens ve Prensesler Daima Taze ve Bol Masal Sosu ile Sunulur*. Kriton Dinçmen, Scala Yayıncılık.

KEY TERMS AND DEFINITIONS

Communication Research: Media-related systematic investigation and the study of materials and sources in order to establish facts and to reach new conclusions.

Feminism: The advocacy of women's rights on the grounds of political, social, and economic equality to men.

Gender: The state of being male or female (typically used with reference to social and cultural differences rather than biological ones).

Media: The main means of mass communication (especially television, radio, newspapers, and the internet) regarded collectively.

Television: A system for transmitting visual images and sound that are reproduced on screens, chiefly used to broadcast programs for entertainment, information, and education.

Violence: Physical and non-physical harm that causes damage, pain, injury, or fear.

Violent: Using or involving physical force intended to hurt, damage, or kill someone or something.

Woman Programs: Women's programs on television.

Chapter 3
The Politico-Poetic Representation of Turkish Women in *Türk Kadını* Magazine (1966-1974)

Fatma Fulya Tepe
Istanbul Aydın University, Turkey

ABSTRACT

This chapter aims to explore the ways women are represented in the context of 20th century Turkey by analyzing four poems, namely "Türk Kadını" (Turkish Woman), "Anadolu Kadını" (Anatolian Woman), "Kadın–Ana" (Woman-Mother), and "Ayşe," published in the Türk Kadını magazine in the 1960s. Purposive sampling was used in the selection of the poems, which were later interpreted with the strategies of descriptive content analysis. In these poems, the Turkish woman is being represented and celebrated in at least the following four ways: (1) by being celebrated for combining heroism, goodness, and naturalness; (2) by having her struggle with primitive conditions of life celebrated as yet another form of heroism; (3) by being celebrated as a creative mother of the nation, charged with finding solutions to the problems of the country; (4) by being celebrated as a hardworking daughter of the nation to whom the country owes recognition and support.

DOI: 10.4018/978-1-7998-0128-3.ch003

INTRODUCTION

The *Türk Kadını* (Turkish Woman) was a monthly magazine of opinion, art and education, published in Turkey between 1966 and 1974. This chapter explores how Turkish women are represented in the 1960s' Turkey by a detailed study of four poems published in this magazine. The present study departs from the following idea: Although researchers have paid attention to the history of Turkish women and developed general themes and conceptual approaches to them, detailed and vivid historical representations of Turkish women and Anatolian women are still missing. The author of this chapter believes that rich and vivid representations of Turkish women could be fruitfully uncovered from literary sources, such as poetry. Thus, the primary aim of this chapter is to provide and analyse examples of politico-poetic conceptualizations of Turkish women. A secondary aim is to show how literature can contribute to the field of Turkish women's studies and political theory.

BACKGROUND

In political poetry, politics and poetry can be connected in various ways. One such relation was defined by Percy Bysshe Shelley. In his *A Defence of Poetry* (1840), Shelley argues not only that poetry is "divine", but that it "is at the same time the root and blossom of all other systems of thought", and he asks, rhetorically, "What were virtue, love, patriotism, friendship ... if poetry did not ascend to bring light and fire from those eternal regions where the owl-winged faculty of calculation dare not ever soar?" (Shelley, 1840, p. 47). Here poetry is superior to both political and moral beliefs in that it makes these beliefs vivid and relevant to people in a way that purely factual accounts cannot achieve. According to the more contemporary view of David Orr, political poetry is "concerned with a specific political situation; rooted in an identifiable political philosophy; addressing a particular political actor; written in language that can be understood and appreciated by its intended audience; and finally, offered in a public forum where it can have a maximum persuasive effect" (Orr, 2008, p. 415). What both Shelley and Orr have in common is the idea that political poetry works persuasively, bringing "light and fire" to political beliefs. In this chapter, this motivating function of political poetry will be studied and analysed from the point of view of Turkish nationalist ideas concerning the role of Turkish woman.

The poetry of nationalism is a specific form of political poetry, born out of the nationalist ideologies that were born in the aftermaths of the French Revolution. The poets of nationalist movements aim to catch what they believe to be the "spirit" of their nation: "They use its own language to describe its landscape, customs, past, myths, and hopes for the future. They inspire their people with a proud identity – and at times self-criticism and shame, hatred and militancy" (Aberbach, 2003, p. 256).

The poetry of Turkish nationalism, too, has emerged as a repercussion of historical and political developments following the French Revolution (Türkeş, 2009). Kemal Karpat notes that with the influence of the Westernization movement in the cultural domain since the mid-1800s, Turkish literature adopted social themes and "(t)he greatest literary names during this period drew their reputations more from political and social views connected with the fate of the society than from the actual literary value of their words" (Karpat, 1960: 29). For instance, "Ziya Gökalp, the formulator of Turkish nationalism and of the ideas of modernization subsequently accepted in the Republic, expressed his views first in the form of poems and advocated the use of literature to spread the ideas of nationalism and bring about society's modernization" (Karpat, 1960, p. 29).

After the establishment of the Republic of Turkey in 1923, Mustafa Kemal Atatürk adopted Westernization as a political path for the new republic, and, as part of this Westernization policy, laws changing the legal status of women were introduced (Arat, 2001, p. 27). In this context, the shari'a law, a remnant of the Ottoman Empire, was replaced by the 1926 Swiss Civil Code. According to this, women and men were equalized in relation to divorce and inheritance while polygamy was abolished and civil marriage was made a requirement (Arat, 1996, p. 29). In 1924 women were granted equal rights with men to receive education, including higher education, and in 1930 they received the rights to vote and to be elected in local elections, from 1934 also in national elections (Arat, 2005, p. 105). This period (1926–1945), which is known as the golden years of the Kemalist Age (Zürcher, 2016, p. 18), contained the emergence of a distinction between the Istanbul woman and the Anatolian woman (Toska, 1998; Çaha, 2011; Durakbaşa, 2011). Mustafa Kemal Atatürk himself applies this distinction in some of his speeches, defining the Anatolian woman as the real woman of the republic (Toska, 1998, p. 77). Here, the term "Anatolian woman" is used in contrast to educated urban upper class women; mostly it refers to peasant Turkish women living in the rural Anatolian part of Turkey. Ömer Çaha, reporting a memory of İffet Halim Oruz, writes that Atatürk wanted Oruz, who demanded voting rights for women in 1930, to give up on this question and instead educate the peasant women about the revolutions that had taken place (Çaha, 2010). Likewise, Yaprak Zihnioğlu notes the following statement made by the Kemalist women's movement after 1946: "The women did not know the rights granted to them by the 'Great Leader' Atatürk. These rights should be taught to them" (Zihnioğlu, 2009, p. 808). Teaching Anatolian women about their rights would be the task of urban educated women. Durakbaşa, too, mentions that the modernizing women's movement in the early years of the republic focused on saving women from backwardness in order for the nation to progress (Durakbaşa, 2011, p. 463).

Later, during the Cold War years, a literature praising Kemalist reforms regarding the status of Turkish women emerged, equating the legal rights given to women with the near completion of urban women's liberation, at least for those who were educated. In 1982 Binnaz Toprak, in a critical evaluation of the Kemalist literature, argued that despite the existence of rights for women, even educated urban Turkish women were still far from liberation. In her analysis, Toprak distinguished women's liberation from their emancipation. While emancipation meant gaining legal and political rights, liberation meant making choices of their own. Emancipation was a pre-requisite of liberation, but it did not guarantee liberation itself (Toprak, 1982, pp. 361–362). The "Emancipated but Unliberated Turkish Women argument", as summarized above, was later supported and applied by other scholars such as Deniz Kandiyoti (1987), Nermin Abadan-Unat (1991), and Zehra Arat (1998). Similar arguments were made in different terms by other scholars, such as Ayşe Durakbaşa (1998a; 1998b), Ayşe Durakbaşa and Aynur İlyasoğlu (2001). Yeşim Arat (2000) complements Toprak's work in two ways: First, while Toprak's work focuses on structural aspects, Yeşim Arat's work is based on data concerning the collective agency of post-1980 women. Second, Arat's article develops the Toprak argument, stating that Turkish women became both emancipated and liberated in the post-1980 period. This discussion contained the Istanbul woman (urban women) and Anatolian woman (rural women) distinction only implicitly and the issue of Anatolian woman and its relation to Turkish woman category was not elaborated further in this literature. For a more recent discussion of the emancipated by unliberated argument, see Tepe and Bauhn (2017).

Recently Tanıl Bora (2017) has provided a narrative about the emergence of the distinction between Istanbul ladies and Anatolian women. Bora connects the emergence of these two categories of women to a campaign that was aimed to bring down and isolate Nezihe Muhiddin, the president of Turkish Women's Union. According to Bora,

In a context in which the Sheik Said Rebellion was being suppressed, the Progressive Republican party was closed down, and the press was placed under government control, a smear campaign started against Nezihe Muhiddin… The Anatolian woman image, which was to become a strong and durable motive of anti-feminist discourse, came into circulation in this campaign. The portrait of the dignified, courageous Anatolian woman, making sacrifices for her country without any fuss, performing the duties of motherhood as well as working in the fields, was polished into an ideal type, which made the spoiled urban snob type of woman lose esteem. According to this depiction, that parasitic select minority, who were strangers to the reality of the Anatolian woman's suffering, had demanded equal rights for the sake of their own pleasure and as a way of escaping the duties of mothers and wives. This smear campaign was completed with a series of caricatures in which women struggling for rights were depicted as "tango women" who were after makeup, fashion, satin and silk. This sexist caricaturization would continue to prevail for several decades (Bora, 2017, pp. 755–756).

With the emergence of the Istanbul lady and Anatolian woman categories, the Kemalists had involved themselves in a war on two fronts. On the one hand, they faced religious-conservative opposition in the countryside, and here they wanted to bring modern views to Anatolian women. On the other hand, they faced demands for equal women's right from educated urban women, and in order to push them back they invoked the ideal of rural Anatolian woman. In this context, the Anatolian woman was idealized as an icon of republican virtues, but at the same time she was to be educated to be of service to the republic rather than a victim of the religious superstition and fanaticism of the rural areas. Urban women could be seen as either a problem (if they demanded rights as women rather than as Turkish citizens) or a solution (if they could be of service to the national educational project): "The village woman with her self-sacrificing, hard-working, dignified personality, dedicating her very being to motherhood, was perceived as the "correct" and ideal Turkish woman. While on the one hand republican women would teach village woman how to read and write, on the other hand they should take inspiration from her" (Bora, 2017, p. 759).

In this story of the categories of Istanbul ladies and Anatolian women, Bora presents the Anatolian woman image as part of a discourse aimed at controlling Istanbul feminists. However, from the viewpoint of the political leadership, and given that Anatolian women constituted the majority of Turkish women at the time, it can also be conceived of as a discourse of necessity. After all, the political leaders had to develop a policy for the inclusion of the majority of the country's population as part of their programme for republican national unity.

The poems that will be studied here come from the *Türk Kadını* (Turkish Woman), a monthly magazine of opinion, art, and education, published in Turkey between 1966 and 1974. It was one of a small group of magazines in the 1960s and 1970s that were explicitly dedicated to Turkish women. In four poems published in the *Türk Kadını* magazine in 1966 – "Türk Kadını" (Turkish Woman), "Anadolu Kadını" (Anatolian Woman), "Kadın-Ana" (Woman-Mother), and "Ayşe" – the Turkish woman is being represented in at least the following four ways: (1) as combining in her person the seemingly opposite qualities of passive femininity and female heroism; (2) as having her struggle with limited resources purified and idealized by being nationalized; (3) as a mother of the nation who will find solutions to the problems of the country; (4) as a hardworking daughter of the nation to whom the country owes recognition and support. These findings support the ideas of Anthias and Yuval-Davis regarding the ways in which women participate in national projects, namely, biological reproduction (related to motherhood) and reproduction of state ideology (related to citizenship) (1989, p. 7).

WOMEN OF THE TURKISH NATION IN FOUR POEMS FROM 1966

A previous study on *Türk Kadını* magazine has emphasized that the Turkish Cold War concept of the Mother Citizen and a certain conception of homefront duties was central to this magazine (Tepe, 2017). Motherhood, citizenship, and duties also figure prominently in the poems studied in this chapter.

Methods

Model of the Research

The present study relies on qualitative rather than quantitative methods, taking its point of departure in four poems published in the *Türk Kadını* magazine in 1966. The point of this qualitative approach is not to provide statistically valid generalizations but rather to establish the existence of a particular discourse and to suggest new research directions (Reinharz, 1992). The analysis of the poems will rely on sensitivity, in the sense of "having insight as well as being tuned in to and being able to pick up on relevant issues" (Corbin and Strauss, 2015, p. 78) and contextual inferences, based on relevant background knowledge.

Sample Group

In this study, non-probability sampling is used as in most qualitative research. As Honigmann has noted, non-probability sampling aims to solve qualitative problems, such as "discovering what occurs, the implications of what occurs, and the relationships linking occurrences" (1982, p. 84). The most common form of non-probabilistic sampling is called purposive (Chein, 1981) or purposeful (Patton, 2002). Merriam explains that "purposeful sampling is based on the assumption that the investigator wants to discover, understand, and gain insight and therefore must select a sample from which the most can be learnt" (2009, p. 77). In this study purposive sampling has been used in selecting a magazine that could be expected to provide examples of representations of Turkish women. Four poems were selected to be analysed, based on the ways in which they represent different aspects of Turkish women. In this study, the researcher selected the magazine and the poems according to the relevance of their themes to womanhood and nationality in Turkey in an interchangeable order.

The authors of the poems that are under consideration here are all women. The first poem, "Turkish Woman" is written by Halide Nusret Zorlutuna; the second, "Anatolian Woman", by Asuman Kavak; the third, "Woman-Mother" by Neriman Saryal; while the fourth poem, "Ayşe", is written by Şükûfe Nihal. Two of these writers, namely Şükûfe Nihal and Halide Nusret Zorlutuna, are classified as national romantics (Korkmaz and Özcan, 2007). Neriman Saryal is a teacher-poet who worked at state schools and universities. As for Asuman Kavak, she cannot be traced in any anthologies or internet sources. Çelik Aruoba, the son of the publishers of the *Türk Kadını* magazine, told the author of this chapter in a telephone communication (on 19 February, 2019) that he does not remember the name of Asuman Kavak and that most likely she was an amateur poet who sent her poem to his mother, Muazzez Aruoba, who liked it and decided to publish it.

Data Analysis

The kind of material used in this research, that is, the four poems selected from the *Türk Kadını* magazine, are classified as popular culture documents in the relevant methodological literature (Merriam, 2009: 143). As such, the poems will be analysed according to the strategies of textual analysis, having their conceptualizations and images of Turkish women illuminated by an imaginative interpretation that is informed by relevant historical and social background knowledge.

The original language of the poems under study is Turkish. The English translation that appears in this chapter has been made by its author. The analysed poems are linked to each other by a thematic structure. The first poem starts with depicting the *Turkish woman*, using motives from nature and stating her heroism. The second poem further develops this heroism as a feature of how *Anatolian women* deal with their harsh conditions of life. The third poem connects this heroism to the role of Turkish women as *mothers of the nation*, assuming responsibility for the development of the country. The fourth poem addresses Turkish women as the *daughters of the nation*, bringing back the theme of nature from the first poem and combining it with the heroism of the second poem and the national mission of the third poem. Accordingly, the fourth poem integrates elements of all the previous poems. Taken together, the four poems combine to produce a politico-poetical narrative of Turkish women.

Turkish Woman

Elegant like a flower, pure like water
Goodness emanates from her soul, like the scent of a rose
Her name became legendary on the side of heroism
History knows her well: TURKISH WOMAN is her name.

In the title of the poem, the speaker constructs a character by combining a national axis with a gender axis. The character that is being described in the poem is accordingly identified first with her national and second with her gender belonging; she is a Turkish woman rather than a woman in Turkey. This reflects the nationalist priorities of the speaker. Despite this, in the poem the feminine qualities of the character are described first, before the political quality of heroism.

In this poem, an image of the Turkish woman is constructed on hierarchical binary oppositions. The speaker relies heavily on attributes derived from nature – flower, water, rose – which brings out the classical essentialist dichotomy in which nature and women are contrasted with men and culture (see, for instance, Ortner (1972) and Mathieu (1978)). The speaker goes on by associating the natural qualities of women with various aesthetic attributes, such as elegance, purity, and sweetness, but also the moral quality of goodness. It should be noted here that the property of purity has a religious connotation as well. Here it is also important to note what is being negated. By implication it is ruled out that a Turkish woman could be rude, dirty and sinful. For all her goodness and sweetness, the Turkish woman is here conceived of as a passive object rather than an active subject. It is as if this woman cannot have any interests and drives of her own, she does not want or seek anything, she just embodies various qualities that might be attractive or useful to others. The speaker describes the Turkish woman in visual terms, as an icon of beauty and goodness to behold rather than as an agent with purposes of her own; moreover, she is described from the perspective of a distant and abstract audience ("history") as "legendary", that is, as a mythical creature rather than a living and breathing woman. She is assigned the property of heroism, but the reader is given no explanation why. It appears a bit strange, to say the least, that this flowerlike creature also should embody heroic qualities.

In short: The Turkish woman is perceived as having a character closely related to nature or that is associated with positive, but also passive natural qualities. Underlying this is an at least implicit essentialist argument: women are associated with nature, men with culture. Moreover, it could be argued that the speaker at least implicitly relies on a set of common hierarchical binary oppositions. She has her account of the Turkish woman rely on characteristics that she expects her audience to approve of; by implication the opposite characteristics represent qualities that a Turkish woman should *not* be associated with. The set of hierarchical binary oppositions can be listed as follows:

1. Turkishness vs. foreignness;
2. Female vs. male;
3. Nature vs. culture;
4. Elegance vs. roughness;
5. Cleanliness vs. dirtiness;
6. Purity vs. sinfulness;
7. Goodness vs. evil;
8. Passivity vs. activity;

In this way, with positive qualities of plants and water, Turkish woman is being sterilized and it is implied that she can exist only in this sterilized way or she can be accepted only in this way. Thus, the speaker creates an image of the Turkish woman that is abstract and idealized, free of any features characteristic of real life women. This image is also strangely contradictory, depicting a creature who is both harmless and heroic, both passive and "legendary", both submissive and historically remarkable, and who is both a child of nature and an icon of society. In other words, the woman described here is idealized beyond reason. She is elevated to a level of abstraction at which we cannot have even an image of a real woman. This is also consistent with Boland's comment about nationalist poetic conceptualizations of women that "once the feminine image … became fused with a national concept then both were simplified and reduced" (1987, p. 152). Thus in nationalist poetry, women become icons rather than really existing women.

Another interesting aspect here is how the speaker actually masculinizes the Turkish woman by attributing to her the typically male quality of heroism – it is her capacity for heroism that makes her "legendary". Heroism is typically associated with bravery in war, involving a willingness both to kill and to be killed when necessary. It is difficult to see how such a quality can easily coexist with the other attributes of the poem, signifying a harmless, flowerlike, elegant, and goodhearted being. Moreover, the speaker not only masculinizes the Turkish woman but also moves her from the private to public sphere, which traditionally has been inhabited by men: Heroism relates to actions that are performed for others, for a group or society or a state. Although this could be considered as a way of honouring and praising the Turkish woman, it in fact suggests that in order for her to earn such honouring and praise, she must acquire typically male qualities. Hence, the celebration of the Turkish woman in this poem is ambiguous – she is indeed celebrated, by not as a real life woman, struggling with the vast gender inequalities characterizing the Turkish republic at the time, but rather as one who is already embodying the most significant male qualities and hence implicitly equal to men.

According to this poem, the Turkish woman takes her place in history by performing "legendary" acts of heroism; in other words, she does it by performing typically male acts of war, destroying or helping to destroy the enemy (as some Turkish women actually did during the War of Independence (1919–1922)). Hence, the Turkish Woman enters history by combining her "natural" feminine qualities with heroic masculine qualities typical of war time activities. By implication, it seems it would not be possible for her to take place in history or become legendary otherwise. Still, the Turkish woman's "natural" qualities of elegance, sweetness, purity, and goodness are also essential: the speaker does not idealize a woman who turns into a man, but rather a woman who combines qualities associated with femininity with qualities associated with masculinity. The feminine qualities also provide a contrasting background for the masculine ones, making the Turkish woman appear as someone very special and unique.

The last line of the poem – "History knows her well: TURKISH WOMAN is her name" – takes on a somewhat intimidating tone. Here the name "TURKISH WOMAN" is written in capital letters as the speaker wants to underline that this is a very unique kind of woman, to be admired by the whole Turkish nation and to be feared by all its enemies. The capitalization of "Turkish Woman" also serves to promote the idea of a singular monolithic Turkish Woman category, homogenizing and stereotyping the qualities of Turkish women (in plural) and creates. Obviously, this Turkish Woman category functions as an ideal with normative power.

Anatolian Women

Is it the sweat or tears collected on your forehead, my Fadime?
Your hands are calloused, in your eyes, there is faith
Tell me, my Zeyneb, my Ayşe!
When you are running between your hut and the field,
Don't the thorns that pierce your feet hurt?
The thing, which makes you lost in thought,
Is it the meal you plan for the evening?
Is it bulgur, is it tarhana, is it curd what you eat?
Is it your fate or luck?
That cry of the baby
Whose belly cord you cut between two stones.

The Politico-Poetic Representation of Turkish Women in Türk Kadını Magazine (1966–1974)

Anatolia is the name of a geographical region of Turkey which in the 1960s consisted of mostly rural areas. In the title of this poem, it is first Anatolianness, connoting a rural background, that is highlighted, followed by the gender identity of woman. The subjects that fall in the intersection of these two social markers respectively constitute the topic of this poem. Thus, the main subject of this poem is Anatolian Woman with a capital A and capital W. It should be noted here that this singular category is different from the category of Anatolian women, which is a plural category that could comprise the diversity of women living in Anatolia. However, here, from this category of singular Anatolian Woman, we understand that the speaker is not interested in diversity (religious or ethnic) among Anatolian women. The speaker wants to construct a homogeneous Anatolian Woman category assigning to it certain fixed qualities. Accordingly, we should expect some generalizations to follow, revealing a particular kind of Anatolian woman imagery. From these generalizations we will be able to draw conclusions about the speaker's priorities and preconceptions.

In the poem, the Anatolian Woman is addressed with several common woman's names, suggesting that she represents every woman. The names used to address the Anatolian Woman is Fadime, Ayşe, and Zeynep. These are mainly Turkish names. However, Anatolia has a very mixed population of different ethnic as well as religious backgrounds. The use of mainly Turkish woman's names contributes to the homogenization of the Anatolian woman category. From this the reader can deduce that the speaker has a view of Anatolian woman that equates her with Turkish woman. But what kind of Turkish woman is this? What qualities are emphasized?

First the speaker observes Fadime and addresses her and asks her if it is sweat or tears that shows on her forehead. In this way, the speaker approaches Fadime in a sympathetic way, empathizing with her condition. The speaker recognizes Fadime's hard physical work and suffering. From this, it is understood that the speaker takes an interest in Fadime and that she can perceive the hardships characterizing Fadime's life. Hence, as the poem develops we do not only learn about Anatolian Woman but we also learn something about the speaker, too. Another interpretation that suggests itself here is that the speaker admires Anatolian women's toughness, endurance, and capacity to bear pain and suffering. It is a kind of soldierly qualities that the speaker sees in these women. This, of course, also fits with the nationalist agenda, that women are conceived of as soldiers without uniform, worthy of respect for their everyday courage (just as soldiers are expected to be courageous in war).

The speaker further observes that Fadime's hands are calloused and her eyes are full of faith. This further adds to the recognition of Fadime's hard manual work as well as confirms her spiritual qualities, too. Fadime believes in God and it could be suggested that the speaker wants the readers to understand that Fadime's faith makes her stronger in her manual work. So Fadime is portrayed as an active woman who does physical or manual work in rural Anatolia and this is combined with her having a religious faith. Hence, her world is not limited to the negative conditions of this world (poverty, toil, and so on) but she is also connected to another world, the world of God and of her religion.

Then the speaker addresses other Anatolian women, Zeyneb and Ayşe, wanting them to tell her if it does not hurt when the thorns in the field pierce their feet. Here, the speaker wants to reveal the difficult rural conditions of Anatolian women. These are women who have to walk barefoot on the unpaved ground (no shoes, no means of transportation) to do hard physical labour in the fields. Moroever, the fact that the home of these women is a "hut" rather than a house further underlines how underprivileged they are. The poverty and primitivity of their lives are brought out vividly. The speaker expresses not only her sympathy with these Anatolian women but also her admiration for them and their struggle to make a living for themselves. By asking how they can manage or stand this kind of life, the speaker implies that she herself would not be able to cope with conditions such as these.

The speaker asks the Anatolian woman if it is the dinner that she will cook for tonight that makes her lost in thoughts. The food that is mentioned here is of a quite modest kind, involving no meat and no fish. Once more, the difficult living conditions of Anatolian woman are underlined. The Anatolian woman is presented as an active and hardworking woman but also as one who is living with very limited resources. When the speaker asks "Is the cry of the baby whose belly cord you cut in two stones?" this suggests the absence of any hospital or medical services: women give birth on their own and have to cope with this one their own as well. The question "Is it your fate or your luck?" suggests that although these difficult conditions cannot be escaped, the Anatolian woman is capable of embracing them in a hopeful manner. What an observer might think of as just a harsh fate, she might think of as luck – it could have been even worse, and she will manage.

Here it is important to note that while the Anatolian woman is presented as an active and courageous woman with few means at her disposal, her connection to other people is unclear. She is represented as being on her own and the existence of others (like the ones she is cooking for or the baby in the poem) is only implied. Nor is the reader told anything about her relations to other women. Hence, she is represented as a rather isolated person, imprisoned by conditions of poverty and hardship. Perhaps the speaker intends to offer the prospect of a wider solidarity with the Anatolian woman and so bring her out of her isolation.

One should also pay attention to other aspects of the Anatolian woman's condition that are not mentioned in the poem. For instance, women who die young in childbirth, women who are forced into marriage, women who are beaten by their fathers and husbands, women who cannot read and write and for this reason are barred from sharing in the wider society – all these aspects of Anatolian women's lives are excluded from the speaker's attention, although they are very much present in the rural conditions that she describes. One can speculate about the reasons for this. For instance, that the poem does not mention women being beaten (and sometimes killed) by husbands and fathers could be explained by the fact that it is not only about celebrating Anatolian woman, but also about creating a nationalist narrative, elevating the Anatolian woman into an icon of Turkishness. It would be difficult to succeed in such an aim if one has to admit that this iconic woman is actually also the victim of Turkish men's abuse and violence. To admit this aspect of Anatolian women's reality would be to introduce a narrative in which Turkish men oppress Turkish women, which would be divisive rather than unifying from a nationalist point of view.

To sum up, the speaker focuses on the tough and enduring women, but ignores those are who instead broken by the adversities that they have to face and because they are denied of opportunities for development. The speaker wants to raise a monument to the Anatolian women, but she does not make an argument in favor of social reform or equal opportunities, nor does she pay any attention to the abuse and gender inequalities that Anatolian women had to live with.

Woman-Mother

Responsibility means
To see and solve
The piled up problems
Of the backward country
You are a woman and you are a mother
Without being afraid of the unfriendly gazes
Without being daunted by and being tired
You will know your responsibility
And you will know...
That the one who make a nation live is the mother
That the one who develops a nation is the woman

This poem, written by a woman for other women, highlights altruism. The title of the poem is Woman-Mother. Hence, first the gender and then the motherhood identity have been chosen to be emphasized. In this case, and unlike the previous poems, the nationality marker has been left out in the title. Despite this, in poem itself country, nationality, and responsibilities play an important part. Moreover, the relevant responsibility here is defined in terms of concern for the nation and its problems. This responsibility is then related to the (Turkish) woman in her capacity as a mother. Implicit here is a traditional view of mothers as responsible caregivers in the family context. Just as women as mothers are expected to care for their children (and for their husbands), so they are expected to care for the whole nation of which they are members. Another implication here is that the nation is to be thought of as an extended family. Hence, the problems of the nation become the natural concern and responsibility of women-mothers. (This politicized role of women-mothers has in another context been conceptualized as the *Mother Citizen* (Tepe, 2017).) It has been argued that nationalists often identify women as mothers "to protect the patriarchal division between the private and the public domains" (Adak, 2010, p. 83). While this may well be true for certain anti-feminist nationalists, it is certainly not the case here. Instead this poem encourages, indeed exhorts women to enter the public sphere, assuming responsibility for the nation and its problems. Rather than suggesting that women should confine their motherhood responsibilities to their families, it urges them to extend these responsibilities to the entire nation.

In this poem, the speaker praises the woman-mother as one who is not "afraid of, daunted by, tired of unfriendly gazes". From where do these unfriendly gazes come? Presumably from sexist opponents to emancipated women who are reluctant to allow these women a role in the public sphere. The speaker however takes women's participation in public life as not only permissible but as required and indeed as a duty for women to realize: "you will recognize your responsibility". This perspective, combining a nationalist view of civic duties with a traditional conception of mothers as caregivers, places the woman-mother in an active public role. The speaker wants the woman-mother know that it is woman who makes a nation live and develop. According to the logic of this discourse, everything depends on woman. There is no mention of man. The responsibility for resolving public problems are on the shoulders of the women. Accordingly, it can be questioned whether this is a liberating perspective. Certainly, it gives woman a public role, and to this extent it can be considered as emancipatory. However, the speaker's approach places all the burdens of the nation on the shoulders of woman, just as traditional gender roles place the burden of caring for children and husband on her shoulders. Merely because of her being a woman and a mother, public as well as private duties are assigned to her. Moreover, the perspective of this poem promotes a view of woman as mother that by implication denies room for women who cannot or do not want to become mothers. In this way, for all its possible emancipatory intention, the poem reinforces a traditional essentialist and biologist view, according to which "woman's body seems to doom her to mere reproduction of life" (Ortner, 1972, p. 14). Hence, the poem both underestimates women (by implicitly reducing them and their social role to motherhood) and overestimates them (by making them responsible for the well-being of the nation in virtue of their gender and capacity for motherhood). Likewise, there is in this poem a tension between a kind of nationalist feminism, that gives women the right as well as the duty to assume responsibility for the whole nation, and a more traditional and essentialist view of women as primarily mothers and caregivers. There is also a similarity with the previous two poems in that women are assumed to possess heroic qualities – in the context of this poem, these heroic qualities are demonstrated not only in women's tireless efforts to solve the problems of the nation, but also in their willingness to fulfil their extended motherhood duties to the nation regardless of the disapproval of their environment. It is also these heroic qualities that makes woman a suitable subject for her mission to save the nation. Hence, the poem expresses the viewpoint of a special kind of state feminism, according to which women are perceived to have the ability as well as the responsibility and duty to observe and solve the problems of the country. This approach gives woman an active and central role in the public life of the nation, while at the same time preserving a traditional conception of woman as mother and caregiver.

Ayşe

I am out on the roads, wandering, asking for you AYŞE
I wouldn't stop even if I encounter fire or tempest
I found you sometimes in the fields, sometimes at the spring;
Sometimes I found you, like a gazelle on a sharp abyss
Wherever you are, you are emotional, wherever you are, you are reserved;
Your great soul is in love with nature from the birth
For a lifetime you conversed with the stars, the moon and the sun,
For a lifetime you were in the company of poor birds
At the bottom of a valley, in the shadow of a fence
In your voice there is the epic of your torak1 roofed home
Open the secrets of your sad heart to me, too,
Then maybe tomorrow of this night becomes heaven
Even if you keep silent, the waterfall in the mountain would speak
For the ones who cried silently, pouring their tears there
You are the own daughter of the soil; the country owes you
Your labor is invaluable; my poem is a reminder to you
Ayşe, your home is your own country, and the foreigners should withdraw
Give me a space, too, in your dinner table with bulgur meal

The title of the poem is Ayşe. This is a common Turkish name and it is also a name with religious significance, being the name of the prophet Mohammed's wife. The speaker talks about her experience of being on the roads on a quest for Ayşe. The speaker is determined to find Ayşe and she will not desist from her quest even in the face of fire or tempest. Here one can understand that this is not just about looking for some particular and actually existing woman called Ayşe, but rather about a much more important mission, namely, to find an iconic representation of the Turkish Woman (with a capital T and a capital W) to whom the speaker has given the significant name of Ayşe.

The speaker says that sometimes she has found Ayşe in the fields and sometimes at the spring, thereby referring to the work activities of Ayşe. She is depicted as a rural woman, working in the fields and collecting drinking water for her household from the spring. Here the reader is reminded of the hardworking Turkish woman of the second poem, who has to fend for herself under primitive conditions. This is a woman who has to bring water home from a spring – we can conclude that there is no running water in her home. One could add that there is in Ayşe's daily struggle an implicit heroism of the kind that was celebrated in the first poem, although here it is a kind of domestic heroism, confronting everyday adversities rather than contributing to a war effort. The speaker also describes encountering Ayşe on a sharp abyss where she appears "like a gazelle". Here we are once again reminded of the first poem, in which the Turkish woman was described as a gentle and gracile creature of nature. The speaker hence presents Ayşe as both an active hardworking woman, heroically struggling with poverty and harsh conditions to make a home for herself and her family, and as an aestheticized and romanticized part of nature. In the latter respect, the reader is once again reminded of the essentialist distinction between women as creatures of nature and men as agents of culture (Mathieu, 1978).

However, as was the case with the woman of the second poem, Ayşe appears as a rather isolated woman. She is not described in relation to other people and the existence of her family is only implied by the account of her household responsibilities – taking part in the work in the fields and fetching water from the spring. She is described as conversing with the stars, the moon, and the sun – but not with other human beings. She has birds for companions, not other women – and even the birds are described as "poor", to further emphasize Ayşe's own poverty. The speaker has depictions of Ayşe's natural environment illustrate her dismal conditions of life. She has spent her life "at the bottom of a valley", suggesting a rather dark place; the absence of light in her life is further underlined by the speaker pointing out that Ayşe has lived in "the shadow of a fence". This last observation deserves some attention. Why a fence? The most typical function of a fence is not to provide shade from the sun, but rather to limit possibilities of access or exit. In the context of Ayşe, the fence can easily be interpreted as a metaphor for those barriers that rural Turkish women had to face, should they ever want to improve the conditions of their existence. The speaker of this poem, like the one of the second poem, remains silent about other barriers than poverty and primitive standards of housing. There is no mention of abusive husbands, honour violence, or conservative religious practices, or any other obstacle to women's freedom and well-being that emanate from the local culture. The only enemy identified in the poem is "the foreigners", that is, non-Turkish people, which is also what one should expect from a piece of nationalist poetry. The message of the poem is to express admiration for a woman who endures a difficult life rather than pointing a finger against the domestic social and cultural structures that make her life difficult in the first place.

Ayşe is not a rebel. She endures her hard life with a "sad heart", seeking comfort in nature. The speaker seems to trust nature to compensate Ayşe in some way for the difficulties she encounters. The stars, the moon, the sun, the birds are described as providing company and comfort for her. And nature itself is relied upon to express the complaints that Ayşe herself does not give words to. The waterfall in the mountains, pouring out its mighty cascades of water, will speak for Ayşe and all others who have to cry in silence. This poem is far from a call for social and cultural change. Instead what the speaker does is to recognize Ayşe as a "daughter of the soil". By so doing, the speaker gives the appearance of nobility and heroism to the hardships that Ayşe has to endure. Instead of suggesting how these harsh conditions should be removed, the speaker proposes that Ayşe should be proud of the service she is doing to her country and that her country for its part should recognize her as its daughter. Here there is an interesting development from the third poem, in which the Turkish woman was depicted as a mother of the nation. Here Ayşe is depicted in the role of a daughter of that same nation. In both cases, the Turkish woman is represented not just as a citizen with the same rights and duties as men, but rather as embodying the role of a family member, belonging either to the generation of mothers or to the one of daughters. By implication, the Turkish nation is presented as an extended family. Accordingly, the Turkish woman's civic duties are modelled upon the duties she is expected to have within the family, that is, duties of care and support as well as the duty to contribute to the work needed to bring food on the table. The family duties of looking after children, supporting one's husband, and working in the fields are implicitly translated into a generalized duty of women, whether as mothers or as daughters, to contribute their share of support for the entire nation. In return, they will be recognized as something more than just family members – they will be the mothers and daughters of the nation. Hence, Ayşe can claim the role of a *Daughter Citizen*.

The speaker also places herself in a relation to Ayşe, reminding her that her real home is her country and asking Ayşe to invite her to share a bulgur meal. This provides an interesting and revealing conclusion to the poem, as it brings out its didactic purpose. Presumably, the speaker is one of those Istanbul ladies who, according to Kemalist ideology, should establish a mutually rewarding relationship with Anatolian women, learning from the latter a self-sacrificing commitment to the republic and in turn providing them with enlightenment and knowledge of the wider world.

Ayşe is portrayed as being emotional, but also as being introvert or reserved, seeking consolation in nature rather than in other people. In spite of having to work hard to survive, she does not complain, but rather looks to nature for comfort. It could be argued that this not only pacifies her but also immobilizes her, preventing her from making demands on society and trying to change her situation. In this respect, she appears to be frozen in the conditions of her hardworking life. Here one can once again speculate about the role of the speaker in this poem. Perhaps it is she, a representative of the Istanbul ladies, who should give a voice to Ayşe? After all, this is what the poem does, to some extent, by giving the reader a perspective on the life and struggle of Ayşe. However, while the voice of the speaker celebrates Ayşe as the daughter of the nation, she does not call for the state to intervene and put an end to the difficulties that Ayşe has to confront. The poem expresses admiration for the heroism of Ayşe but does not suggest any kind of social intervention that could make this heroism unnecessary.

Moreover, while the Istanbul lady speaker offers solidarity and sisterhood to Ayşe, this is not a sisterhood of equals. By implication, the speaker claims that her conditions of life are better than Ayşe's. She describes Ayşe from the point of view of an admiring outsider, thereby suggesting that Ayşe lives under more primitive conditions than she does herself.

The fourth poem brings together themes for the previous three. Here is the theme of woman and nature from the first poem, as well as the theme of woman and heroism of the second poem, and the theme of woman and nation of the third poem. Moreover, the fourth poem develops a theme from the third poem, by depicting the nation as an extended family. According to this theme, woman can be conceived as the mother of the nation as well as the daughter of the nation.

FUTURE RESEARCH DIRECTIONS

The study of the history of women in Turkey is a growing field. However, very little use has been made of literary sources, such as poetry. Political poetry invites a kind of analysis common to literary studies, in which metaphors, images, and ambiguous meanings are explored for a content that not even the poet herself might be aware of, and in which silences and omissions may be as important as explicit statements. By applying literary analysis to political poetry relating to Turkish women, a richer and more nuanced understanding of the historical and socio-cultural conditions of these women will be gained, one that goes beyond official declarations and statistical reports.

CONCLUSION

This chapter focused on four poems which took place in *Türk Kadını* magazine in 1966, namely "Türk Kadını" (Turkish Woman) by Halide Husret Zorlutuna, "Anadolu Kadını" (Anatolian Woman) by Asuman Kavak, "Kadın-Ana" (Woman-Mother) by Neriman Saryal, and "Ayşe" by Şükûfe Nihal. While Halide Nusret Zorlutuna and Şükûfe Nihal are well-known as national romantics in the literature, Neriman Saryal could be labelled as a teacher-poet and Asuman Kavak is believed to be an amateur poet of her time. While the common denominator of all poems is women in general, there is a variation in the women as the subject of these poems. The woman addressed is the Turkish woman in the first poem, she is the Anatolian woman in the second poem. While the woman-subject is the mother of the nation in the third poem and she is the daughter of the nation in the last poem.

Despite variations in the woman-subjects of the poems, the detailed features provided about them show that the Anatolian woman is the Turkish woman. In the "Turkish Woman" poem, although it is not at first clear whether it is about urban or rural woman, it is understood from its last lines, stressing the heroism of the woman, that it is the Anatolian woman who is described here. It is well-known that Anatolian women were very efficient both in supporting the front war and in defending the homefront in the Independence War of 1919–1922. Thus, in this poem, the concepts of Turkish woman and Anatolian woman are used interchangeably and they are actually merged into each other to become one and the same thing. In "Anatolian Woman" and "Ayşe", Anatolian woman, whom the Kemalists regarded as the true Turkish woman, is depicted in great detail. In both poems, the everyday hardships and heroism of rural women are described and celebrated. The Turkish woman that appears in these poems is not only Anatolian but also a family member and the Turkish nation is described as her extended family. Hence, women is celebrated as the mother of the nation in the poem "Woman-Mother" and as the daughter of the nation in "Ayşe". The poems have in common that they celebrate the Anatolian woman as an icon of the Turkish nation, while at the same time reminding her that she belongs to this nation and that she has duties to it, just as the nation has duties to her. To this extent, the four poems exemplify nationalist poetry.

The nationalist poetry discussed here is interesting not only because of what it says but also because of what it does not say. While the Anatolian woman is idealized and celebrated for her heroic struggle against poverty and primitive conditions of life, there are adversities faced by real life Anatolian women about which the poems remain silent. Examples of such adversities are women being beaten by their husbands and fathers, women forced into child marriage, women being raped, and women being the victims of honour killings. The reason for the exclusion of these kinds of threats against women is, in all probability, that mentioning them would contradict the unifying purpose of nationalist ideology. If Turkish men are depicted as oppressors and abusers of Turkish women, it would make it difficult, to say the least, to present a harmonious picture of the Turkish nation as an extended idealized family in which everyone is supportive of each other and in which the enemy can only be a foreigner, that is, non-Turkish people.

In the examples of nationalist poetry analysed above, Anatolian woman is made into an icon of the Turkish nation in four ways: (1) by being celebrated for combining heroism, goodness, and naturalness; (2) by having her struggle with primitive conditions of life celebrated as yet another form of heroism; (3) by being celebrated as a creative mother of the nation, charged with finding solutions to the problems of the country; (4) by being celebrated as a hardworking daughter of the nation to whom the country owes recognition and support. If one thinks of the woman celebrated in these poems as a person (and not only as an idealization), one could also see her as the subject of a nationalist biography. According to such a biography, the Anatolian woman starts out as a daughter of the nation; as she matures, she becomes a mother of the nation, and, because of her heroic contributions to the nation, she finally becomes one with the nation, identified as the *Turkish* woman. Hence, the poems analysed here can be seen as different chapters of a nationalist biographical narrative, contributing to an idealized image of the Turkish woman as well as to an idealized view of the Turkish nation itself.

In addition to shedding light on politico-poetical representations of Turkish women, a further aim of this chapter has been to show how the study and analysis of literature can contribute to the field of Turkish women's studies and political theory in general. In poetry and literature we often find discourses that aim not only to provide fictional narratives, but also to transmit norms and values. Accordingly, it will often be fruitful to approach such narratives not only from the point of view of their aesthetic qualities, but also from the point of view of their explicit as well as implicit normative content.

ACKNOWLEDGMENT

This research was supported by the Scientific and Technological Research Council of Turkey (TÜBITAK) with project number 114K103.

REFERENCES

Abadan-Unat, N. (1991). The impact of legal and educational reforms on Turkish women. In N. R. Keddie, & B. Baron (Eds.), *Women in Middle Eastern history* (pp. 177–194). New Haven, CT: Yale University Press.

Aberbach, D. (2003). The poetry of nationalism. *Nations and Nationalism*, 9(2), 255–275. doi:10.1111/1469-8219.00085

Adak, S. (2010). Construction of gendered identities in Turkish national memory: 'Our' women and 'other' women in the stories of Ömer Seyfeddin. *Çankaya University. Journal of the Humanities and Social Sciences*, 7(1), 75–100.

Anthias, F., & Yuval-Davis, N. (1989). Introduction. In *N. Yuval-Davis, & F. Anthias (Eds.), Woman-Nation-State* (pp. 1–15). London, UK: Palgrave Macmillan. doi:10.1007/978-1-349-19865-8_1

Arat, Y. (1996). On gender and citizenship in Turkey. *Middle East Report (New York, N.Y.)*, 198(198), 28–31. doi:10.2307/3012873

Arat, Y. (2000). From emancipation to liberation: The changing role of women in Turkey's public realm. *Journal of International Affairs*, 54(1), 107–126.

Arat, Y. (2001). Women's rights as human rights: The Turkish case. *Human Rights Review (Piscataway, N.J.)*, 3(1), 27–34. doi:10.100712142-001-1003-9

Arat, Y. (2005). Women's challenge to citizenship in Turkey. In F. Birtek, & T. Dragonas (Eds.), *Citizenship and the nation-state in Greece and Turkey* (pp. 104–116). London, UK: Routledge. doi:10.4324/9780203311462_chapter_7

Arat, Z. (1998). Educating the daughters of the republic. In Z. F. Arat (Ed.), *Deconstructing images of Turkish woman* (pp. 175–181). New York, NY: St. Martin's Press.

Boland, E. (1987). The woman poet in a national tradition. *Studies: An Irish Quarterly Review*, 76(302), 148–158.

Bora, T. (2017). *Cereyanlar: Türkiye'de siyasi ideolojiler*. İstanbul, Turkey: İletişim.

Çaha, Ö. (2010). *Sivil kadın Türkiye'de kadın ve sivil toplum (Genişletilmiş 2. Baskı)*. Ankara, Turkey: Savaş Yayınevi.

Chein, I. (1981). Appendix: An introduction to sampling. In L. H. Kidder (Ed.), *Selltiz, Wrightsman, and Cook's research methods in social relations* (4th ed.; pp. 418–441). Austin, TX: Holt, Rinehart and Winston.

Corbin, J., & Strauss, A. (2015). *Basics of qualitative research: Techniques and procedures for developing grounded theory* (4th ed.). Thousand Oaks, CA: Sage.

Durakbaşa, A. (1998a). Kemalism as identity politics in Turkey. In Z. F. Arat (Ed.), *Deconstructing images of Turkish woman* (pp. 139–156). New York, NY: St. Martin's Press.

Durakbaşa, A. (1998b) Cumhuriyet döneminde modern kadın ve erkek kimliklerinin oluşumu: Kemalist kadın kimliği ve 'münevver erkekler'. In A. B. Hacımirzaoğlu (Ed.), 75 Yılda kadınlar ve erkekler, "Bilanço 98" kitap dizisi (pp. 29–51). İstanbul, Turkey: Türkiye Ekonomik ve Toplumsal Tarih Vakfı.

Durakbaşa, A. (2011). Türk modernleşmesinin kamusal alanı ve "kadın yurttaş". In S. Sancar (Ed.), *Birkaç arpa boyu... 21. yüzyıla girerken Türkiye'de feminist çalışmalar* (pp. 461–475). İstanbul, Turkey: Koç Üniversitesi Yayınları.

Durakbaşa, A., & İlyasoglu, A. (2001). Formation of gender identities in republican Turkey and Women's narratives as transmitters of 'herstory' of modernization. *Journal of Social History, 35*(1), 195–203. doi:10.1353/jsh.2001.0082 PMID:17600966

Honigmann, J. J. (1982). Sampling in ethnographic fieldwork. In R. G. Burgess (Ed.), *Field research: A sourcebook and field manual* (pp. 79–90). London, UK: Allen &Unwin.

Kandiyoti, D., & Kandiyoti, D. (1987). Emancipated but unliberated? Reflections on the Turkish case. *Feminist Studies, 13*(2), 317–338. doi:10.2307/3177804

Karpat, K. (1960). Social themes in contemporary Turkish literature. *The Middle East Journal, 14*(1), 29–44.

Korkmaz, R., & Özcan, T. (2007). 1950 sonrası. In T. S. Halman (Ed.), *Türk edebiyatı tarihi 4* (2nd ed., pp. 63–124). Ankara, Turkey: Kültür ve Turizm Bakanlığı Yayınları.

Mathieu, N.-C. (1978). Man-culture and woman-nature? *Women's Studies International Quarterly, 1*(1), 55–65. doi:10.1016/S0148-0685(78)90362-7

Merriam, S. B. (2009). *Qualitative research: A guide to design and implementation*. San Francisco, CA: Jossey-Bass.

Orr, D. (2008). The politics of poetry. *Poetry, 192*(4), 409–418.

Ortner, S. B. (1972). Is female to male as nature is to culture? *Feminist Studies, 1*(2), 5–31. doi:10.2307/3177638

Patton, M. Q. (2002). *Qualitative research and evaluation methods* (3rd ed.). Thousand Oaks, CA: Sage.

Reinharz, S. (1992). *Feminist methods in social research*. Oxford, UK: Oxford University Press.

Shelley, P. B. (1840). *Essays, letters from abroad, Translations and fragments*. London, UK: Edward Moxon.

Tepe, F. F. (2017). Turkish mother citizens and their homefront duties: The cold war discourse of the *Türk Kadını* magazine. *Feminist Formations*, *29*(1), 25–52. doi:10.1353/ff.2017.0002

Tepe, F. F., & Bauhn, P. (2017). Two arguments about women's rights in the *Türk Kadını* magazine 1966–1974. *Galatasaray University Journal of Communication*, *27*, 135–152.

Toprak, B. (1982). Türk kadını ve din. In N. Abadan-Unat (Ed.), *Türk toplumunda kadın* (2nd ed., pp. 361–374). İstanbul, Turkey: Araştırma, Eğitim, Ekin Yayınları.

Toska, Z. (1998). Cumhuriyet'in kadın ideali: Eşiği aşanlar ve aşamayanlar. In A. B. Hacımirzaoğlu (Ed.), 75 yılda kadınlar ve erkekler (pp. 71–88). İstanbul, Turkey: Tarih Vakfı.

Türkeş, A. Ö. (2009). Milli edebiyattan milliyetçi romanlara. In T. Bora & M. Gültekingil (Eds.), *Modern Türkiye'de siyasi düşünce, cilt 4: Milliyetçilik* (pp. 811–829). İstanbul, Turkey: İletişim Yayınları.

Zihnioğlu, Y. (2009). Kadın kurtuluşu hareketlerinin siyasal ideolojiler boyunca seyri (1908–2008). In T. Bora & M. Gültekingil (Eds.), *Modern Türkiye'de siyasi düşünce, cilt 9: Dönemler ve zihniyetler* (pp. 805–817). İstanbul, Turkey: İletişim Yayınları.

Zürcher, E. J. (2016). *Modernleşen Türkiye'nin tarihi* (33rd ed.). İstanbul, Turkey: İletişim Yayınları.

ADDITIONAL READING

Abadan-Unat, N. (Ed.). in collaboration with Deniz Kandiyoti and Mübeccel B. Kıray. (1981). Women in Turkish society. Leiden: Brill.

Abadan-Unat, N. (Ed.). (1982). *Türk toplumunda kadın* (2nd ed.). İstanbul: Araştırma, Eğitim, Ekin Yayınları.

Arat, Z. F. (Ed.). (1998). *Deconstructing images of Turkish woman*. New York: St. Martin's Press.

Bora, A., & Günal, A. (Eds.). (2014). *90'larda Türkiye'de feminizm* (5th ed.). İstanbul: İletişim.

Hacımirzaoğlu, A. B. (Ed.). (1998). *75.Yılda kadınlar ve erkekler, "Bilanço 98" kitap dizisi*. İstanbul: Türkiye Ekonomik ve Toplumsal Tarih Vakfı.

Tekeli, Ş. (Ed.). (1990). *1980'ler Türkiye'sinde kadın bakış açısından kadınlar*. İstanbul: İletişim.

Tepe, F. F. (2018). *Milliyetçi devlet feminizmi söylemi: Türk Kadını dergisi (1966-1974) örneği*. Ankara: Gece Kitaplığı.

Toprak, Z. (2014). *Türkiye'de kadın özgürlüğü ve feminizm (1908-1935)*. İstanbul: Tarih Vakfı Yurt Yayınları.

KEY TERMS AND DEFINITIONS

Anatolia: The territory of Turkey that is located in the Asian continent.

Anatolian Women: A category of women that dates back to the 1920s, referring to women of Turkish ethnic and Muslim background living in rural Anatolia.

Istanbul Ladies (Also Known as Istanbul Women): A category of women that dates back to the 1920s, referring to big city upper class and educated women with a Turkish ethnic and Muslim background.

Nationalist Poetry: A specific form of political poetry, emanating from the nationalist ideologies that were born in the aftermaths of the French Revolution.

Political Poetry: A kind of poetry that expresses political beliefs and ideals, aiming to persuade the reader to share them.

Republican Women: Women who supported the ideals and values of the Kemalist Turkish Republic.

Westernization: A set of reforms which were launched by Mustafa Kemal Atatürk, the founder and first president of the Turkish republic, in areas like law, clothing, alphabet, industry etc.

ENDNOTE

[1] A *torak* is a conical mud structure, containing wood to char or bricks to prepare.

Chapter 4
Inter-Family Communication Languages via the Discourse in Women's Roles in Turkish TV Series

Şebnem Gürsoy Ulusoy
Istanbul Gelişim University, Turkey

ABSTRACT

Modernization and urbanization have changed many phenomena. One of these changes is the representation of mother and women. It is seen that the modernization and urbanization and motherhood concept of women have changed. Maternity representations have recently changed in Turkish series. Within the scope of the study, the language of the woman in the family as a mother and her place in the family were examined. It is also an important issue whether urban culture changes the representations of motherhood. In this sense, social media, urbanization, modernization, and the changes in women's representations are all interrelated.

INTRODUCTION

Communication is an important process of human life. The representation and forms of communication of women in recent Turkish TV series is an important area of study. The role of female characters in the family and the ways in which they communicate with their environment forms the basis of the examination. In this context, the changing discourse on the representation of female characters who appeared in 5 TV series in the 2015-2018 period and their participation in family

DOI: 10.4018/978-1-7998-0128-3.ch004

communication processes were examined and investigated. Between these years, the differences between the types of series played by female characters were investigated. In particular, the effects of female characters on family communication processes in the regulation and establishment of family communication were investigated. The role of the discourse language in the role of women in the changing representation of women and the roles of women in the series were investigated and examined.

In this context, the role of women in the television series, the role of women in family communication processes, and the role of women in the changing family communication processes were investigated in television series. This research was carried out on 5 TV series which played on TV in the 2015-2018 period.

All of the selected series were selected as family series with crowded families. The aim of this study was to determine and reveal the selected groups in the family communication process.

In this context, the studied series were examined from the first part to the last part. Among the selected series, research and examinations were performed on the roles of women in the series 'İstanbullu Gelin – The Bride from Istanbul', 'Aşk Yeniden – Love Again', 'Hayat Şarkısı – Life Song', 'Cesur ve Güzel – The Bold and the Beautiful', and 'Fazilet Hanım ve Kızları – Ms. Fazilet and her Daughters'. In this context, the concepts of the public space and the private space were mentioned together with women limiting women within their private sphere and subordinating them to the patriarchal order (Özdemir, 2017: 108). In this research, how the female representations appeared through motherhood in the mentioned series were examined. In this sense, investigating the motherhood representations in the series shot in metropolitan areas, which are the basis of the modernized social structure, constitutes the basic framework of the study.

BACKGROUND

The social roles have changed with the modernizing society. Especially the changes in the representation of women roles in television series are considered important in this sense. It is seen that the urbanization culture, which is the return of modernization, is actively involved in the series. Representations of modernizing and modern mothers in Turkish series constitute the general framework of the research.

Modernization, Changing Culture, and Its Reflections to Society

Industrialization of Turkey since 1950 and the resulting rural migration have revealed the fact that people have started to leave their towns and cities and have started to live in urban areas. One of the most important returns of industrialization is the replacement of manpower with the use of machinery for industrial power. The need for manpower is reduced when manpower is replaced by machinery in rural areas. "Thus, development of poverty as an important fact with its associated subjects advanced together with the matters in the process of urbanization caused by a rapid migration." (Romano and Penbecioğlu, 2009: 136). One of the basic facts that emerge with migration is the concept of poverty and people living in the slums. In the West, the concept of squatting and being the residents of slums emerged in the 19th century. In Turkey, the formation process of slums started around the year 1945 as a result of the process of urbanization and the increased internal migration in connection therewith (Mirza, 2016: 21). The concept of the slum, which has emerged as a result of the settlement process of poor people from rural areas to big cities, refers to the neighborhoods that are usually established near factories. The concept of poverty culture identifies the common conditions in the lifestyles of poor peasants and poor workers in large urban areas. In this case, the people living in this culture are in a group that does not integrate with national institutions and is struggling to maintain their lives in a low-level social structure. (Mirza, 2016: 22) People looking after each other's fellow townsmen in this culture of poverty has emerged as an urbanite-peasant ideology. Within the concept that has been expressed as poverty culture, looking after each other's fellow townsmen has been formed also in the sense of looking after one's own past. In this sense, the period during which the concept of fellow-townsmenship and fellow townsmen associations have become functional and have increased in Turkey is the same as the rural to urban migration period. Migration is the movement of individuals or masses in a residential area from a certain group or piece of land, to another piece of land (Dural, 2007: 22). This mass movement generally refers to a process that starts individually and then leads people to take their relatives and friends with their fellow-townsmenship approach. Economic and social developments also play a role in the growth tendencies of cities (Kaçer, 2017: 36). Industrialization and increasing population are influential in urban growth. Population growth leads to increased needs. Urban growth consists of processes that involve many different morphological structures in urban growth (Millward, 2011: 53-54). The basis of the concept of migration is the desire to reach a better social life. "The phenomenon of migration has continued to be important in every section of human history, in parallel to the increasing search for the better" (Güngör, 2006: 229). It is observed that immigrants facilitate the process in which they encourage and assist the migration of also their family members and friends, and that the fact that immigrants (sometimes all the individuals living in a single region) migrate to a single place is the result of this solidarity of fellow-townsmenship (Öksüz, 2018: 88). There is a great connection between the migration process and the relationships of fellow-townsmenship. The immigrant draws relatives and kins to the same city or even to the region. Or the immigrant becomes the greatest supporter of others in the process of settling and establishing a new life. Groups and small groups that are marginalized especially in urban areas, set up some associations in order to adapt to the new environment, to protect their culture and to maintain their own existence. These associations are mostly established through "fellow-townsmenship". For example, the group of people who migrated from the district of 'Of' in Trabzon to Trabzon city center establish the "Association of the People of of" and the ones who migrated from Trabzon to Ankara can establish the "Association of the People of Trabzon" in Ankara (Öksüz, 2018: 88-89). When the phenomenon of fellow-townsmenship is examined, it is seen that these people generally consist of the migrating part of the society and they attach importance to the concept of fellow-townsmenship in their lives as a social fact. The notion fellow-townsmenship is a concept of social and organizational importance, but sufficient research has not been conducted on the field. While the concept of 'fellow-townsmenship' is basically a spatial approach, it symbolizes a secondary space created by the people who are drifted away from the space (Kurtoğlu, 2018). The migrant population is observed to be generally located close to each other within the framework of community and fellowship relations. Among the features of urbanization in Turkey, it is seen that the migrants from villages, districts, provinces and generally the same geographical region are gathered in the same neighborhoods and even in the same streets of the cities (Altay et al., 2010: 232). Alienation constitutes the most important point in the processes of both civilizations. People are more in need of fellow-townsmenship closeness because they are unfamiliar with themselves and their environment (Öksüz et al., 2017: 1182). After the 1950s, with the industrialization, the phenomenon of migration has become more prevalent and the concept of fellow-townsmenship has gained more importance. With the replacement of manpower in the villages, the need for people decreased and a certain group began to migrate from the village to the city. The groups that did not want to lose their own identity during this migration process started to establish associations among themselves. As a result of this process, associations are established in cities generally named in the sense of local solidarity associations. These associations aim to establish solidarity among the people of the city, to provide cooperation, to develop the image of fellow-townsmenship, on the other hand, to ensure the continuation of their customs and traditions and to transfer this consciousness to the future generations (Terzi et al., 2014: 138). The facts, which fellow-townsmen look after and protect each other and maintain the common customs and traditions of the region they come from, are seen as a process that emerges as a result of this process. The fellow townsmen people help each other when they start a job. The person who is the owner of the workplace or the person responsible for the job can give priority to the fellow townsmen in the recruitment process. After the 1960s, new policies in the field of tourism began to be determined. Ecological and economic policies have been implemented (Kozak et al., 2006: 5). The main reason for these practices is based on industrialization and migration from rural to urban areas. The main reason for the increase and diversification of industrial products is that people living in rural areas have started to work in factories in cities.

The relationship between community and congregation should be considered as a private space as well. "In short, the country where there has been immigration is imaginary geography and the fellow townsman is the member of the imaginary community coming from that imaginary area" (Kurtoğlu, 2018). Fellow townsmen represent the people who feel as members of a particular group and as loyal to that group. Fellow-townsmenship is a social bond and belonging (Kurtoğlu, 2001). People exist and continue their existence in social groups and these social groups are basically linked to the region they live in. In this sense, being fellow townsmen from the same city or region gains importance. Fellow townsmen immigrants try not to break their cultural and social ties with each other with the associations they establish. The people who keep this social bond alive feel themselves in the land where they come from. This prevents them from experiencing social loneliness and satisfies their wish to be part of a group. In conceptual terms, the word "fellow townsman" refers to a situational relationship between fellow townsmen. When this situation is defined, fellow-townsmenship is a phenomenon that shows one of the two people whose common aims are structured in the same geographical area relative to the other. With its second meaning, fellow-townsmenship defines the interrelationships between people whose hometowns are in the same geographical location or who feel that they belong in the same geographical region and also the relationships, social ties, and identities arising from these ties (Kurtoğlu, 2018). In this sense, social media is seen as a link that connects people socially. Campaigns through social media are frequently used to reach masses (Carlson et al., 2014: 24-24). The two most important links between people are the community and congregation relations. In this sense, having lived in the same territory or having common relatives and friends emerges as a situation that makes it easier for people to connect with their roots and backgrounds. For the individuals who drift apart from their traditional ties, who struggle to exist in a foreign place and who are in search of belonging, 'coming from the same place' is of great importance. In order for the new inhabitants of the city to adapt to their new lives, the fellow-townsmenship associations, which are an example of community ties, undertake major functions" (Köse, 2008: 221). From a community point of view, the social media system is observed to make a certain group the members of a community in the direction of common goals and expectations. Shares of the same style, similar words, similar discourses, and expressions standardize people and transform them into similar people and the members of similar associations. The concept of fellow-townsmenship is seen to be closely intertwined with the concept of favoritism in social structure

(Kurtoğlu, 2012: 141-142). The institutional spaces of the immigrants who want to make themselves visible in the city have been associations. Associations inform people about other people whom they do not know and provide that people help each other about public institutions, hospitals and schools (Fliche, 2005; Hersant et al., 2005). It is possible to indicate that the proximity of fellow townsmen is a state that continues among occupational groups as well. It is also possible to state that the fellow-townsmenship approach and the trust and closeness that fellow townsmen feel for each other is also seen among the teachers (Güven et al., 2014: 3210-3212). Being part of a group is always important in human life. The easiest group to become members of the rural people coming to the city are the fellow-townsmenship associations and groups. Social media makes this process much easier. In the concept of urban culture, social media both creates the notion of fellow-townsmenship and plays a role in the promotion of the city. The content shared on social media can spread rapidly in traditional media and the topics, texts and pictures that appear in traditional media can spread rapidly in social media. The sharing and discourse speed of social media and the number of people it reaches are much higher (Izmirli Olmak Symposium Book 2009: 229-230). In general, what underlies social media to spread very fast is that social media is easy to use and that it can be easily accessed on smartphones. As the new media is changing and becoming increasingly widespread, mass media have gone through a massive process of transformation and improvement (Yağız and Demirel: 1).

Social movements and social organization are everywhere with people. The basis of social media is the gathering of groups of people and of people who know each other from a particular group. Social movements reveal their strength and emergence processes by how much they are supported by society. Generally, this support is provided by the fluent relations established with the media (Kılıç, 2009: 151).

The concept of social networking is often conceptualized under social capital theory. Although the literature on social capital is different from the social network literature, it is largely convergent. For this reason, it may be useful to briefly define social capital before the concept of social networking. Putnam (2000) describes social capital as "social organization features such as networks, norms, and trust that facilitate coordination and cooperation for mutual benefit", while Bourdeieu (1986) stated it as "the sum of potential resources in durable or permanent social networks" and Woolcock (1998) interpreted social networks as "the mutual exchange of knowledge, trust, and norms" (Akgiş, 2018: 22-23). The concepts of social network and social capital are seen as close concepts. Although social capital and social network concepts are seen in a different understanding and literature, they stand close to each other. Putnam indicated social networks as common networks and social organization structures that seek mutual benefit and provide cooperation (Akgiş et al., 2018: 22-23). Bourdieu gave a different perspective on the topic and indicated it as the total of resources with potential in social networks (Bourdieu 1986). Although social media is used for different purposes, it also continues its existence as a medium where people can share pictures, poems, videos and writings which are part of their origins and the lands that they feel belong in, regardless of time and place. In this sense, it is seen as a field where the sense of fellow-townsmenship is formed and kept alive. Since social media provides ease of communication, it is seen as a field where communities are easily formed and gathered. People can share and talk about topics of interest such as political speeches, common photo tastes, and television programs. Individuals who do not know each other can define themselves as 'us' within the context of the fellow townsmen concept. The ties between people who have the feeling of belonging to the same geographical location sometimes affect their personal identity. The number of social networks gathered around the notion of fellow-townsmenship in social media is observed to have exceeded thousands.

Our daily life consists of a trust relationship built on institutional and social relations. Social capital is an important concept. It represents the trust in friendship relationships that people establish with each other. In general, the emphasis of social capital is in social relations (Topçuoğlu et al., 2013: 128). On the one hand, economic relations in urban environments have developed the processes of fellow-townsmenship, which function as an important institution in the process of urbanization, and on the other hand, they have created some forms of private life in this social-economic and social-cultural environment. Fellow-townsmenship relations (traditional, based on solidarity, community relations) have not only provided the people, who migrated from the village, to settle in the city and created their prior knowledge, but also prevented the disappearance of people in the city and re-established their traditional solidarity patterns by moving them into the urban environment. For example, people from the provinces of Sivas, Erzurum, Kars, Trabzon, and Kastamonu settled in neighborhoods and districts in the cities. They built their own houses and workplaces, they established their fellow-townsmenship associations and they carried out their relations in this way (Kahya, 2008: 18). All these relationship processes reveal that these relations are formalized with associations and the members of the associations protect and favor each other. Fellow-townsmenship associations are an area where different groups of the society can be represented together and where people come together to find solutions to the problems of the city and people (Usta et al., 2017: 225). In addition, the masses, who were detached from the countryside as a result of the migration from the countryside, and who were gathered in the cities, were not able to adapt to the urban life and could not adopt the urban values and as a result, they are stuck between rural life and urban life and they remain strangers to urban life. This process is observed to be related to fellow-townsmenship relations (Aktas et al., 2006: 53). The family and the people who complete the family are observed to have many social relations and strong ties including kinship and neighborhood.

For example, friendship, citizenship, and membership in communities represent the other ties that the individual and family are in (Özbay, 2014: 2). While explaining the concept of social community, it is necessary to mention the concepts of public space and private space. Social media creates both a public space and constitutes a private space. "The distinction between the public space and the private space is a contradiction discussed by social scientists for centuries. The fact that the public space is attributed to men and the private space is attributed to women has led to the reinforcement of the distinction between men and women in the social order" (Özdemir, 2018: 143).

THE CONCEPT OF MOTHER REPRESENTATION IN TELEVISION

The inclusion of mother and female identity within the structure of the society shows a social, political, economic, and cultural-related situation. Starting from the first societies, the way women are presented in society has been changing with modernization. The main point of this difference is that women's participation in society on the basis of gender is gaining importance. One of the important points in this process is the transition from a patriarchal society to matriarchal society. In this sense, the identity of women declines and it is seen that there is also a social loss for freedom. Developments in the Western world and developments in human rights have led to the re-examination of women's identity and freedom issues. Especially the media is the most active in this sense (Aytekin, 2018: 449-451). The representation of motherhood and women in the media also represents an important area to be investigated and examined in this respect. The media has a great deal of interaction with society, so it has an important place in the representation of women (Aytekin, 2018: 462). Especially in recent times, motherhood concept and mother representations of women have been used actively. In this sense, the main purpose of the character playing the role of the mother in front of the audience with anecdotes from everyday life is that the audience identifies themselves with the characters in the series. "In the series, the reason why people are allowed to connect with the characters in the series is that the daily lives of the people and parts of their lives are included" (Haywood, 1994: 196-197). Recently, old age representations are also shown in television series. The character of Turkish society and the image of motherhood of Turkish women are brought to the fore with the struggle of a mature mother character to keep her family and children together. In this sense, old age is no longer ignored, regardless of the age of each mother's children who are shown to be worth fighting for. In this sense, the processes of representation of old age in television series have a socio-cultural dimension (Kılın and Uztuğ, 2016: 477).

Especially in this sense, there are recent changes in the representation process of a woman with advanced age (60 and above). "In modernist culture, which includes a future-oriented discourse, reminding disease, weakness, death, the inclusion of a conflict with the ideal body perception, and the fact that the elderly are often excluded from the economic production area, over time, the perception of old age, representation and perceptions of old age have changed" (Kılın and Uztuğ, 2016: 478). Old age, motherhood and female image represent an area that has been actively used in Turkish series. In particular, the concept of mothers trying to prove the social identity of the lonely mothers and the series about the self-existence effort are presented to the audience frequently. Looking at the series sector, which is planned according to the needs of the audience and shaped according to the preferences, it is possible to observe that those who watch these series are similar to the characters in the series. It is seen that the representation of power is the main determinant of interpersonal communication and social communication in order to activate the audience's attention in the process of communicating with the audience in television series. This power concept is also seen as the leader of the family. The series in which the concept of power representation is actively loaded on the mother character is seen recently (Karadaş, 2013: 67). The mother's family gathering function is seen as the basic stone that holds the family together in case of loss of the father. It is observed that this concept is actively used in the series after 2010. The beauty of having a large family, the social tasks of women and men are seen as the subjects that are actively involved in the series. Weak and delicate, more attractive and beautiful women are perceived as a positive adjective but when the same words are used for men, they are considered weak i.e. having a negative title. It is possible to indicate that the majority of female characters appearing in the series are created in accordance with the concept of physical beauty imposed by popular culture and consumer culture on femininity (İnceoğlu and Akçalı, 2018: 27-28). The representation of the woman in the series is usually seen as the most commonly used image. The mother, who is the woman's naïve and weak state, is given only to the side characters. It is observed that the main character of the series is weak. From a critical point of view, it is possible to say that the media is male-dominated and therefore supports the patriarchal mentality. According to critical approaches such as the Frankfurt School and the Birmingham School of Cultural Studies, which assert that the power of the media is unrestricted, the individual tends to be true in what they see in the media. This situation can sometimes be concluded that individuals adopt the content offered through the media without questioning (Ünür, 2013: 32). The fact that the mother takes over the father's mission in the families who have a loss of the father, especially in the representation of the patriarchal structure in the series and the attempt to keep the family together actually refers to a male-dominated society. The concept that women should have priority in taking care of children when they are mothers is a concept that is often given place in series. The family's recovery is associated with the mother so the mother is actively used in the series. In the series, when the communication language of the concept of motherhood is considered, the mother is seen as the executive and also the executive of the communication. It is also observed that the series following series is also for an expectation in this direction. In this sense, the Turkish series is a continuation of a patriarchal structure.

RESEARCH

Within the scope of the research, all parts of the five Turkish TV series which were shown between the years 2015-2018 were examined. In the examination, the communication language used by the mother character in the series, the communication processes within the family, the place and importance of the mother in the family, the education of the mother character, and the communication with her husband were sought. After examining in five series, the characteristics of the mother characters in the series were compared with each other. As the hypothesis, the study tried to prove that the Turkish mother character is supposed to be represented in a similar way with a common language of discourse in Turkish series. In this context, within the scope of the research, a second research was carried out by analyzing the own accounts of the series on social media and the audience comments about the mother characters in the series were examined one by one. The research was conducted in two phases. Finally, the findings of the social media viewers and the series were revealed and compared with each other.

Due to the ethical principle of the series, only the initials of their names are given.

1. Series – İ. G.

Starting from the first episode of the series, a mother character that holds and manages the family comes forward. The basic structure of the character of Esma Boran, who is over-bound with her roots and family history, shows the image of a woman who could not find the happiness she was looking for in her marriage from a rich and rooted family. It is one of the cornerstones of a mother figure, who has grown up with social pressure, has lived, married and tried to apply the same social pressure to her children and brides. Later in the series, the marriage of the children, with the presence of their own children as they sit with the mother figure begins to pass to the sons and brides. In general, however, the mother figure carries the traces of a Turkish family structure.

2. Series – A. Y.

In the series, which tells the story of a Black Sea family in Istanbul, there is a dominant father figure and a mother figure dominated by him. As the mother figure in the series, the lead actress plays a dominant role for her own son as a mother. It is observed that the concepts of taking care of your child and protection are important and this is explained in a funny language. Issues such as the importance of the family on the basis of the series, the importance of the mother in the family communication processes together and the importance of the growth of the mother and father are discussed.

3. Series – H. Ş.

The series reveals that there is an Anatolian family living in Istanbul and the family is between modernization and non-modernization. It is seen that the family lives together collectively and the mother figure has a desire to put pressure on her children, but not all the time. The mother seems to be more in the background, especially since she has a dominant father figure in the house. But the bride and her sons want to do what they want.

4. Series – C. G.

In the basic structure of the series, it is seen that it is a family series and a crowded family lives in the same house. The series reveals that there is a dominant father figure and it is based on him as the gathering figure of the family. It is seen that the mother character is shown as a woman who is naïve and needs help.

5. Series – F. H. and K.

In this series, which tells the story of a mother who is in love with a man and who brings her two daughters to a rich family, the figure of a mother, who grew up in the culture of pressuring and fighting, is used for every event. It is observed that children have many problems due to their mother being involved in their jobs and in their entire lives. In general, a crowd of people living in the same house is seen again in the series. It is seen that the mother figure and her character are identified especially in the place where they earn income and socially grow up.

SOCIAL MEDIA ANALYSIS

In the social media analysis, the collected information was shared by reviewing the comments written under 3 pictures and videos randomly selected from the videos and image sharing of each series, where the mother character is shown in the most recent part of the series. The analysis is restricted in this way because there are too many choices.

1. Series. İ.G. – Audience Reviews

Video Sharing and Audience Reviews on October 22, 2018

It is seen that the character, who is the figure of the mother, is generally sympathetic to the audience and the audience comments that she gathers the family.

Video Sharing and Audience Comments on November 21, 2018

In general, it is observed that the audience liked the positive and happy family life in the series. It is seen that the Turkish audience enjoys the wings of the family and adopts the concept of extended family. In this sense, it is seen that the mother figure in the series has a positive attitude towards the regulation of family communication.

Video Sharing and Audience Comments on December 24, 2018

It is generally stated by the viewers that every mother should have a son in the family and that the dominant and authoritarian mother of the series is entitled to be happy. The audience seems to be sympathetic to the dominant and authoritarian mother character.

2. Series A.Y. – Audience Reviews

January 22, 2018: The mother-in-law in the series does not want her bride to be seen. Although the mother figure is dominant in the life of her son, she is a mother character who makes plans to become active in her son's life because he does not listen to her.

The followers of the mother character stated that they generally expect new parts of the series.

March 20, 2018: It seems that the person with the mother character naively tries to enter into every event and to dominate the events. It is seen that the viewers generally find the events funny.

3. Series H. Ş. – Audience Reviews

May 29, 2016: It is seen that the audience of the show loved the family structure in the series and felt themselves like a part of this family. It was determined that the mother figure was not shared by many in general and she was not seen as active in any share. In general, the comments appear to be related to the leading actors of the series and the father figure, who is seen as the family's recovery.

June 14, 2016: It is seen that the series and its family relations are interesting for the followers. The mother character is shown with a funny language and attracts the attention of the audience. The comments made are also in this direction.

June 19, 2016: It is seen that the crowd generally liked the crowded family image. 25 comments were also shared how the series was loved and followed.

4. Series C. and G. – Audience Reviews

May 5, 2017

The mother character in the series has died but no comments are found in the user comments.

None of the interpretations and analyses of the series were found to be related to the mother character.

June 6, 2017

Comments on the death of the mother character in the series can be seen. It is seen that the followers generally comment on the leading roles of the series. The passive character is not commenting on the mother.

In the series, some comments have been made about the leading actors. Therefore, there are no other findings.

5. Series F. H. and K. – Audience Reviews

May 5, 2018: It was written by a viewer that the name changed to Grind Lady because of the mother character in the series.

June 2, 2018: In the series, the actress who wants to protect her two daughters is shown with compassion and sentimental messages by her followers are observed.

June 9, 2018: The show features a father character and a mother character. The mother character seems to be badly criticized by the followers in the comments of the audience following her anger. In addition, as the mother character at the end of the series regrets what she has done, the criticisms of the followers are seen to be full of pity.

RESULTS OF THE RESEARCH

When the official accounts of social media were analyzed and the shares about the mother characters in the series were examined, it was observed that the mother character was dominant in each series and the mother character played an active role in shaping and changing the lives of the children of the family. According to the father's family, the mother character is more in the background in the series. However, especially in the series I.G., since there is no active father character with the mother, the mother character plays an active role. It is obvious that the mother is seen as the main character in the four series. The protecting and collecting person is seen as a guide in the inter-family relations and as a safe harbor. In general, it is seen that the following masses are warm to the mother role models and affirm their behaviors. When the parts of the series are examined, the comments made on the social media accounts of the followers overlap the observations made in the series. Recently, dominant, authoritarian, family collector, maternal models that have the right to speak in the lives of the children, brides and grooms have been used actively in Turkish TV series. In accordance with the hypothesis of the study, the study tried to prove that the Turkish mother character is supposed to be represented in a similar way with a common language of discourse in Turkish series. It is possible to indicate that the hypothesis has been proven. In the absence of a prominent father figure in the family, the mother is included in the series as a building block that provides the continuation of the main body of the communication provider.

CONCLUSION

Within the scope of the research, the transformation of the concept of motherhood together with the modernizing society is examined. The notions that the concepts such as technological transformation, urbanization, and modernization create a change in the image of women, and that the concept of motherhood also create a change in the processes of representation in the Turkish series are examined through the concept of gender. In general, it is seen that the concept of maternity in Turkish TV series proceeds from the concepts of oppression and replacement in the structure of mainstream and ancestral style of society. It is seen that the mother character plays a more active role in the communication processes in the absence of an active father role. It is also observed that the parents of the followers have a positive attitude towards their mothers' character in dominating their children and interfering in their private lives. In general, families are large families living in large houses. Being the mother and a woman and being a woman's mother and her husband's mother can all be considered as being a mother in society and the concepts of gender are actively appear in series. The mother character seems to assume a binding, transformative and most important unifying and gathering mission. In this sense, the mother character is seen as the indispensable foundation stone of the family. In fact, the basis of being a happy, peaceful, beautiful family that dominates events is the concept of an active mother in the process of communication within the family.

FUTURE RESEARCH DIRECTIONS

Within the scope of the research, maternity representations were examined through Turkish series. Similar studies to be carried out in the future may not be limited to social media for more comprehensive research, but observations can be suggested for people who follow the series to make clear findings and to advance the research.

REFERENCES

Akgiş, Ö., & Karakaş, E., (2018). Bir Sosyal Ağ Olan Hemşehri Derneklerinin Yoksullukla Mücadeledeki Rolü Üzerine Uygulamalı Bir Araştırma. *Ege Coğrafya Dergisi, 27*(1), 21–34.

Altay, N., & Gümüş, N., (2010). Hemşehrilik ve İzmir'deki Hemşehri Dernekleri. *e-Journal of New World Sciences Academy, 5*(3), 231-239.

Bourdieu, P. (1986). The Forms of Capital. In J. G. Richardson (Ed.), Handbook of theory and research for the sociology of education. New York, NY: Greenwood Press.

Dural, A. B., & Yas, S. (2007). Göç eden nüfusta grup içi tabakalaşma ve siyasetin yeniden şekillenmesi. *Akademik Fener,* 22-31.

Haywood, I. (1994). Fathers and sons: Locating the absent mother in 1960s children's television series. *JSTOR, 6*(2), 195–201.

Fliche, B. (2005). The Hemşehrilik and the Village: The Stakes of an Association of Former Villagers in Ankara. *European Journal of Turkish Studies, 2*. Retrieved from http://ejts.revues.org/385

Göngör, N. (2006). Göç Olgusu ve Arabesk. Aralık Uluslararası Göç Sempozyumu, Sistem Matbaacılık, İstanbul.

Terzi, E., & Koçak, Y. (2014). Hemşehri Dernekleri, Hemşehrilik Bilinci ve Kentlileşme İlişkisi Üzerine Bir Araştırma: İstanbul/Sultangazi'deki Karslı Hemşehri Dernekleri Örneği. *Selçuk Üniversitesi Sosyal Bilimler Enstitüsü Dergisi, 32*, 137–150.

İzmirli Olmak Sempozyum Kitabı. (2009). *İBB Ahmet Pirifltina Kent Arflivi ve Müzesi*. İzmir.

Mirza, A. (2016). Kenar Mahalleliğin Sinemadaki Yansımaları. *Abant Kültürel Araştırmalar Dergisi, 1*(2), 21–33.

Kurtoğlu, A. (2001). Hemşehrilik ve şehirde siyaset. İletişim Yayınları, İstanbul, Turkey.

Kurtoğlu, A. (2012). Siyasal Örgütler ve Sivil Toplum Örgütleri Bağlamında Hemşehrilik ve Kollamacılık. *Ankara Üniversitesi SBF Dergisi, 67*(1), 141–169. doi:10.1501/SBFder_0000002241

Kurtoğlu, A. (2005). Mekansal Bir Olgu Olarak Hemşehrilik ve Bir Hemşehrilik Mekanı Olarak Dernekler. *Social Sciences on Contemporary Turkey*. Retrieved from https://www.researchgate.net/publication/30453637_Mekansal_Bir_Olgu_Olarak_Hemsehrilik_ve_Bir_Hemsehrilik_Mekani_Olarak_Dernekler

Loon, N. M. V., Gummuluru, S., Sherwood, D. J., Marentes, R., Hall, C. B., & Dewhurst, S. (2019). Direct Series Analysis of Human Herpesvirus 6 (HHV-6) Series from Infants and Comparison of HHV-6 Series from Mother/Infant Pairs. *Oxford Journals Press,* 1017-1019.

Kozak, M., & Kizilirmak, I. (2006). Turistik Ürün Çeşitlendirmesi Kültür ve Turizm Müdürleri Görüşlerine Dayalı Bölgesel Yaklaşımlar. *Mustafa Kemal Üniversitesi Sosyal Bilimler Enstitüsü Dergisi, 3*(5), 1–24.

Millward, A. A. (2011). Urbanisation viewed through a geostatistical lens applied to remote-sensing data. *Area, 43*(1), 53–66.

Muhammet, Ö. (2018). "Buralarda yabancı yok": Hemşehri derneklerinin kentlileşme üzerine etkisi, Ankara'daki Oflular örneği. *Türk Coğrafya Dergisi, 70*, 87–98.

Necmettin, Ö., & Yavuz, K. (2008). Organize Suç Örgütlerinin Oluşumunda Hemşehrilik İlişkilerinin Rolü. *Polis Bilimleri Dergisi, 10*(4), 15–42.

KilincÖ, ., & UztugF, . (2016). Televizyon Dizilerinde Yaşlılığın Temsili. *Sosyoloji Dergisi, 36*(2), 477–506.

Özbay, F. (2014). Türkiye Aile Yapısı Araştırması İleri Analiz Raporu. Ankara: TC Aile ve Sosyal Politikalar Bakanlığı ve İPSOS.

Özdemir, B. G. (2017). Türk Sinemasında Özel Alan Kamusal Alan Karşıtlığında Anlatıda Mekan Ögesinin Kullanımı. IBAD Uluslararası Bilimsel Araştırmalar Dergisi, 108-118.

Pelin, A. (2018). Yerli Dizilerde Kadın Kimliğinin Temsili Üzerine Bir Örnek; "Yaprak Dökümü" Dizisi. *Erciyes İletişim Dergisi*, *5*(4), 447–463. doi:10.17680/erciyesiletisim.371332

Romano, Y., & Penbecioğlu, M. (2009). From Poverty in Turns to New Poverty: A Scrutinize to Changing Dynamics of Urban Poverty in Turkey. *Toplum ve Demokrasi*, *3*(5), 135-150.

KilicS, . (2009). Kamuoyu Oluşum Sürecinde Sosyal Hareketler ve Medya. *Niğde Üniversitesi İİBF Dergisi*, *2*(2), 150–167.

Usta, S., & Bilgi, E. (2017). Hemşehrilik Bilinci ve Kent Konseyleri: Karaman İlinde Bir Araştırma. *Süleyman Demirel Üniversitesi Sosyal Bilimler Enstitüsü Dergisi*, *1*(26), 223–252.

Topçuoğlu, A., & Eroğlu, S. E. (2013). Sosyal Sermayenin Akrabalık Hemşehrilik ve Güven İle İlişkisi: Konya Sanayi İşletmeleri Örneği. *HAK-İŞ Uluslararası Emek ve Toplum Dergisi*, *2*(3), 124–145.

CarlsonT, ., & DjupsundG, . (2014). Taking Risks in Social Media Campaigning: The Early Adoption of Blogging by Candidates. *Scandinavian Political Studies*, *37*(1), 21–40. doi:10.1111/1467-9477.12011

Yağiz, A., Demirel, A. S., Karabay, D., Yalçin, G., Egemen, M. S., & Utku, Y. (n.d.). *Yerel Medyanın Dijital Teknolojilere Uyumu: Türkiye'deki Yerel Gazetelerin Dijital Medyayı Kullanımı Üzerine Bir İnceleme*. Retrieved from http://www.academia.edu/9728266/Yerel_Medyan%C4%B1n_Dijital_Teknolojilere_Uyumu_T%C3%BCrkiye_deki_Yerel_Gazetelerin_Dijital_Medyay%C4%B1_Kullan%C4%B1m%C4%B1_%C3%9Czerine_Bir_%C4%B0nceleme

Yücel, Ö., & Melek Baba, Ö. (2017). Relationship between Levels of Student Alienation and Hemsehrilik Attitudes of University Students: A Study on Kırgız-Turkish Manas University Students, Universal. *The Journal of Educational Research*, *5*(7), 1182–1191.

KEY TERMS AND DEFINITIONS

Family Communication: They are all the communication and dialogues built into the family.

Maternity Representations in the Series: How the mother character appears in the series is examined.

Modernization: It is the adaptation to the innovations and changes brought by the age.

Social Identity: It is a concept that defines the point of view of society and explains the communication processes established between groups over social roles.

Social Media: It is the medium that allows for instant sharing and discourse with the new media.

TV Series: They are a series of related fiction stories on television.

Urban Culture: It is the language of communication used by people living in metropolitan areas coupled with modernization.

Women's Roles in the Series: The concept of the role of the female image in the series is examined.

Chapter 5
A Feminist Reading of an Oriental Tale:
"Crystal Manor and Diamond Ship"

Derya Çetin
Bolu Abant Izzet Baysal University, Turkey

Mevlüde Deveci
Fırat University, Turkey

ABSTRACT

Tales, which have an important place in the process of socialization, contain various ideological constructions like other narratives. This study aims to analyses an important tale of Turkey's tale corpus named "Crystal Manor and Diamond Ship" by the terms of feminist critics. This tale is considered among the tales of Anatolian field and is similar to some western tales such as Rapunzel. However, in terms of subject positions, which are one of the focal points of feminist criticism, the main female character, unlike most fairy tales, seems to be planning and implementing the actions that advance the plot, rather than waiting for a man to rescue her.

INTRODUCTION

Tales, which have an important place in the process of socialization, contain various ideological constructions like other narratives. Tales, which are an important part of culture, are collective cultural products and one of the tools that reflect and reconstruct the dominant ideology in society. They, which are an important actor

DOI: 10.4018/978-1-7998-0128-3.ch005

in the socialization of children, are often examined with their role in education. However, feminist theory is an area of interest as fairy tales are one of the areas where gender definitions are made and these are transferred to new generations. "Although feminisms are multiple, feminists do share certain beliefs. Feminist critics generally agree that the oppression of women is a fact of life, that gender leaves its traces in literary texts and on literary history, and that feminist literary criticism plays a worthwhile part in the struggle to end oppression in the World outside of texts." (Eagleton, 2013: x). This study aims to evaluate an important tale of Turkey's tale corpus which named "The Crystal Manor and The Diamond Ship" by the terms of feminist critics. This tale is considered among the tales of Anatolian field and is similar to some western tales such as Raphunzel (Saluk, 2018). However, when it is evaluated through some concepts of feminist theory –such as subject positions-, it can be said that it remains outside the patriarchal discourse.

FEMINIST CRITICISM AND TALES

Feminism is an intellectual movement, which, *before all*, is concerned with the social roles and positions of the women and the men. Feminism is a doctrine that aims at the women's having the same rights with the men, and the eluding of the women from the legal and social inequalities (Bolay, 2004: 229). Despite being a women or a men is a result of a biological process, today the women and the men have been casted different roles in today's society. In that sense feminism is against sexism. It criticizes the behavior of the men; such as the insulting and disregarding of the women. (Butler, 2012: 87). Feminism criticism, with its works, reveals the commoditization of the women-body and the gender apartheid during the course of the history (Antmen, 2012: 8).

Feminist criticism had appeared in the sixties as a result of the social and political struggles in USA, Britain, and France; and then had been adapted in the field of literature (Moran, 2002: 249). The first modern work of feminist criticism is Virginia Woolf's "A Room of One's Own", which was published in 1929. Woolf, in her masterpiece, mentions that even the language itself is a means for gender apartheid (Güzel, 2007: 26), and that in general the position of the women in the society is lower than the men's. The book emphasizes the discrepancy of the women in the social, literal, and cultural senses (Humm, 2002: 18).

Feminism has three basic issues. The first is the means of oppression against the women, and their differences with the men in the sense of power. In that sense, the principles to minimize the differences have been investigated. The second is mainly about the biological gender. It tries to show up the reasons for the differences between the women and the men, and within that scope it includes the biological, social, etc. aspects into the research. The third issue is the gender relations, which it deals with by focusing on the differences (Yuval-Davis, 2003: 24-25).

Feminist critics present two main approaches in the field of literature (Moran, 2002: 250):

1. Towards women as the reader
2. Towards women as the writer

At the criticism against women for being the reader, which forms the first phase of the feminist criticism, the concern is the sexual ideology, how the women are represented, the pictured women types, and the evaluating of those with a feminist perspective. The critics, which had made the exposing of the ideological attitude possible, draw the attention to the exploiting of the women. The criticism against women for being the writer forms the second phase. Here, the connection of the women's representation with the patriarchal system is assessed. The concern is how the women, who had formed a subculture as a result of the social oppression, are narrated by the women authors (Moran, 2002: 250-255).

Feminist criticism takes the literature as a cultural phenomenon. It questions the work in the sense of the characters formed, the values, and the effects of the language on the women's life (Kırtıl, 2003: 128). It deals with issues; such as the relations between the women and the men, and the representation of the women. The feminist criticism, which basically rests against the feminist ideology, is mostly understood in conjunction with the concept "gender". However, it also utilize the psychoanalysis (Kabadayı, 2014: 85-86).

Gender, as a concept, is particularly important for the feminist criticism, which aims at raveling out the women identity determined with an ideological manner. The social roles of the women and the men are in fact ideological structures (Butler, 2012: 209-210). According to the feminist point of view, gender is always shaped according to the discourse and power conditions (Butler, 2012: 85).

Gender is a reflection of the culture that we have erected. In that sense, the roles assigned to the women and the men are tried to be revealed. Especially, the roles assigned to the women in the men author's works are focused. How the women, who are under social pressure, are represented in in the texts is a topic of query. It objects to the hegemony of the men by disclosing the tacit messages in the texts (Showalter, 1996: 99).

The feminist critics pay importance to how the women are approached in the works. They assess the work not only in terms of literature, but also in terms of popular culture. In addition it is assessed whether or not it has a conditioning effect on the women readers (Sümer, 2009: 173). The patriarchal system is being taken as an object serving the men, and living under their dominance. The structure of this system has also reflections on the narrative systems. The generally viewed frame is the superiority of the men against the women.

The source of the literal works is the humans. In that sense it is the mirror of the society that it is produced at (Yüce and Kazan, 2006: 18). At the main works, the women are generally encountered in two formats; namely as the angel-woman or evil-woman. According to Althusser, this artificial duality is misleading and disturbing (1994: 62-65).

Works of literature bears traces of its artist's emotions and ideas for sure. The artists use psychoanalysis typically in their works. In that sense the fields of psychology and psychoanalysis are strictly related. The main subjects of the psychoanalytic approach are the state of mind, the concerns, fears, passions, pains, and dreams. Thus, the tacit meanings at the works are particularly important (Yavaş, 2018: 19-21).

Feminist criticism is utilizes the theory of psychoanalysis. Expression of the subconscious and the analyzing of the mental state are also parts of the feminist criticism (Özden, 2004: 179-180).

Psychoanalytic ideology aims at analyzing the persons and to dive into the universes they hide inside (Aliçavuşoğlu, 2012: 2). Freud, who initiated the psychoanalytic criticism, had first examined the works of artists; such as Sophocles, Leonardo Da Vinci, Shakespeare and Dostoyevsky (Özden, 2004: 180). According to Freud the human beings somehow reveal their feelings those they suppress into their subconscious for whatsoever reason. The main reason for suppressing such feelings is the social pressure that they are imposed upon. However, the subconscious desires are expressed in a symbolic style by the means of the tongue slip, faulty acts, and dreams (Tura, 2016: 53).

The meaning that is reached as a result of psychoanalytic criticism is connected to all other interpretations with a special tie; because psychoanalysis enables the exploring of a fantasy that exists at the roots of the literal work and that has a special place for our intellectual life. Since such types of fantasies are subconscious, childish, and loaded in the sense of feelings, their exploration may only be possible by the means of psychoanalysis. Within that framework, to argue that a story has a certain meaning, means the transforming of the subconscious fantasy of the specific story into social, moral, intellectual, and mythical terms. (Cebeci, 2015: 188).

The psychoanalytic theory aims at entering the inner-world of the writer. The language, images, characters and events, and the means of expression to the reader are the most important elements of the method (Karakuş, 2018: 184). Psychoanalytical method, while used by some researchers in order to expose the psychology, subconscious, sexual complexes, etc. of the artists, is used by the others in order to comment on the works of the artist (Gariper and Küçükcoşkun, 2009: 23).

One of the most important tools that engrave the gender on to the subconscious is the tales. Tales, while reflecting the culture of the society they are produced at on one hand, they enable the transferring of the concerned culture to the next generations. Accordingly, tales are both national and global. It is generally considered that the tales are read by the children; however, also the adults read tales. Despite the tales have no claim for being real, everyone make an implication from the tales (Erken, 2018: 164).

The religion of the society is also an aspect determining the gender roles. The religious discourse surrounding the world with definite borders is in fact the source of the power (Sabbah, 1995: 97).

Tales, being perceived imaginary stories, in fact take their forms in the direction of the society's needs; they prepare the newborns to the future with the messages they contain (Gezgin, 2007: 35). The messages, which are intended to be given, are injected to the subconscious of the readers without their awareness. The messages engraved in early ages appear during adulthood in various forms (Sezer, 2017: 21). The tales, which are defined as a fruit of the imagination are in fact a reflection of the idealized and symbolized forms of the real life. Thus they may not be construed apart from the consciousness (Sarı and Ercan, 2008: 28-29).

The main characters of the tales are the women. We generally see witches, sorceresses, and fairies (Ölçer, 2003: 9). The tales, as a product of the collective memory of the society, reproduce the traditions. The gender roles at the tales, similar to the daily life, are transmitted via the functional usage of the places (Ölçer, 2003: 12-13).

The tales, consisting of conscious and subconscious factors, bring with different reading styles. Tales make the children meet with the things and events they had not experienced before. Accordingly, they learn the moral messages and advices and the gender codes firstly from the tales. (Sekmen, 2017: 832).

The tales in fact represent a sexist attitude with the messages they involve. The difference of the messages given to the boys and the girls do support that opinion. The language of the tales are full of symbols (Gezgin, 2007: 36). Each discourse reconstructs the men and the women (Sabbah, 1995: 86). The patriarchal discourses found in all the stories also appear before us at the tales.

The message generally used in the tales is that the salvation of the women will be possible by the virtue of the men. This men type can be categorized under two types; the father or the strong prince. The women, who are given limited roles at the tales, do not have much of a chance of choice. In that sense the roles of the women and the men are quite different (Erken, 2018: 166).

According to Foucault the discourse and the language are two different factors, and the discourse draws its strength from oppression. The discourse forces the individuals to practice definite behavioral patterns (2006: 123). In that sense, the tales can be named as the arena of the dominant discourse and ideology.

AN ORIENTAL TALE: THE CRYSTAL MANOR AND THE DIAMOND SHIP

Story

The story takes place in Istanbul and Yemen at an unknown time. Its general flow bears traces from the Snow White and Rapunzel. Neither of the King's kids had survived, and relying on the recommendations of the physicians and the men of the cloth, he closes down his newborn daughter in a secure underground cave. The Princess had been grown-up by her Nurse in that cave. When she reaches the age of maturity she wonders the out of the cave, and stacking her belongings she reaches the window at the ceiling of the cave. She breaks the glass and looks outside. Fascinating from what she saw, the Princess wants to go out, and stops to eat and talk after saying that she would kill herself if she won't be let out. The Nurse delivers the message of the Princess to the King. First the physicians and the men of the cloth are referred for their opinions. They agreed on the idea that the Princess shall be let out slowly. The Princess everyday takes walks in the garden. After a while, charmed by the sea, she wants her father to construct a crystal manor; and starts to live in there. The crystal manor's fame becomes known all over the world, and one day the Prince of Yemen comes to Istanbul to see the manor. Passing through the manor, he sees the Princess in the balcony, and the Princess sees him, and they both fall in love. The Prince passes out seeing the beauty of the Princess, and this makes the Princess cry. This makes the Prince become arrogant, and leaves there. The Princess decides to take her revenge. She dresses as a captain, and sails to Yemen with a ship made of jewels. She settles across the palace of the Prince with her slaves. The Prince sees the Princess from a distance. He does not recognize her, but falls in love. The Princess asserts very heavy conditions for accepting his proposal. The Prince satisfies all the requests of the Princess, and then she tells him her identity; and they move to Istanbul and marry; and the tale ends.

Subject Positions

The main character of the tale is the daughter of the Istanbul's King. The name of the Princess is not mentioned in the story; but called as the "King's Daughter",

A Feminist Reading of an Oriental Tale

"Lady Princess", or the "Princess". The story has a similarity with the western tale Rapunzel, since she was locked in an underground cave by her father. However, in the tale of Rapunzel the reason for her being locked in the tower was the black magic of an evil hearted witch, but in this tale the reason for the bad luck has not been mentioned. On the other hand, different from Rapunzel, the Princess does not accept the safe life she was forced to live, and after exploring the possibilities of the outer-world she insists to leave the cave. Despite the method she used to get out of the cave was quite passive (not eating, keeping silent, threating other with suicide), she gets permission from the King to get out of the cave. The Princess, affected from the beauty of the sea, wants to live in a crystal manor in the middle of the sea. The crystal manor becomes famous worldwide within a short time, and turns into a spectacular structure to watch. The other character of the tale, the son of the King of Yemen, the Prince hears about the manor, and takes a trip to see it. The Prince reaches the manor during a night time, sees the Princess and falls in love with her, and passes out on the ship's board because of his love. Similarly the Princess falls in love with the Prince as she sees him, and starts to cry because of her sorrow. The Prince sees the Princess crying, feels arrogant, and leaves. At the following part, which we may name as the second section, the Princess set out on a journey with a vengeance plan. She makes the Prince fall in love with her; and refuses his proposals. After putting the Prince and his mother into various troubles by playing tricks on them, she makes the Prince understand that she was the girls who he left in Istanbul. The Prince recognizes his mistake and the Princess forgives him. The tale ends as they return to Istanbul, tell all about the King, and marry.

There are five main characters in the tale, the Princess, the King (father), the Nurse, the Prince, and the Prince's Mother. The King, one of the two men in the tale, takes no action other than providing the wills of his daughter, giving permission, not giving permission, and asking for opinion to his consultants. It can be said that the most effective act of the King is closing his daughter into a cave to protect her from the fate of his other children, who all died because of misfortune. However, this idea had been given to him by his consultants (physicians and the men of the cloth). The second biggest act of him is letting the Princess out of the cave, which again was not his idea, but the suggestion of the physicians. The decisions he made by himself was letting his daughter to travel with the jewel-made ship, and approving her marriage with the Prince. As a matter of fact, it is not very clear whether or not the lovers for his permission.

The Princess came to the board, holding the Prince's hand, directly sailed to her father, the King, and told him all from the very beginning. Her father was so surprised, and became so happy seeing the joy felicity of his daughter. Starting from that very day the wedding feast started. (Alangu, p.30, 2010).

At that quotation the wedding feast is notified with a passive attitude, which makes the reader that a collective decision had been made and practiced. The other man character of the tale, the Prince, does not have the role of the savior, unlike the princes of many other tales. He sailed miles to see the crystal manor, fell in love with the Princess incidentally, and move off, after feeling arrogant because of a reason that is not quite clear.

This situation forms the basic contradiction of the tale. The Princess wants both to take the revenge of being let down and to make the man she loves love her again. After going to Yemen with her diamond ship, as she settles before the palace of the Prince, the Prince thinks she is somebody else and falls in love with her again. However, the Prince never meets the Princess till to the end of the story, from the time he falls in love with her. Instead, the communication is established by his mother by coming and going between their palace and the Princess's palace. It is the Prince's mother who proposes to the Princess and who selected the gifts. All that the Prince does, till to the end of the story, is to wait in anxiety. In that sense we can argue that he has a passive image, just like the other man character, the King.

Other than the main character of the tale, Princess, the other two women characters of the tale are the Nurse and the mother of the Prince. The Nurse between the King and the Princess, and the mother between the Princess and the Prince, take acts as messengers. However, unlike the Nurse, the mother gives advices to her son, tells her opinions and impressions about the Princess, and has impacts on the flow of events. Furthermore, she speaks her own wishes, and dissents with her son. At the first visit the mother gives a golden shoe to the Princess, which she then gives to her servant. In her second visit she gives a pearl neckless to the Princess, thinking that it would be more appropriate, but the Princess returns it with a rude attitude. His mother tells to the Prince that:

Oh, my poor son, I gave my pearl neckless to her, and she fed before me her parrot with its pieces one by one, just to spite. The evil bird it is; it ate the pearls crunching and laughing "Ha, ha, ha!" I do not know for what I shall be sorry for, the pearls or her spite! I felt nauseated, I lost all my energy. I was confused; you shall forget about her as soon as possible. She is foxy, a bloody woman, a pedant. Nobody can cope with her. I give in; do what the hell you want. (Alangu, 2015: 25)

The Prince begs her mother, threatens her with going away; and finally convinces her to go between. In that sense the Prince is quite similar with the Princess, since the Princess had threatened her father with suicide in order to leave the cave.

The last woman character of the tale is the Princess, the main character. The Princess is the strongest character, who has her own will, speaks of her will, and realizing her will. It is the Princess, who desires, plans, and practices all the acts as

A Feminist Reading of an Oriental Tale

she reaches puberty. The only act in the tale that the Princess is not the subject of is the Prince's leaving her at the very night he sees her. Instead of accepting that act she makes a plan for vengeance and practices it; and redirects the events according to her own will.

The Princess starts to make her presence felt as she reaches puberty. As she becomes fifteen she puts the things in the cave on each other and reaches the window, and breaks the glass and sees the outer-world. When her Nurse asks why the glass is broken, she responses:

It is me who puts on and on, who breaks the glass, who is the poor princess. Though there was another world on that world, which the glitter of whiteout me, which the beauty of took my mind and my heart. Please take me out of this small place, or I will commit suicide. (Alangu, 2015: 11)

The second will of the Princess from her father is a crystal manor. Astonished from the beauty of the sea and wanted to live there, the Princess directly speaks to her father this time:

Oh my kind father Please build a crystal manor on that sea, and furnish with golden and silver furniture, adorned with jewels, brocaded satin clothes, silk carpets. This is what my heart wants from you to do. (Alangu, 2015: 11)

The last wish of the Princess from her father is a diamond ship to follow the Prince who left her and returned to Yemen. She speaks her wish this way:

Ah! My father, the king! I this time want a ship from you. Its vessel shall be made of pearl, cabins shall be made of jewels, mast shall be made of ruby, furniture shall be coated with satin. 40 young and beautiful slaves shall be placed in it. These shall be the most beautiful ones. If you will not make this happen I will kill myself. (Alangu, 2015: 15)

The Princess does not meet her father till to the end of the tale, after she leaves Istanbul. The Nurse, who was with her since she was born, is no more mentioned. The Princess takes and practices her decisions alone for almost the course of the story. In that sense we can argue that the Princess is the strongest subject of the tale[1].

FUTURE RESEARCH AND DIRECTIONS

It is thought that some perspectives that are not covered by this study will open useful discussion areas for future studies. A comparative analysis of the tale may be useful for cross-cultural studies. Similarly, a psychoanalytic analysis of the symbols in the fairy tale can raise considerable questions. In addition, the evaluation of the fairy tale from an orientalist perspective may create fruitful discussion areas.

CONCLUSION

This study aims to evaluate an important tale of Turkey's tale corpus which named "The Crystal Manor and The Diamond Ship" by the terms of feminist critics. This tale is considered among the tales of Anatolian field and is similar to some western tales such as Raphunzel. Although the fairy tale resembles some patriarchal narratives -the king closes her daughter to protect her from evil fortune-, it exhibits a quite woman-centric appearance in terms of the role of female characters in the advancement of the plot. Rather than expecting a prince to save herself as in many fairy tales, the female hero stands in the position of a powerful subject who, acting in accordance with her own desires throughout the tale, pursues the prince by going to another country alone. The other main character of the tale does not take any action other than to come to see the princess and then to escaped to his country at the beginning of the tale. It can be said that other actions of prince which in line with the princess's wishes, performed by his mother, another strong female subject in the tale. Similarly, the king does not show any existence other than fulfilling the suggestions of the physicians and counselors according to his daughter's wishes. Another point worth mentioning in the study is that the princess expresses her own desires in a loud and direct way. The princess wanted to get out of the cave, to live in a crystal mansion, to go after the man she wanted to win with a diamond ship, she voiced it, and then achieved it. This situation, which is not frequently encountered in patriarchal narratives, reinforces the princess's strong subject position. As a result, it can be said that "The Crystal Manor and the Daimond Ship" is out of patriarchal discourse with strong female subjects.

REFERENCES

Alangu, T. (2015). *Billur Köşk Masalları*. İstanbul, Turkey: Yapı Kredi Yayınları.

Aliçavuşoğlu, E. (2012). Psikanaliz, Freud ve Sanat. *Sanat Tarihi Yıllığı*, (20), 1–16.

Althusser, L. (1994). *İdeoloji ve Devletin İdeolojik Aygıtları*. Mahmut Özışık ve Yusuf Alp (çev.). İstanbul, Turkey: İletişim Yayınları.

Antmen, A. (2012). *Sanat / Cinsiyet: Sanat Tarihi ve Feminist Eleştiri*. İstanbul, Turkey: İletişim Yayınları.

Bolay, S. H. (2004). *Felsefe Doktrinleri ve Terimleri Sözlüğü*. Ankara, Turkey: Akçağ Yayınları.

Butler, J. (2012). *Cinsiyet Belası: Feminizm ve Kimliğin Altüst Edilmesi*. İstanbul, Turkey: Metis Yayınları.

Cebeci, O. (2015). *Psikanalitik Edebiyat Kuramı*. İstanbul, Turkey: İthaki Yayınları.

Eagleton, M. (2013). *Feminist Literary Critism*. New York, NY: Routledge.

Erken, J. (2018). Feminist Teori Işığında Muğla Masallarında Kadın Algısı. *Sosyal ve Beşeri Bilimler Araştırmaları Dergisi Kadın Çalışmaları Özel Sayısı, 19*(42), 163–186.

Foucault, M. (2006). *Sonsuza Giden Dil, çev. Işık Ergüden*. İstanbul, Turkey: Ayrıntı Yayınları.

Gariper, C., & Ve Küçükcoşkun, Y. (2009). *Dionizyak Coşkunun İhtişam ve Sefaleti, Yakup Kadri'nin Nur Baba Romanına Psikanalitik Bir Yaklaşım*. İstanbul, Turkey: Akademik Kitaplar.

Gezgin, İ. (2007). *Masalların Şifresi*. İstanbul, Turkey: Sel Yayıncılık.

Güzel, N. S. (2007). *Edebi Metin Çözümlemelerinde Dilbilim-Biçembilim-Kuram*. Manisa: Kendi yayını.

Humm, M. (2002). Feminist Edebiyat Eleştirisi. İstanbul, Turkey: Sal Yayınları.

Kabadayı, L. (2014). *Film Eleştirisi*. İstanbul, Turkey: Ayrıntı Yayınları.

Karakuş, G. (2018). *Nazan Bekiroğlu'nun Roman Ve Hikayelerinde Postmodernizm-Büyülü Gerçekçilik, Tasavvuf Ve Psikanalitik, Ordu Üniversitesi, Sosyal Bilimler Enstitüsü*. Ordu, Turkey: Yüksek Lisans Tezi.

Kırtıl, G. A. (2003). Feminist Edebiyat Eleştirisi Açısından Sevim Burak. *Kadın Araştırmaları Dergisi, 0*(8), 127–151.

Marshall, G. (1999). *Sosyoloji Sözlüğü*. Ankara, Turkey: Bilim ve Sanat.

Moran, B. (2002). *Edebiyat Kuramları ve Eleştiri*. İstanbul, Turkey: İletişim yayınları

Mutlu, E. (2004). *İletişim Sözlüğü*. Ankara, Turkey: Bilim ve Sanat.

Ölçer, E. (2003). *Türkiye Masallarında Toplumsal Cinsiyet ve Mekân İlişkisi. Bilkent Üniversitesi Ekonomi ve Sosyal Bilimler Enstitüsü*. Ankara, Turkey: Yüksek Lisans Tezi.

Özden, Z. (2004). *Film Eleştirisi*. Ankara, Turkey: İmge Kitapevi.

Sabbah, A. F. (1995). *İslam'ın Bilinçaltında Kadın*. İstanbul, Turkey: Ayrıntı Yayınları.

Saluk, R. G. (2018). Menzel'in Dilinden Billur Köşk Masalları. *Akademi Dil ve Edebiyat Dergisi, 1*(2), 41–51. doi:10.34083/akaded.410063

Sarı, A., & Ve Ercan, A. C. (2008). *Masalların Psikanalizi*. Erzurum, Turkey: Salkımsöğüt Yayınları.

Sekmen, M. (2017). Masallar ve 'Anlat İstanbul' Filminin Toplumsal Cinsiyet Eleştirisi. *Atatürk Üniversitesi Sosyal Bilimler Enstitüsü Dergisi, 21*(3), 827–845.

Sezer, M. Ö. (2017). *Masallar ve Toplumsal Cinsiyet*. İstanbul, Turkey: Kor Kitap.

Showalter, E. (1996). Towards a Feminist Poetics. In P. Rice & P. Waugh (Eds.), Modern Literary Theory: A Reader. London, UK: Arnold.

Sümer, Z. S. (2009). *Tarih İçinde Görünürlükten, Kadınların Tarihine: Amerikan Kadın Romanında Feminist Bilinç Ve Politika. Selçuk Üniversitesi Sosyal Bilimler Enstitüsü* (Doktora tezi).

Tura, S. M. (2016). *Freud'dan Lacan'a Psikanaliz*. İstanbul, Turkey: Kanat Kitap.

Yavaş, S. (2018). *Oğuz Atay'ın Roman Ve Öykülerinin Psikanalitik Açıdan İncelenmesi, Adıyaman Üniversitesi Sosyal Bilimler Enstitüsü*. Adıyaman: Yüksek Lisans Tezi.

Yüce, K., & Kazan, Ş. (2006). Edebiyat Bilgi ve Teorileri. İstanbul, Turkey: Arı Matbaacılık.

Yuval-Davis, N. (2003). *Cinsiyet ve Millet*. İstanbul, Turkey: İletişim Yayınları.

ADDITIONAL READING

Bhasin, K. (2003). Toplumsal Cinsiyet: Bize Yüklenen Roller, İstanbul:Kadav yayınları.

Conne!l, R. W. (1998). Toplumsal Cinsiyet ve İktidar, Ayrıntı Yayınları, İstanbul:Ayrıntı yayınları.

Demir, Z. (1997). Modern ve Postmodern Feminizm, İstanbul: İz yayınları.

Dökmen, Y. Z. (2010). *Toplumsal Cinsiyet*. İstanbul: Remzi Kitabevi.

Fine, C. (2011). *Toplumsal Cinsiyet Yanılsaması*. İstanbul: Sel Yayıncılık.

Freud, S. (2014). *Cinsiyet Üzerine*. İstanbul: Say Yayınları.

Keller, F. E. (2007). *Toplumsal Cinsiyet ve Bilim Üzerine Düşünceler*. İstanbul: Metis Yayıncılık.

Ölçüner, Ö. E. (2006). Masal Mekanında Kadın Olmak - Masallarda Toplumsal Cinsiyet Ve Mekan İlişkisi, Ankara:Geleneksel yayınevi.

Sakaoğlu, S. (1999). Masal Araştırmaları. Ankara: Akçay yayınları.

Sezer, E. Ö. (2011). *Masallar ve Toplumsal Cinsiyet*. İstanbul: Evrensel Basım Yayın.

ENDNOTE

[1] In addition to those five main characters, there two side characters at the tale. Since those characters take relatively less place at the story they only had been referred briefly at the footnotes. One of those two characters is the King of Yemen, the father of the Prince. This character has no role other than giving permission to the Prince to travel Istanbul. The other is the tutor of the Prince, whose only role is to act as the messenger who informs the Yemen King and the Prince about the diamond ship after it arrives Yemen.

Chapter 6
Gender Representations in Cartoons:
Niloya and Biz Ikimiz

Arzu Karasaç Gezen
Bolu Abant Izzet Baysal University, Turkey

ABSTRACT

The concept of gender refers to the roles, learned behaviors and expectations determined by the society for women and men, apart from the biological differences between women and men. These expectations differ from society to society and even within different sections of the same society; based on such distinctions as rural/urban, class and ethnicity, etc., they may vary depending on the distinctions. It is important how these roles are offered in terms of shaping the children's views on gender roles at very young ages. The aim of this study is to analyze the cartoons within the frame of rural and urban life in terms of gender representations. In this study, 30 episodes of cartoons were analyzed by using the content analysis technique. The study strives to reveal how male and female characters are represented within the context of gender. The findings have shown that despite the existence of egalitarian representations in terms of gender, the contents emphasizing inequality are more dominant.

INTRODUCTION

The difference between men and women has been presented as a contradiction since the early ages. This contradiction has been reproduced and brought to the present through myths and stereotypes. The presentation of the difference between women and men in the form of a contradiction is important in the sense that an unequal structure in favor of the men has been brought to the present in social life.

DOI: 10.4018/978-1-7998-0128-3.ch006

The gender roles and the resulting division of labor within this unequal structure determined the place and limitations of women and men in society. In this process, discrimination based on gender served the reproduction of stereotypes about women and men. While women were considered belonging to home, in other words, the private space; men were considered belonging to outside the home, that is, the public space (Becerikli, 2005, 978).

In industrialized societies, it might be thought at first glance that this picture has changed and both genders share the roles inside and outside the home in a more equal manner due to changes in the family structure and the fact that women begin to take more part in the work life. However, studies show that this is not the case, and that the role of businesswoman is added to women's role of a housewife as a new role (Bora, 2011). Although the spread of the core family structure in the urban life contrary to rural life, as well as the working conditions bring into question the men's undertaking a more active role in the house, the house responsibility again seems to be falling to women.

Gender refers to the definitions of femininity and masculinity that the society wants to see. The individual basic characteristics of women or men are expected to be in line with the norms of society. Social institutions and practices become important in the creation and maintenance of such harmony. While social institutions such as family, friends and school convey the roles of masculinity and femininity they want to see to individuals, they also provide the continuity of this information among generations.

The media, which has an important place in our daily life, is as important as the family, school and friends in terms of shaping the individuals' perceptions of gender. The media contents and the representations in these contents provide clues to social life and culture. In media, the ways in which gender roles are presented play an important role in shaping the perceptions of children about gender roles.

As with other media content, the cartoons also encompass many codes regarding social life. As cartoon viewers, children tend to directly accept the contents that are offered, because they have not reached the cognitive level through which they can critically read and interpret media (Keloğlu İşler, 2014,68). The individuals' perceptions of gender start to form at early ages and continue to take shape throughout their lives, which makes the role of media more understandable in terms of providing children with egalitarian perspectives as from childhood. In this respect, the main problem of this research is that the sex roles in cartoons are presented mostly on the basis of gender inequality. The aim of this study is to analyze the cartoons "Niloya" and "Biz İkimiz" within the frame of rural and urban life in terms of gender representations.

The episodes of mentioned cartoons that were broadcasted in the first month (30 episodes) were analyzed through the content analysis technique. Within the scope of study, efforts were made to reveal how the male and female characters are represented as part of gender equality/inequality and whether there is any difference between these representations in terms of rural and urban life through such categories as the characters' works, occupations, clothing types and colors, individual talents, suggestions, emotional responses, use of space, the games that the children play, the responsibilities allocated to children and the children's choices of profession. This study is important in terms of trying to analyze how gender representations are presented within the framework of rural and urban life.

Sex and Gender

The human species is divided into two as the male and female. Nevertheless, such distinction between men and women is not solely based on a biological difference. It's been generally accepted since the early ages to the present that the men and women are different and such acceptance incorporates unequal power relations as well. In the historical process, women have been identified with nature, whereas the rational information associated with men has been accepted as the transformation and control of nature. The distinction between men and women also constituted a criterion in such acceptance. Accordingly, while the men have been associated with the clear, explicit and definite side of thought, the women with its ambiguous and unclear side. While the men represented an effective, defined form, the women represented the passive and undetermined substance (distinction between form and substance). It is the rational and rational knowledge that represents the man who shapes the unidentified substance in nature (Lloyd, 2015). The power of transformation, namely, the power has been considered to be in the hands of men.

The distinction between femininity and masculinity has also been dealt with by Freud and defined in three different contexts: the first one is at the efficacy-passivity level as in Greek philosophy, the second one concerns biology and the third one is at the social level. Freud argues that the individual is a combination of efficacy and passivity, regardless of their biological sex (as cited in Yüksel 1999,68-69). Similarly, Illich does not deal with femininity and masculinity merely in the context of the principle of contradiction. According to him, femininity and masculinity are the same concepts that also complement each other in addition to such contradiction (1996,91).

Bora argues that it cannot be asserted that the categories of "female" and "male" in the biological difference of sex are based on a universal basis. According to him, differences of sex can also vary from society to society, just like the gender can undergo changes depending on culture. For example, people in Nepal believe that all humans embody femininity and masculinity in different amounts. These features are not considered as belonging to only one sex (as cited in Bora, 2011,38-39).

The meanings and expectations attributed to femininity and masculinity might differ from society to society and culture to culture as mentioned above. It is clear that the difference between men and women cannot be explained solely on a biological basis. As a result, to start with the explanation of the concept of sex when dealing with gender is regarded important in terms of revealing the relationship between these two concepts.

The term "sex" refers to the anatomical and physiological differences that define the male and female bodies, while the term "gender" refers to psychological, social and cultural differences between women and men. Gender, which is associated with the socially constructed categories of masculinity and femininity, is not a direct product of the biological sex of an individual. Gender is the process of cultural interpretation of what is biologically given. From the moment when an individual's perception of gender starts to emerge, the society expects him/her to act in accordance with his/her role. As a result, the expectations of society are reproduced, and sex is socialized and transformed into a feature of society and culture beyond being a feature of the individual by socializing (Giddens, 2012, 600-602). The concept of gender has expanded to include not only the individual identity from the moment it was initially introduced, but the cultural ideals of masculinity and femininity at a symbolic level, and the division of labor in institutions and organizations on the structural plane (Marshall,1999,98).

Oakley (1972), who has introduced the term gender in sociology, points out that gender refers to a socially unequal division between masculinity and femininity in addition to biological differences and underlines the socially-established aspects of differences between men and women.

Butler considers gender as a mechanism by which notions of masculine and feminine are produced and naturalized and deals with gender as a regulatory norm (2009; 75). Each society incorporates some norms, which they attribute to men and women and distinguish them from each other. While these norms differ from society to society, they generally define women as warm, compassionate, gentle, intuitive, caring and flexible, and men as assertive, strong, sociable, productive, risk-taking and self-confident (cited from Davis by Horrock, 1994, 143). The gender patterns created by society not only differentiate women and men from each other, but also significantly affect access to social resources, use of opportunities and distribution of responsibilities and resources. They develop social expectations about what kind of behaviors are suitable for men and women and which rights, resources and power should these two sexes have and to which extent they should be (Ecevit,2003,83).

The two types are positioned as opposed to each other within the social structure. According to Illich, the concept of gender bespeaks a complementarity that is enigmatic and asymmetrical. The works, places, clothes, colors and speech forms that are integrated with the men and women through gender stereotypes differ from each other (1996,13-14). The criteria of this distinction are determined by social, cultural norms. For example, clothing is one of the fundamental indications of gender. Women are encoded with skirt, whereas men are encoded with trousers. The encodings regarding the costumes peculiar to certain professions and occupations (e.g. kitchen aprons) give clues to gender-compatibility. These encodings also provide continuity of existing gender patterns. (Yüksel,1999,71).

Sex Roles

As mentioned above, gender refers to expectations and meanings that are attributed by a society and culture to a woman or a man. These expectations constitute the sex roles.

Sex roles refer to how women and men should behave and the different tasks they are expected to perform. The roles of most of women consist of doing housework and working in service works, in other words, conducting the "womanly work." The roles of men include working outside the home at better wages usually and higher-status jobs, compared to women (Marshall, 2005, 109). Social expectations put pressure on people to comply with these roles.

Why did differences in sex roles emerge?

There are different theoretical approaches dealing with this issue. According to the social learning theory; innate biological differences are not sufficient to explain differences in sex roles. Learning occurs through selective reinforcement, model taking and imitation in the process of gaining sex-related identity. Children are more likely to take the behavior of the parent with whom they share the same sex as a model. If the behavior of the model is rewarded, the observer gets more likely to display the same behavior. If the model is punished as a result of his/her behavior, the observer's tendency to display that behavior decreases or disappears. Bandura has added a new dimension to this theory, arguing that the children tend towards observational learning in addition to imitating the adults' behaviors. Learning occurs by taking as a model through observation and by watching. Bandura has considered imitation as a part of observational learning. Children are more likely to imitate strong people than less powerful ones and more important people than less important ones (Kağıtçıbaşı, 2017; Onur, 2004).

According to cognitive theory, children maintain their cognitive consistency by imitating the behaviors of people with whom they share the same sex, once they realize their gender. According to this theory, the development of sex roles occurs, when children reach a certain level of cognitive development. The children firstly accept themselves as male or female, and then tend towards achieving the behaviors that are appropriate to categories of their own sex. According to Kohlberg, children form a stereotyped concept of masculinity and femininity. They then use this template image to organize their environment. They select and develop the behaviors that match the concepts of their sex (Kağıtçıbaşı, 2017; Onur, 2004; Vatandaş, 2011, 35).

Learning the gender roles is a dynamic process, which starts from early childhood and continues for a life time. Teachers and the media, as well as parents play an important role in this process. As a result, presenting the difference between men and women on a non-sexist basis is very important in terms of providing children with egalitarian thinking and behavioral patterns. Within this framework, the representation of women and men in media, their relations with each other and how their gender roles are presented become more important. There are many studies on media and gender. In the following section, especially the studies on cartoons are briefly mentioned and the aspect of this study differing from them is revealed.

There are studies dealing with the presentation of gender roles in cartoons. The next section briefly touches upon the studies about the issue and reveals the aspect of this study that differs from others.

BACKGROUND

The subject gender is dealt with by many disciplines with its different aspects. In recent years, various studies on gender representation were carried out in various media contents. Some of these studies -especially those depicting the cartoons - are as follows;

Gürel and Alem (2010, 332-347) analyzed the cartoon Simpsons in connection with the concept of postmodernism in their study entitled "Content Analysis on a Postmodern Sit-com: Simpsons." In the cartoon that draws attention with its satires about social institutions; Homer, the father of the Simpson Family, is presented as the pillar of his family, a devoted husband and a self-sacrificing father who brings home the bacon, whereas Marge is displayed as a skillful housewife who is deeply in love with her husband and as a mother who would do anything for her children; and it was suggested that this situation makes important references to "family myth" of the patriarchal social structure.

Another study on the subject is a dissertation entitled "Presentation of Gender Roles in Children's Programs: TRT Çocuk and Yumurcak TV" by Günaydın (2011). Günaydın has analyzed in her study the cartoons on TRT Çocuk and Yumurcak TV, which are among the thematic children's channels broadcasted in Turkish, with the content analysis technique by their age categories. The study concludes that the girls and boys are not represented evenly in cartoons, the boys are represented more frequently, the protagonists are usually male, men deal with jobs that require power, adventure, intelligence and self-confidence and use the related tools in most of the shows, while the girls are represented with roles secondary to that of men, which do not require intelligence and skills, and also using the compliant tools.

Keloğlu İşler (2014) analyzed the cartoons "Pepe," "Canım Kardeşim" and "Biz İkimiz" within the concept of Gerbner's Cultivation Theory in her study entitled "Turkey-Made Cartoons and Creation of Children's Awareness in the context of Cultural Cultivation." Keloğlu argues that the domestically produced cartoons play an important role in cultural construction, universal human elements are emphasized in cultural construction in globally broadcasted cartoons and local cultural elements are emphasized in domestically produced cartoons and defines this situation as natural. The researcher argues that the transfer of culture and cultural practices is not a problem and not a case peculiar to Turkey, noting that the problematic issue at this point consists of the ways of representation in cultural transmission. Having found the manipulation of child's consciousness based on the normative assumption regarding "what kind of a human being should the child be in the future" was problematic, Keloğlu İşler argues that the definition of the role of women/men (housework, childbirth, taking care of children/going to work and earning money) in a separated manner in the cartoons that are watched is enormously autocratic.

In her study entitled "Analyses of the Cartoon Series from a Gender Equality Perspective: Pepe," Kalaycı (2015) analyzed the cartoon movie Pepee in terms of the concept of gender equality. As a result of the study in which semiology and content analysis technique were used, it was concluded that both male and female characters contain some stereotypes confined to sex roles in terms of their work, clothing types and colors, as well as messages containing sexist perspectives.

Güder et al. (2017) examines the mentioned cartoon through the content analysis method in their study entitled "An Examination of Cartoons Watched by Preschool Children in terms of Gender Stereotypes: Case of Niloya." The study analyzes the gender stereotypes through such variables as domestic/external works, colors and types of clothes, play and toy preferences and parents' care for their child. The study concludes that the cartoon consists of traditional stereotypes about men and women. The female characters are deal with cooking, house cleaning and childcare, whereas male characters handle activities such as driving, garden works and animals.

The researches summarized above commonly conclude that the male and female characters in cartoons are presented in a way that the gender roles are sharply confined. According to researches, cartoons contain stereotypes regarding gender and include patterns of thinking and behavior, which are extensions of a patriarchal culture.

This study analyzes how male and female characters are represented in the context of gender equality and inequality in cartoons. Unlike other studies, it has been tried to reveal whether there is any difference between these representations within the framework of rural and urban life.

RESEARCH METHOD

The basic assumption of the study is that the sexist ways of thinking and behavior are reproduced in cartoon contents.

The aim of this study is to analyze the cartoons "Niloya" and "Biz İkimiz" in terms of gender representations within the framework of rural and urban life. The analyzed cartoons are the examples that are prepared for preschool children and also representing rural and urban life. In this study, a descriptive research method was used and analyzes were performed through the content analysis technique as a convenient method in terms of learning how certain clusters – the poor, different ethnic identities, sexes, etc. – are represented in the media (Geray, 2017, 147). As part of study, some episodes of cartoons were chosen as the unit of analysis. The instructions for encoding were developed by the researcher as a data collection tool. After a detailed literature search on the subject, cartoons were watched and categories were formed in the process of creating categories in the instructions for encoding. A pilot study was conducted, and thus the categories were finalized. The data were obtained by watching the first 30 episodes of cartoons Niloya and Biz İkimiz on YouTube channel.

In the study, it was tried to analyze how male and female characters are represented in the context of gender equality and inequality, whether there is any difference between these representations in terms of rural and urban life through such categories as the characters' domestic/external works, professions, cloth types and colors, individual talents, suggesting ideas, emotional responses, the places they are associated with, the games children play, responsibilities allocated to children and children's choices of profession.

Definition of Cartoons

Cartoon Niloya

Niloya is a domestic cartoon especially designed by Yumurcak TV for the pre-school age group. It was also broadcasted on the TRT Çocuk Channel. Niloya lives in a village by the river. In each episode of the cartoon, different themes are depicted. Among these themes are the cultural values such as feasts, wedding and Noah's pudding, as well as individual values and aspects such as honesty and patience. Niloya has a curious mind and she lives in a large and loving family. The cartoon describes Niloya's daily life with her family and friends. The characters of the cartoon consist of Niloya, Tospik (her turtle), her friend Mete, her elder brother Murat, her mother, her father, her grandmother and grandfather.

Cartoon Biz İkimiz

Biz İkimiz is a cartoon designed by Siyah Martı Advertising and Animation Company for the TRT Çocuk Channel. Its target group consists of preschool children. The cartoon depicts the daily life of twin siblings of different sex – a boy named Arda and a girl named Ceren – who live in a house with garden in Istanbul. Different themes are depicted also in each episode of the cartoon. Ceren and Arda live in a nuclear family with their parents. Their grandmother, who seems to be living in a separate house, occasionally visits them. The characters of the cartoon consist of the twins Ceren and Arda, their parents and grandmother.

Research Findings

The episodes of Niloya that are watched show that the female and male characters are represented solely as married (Table 1).

Similarly, the cartoon Biz İkimiz represents the female and male characters as married.

In the two cartoons that were watched, the ideal woman and man were presented as married with children. There were no representations of single, divorced, widowed women and men. These statuses, which are a part of social reality, are also included

Table 1. Distribution of adult characters by marital status (Niloya)

Marital Status	Number	Percentage (%)
Married Woman	8	26.7
Married Man	4	13.3
Single Woman	0	0
Single Man	0	0
Divorced/Widow Woman	0	0
Divorced/Widow Woman	0	0
Together (Married Woman and Man)	12	40.0
Could not be Encoded	6	20.0
Total	30	100

Gender Representations in Cartoons

Table 2. Distribution of adult characters by marital status (Biz İkimiz)

Marital Status	Number	Percentage (%)
Married Woman	1	3.3
Married Man	1	3.3
Single Woman	0	0
Single Man	0	0
Divorced/Widow Woman	0	0
Divorced/Widow Woman	0	0
Together (Married Woman and Man)	28	93.3
Total	30	100

in the content of cartoons, which is important for the development of children's gender identity. In both cartoons, men and women are presented in a uniform manner. This presentation is problematic in terms of gender equality and social diversity. It is considered that the representation of different but equal characters is important.

As can be seen on Table 3, kitchen works come first among the work done inside and outside the home. This is followed by the childcare, house cleaning and other

Table 3. Distribution of domestic/external works by gender (Niloya)

Domestic/External Works	Female Characters Number*	%	Male Characters Number*	%	Together (Female and Male) Number*	%	Total Number*	%
Kitchen works	10	100	0	0	0	0	10	100
Child care, education	4	100	0	0	0	0	4	100
House cleaning and other housework	4	100	0	0	0	0	4	100
Garden works	1	25	0	0	3	75	4	100
Playing games with children	0	0	0	0	0	0	0	0
Care of animals	0	0	1	50	1	50	2	100
Repair works	0	0	2	100	0	0	2	100
Helping with house cleaning	0	0	0	0	0	0	0	0
Helping with childcare	0	0	0	0	0	0	0	0
Other	0	0	2	100	0	0	2	100

*The number was calculated over the number of markings, not over the number of cartoons.

Table 4. Distribution of domestic/external works by gender (Biz İkimiz)

Domestic/External Works	Female Characters Number*	%	Male Characters Number*	%	Together (Female and Male) Number*	%	Total Number*	%
Kitchen works	11	100	0	0	0	0	11	100
Child care, education	11	73.3	1	6.7	3	20.0	15	100
House cleaning and other housework	4	100	0	0	0	0	4	100
Garden works	0	0	2	66.7	1	33.3	3	100
Playing games with children	3	33.3	2	22.2	4	44.4	9	100
Care of animals	0	0	0	0	0	0	0	0
Repair works	0	0	0	0	0	0	0	0
Helping with house cleaning	0	0	1	100	0	0	1	100
Helping with childcare	0	0	0	0	0	0	0	0
Other	1	50	0	0	1	50	2	100

*The number was calculated over the number of markings, not over the number of cartoons.

housework. All of these works are done by female characters. Women are responsible for housework and childcare. The work carried out by male characters consist of taking care of animals, repair works, as well as wheat milling and organizing the old belongings in the storeroom that fall in the category of "other." Garden work is presented as the joint work of both sexes. Considering the distribution of works by gender in Niloya, there is a very clear inequality. Domestic works are presented as belonging to female characters as the "womanly work", while external works are presented as belonging to male characters. The "motherhood myth" of the patriarchal society seems to be reproduced here as well.

Considering the works carried out and the distribution of works by gender in the cartoon Biz İkimiz, similarly, the kitchen works, childcare and house cleaning and other house works are placed near the top and carried out by female characters. Male characters are in charge of garden works. Unlike Niloya, "playing games with children" is presented as a joint work of both sexes.

In the cartoon Biz İkimiz, although the male character seems to have played a more active role in terms of the children's education and playing games with children, the responsibility for these works again falls to the woman. We can argue that the division of labor has a traditional character which has been continuing and unchanged to a great extent. For example, in the episode "Camera," while the mother cooks in the kitchen, the father shoots a video of children with the new camera he has just bought. In the episode "Climbing the Tree," the mother calls out to her children, saying, "Your father woke up, children, let's have breakfast." The mother is the person who prepares the family breakfast early in the morning and huddling the family together. In many other episodes, the mother was seen calling out to her children by saying, "the meal is ready, children."

Different representations of women and men need to be presented in order to develop more egalitarian perspectives in terms of gender roles in children. For example, representations of strong and independent women who are engaged in jobs other than housework (e.g. jobs related to technology); and representations of men who take care of children, cook, iron and express emotions should be included.

Dresses, skirts and the kitchen apron are placed near the top in the clothes worn by female characters. Niloya's mother and almost all other female characters appear to be wearing a kitchen apron. The mother does not remove her kitchen apron and welcomes her guests in this manner even during the "feast" days, which are special occasions. The work-related costumes give important clues about compatibility to gender. The fact that Niloya's mother is usually seen in her kitchen apron is an extension of the understanding that the woman's place is the kitchen. Among the female characters, only the grandmother (married, old and a senior member of the family) does not wear a kitchen apron. It could be argued that this situation allows a reading that the kitchen work is among the traditional roles of women and that it will be handed over to younger women, when the time comes.

Table 5. Distribution of clothes/accessories by gender (Niloya)

Type	Female Characters Number*	Female Characters %	Male Characters Number*	Male Characters %	Worn by Both of Them Number*	Worn by Both of Them %	Total Number*	Total %
Dress	21	100	0	0	0	0	21	100
Jumpsuit	11	91.7	0	0	1	8.3	12	100
T-shirt	5	17.9	0	0	23	82.1	28	100
Trousers	1	3.3	23	88.5	2	7.7	26	100
Vest	9	39.1	5	21.7	9	39.1	23	100
Hat	0	0	10	83.3	2	16.7	12	100
Kitchen apron	13	100	0	0	0	0	13	100
Skirt	20	100	0	0	0	0	20	100
Shirt	11	50	2	9.1	9	40.9	22	100
Scarf/Headscarf	6	100	0	0	0	0	6	100
Other	0	0	5	50	5	50	10	100

* The number was calculated over the number of markings, not over the number of cartoons.

Trousers, vests and shorts (in the "other" category) are placed near the top in the use of clothing in male characters, while the cloth used by both sexes was the t-shirt. The grandmother and grandfather, who are the elders of the family, are seen wearing a scarf/ headscarf and a hat as traditional clothes. As mentioned earlier, clothing is one of the fundamental indicators of gender. The women are encoded with skirts and dresses, whereas men with trousers. These encodings also provide continuity of existing gender patterns.

The skirt has been the type of clothes which are most commonly worn by female characters who are represented in urban life. Men's clothes are presented as the trousers and shirts. The trousers and shirts are also the clothes pertaining to the professional life. The father of Ceren and Arda were frequently seen in these clothes, as he is frequently represented on the way back from the office in the episodes that were watched. The clothes worn by the girls and boys (Ceren and Arda) were jumpsuits and T-shirts. Arda and Ceren, who are twins, wear similar clothes. It is considered that the fact that they are twins had influence on the use of similar clothing. It is common for twin siblings to dress in this way in Turkish society. There is no significant difference between rural and urban life in terms of the use of clothing.

Considering the clothing colors in Niloya, it was seen that the female characters wear mostly pink and yellow colors, while the male characters use red and blue. In addition to pink, which is regarded as the "girly color" in society, Niloya, one of the main characters, was seen using green, blue and orange – though to a lesser

Table 6. Distribution of clothes/accessories by gender (Biz İkimiz)

Type	Female Characters Number*	%	Male Characters Number*	%	Worn by Both of Them Number*	%	Total Number*	%
Dress	0	0	0	0	0	0	0	0
Jumpsuit	0	0	0	0	29	100	29	100
T-shirt	0	0	0	0	29	100	29	100
Trousers	0	0	27	96.4	1	3.6	28	100
Vest	0	0	0	0	0	0	0	0
Hat	0	0	0	0	0	0	0	0
Kitchen apron	0	0	0	0	0	0	0	0
Skirt	29	100	0	0	0	0	29	100
Shirt	0	0	29	100	0	0	29	100
Scarf/Headscarf	0	0	0	0	0	0	0	0
Other	1	20	0	0	4	80	5	100

* The number was calculated over the number of markings, not over the number of cartoons.

Table 7. Distribution of clothing colors by gender (Niloya)

Colors	Female Characters Number*	%	Male Characters Number*	%	Used by Both of Them Number*	%	Total Number*	%
1. Pink	27	100	0	0	0	0	27	100
2. Yellow	22	100	0	0	0	0	22	100
3. Orange	3	14.3	10	47.6	8	38.1	21	100
4. Green	7	53.8	5	38.5	1	7.7	13	100
5. Red	2	14.3	11	78.6	1	7.1	14	100
6. Blue	1	3.4	11	37.9	17	58.6	29	100
7. Lilac	7	50	1	7.1	6	42.9	14	100
8. Purple	0	0	1	100	0	0	1	100
9. Brown	0	0	10	100	0	0	10	100
10. Maroon	0	0	0	0	0	0	0	0
11. Other	5	62.5	3	37.5	0	0	8	100

*The number was calculated over the number of markings, not over the number of cartoons.

Table 8. Distribution of clothing colors by gender (Biz İkimiz)

Colors	Female Characters Number*	%	Male Characters Number*	%	Used by Both of Them Number*	%	Total Number*	%
1. Pink	29	100	0	0	0	0	29	100
2. Yellow	1	100	0	0	0	0	1	100
3. Orange	28	96,6	1	3,4	0	0	29	100
4. Green	6	100	0	0	0	0	6	100
5. Red	0	0	0	0	0	0	0	0
6. Blue	0	0	2	6,7	28	93,3	30	100
7. Lilac	0	0	0	0	0	0	0	0
8. Purple	2	100	0	0	0	0	2	100
9. Brown	2	100	0	0	0	0	2	100
10. Maroon	0	0	28	100	0	0	28	100
11. Other	1	100	0	0	0	0	1	100

*The number was calculated over the number of markings, not over the number of cartoons.

extent. The colors most frequently used by male characters are red, blue, brown and orange. This finding corresponds to the fact that pink is considered as the "girly color" and blue is regarded as the "boy color" in society. Nevertheless, blue is also the color used commonly by both sexes.

In the cartoon Biz İkimiz, it was seen that the female characters use mostly pink and orange colors, while male characters prefer maroon and blue. The most common color used by both sexes was blue.

The color choices for boys and girls appear to be closer to social acceptances during their childhood (such as dressing the girls in pink and the boys in blue). This distinction is considered to decrease gradually in later ages. There is no significant difference between rural and urban lives in terms of the color of clothes.

In the cartoon Niloya, girls often play in the garden of their house or in the countryside; boys are seen flying kites and playing with marbles. While Niloya was also seen playing with dolls in a way that is expected from girls, she was mostly seen playing in the garden or in the countryside. Playing with ball and racing are placed near the top among the games the girls and boys play together. In patriarchal societies, playing with dolls is considered as the games played by girls, whereas playing with marbles and flying a kite as the games played by boys. Although this categorization is small, it is also present in Niloya. The games played by children are presented in relation to the living environment. Living in the village environment and being intertwined with nature are often associated with children being represented outside the home, in the garden and in the countryside.

In the cartoon Biz İkimiz, it was seen that the girls mostly play with dolls, while the boys were seen playing with toy cars, airplanes, etc. Among the games that girls and boys played together, playing ball and building things with the help of equipment took the first place (Table 10). We have seen that both boys and girls play the games that are expected from their gender roles while playing alone, and they prefer different games in the course of playing together. It is noteworthy that the games played jointly are close to the boys' game preferences. It is very important to present girls and boys playing similar games in the development of egalitarian ways of thinking and behavior as from these ages.

The games played by children are presented in relation to the living environment. As Niloya and her friends live in the village environment and they are in touch with nature, they are seen usually playing outside the home, in the garden and in the countryside. Ceren, Arda and their friends are mostly presented as playing at home due to the urban life.

Representations of professions peculiar to men and women are an important indicator of gender. A few representations of professions were observed in the episodes of Niloya which were watched. These professions are compatible with the rural lifestyle. Female characters are represented only as a housewife (Niloya's

Gender Representations in Cartoons

Table 9. Distribution of the games played by gender (Niloya)

Games	Girl Number*	%	Boy Number*	%	Together (Girls and Boys) Number*	%	Total Number*	%
Playing ball	0	0	0	0	5	100	5	100
Playing with doll	1	100	0	0	0	0	1	100
Playing marbles	0	0	2	100	0	0	2	100
Blind man's buff/Hide and seek	0	0	0	0	1	100	1	100
Drawing	2	100	0	0	0	0	2	100
Playing with toy cars, airplanes, etc.	0	0	1	50	1	50	2	100
Rope jumping	1	33.3	0	0	2	66.7	3	100
Racing (foot-racing, etc.)	0	0	0	0	3	100	3	100
Cycling	1	100	1	100	0	0	2	100
Hopscotch	0	0	0	0	2	100	2	100
Games related with technology	0	0	0	0	0	0	0	0
Skating	0	0	0	0	2	100	2	100
Swinging	0	0	0	0	0	0	0	0
Playing in the garden/countryside	4	80	0	0	1	20	5	100
Flying a kite	0	0	3	100	0	0	3	100
Building something with tools	0	0	0	0	0	0	0	0
Solving riddles	0	0	0	0	0	0	0	0
Other	0	0	1	33.3	2	66.7	3	100

* The number was calculated over the number of markings, not over the number of cartoons.

mother, grandmother, neighbors). On the other hand, male characters are presented as a farmer, baker, Ramadan drummer and imam/mosque teacher. The professions of Niloya's father and grandfather are not clearly shown. The father and grandfather were shown in a way to create a feeling that they are coming from work by showing them entering home from outside on a pick-up truck. When the occupations are evaluated in terms of gender, there seems to be a strict distinction in the sense that women deal with domestic work, whereas men with external work.

Table 10. Distribution of the games played by gender (Biz İkimiz)

Games	Girl Number*	%	Boy Number*	%	Together (Girls and Boys) Number*	%	Total Number*	%
Playing ball	0	0	1	14.3	6	85.7	7	100
Playing with doll	4	100	0	0	0	0	4	100
Playing marbles	0	0	0	0	0	0	0	0
Blind man's buff/Hide and seek	0	0	0	0	1	100	1	100
Drawing	1	16.7	2	33.3	3	50	6	100
Playing with toy cars, airplanes, etc.	0	0	4	100	0	0	4	100
Rope jumping	0	0	0	0	1	100	1	100
Racing (foot-racing, etc.)	0	0	0	0	0	0	0	0
Cycling	0	0	0	0	0	0	0	0
Hopscotch	1	33.3	0	0	2	66.7	3	100
Games related with technology	0	0	0	0	0	0	0	0
Skating	0	0	0	0	0	0	0	0
Swinging	0	0	1	50	1	50	2	100
Playing in the garden/ countryside	0	0	0	0	2	100	2	100
Flying a kite	0	0	1	100	0	0	1	100
Building something with tools	1	11.1	2	22.2	6	66.7	9	100
Solving riddles	0	0	0	0	5	100	5	100
Other	2	28	1	14	4	58	7	100

* The number was calculated over the number of markings, not over the number of cartoons.

In the cartoon Biz İkimiz, being a housewife ranks the first in representations of professions peculiar to women, which is followed by teaching. Women were represented as a housewife, teacher, etc. which are defined as a woman's work.

As the male character, the father of the family was shown on the way home from work, but what his profession is not clear. The professions of other male characters were represented as firefighters, security guards and garbage men. These professions are indicative of the urban life (Table 12).

In rural and urban life, female characters were mostly represented as housewives. In both cartoons, children's fathers were shown on the way home from work at all times. Although their professions are not clearly understood, the father's task

Gender Representations in Cartoons

Table 11. Distribution of professions by gender (Niloya)

Professions	Female Characters Number*	%	Male Characters Number*	%	Conducted by Both Number*	%	Total Number*	%
Farmer	0	0	2	100	0	0	2	100
Housewife	13	0	0	0	0	0	13	100
Baker	0	0	1	100	0	0	1	100
Teacher	0	0	0	0	0	0	0	0
Doctor	0	0	0	0	0	0	0	0
Ramadan drummer	0	0	1	100	0	0	1	100
Imam/Mosque teacher	0	0	1	100	0	0	1	100
Other	0	0	0	0	0	0	0	0

* The number was calculated over the number of markings, not over the number of cartoons.

Table 12. Distribution of professions by gender (Biz İkimiz)

Professions	Female Characters Number*	%	Male Characters Number*	%	Conducted by Both Number*	%	Total Number*	%
Farmer	0	0	0	0	0	0	0	0
Housewife	20	100	0	0	0	0	20	100
Baker	0	0	0	0	0	0	0	0
Teacher	3	100	0	0	0	0	3	100
Doctor	0	0	0	0	0	0	0	0
Ramadan drummer	0	0	0	0	0	0	0	0
Imam/Mosque teacher	0	0	0	0	0	0	0	0
Other	0	0	3	100	0	0	3	100

* The number was calculated over the number of markings, not over the number of cartoons.

was shown as a job outside and providing the livelihood of the family. Other male characters were represented by other "male jobs" in accordance with the requirements of rural and urban life.

Children's choices of profession are an important indicator of gender. In traditional societies, some jobs are seen as women's work by associating them with women, while others are considered men's jobs. In the episodes of Niloya which were watched, children's choices of profession are barely covered. Mete, one of

Table 13. Distribution of children's choices of profession by gender (Niloya)

Professions	Girls Number*	%	Boys Number*	%	Together (Girls and Boys) Number*	%	Total Number*	%
Farmer	0	0	0	0	0	0	0	0
Housewife	0	0	0	0	0	0	0	0
Teacher	0	0	0	0	0	0	0	0
Doctor	0	0	0	0	0	0	0	0
Pilot	0	0	0	0	0	0	0	0
Shepherd	0	0	1	100	0	0	1	100
Ramadan drummer	0	0	0	0	2	100	2	100
Other	0	0	0	0	0	0	0	0

* The number was calculated over the number of markings, not over the number of cartoons.

Table 14. Distribution of children's choices of profession by gender (Biz İkimiz)

Professions	Girls Number*	%	Boys Number*	%	Together (Girls and Boys) Number*	%	Total Number*	%
Farmer	0	0	0	0	0	0	0	0
Housewife	0	0	0	0	0	0	0	0
Teacher	0	0	0	0	0	0	0	0
Doctor	0	0	0	0	0	0	0	0
Pilot	0	0	0	0	1	100	1	100
Shepherd	0	0	1	100	0	0	1	100
Ramadan drummer	1	100	0	0	0	0	1	100
Other	0	0	0	0	0	0	0	0

* The number was calculated over the number of markings, not over the number of cartoons.

the main characters of the cartoon, wants to be a shepherd, whereas Niloya and her elder brother want to be a Ramadan drummer, being impressed by the drummers they saw in the month of Ramadan.

In the cartoon Biz İkimiz, Ceren, who is a girl, wants to be an astronaut. A lesson about space which was taught by her teacher at school had an influence on Ceren's choice. Arda wants to be both a pilot and a football player. Arda's choices of profession are the works usually conducted by men. Their common choice of profession is to be a pilot. The presentation of Ceren' choice of professions which are considered as the men's occupations is an egalitarian discourse in terms of gender. In both cartoons, no content was found with regard to adult male and female characters about what their children want to be when they grow up. The children's choices of profession are presented in compliance with the social environment they live in (Table 13, Table 14).

The responsibilities allocated to children are also an important indicator in terms of gender equality. The cartoons were evaluated in this respect as well. In the episodes of Niloya which were watched, children are not given so much responsibility. However, when responsibility was to be allocated to children, the girl was asked to help with the kitchen work and no responsibility was given to the boy. The common responsibilities allocated to both of them were to carry furniture and to help with the garden work. The presentation of girls and boys with similar responsibilities is necessary in terms of gender equality.

The responsibilities given to children in Biz İkimiz are the same as the responsibilities in Niloya. While the girl is given responsibilities for kitchen work, the boy is given responsibilities for repair work. The common responsibilities given to both of them were related to carrying furniture.

In both cartoons, it was seen that the children were not given much responsibility, but the responsibilities given were consistent with the children's own gender roles.

Table 15. Distribution of responsibilities allocated to children by gender (Niloya)

Responsibilities	Girl Number*	%	Boy Number*	%	Together (Girl and Boy) Number*	%	Total Number*	%
Helping with kitchen work	1	100	0	0	0	0	1	100
Helping with house cleaning	0	0	0	0	0	0	0	0
Helping with carry furniture	0	0	0	0	1	100	1	100
Helping with repair work	0	0	0	0	0	0	0	0
Taking care of his/her sibling	0	0	0	0	0	0	0	0
Helping with garden work	0	0	0	0	4	100	1	100
Other	0	0	0	0	0	0	0	0

* The number was calculated over the number of markings, not over the number of cartoons.

Table 16. Distribution of responsibilities allocated to children by gender (Biz İkimiz)

Responsibilities	Girl Number*	%	Boy Number*	%	Together (Girl and Boy) Number*	%	Total Number*	%
Helping with kitchen work	2	100	0	0	0	0	2	100
Helping with house cleaning	0	0	0	0	0	0	0	0
Helping with carry furniture	0	0	0	0	1	100	1	100
Helping with repair work	0	0	1	100	0	0	1	100
Taking care of his/her sibling	0	0	0	0	0	0	0	0
Helping with garden work	0	0	0	0	0	0	0	0
Other	0	0	0	0	3	100	3	100

* The number was calculated over the number of markings, not over the number of cartoons.

Table 17 shows how the men and women in Niloya are associated with places. Accordingly, female characters were mostly seen in the kitchen and other domestic spaces. It was seen that the male characters were not present at any place alone. The male characters are seen along with female characters only in the kitchen and other domestic spaces during eating or family conversations. The garden has been the space where female and male characters were seen the most.

Table 17. Distribution of Places by Gender (Niloya)

Places	Female Characters Number*	%	Male Characters Number*	%	Together (Female and Male) Number*	%	Total Number*	%
Kitchen	4	66.7	0	0	2	33.3	6	100
Other domestic spaces	4	80	0	0	1	20	5	100
Street	0	0	0	0	4	100	4	100
Garden	0	0	0	0	24	100	24	100
Zoo	0	0	0	0	0	0	0	0
Children's park	0	0	0	0	0	0	0	0
Other	0	0	0	0	2	100	2	100

* The number was calculated over the number of markings, not over the number of cartoons.

Table 18. Distribution of Places by Gender (Biz İkimiz)

Places	Female Characters Number*	%	Male Characters Number*	%	Together (Female and Male) Number*	%	Total Number*	%
Kitchen	5	41.7	0	0	7	58.3	12	100
Other domestic spaces	1	5.3	0	0	18	94.7	19	100
Street	0	0	0	0	2	100	2	100
Garden	0	0	0	0	25	100	25	100
Zoo	0	0	0	0	1	100	1	100
Children's park	0	0	0	0	3	100	3	100
Other	0	0	0	0	5	100	5	100

* The number was calculated over the number of markings, not over the number of cartoons.

Similarly, in Biz İkimiz, female characters were most commonly seen in the kitchen and other domestic spaces. While male characters were not seen alone, the most common places with female characters were garden, other domestic spaces and kitchen respectively. In places where people are present together, they are seen eating, having family conversations and playing with their children.

In both cartoons, the woman is associated with "home" as a place, while the man is associated with "outside the home." Men's relationship with home was presented as limited to eating and family conversations. The relationship of men and women with space is presented in an unequal way through gender roles. The woman is represented "at home" in relation to domestic reproduction which has no monetary equivalent, whereas the man is represented "outside" in relation to production for the market with monetary equivalent. No difference was found between rural and urban life in terms of associating the men and women to space.

In the episodes that were watched, female characters are more likely to give emotional responses than men. This situation is in line with the gender roles of men and women. The woman is encoded as an emotive person who lets her emotions show, whereas the man as a strong person who does not express his emotions (Table 19).

Niloya, the main character in the cartoon, is represented as a curious, fearless and sensitive girl. She has such individual characteristics as being fearless and brave, which are attributed to men. This has allowed for more equitable representations of girls. For example, in the episode "Zambak," Niloya, Murat and Mete go to the countryside to pick lily flowers for their grandmother. They also take a little goat with them. The little goat goes inside the bushes they see on the way and the sounds come from there. Mete thinks that there is a bear behind the bushes, and thus asks them to come back. Niloya tells Mete not to be scared and says to him that they

Gender Representations in Cartoons

Table 19. Situation of Giving Emotional Response by Gender (Niloya)

Emotional Response	Female Characters Number*	%	Male Characters Number*	%	Together (Female and Male) Number*	%	Total Number*	%
Laughing	3	21.4	0	0	11	78.6	14	100
Crying	1	50	1	50	0	0	2	100
Getting sad	6	60	2	20	2	20	10	100
Getting angry	1	33.3	1	33.3	1	33.3	3	100
Being scared	1	20	2	40	2	40	5	100
Other	0	0	0	0	0	0	0	0

* The number was calculated over the number of markings, not over the number of cartoons.

would be back after taking the goat, and goes inside the bushes. Mete and Murat hear Niloya laughing and go up to her. In many other episodes, Niloya was presented as having individual characteristics such as being fearless and courageous, which are attributed to men. This presentation was found important in terms of providing girls with more egalitarian representations.

In Biz İkimiz, the emotional response rates of women are closer to each other – compared to Niloya.

In both cartoons, both male and female characters are mainly seen laughing together. Nevertheless, there are no scenes were seen in which only male characters laugh. The situation of giving emotional responses was presented more prominently in rural life.

Table 20. Situation of giving emotional response by gender (Biz İkimiz)

Emotional Response	Female Characters Number*	%	Male Characters Number*	%	Together (Female and Male) Number*	%	Total Number*	%
Laughing	1	4.3	0	0	22	95.7	23	100
Crying	1	100	0	0	0	0	1	100
Getting sad	1	14.3	1	14.3	5	71.4	7	100
Getting angry	1	50	0	0	1	50	2	100
Being scared	2	66.7	1	33.3	0	0	3	100
Other	0	0	0	0	3	100	3	100

* The number was calculated over the number of markings, not over the number of cartoons.

Gender Representations in Cartoons

Table 21. Distribution of individual abilities by gender (Niloya)

Abilities	Female Characters Number*	%	Male Characters Number*	%	Together (Female and Male) Number*	%	Total Number*	%
Garden care (Growing and taking care of flowers, etc.)	2	100	0	0	00	0	2	100
Keeping and breeding an animal	2	66,7	1	33,3	0	0	3	100
Repairing	0	0	2	100	0	0	2	100
Playing an instrument	0	0	1	50	1	50	2	100
Dancing	1	100	0	0	0	0	1	100
Engagements regarding technology	0	0	0	0	0	0	0	0
Driving	0	0	2	100	0	0	2	100
Problem solving	1	100	0	0	0	0	1	100
Dealing with a sports branch	0	0	0	0	1	100	1	100
Other	0	0	0	0	0	0	0	0

* The number was calculated over the number of markings, not over the number of cartoons.

Another important indicator is the relation of individual abilities with sex. In Niloya; it was seen that the female characters are shown to be more skilled in growing flowers and keeping/breeding animals. Male characters were more skilled in repairing and driving. The individual abilities of women and men are presented in a manner limited to the sex roles.

In the cartoon Biz İkimiz, it is seen that there are differences in terms of female characters in the distribution of individual abilities by gender. The individual talents of the housewife in urban life are presented in similar categories as the male character. These prominent talents are attributed to men; dealing with technology and problem solving. However, male characters are presented more dominantly in these categories. In the episodes that were watched, driving was shown as a talent only peculiar to male characters (Table 22).

One of the characteristics attributed to men in traditional societies is to be a problem solver. This characteristic is frequently encountered in Biz İkimiz. For example, in the episode "Sonbahar," the twins look for a solution to protect the model house in the garden from the falling leaves. The solution they look for comes from their father, who says, "You need an old and reliable solution. We need a strong shield," and thus he brings a covering from the attic of the house. Children cover

Table 22. Distribution of individual abilities by gender (Biz İkimiz)

Abilities	Female Characters Number*	%	Male Characters Number*	%	Together (Female and Male) Number*	%	Total Number*	%
Garden care (Growing and taking care of flowers, etc.)	0	0	0	0	2	100	2	100
Keeping and breeding an animal	0	0	0	0	1	100	1	100
Repairing	0	0	3	100	0	0	3	100
Playing an instrument	0	0	0	0	0	0	0	0
Dancing	0	0	0	0	0	0	0	0
Dealing with technology	2	22.2	7	77.8	0	0	9	100
Driving	0	0	3	100	0	0	3	100
Problem solving	1	25	3	75	0	0	4	100
Dealing with a sports branch	0	0	0	0	0	0	0	0
Other	0	0	0	0	0	0	0	0

* The number was calculated over the number of markings, not over the number of cartoons.

their model house with this covering and protect it from the falling leaves. In the meantime, their mother goes up to them and says, "When the autumn comes, we need to protect our bodies the most. Wear your shield to protect yourself from diseases" and brings them the vests that she has woven for them. The mother has woven a blue vest for her son and a pink vest for her daughter. The father was presented as undertaking the role of a problem solver and the mother the role taking of care of her children. As a woman, the mother reproduced traditional gender stereotypes both through the role she has undertaken and in her choice of color for the vests she has woven for her children. However, gender roles are presented in a way that have been so internalized and naturalized that the possibility of questioning the unequal role distribution between women and men is prevented from the beginning.

In the episode "Uçak Oyunu," Ceren and Arda build an airplane from an old cardboard box. They want to be a pilot and fly, but they see that the airplane does not fly and try to figure out what is missing. At this point, they tell their fathers who was just back from work that their airplane does not fly. Their father says, "The power arms of the airplane are missing, that's why it does not fly," and thus lifts and flies the airplane. These examples regarding the representation of a "strong" father is common and such a father encompasses all sorts of solutions within the family in patriarchal societies, and such examples are seen in other episodes as well.

Table 23. Distribution of situation of suggesting an action-oriented idea by gender (Niloya)

Female Characters		Male Characters		Together (Female and Male)		Total	
Number*	%	Number*	%	Number*	%	Number*	%
10	83.3	2	16.7	0	0	12	100

* The number was calculated over the number of markings, not over the number of cartoons.

Table 24. Distribution of situation of suggesting an action-oriented idea by gender (Biz İkimiz)

Female Characters		Male Characters		Together (Female and Male)		Total	
Number*	%	Number*	%	Number*	%	Number	%
7	35	9	45	4	20	20	100

* The number was calculated over the number of markings, not over the number of cartoons.

Another important indicator of gender is to suggest ideas. Among the ideas suggested in Niloya are to sledge the flour from the mill to the bakery, to stage a play, to make flowers out of paper and place them in the countryside in order to accelerate the arrival of spring, to race to find out who will win, to play shadow plays as a way to make the elders listen to them and so on (Table 23). As mentioned before, Niloya is represented as a character with such characteristics as leadership, curiosity and courage, etc. Therefore most of the ideas are suggested by Niloya.

Among the ideas put forward in the cartoon Biz İkimiz are to obtain brown paint from the Turkish coffee, to make the ball fall from the tree by making wind, to make a gift by combining family photos into cubes, to explain the solar eclipse through animation, etc. (Table 24).

Although male and female characters suggest similar ideas, male characters appear to be more effective in this regard. Unlike Niloya, the fact that both male and female characters are shown together in developing ideas is important in terms of gender equality.

CONCLUSION

Gender refers to socially created roles and expectations for women and men. These roles and expectations differ from society to society and even within different sections of the same society, based on various elements. Despite these differences, the common point is the existence of gender-based inequalities in all societies (Ecevit, 2003,83). The female/male contradiction is repeatedly created and transferred from generation to generation on the basis of these inequalities. In this process, institutions such as family, school and media play an important role. According to Binark and Gencel Bek, media presents the values that exist in society as they are without questioning them. In this context, sexist and unequal social relations are reproduced and circulated (2010,157).

In the cartoons examined within the scope of the study; despite of the existence of an egalitarian representation, it was seen that the contents emphasizing inequality are more dominant. It was found out that there is no significant difference between rural and urban life in the presentation of gender roles of women and men.

In both cartoons, male and female characters were represented in a balanced way in terms of quantity. There is also equality in the representation of men and women as the main character in cartoon movies.

In the cartoons examined, the ideal man and woman are represented as married with children. It was seen that the women are represented only as married with children and as housewives in a homogeneous manner, but different situations and lives of femininity are not included in the contents. Women are presented solely as mothers and spouses. Single and childless women were not able to be represented. Similarly, unmarried and childless male representations were not observed. In both cartoons, men and women are presented in a uniform manner.

Domestic works are presented as the "womanly work" peculiar to female, whereas external works are presented as peculiar to male characters. In rural and urban life, the division of labor is presented in a similar manner with a traditional character. Research has shown that the domestic division of labor has a traditional character that remains unchanged today. (Vatandaş, 20011, 29-56).

The relationship of men and women with space is presented in an unequal way through gender roles. The role of femininity was built on "home," and thus gender-based inequalities existing between women and men were reproduced. The woman's place is the kitchen, and one of her primary duties is to cook. This function of the woman serves to bring the family together. As a result, the function of the woman in the family is presented as providing the unity and happiness of the family. On the other hand, male characters are usually shown while returning home from work. Although what they do is not clearly understood, the father's task is presented as to work for a job outside and to provide livelihood of the family. No difference was found between uses of space in terms of the rural or urban life.

The family has taken its place as the basic element in both cartoons. The families are presented as warm and friendly environments in which their children are taken care of. In a period such as childhood, which requires special attention and care, it gives a general idea of the type of family environment in which the child grows up, as well as the sort of individual the child will become in the future. In this period, family members play important roles in the lives of children as role models. Among these roles are gender-oriented ones. Both cartoons consist of grandmother and grandfather figures. This presentation places cartoons in an intergenerational context, and thus functions as using them as a means of transferring the common culture to future generations. One of the elements transferred is a certain family structure. In this family structure, while individuals are respectful and warmhearted to each other, loving, they are also presented in a manner limited by sexist roles.

Gender equality means enabling both boys and girls to have the same personality characteristics, undertake the same roles and professions and have the same position in the story. It is a more reliable way for their development to provide children with content that goes beyond gender discrimination. (Lemish, 2013,37).

While some representations of gender equality were observed in the content of cartoons, these representations are very limited in the whole story. As Lemish points out, "boys and girls should be portrayed as those who have the freedom to be as they are."

In this context, presenting Niloya with such characteristics as being brave and fearless, etc. and Ceren's choice of professions which are considered as male professions are crucial with regard to egalitarian ways of thinking and behavior on the basis of sex. The friendship between Niloya and Mete, their cooperation and the presentation of girls and boys as individuals who have a good time together are important in terms of building men-women relationships under equal terms. The men and women should be presented not as an extension of biological dichotomy, but merely as human beings within the framework of egalitarian gender roles.

In the production of discourses on gender equality, it is necessary to represent the woman with a humorous, strong, intelligent, independent and self-confident character, and the man with the roles through which he can exhibit his qualities of taking care of and growing.

While the media is an institution that reproduces and circulates sexist and unequal social relations, it has the potential to contribute to changing these patterns.

FUTURE RESEARCH AND DIRECTIONS

Since the children's ability to critically read, interrogate and consume media contents is not yet developed, it is considered that the future studies will make substantial contributions to the field by focusing especially on the production processes of contents prepared for children and the actors of this process.

REFERENCES

Becerikli Yıldırım, S. (2005). Çocuk Öykülerinde Toplumsal Cinsiyet Göstergeleri: Oya ile Kaya Örneği [Indicators of Gender in Children's Stories: Case of Oya and Kaya]. In *Uluslararası Çocuk ve İletişim Kongresi* (vol. 2). Istanbul, Turkey: İ. Ü. İletişim Fakültesi Yayınları.

Binark, M., & Gencel Bek, M. (2010). Eleştirel Medya Okuryazarlığı [Critical Media Literacy] (2nd ed.). Istanbul, Turkey: Kalkedon Yayınları.

Bora, A. (2011). Kadınların Sınıfı: Ücretli Ev Emeği ve Kadın Öznelliğinin İnşası [Women's Class: Paid Domestic Labor and Building Women's Subjectivity]. Istanbul, Turkey: İletişim Yayınları.

Butler, J. (2009). *Toplumsal Cinsiyet Düzenlemeleri. Cogito: Feminizm [Gender Regulations. Cogito: Feminism]*. Istanbul, Turkey: YKY.

Ecevit, Y. (2003). Toplumsal Cinsiyetle Yoksulluk İlişkisi Nasıl Kurulabilir? Bu İlişki Nasıl Çalışılabilir? [How to Establish a Relationship between Gender and Poverty? How to Work on Such a Relationship?]. *C.Ü. Tıp Fakültesi Dergisi, 25*(4), 83-88.

Geray, H. (2017). İletişim Alanından Örneklerle Toplumsal Araştırmalarda Nicel ve Nitel Yöntemlere Giriş [Introduction to Quantitative and Qualitative Methods in Social Researches with Examples from the Communication Field]. Ankara, Turkey: Ütopya Yayınevi.

Giddens, A. (2012). *Sociology* (6th ed.). Cambridge, UK: Polity Press.

Günaydın, B. (2011). *Çocuklara Yönelik Programlarda Toplumsal Cinsiyet Rollerinin Sunumu: TRT Çocuk ve Yumurcak TV* [Presentation of Gender Roles in Children's Programs]. Ankara, Turkey: Radyo ve Televizyon Üst Kurulu Uzmanlık Tezi.

Gürel, E., & Alem, J. (2010). Postmodern Bir Durum Komedisi Üzerine İçerik Analizi: Simpsonlar [Content Analysis on a Postmodern Sit-com: Simpsons]. *Uluslararası Sosyal Araştırmalar Dergisi, 3*(10), 332–347.

Horrocks, R. (1994). *Masculinity in Crisis. Myths, Fantasies and Realities* (J. Campling, Ed.). New York, NY: St. Martin's Press. doi:10.1057/9780230372801

Illıch, I. (1996). Gender, (Çev. Ahmet Fethi). Ankara, Turkey: Ayraç Yayınevi.

Kağıtçıbaşı, Ç., & Cemalcılar, Z. (2017). *Dünden Bugüne İnsan ve İnsanlar: Sosyal Psikolojiye Giriş [Person and Persons from Past to Today: Introduction to Social Psychology]*. Evrim Yayınevi.

Kalaycı, N. (2015). Toplumsal cinsiyet eşitliği açısından bir çizgi film çözümlemesi: PEPEE [An Analysis of a Cartoon in terms of Gender Inequality: PEPEE]. *Eğitim ve Bilim, 40*(177), 243–270.

Keloğlu-İşler, E. İ. (2014). Kültürel ekme kuramı bağlamında Türkiye üretimi çizgi filmler ve çocuk bilincinin inşası, İletişim ve Diploması Dergisi [Turkey-Made Cartoons and Creation of Children's Awareness in the context of Cultural Cultivation]. *Journal of Communication and Diplomacy, 15*(2), 65-78.

Lemish, D. (2013). I. Türkiye Çocuk ve Medya Kongresi Bildiriler Kitabı [Papers on the 1st Congress on Children and Media in Turkey]. *Cilt, 2*, 35-47.

Lloyd, G. (2015). Erkek Akıl Batı Felsefesinde 'Erkek' ve 'Kadın' [The Man of Reason: "Male" and "Female" in Western Philosophy] (2nd ed.). Istanbul, Turkey: Ayrıntı Yayınları.

Marshall, G. (2005). *Sosyoloji Sözlüğü [Dictionary of Sociology]*. Ankara, Turkey: Bilim ve Sanat.

Oakley, A. (1972). *Sex, Gender and Society*. New York, NY: Pantheon.

Onur, B. (2004). Gelişim Psikolojisi: Yetişkinlik, Yaşlılık, Ölüm [Developmental Psychology: Adulthood, Old Age, Death]. Ankara, Turkey: İmge Kitabevi.

Vatandaş, C. (2011). Toplumsal Cinsiyet ve Cinsiyet Rollerinin Algılanışı [Gender and Perceptions of Sex Roles]. *Istanbul Journal of Sociological Studies*, (35), 29-56. Retrieved from http://dergipark.gov.tr/iusoskon/issue/9517/118909

Yağan Güder, S., Ay, A., Saray, F., & Kılıç, İ. (2017). Okul Öncesi Dönem Çocuklarının İzledikleri Çizgi Filmlerin Toplumsal Cinsiyet Kalıp Yargıları Açısından İncelenmesi: Niloya Örneği [An Examination of Cartoons Watched by Preschool Children in terms of Gender Stereotypes: Case of Niloya]. *Eğitimde Nitel Araştırmalar Dergisi, 5*(2).

Yüksel, N. A. (1999). Toplumsal Cinsiyet Olgusu ve Türkiye'deki Toplumsal Cinsiyet Kalıplarının Televizyon Dizilerindeki Yansımaları [Concept of Gender and Reflections of Gender on TV Series in Turkey]. Kurgu Dergisi, 16, 67-81.

ADDITIONAL READING

Bermal, A. Karbay Edibe Betül ve Kurt Merve (2014). "Kuzey- Güney'in Doğu-Batı Ekseninde Çözümlenmesi: Dizideki Kadınlık Erkeklik Rolleri. Toplumsal Cinsiyet ve Medya içinde. Ed. Huriye Kuruoğlu ve Bermal Aydın. Ankara: Detay Yayıncılık.ss.155-202

Dökmen, Z. Y. (2017). Toplumsal Cinsiyet Toplumsal Psikolojik Açıklamalar. İstanbul: Remzi Kitabevi, 2. Baskı

Gündüz Kalan, Özlem (2010). Reklamda Çocuğun Toplumsal Cinsiyet Teorisi Bağlamında Konumlandırılışı: "Kinder" Reklam Filmleri Üzerine Bir İnceleme". İstanbul Üniversitesi, İletişim Fakültesi Dergisi, Cilt 1, Sayı 38,1. s.75-89.

Kaypakoğlu, S. (2004). Toplumsal Cinsiyet ve İletişim Medyada Cinsiyet Stereotipleri. İstanbul: Naos Yayınları, 1. Baskı

Özlem, S. M. (2018). Masallar ve Toplumsal Cinsiyet. İstanbul: Kor Kitap. 2. Baskı

KEY TERMS AND DEFINITIONS

Cartoon: A film technique that provides continuity of representation based on drawing and shooting each phase of a movement.

Gender: The concept of gender refers to the roles, learned behaviors and expectations that are determined by the society for women and men, apart from the biological differences of women and men.

Gender Equality: Refers to equality between men and women in the use of resources, opportunities and power in social institutions (family, labor, law, education, politics, religion, health, etc.).

Gender Inequality: Refers to inequality between men and women in the use of available resources, opportunities and power in social institutions.

Sex: Refers to the anatomical and physiological differences that define the male and female bodies.

Sex Roles: Expresses how women and men should behave and the different tasks they are expected to perform.

Sexual Discrimination: Unfair discrimination which is applied on the basis of gender.

Stereotypes: Pre-created impressions, which fill the information gaps with regard to a particular event or group and make it easier for us to make a decision on them.

Chapter 7
A Rebellion Against the Metallization of the Female Body:
"Dove Beyond Figures"

Rengim Sine Nazlı
https://orcid.org/0000-0001-9784-766X
Bolu Abant Izzet Baysal University, Turkey

ABSTRACT

Media is used as an important tool in the uniformization of the female body metallized on the axis of consumption culture. Ads are of special importance in order for these bodies, which are standardized by media bodies, to reach every segment of the society. The beauty measures of each period are introduced with these films as the main determinant for women to be happy. Moreover, these measures, which are a means of domination, can cause illnesses in which women sometimes lose their lives. In such an environment, Unilever's Dove, a personal care brand, launched a campaign called mark Beyond Figures. It continued to act with this approach in advertising films. In this study, it is aimed to determine how women analyze advertising films beyond the figures. The interviews that will be evaluated in the context of coding, criterion will be examined by reception analysis.

DOI: 10.4018/978-1-7998-0128-3.ch007

BACKGROUND

Especially due to the magical world of the television, the superstar of the period, the early audience surveys demonstrated that TV audiences were passive assets that surrendered unconditionally to the messages coming from the television. As a matter of fact, it is known that the radio, which was the star of the pre-television era, also had a magical power even though it only addressed the auditory world. It is an undeniable fact that mass media has always had a great influence on people in all periods of history. *The War of the Wor*lds, a novel which Orson Welles presented as a radio play on October 30, 1938, is one of the important events that show the power of mass media.

Welles presented the novel on his radio broadcast on CBS channel as if it were a newscast. The program began by the following presentation: "The Columbia Broadcasting System studio presents Orson Welles and the Mercury Theatre of the Air in War of the Worlds by H. G. Wells. Ladies and gentlemen, the director of the Mercury Theatre and the star of these broadcasts, Orson Welles:

"Ladies and gentlemen, following the news we've just given, the Meteorological Administration gave instructions to large observatories to closely observe the movements on the planet Mars". Meanwhile, the number of listeners had reached 6 million and all listeners started waiting for the news from Mars. The audience was told that a live connection was established with the principal observatory and the play continued as follows:[1]

"The outer cover definitely doesn't belong to our world. It's not a substance found on our planet. Wait a minute. Something is happening. This object doesn't look like anything that I have seen before. Someone's calling. I see something coming out of the black hole in the middle of the illuminated circle. It has gote yes. This could be a face. It is standing on legs. Actually, it is rising on a small type of metal piece. Now it has reached out to the top of the trees. It is unbelievable, but both scientific observations and what we are witnessing with our own eyes lead us to this inevitable hypothesis. These strange creatures that disembarked on the farm near New Jersey tonight are the army of occupation from the planet Mars."

Life was congested in most places during the play. There were thousands of people in the street slunatical yes caping. People were saying good bye to their loved ones on their phones, some were trying to take a few of their belongings and drive to the countryside. On the streets were hunters with hunting rifles looking for aliens and there were people in search of salvation in churches. As a result of all this, the New York City Police Department busted the radio building and asked the radio personnel who were unaware of what was going on outside to make an announcement. Although the announcements were made every 15 minutes, it took a long time for people to change their perception of reality (Derci, 2012).

Welles' program is one of the most important examples of how people are affected by massmedia. In this context, "audience" based studies have defined the audience –the target audience of messages produced in the mass media in the first period and later periods- in a passive manner. However, Hall's encoding/decoding model accepts the possibility that dominant/preferred, negotiated or oppositional readings exist. This model has been later transformed and turned into a model where most of the audience constantly transforms or rejects the dominant ideology in the media content (Morley, 2005: 99-100).

In such an environment, media producers have sought ways which allow viewers to receive messages directly and especially sought to make advertising codes attractive to decoders. The principal ideology of advertising, the visible face of the material output of media texts is to direct the buyers to consumption. In order for the continuation of the capitalist system, individuals must be in a position to continue consumption in every setting. In this context, everything about human beings becomes materials for consumption and the codes created by consumption shape individuals. The molds such as women, men, children, the elderly, the beautiful, the sporty, etc. create their own standards and the standardized individual of the global world is idealized while media products are used to ensure people adopt this ideal. In order to enable each and every person living in the world to take part in the consumption cycle, various universal criteria/determinations have been produced in time and especially advertisements are used to have everyone adopt these criteria.

In all the above-mentioned molds, the frameworks about how the "female" should be positioned are shaped according to various assumptions. The female, who is generally assessed in the context of "beauty" and whose criteria of beauty are defined the axis of consumption culture -the ideological extension of capitalism- acquires the assumptions through media texts about how a female should be. By utilizing the Perception Analysis method via in-depth interviews with two groups who have watched the Dove commercial *"Benimgüzelliğim #rakamlarınötesinde"* *"My beauty#beyond numbers"* on the mass media and social media, this study attempted to determine how the female, the apple of the eye for the consumption society is sought to be included in the system by the consumption industry itself.

CULTURE INDUSTRY AND COMMODIFICATION OF THE FEMALE BODY

The standardization of the female body, in other words, its commodification, especially the concrete and abstract effects of the consumption culture on the female body, have been the subject of many studies. This study addressed the commodification of the female body in the context of the culture industry and consumption culture.

It is known that many approaches to the female body have existed in the historical process. However, the meaning attributed to the female body has changed with the culture industry and consumption culture. Consumption culture is a culture where production of perception is preferred to the production of meaning. According to Baudrillard (2001: 75), in this culture, individuals invest in their physical appearances, not their personal qualities. In this context, it is possible to say that woman who exists in the consumption culture has become a commodity that invests in her body.

Cash (1990), however, says that individuals' physical bodies are related to cognitive constructs. According to Cash, subjectively created images help to understand bodies as objects. Thus, the body becomes an important object of thought. Beautiful body patterns are created by idealizing the bodies. The concept that defines images and body patterns in general is defined in the word "fashion". Fashion which is regarded as the law which instructs the patterns of beauty and the beautiful has been a phenomenon to which the majority has complied or tried to comply. Simmel (2006: 120) states that fashion adds an element of charm to women and their lives, both in their own eyes and in the eyes of others. In this context, it would not be wrong to argue that women participate in the rules created by the general public with the desire to be appreciated and admired.

According to Çabuklu (2004: 118-119), modernity and its sense of fashion have commodified the female body. Women have come under the supervision of the objectified male gaze with their bodies and garments, and female bodies have become supervised passive beings. Fashion has the distinction of being a social discipline based on attire which specifies the rules of social participation. Corsets, brassieres, skirts that make it difficult to walk are elements of pressure on the female body.

Coward (1993: 42) argues that there is a specific type of woman considered culturally ideal:

"This "perfect" female body must have a height of 168 to 177 centimetres, long legs, a bronze skin and a sinewy appearance. But most importantly, this body should not have one ounce of extra body weight. Since the sixties, an ideal female body culminated in the Twiggy image is depicted in the texts and images on fashion and beauty: a woman without any extra fat".

A Rebellion Against the Metallization of the Female Body

Fiske (1999: 22-23) states that the effects of commodities on female body can be varied:

"They range from basic necessities to unnecessary luxury items. Television programs can even expand non-material objects such as the appearance of a woman or the name of a star. All commodities can be used by consumers to create the meaning of the self, social identity and social relations".

In the light of these explanations, it is seen that by using the female bod, the consumption culture creates the need to consume more than the need, that is, consume the image. The perception is that there is an order in which the female body commodifies itself.

According to Adorno and Horkheimer (1996: 8-11) who state that the products generated by the culture industry are standardized, these products are collectively consumed and the mass media plays the most important role in this mass consumption. Undoubtedly, mass media also has a great influence on the commodification of the female body. Akdoğan (2004: 50) argues that the media imposes on women a special purpose as a commodity. According to Akdoğan, the media plays an important role in the effectiveness of cultural imperialism and the female body plays an important role in the effectiveness of media messages. Akdoğan who advocates in this context that broadcasts will watched by larger numbers when the female body is on the screen and goes on to say that using women as a commodity in the media as in all other areas is a product of the economic character of capitalism and the market relations.

Therefore, the female body has become an object of consumption that includes images. Nowadays, the female body has become a commodity that consumes or is consumed very prominently in commercials and the media. Taşkaya (2009: 103-104) stated that women are presented in advertisements as discursively, semiologically and hence ideologically sexist manner and states that again, in advertisements, the female body is positioned as an object to watch and enjoy.

Based on Baudrillard's (2004: 113-114) statement that *"If the woman is consuming herself, it is because her relationship with herself is symbolized and produced by indicators"*, it is possible to argue that the reason why the female body is commodified in the media and especially in women's magazines is related to the fact that women consume themselves. Again in the capitalist system, changing forms of production and division of labour have caused alienation from bodies for all individuals, especially of women. Baudrillard's (2004: 163) following assessment in regards to the effects of capitalism on the body is also important:

"The general status of private property in a capitalist society also applies to the body, social practice and the representation of this practice in the mind. In the traditional order, there is an instrumental / magical vision of the body reached through the process of labour and the relation with nature rather than exaltation of the body, thinking of itself as perfect, the siege of narcissism in the form of worshiping itself and indicative perception (Baudrillard, 2004: 163).

Storey (2000: 101) states that the content presented in the articles in women's magazines creates a successful, enjoyable and pleasant perception of womanhood: *"Follow these practical suggestions, try this product and become a better lover, better mother and a better woman"*.

The body is the social manifestation of the self. The body mentioned here is a social body, the embodiment of the society. In fact, the body is a tool that enables individuals to be visible in their societies. For this reason, the primary aim of the consumer culture and the culture industry, especially the sector that needs many images such as fashion, advertising and media organs, is to reset the deficiencies of personality and emotions with the help of the body. For this reason, consumption culture is frequently involved in body construction. Therefore, what is needed for consumption by the consumer society is the acceptance of a symbolically produced social body concept not only the biological body concept.

The cultural industry strives to standardize masses as if they are commercial commodities. A homogeneous culture of people, similar to each other, is created by imposing standard clothing patterns, hair styles and even body measurements. Therefore, not only the commercial goods produced in mass production in the factories but also the life styles and bodies of individuals are commodified. In other words, individuals' behaviours from eating and drinking habits to their patterns of attire are shaped by the standards imposed by the culture industry (cited in Kongar, Satar, 2015: 49).

Lash and Urry state that a culture is produced now in production facilities as well as products. It is sought that individuals acquire certain standard features by means of the molds created in these facilities (Chaney, 1999: 161). Standards brought to the body are perceived as "fitness indicators" (Miller, 2009: 105). Today, the molds imposed on the ideal body measurement are also perceived as fitness indicators of the people with these measurements. In an effort to give fitness signals to their communities, individuals tend to buy diet products, pay more money for aesthetics and gyms, thus creating a new consumer market. This situation undoubtedly leads to the reification of individuals and the commodification of the body while improving the income of the capitalist capital owners (Satar, 2015: 54).

Mass culture has caused individuals to lose their freedoms in regards to their bodies and facilitated their easy guidance in this regard. In mass society, desires and insights of individuals have become insignificant while the way they are perceived by others have become significant (Dolu, 1993: 60). Therefore, individuals lose their commands over their own bodies and adopt image-oriented lifestyles. Foucault states that capitalism wants to create a new field of "bio-power" in social life based on image and visuality. Accordingly, it is aimed to create "submissive bodies" tamed with the body standards produced by bio-power (Öztürk, 2012: 41).

Examination of the examples in regards to the representation of women in the media demonstrates that the woman has been transformed into an object, usually utilized in areas such as fashion, beauty and shopping and positioned to increase the attractiveness of products in product promotions. While women are included in the media as a visual object in areas related to men-women relationships, it is observed that women's representation in the political, economic and cultural areas is not common or they positioned as a completely independent object independent of the topic. Therefore, women are regarded as objects capable of movement within the boundaries determined by the male-dominated ideology. Women are given a place in the media usually as housewives, mothers or sexual objects and hence they are confined within specific boundaries and a public space dominated by men is sought to be created. In the written and visual media, the masses are presented with an "idealized female body" (Akmeşe, 2012: 541). Thus, a perception is created in women that women should have ideal body measurements, while body measurements are bound to certain criteria for men in the selection of spouses or partners.

Beauty criteria are redefined by ensuring that women characters with beautiful and ideal sizes are included in advertisements. Women's privacy is exploited especially in cosmetics, lingerie and apparel advertisements and the female body is transformed into a "ransom of capitalism" (Topcuoglu, 1995: 213). Consumption capitalism, therefore, suggests that consumers should consume with the lust of the advertised products and always want more by not feeling contented with what they already have (Yanıklar, 2006: 110). In advertising, the ideal female body is used both to direct female consumers, the target audience, to purchase these products and to ensure that the product in the advertisement is bought by male consumers by attracting their interest.

CULTURAL STUDIES AND RECEPTION ANALYSIS

From the moment when the mass media has entered our lives, it has been questioned where the viewers are positioned in regard to media and how these viewers are affected by these media which are institutionalized today as the media. The Centre for Contemporary Cultural Studies, founded in Birmingham and based on Marxist tradition, has shaped the "impact studies", based on the discussions usually within the critical paradigm of whether the audience interprets media messages, how the audience interprets these messages or the fact that the audience is subjected to direct messages. The fundamental point the Centre focuses on is defining the problem of ideology, language and subject with a dynamic and holistic approach by reconsidering the structuralist Marxist point of view in the light of linguistic developments. Opening the problem of reception up to discussion and questioning the reading styles of the different genres included in the communication tools within the encoding/decoding model (has been the area that made the Centre significant in this regard (İnal, 1996: 42-43).

Sardar (1999) summarizes the five characteristics of cultural studies that examine the meanings attributed to particular objects and activities by individuals and their forms of action during these activities (cited in: Çakar Mengü and Mengü: 2009: 344-345).

1. Cultural studies examine the cultural practices and their relationship with power. For example, a study of subcultures examines the social practices of the young and white working people in London in the context of their relationship with ruling classes.
2. Cultural studies aim to understand culture in the context of all complex forms, as well as to examine the social and political context in which culture manifests itself.
3. Cultural studies are both a field of study and a field of political action and criticism. For example, a study in this area could be expanded to be a political project.
4. Cultural studies seek to ensure that distribution of information is clear and consensual in order to eliminate the disparity between the cultural information accepted without any explicit or implicit application and the objective or universal forms of knowledge.
5. Cultural studies to evaluate modern society in ethical terms and to radically regulate the political action.

Although Saussure's perspective was followed in the first period of the Centre, Stuart Hall's "Encoding / Decoding" (1980) model paved the way for analysing the "text-reader" relations. By recognized the potential asymmetry between encoding and decoding processes, Hall exposed the struggles of meaning based on Volosinov's "multi-accentuality" concept (Wood, 2006: 75-76). Again "audience reception analysis", "reception studies" or "audience ethnography" have emerged and developed in cultural studies with great success from the 1980s until now (Livingstone, 1991).

A Rebellion Against the Metallization of the Female Body

Unlike the early impact studies that addressed the audience in a passive manner and accepted the assumption that audiences had the unconditional acceptance of all messages produced in the media, the reception analysis which gives viewers visibility and an active voice, has provided researchers with different arguments to identify the relationship between media texts and viewers (Livingstone, 1998). Mass media research has traditionally considered the communication process as a kind of circulation circuit or cycle. This model has been criticized for its linearity (sender / message / receiver) due to its concentration only at the level of message exchange and for its lack of various elements with complex relations. It should be accepted that as a whole, the consumption "encoding" and "decoding" elements (the discursive form of the message is subjected to communicative give and take) where meaning comes through with discursive practices are determined/specific elements even if they are relatively autonomous from the communicative process. In the words of Marx, circulation and reception are indeed elements of the construction process on television, and they are reintroduced into the construction process through roundabout feedback. Therefore, although it is not possible to say that the production of television messages and their reception are not same things, they are in fact related to each other (Hall, 2005: 85-87).

The basic paradigm in the conceptualization of the question of power in emerging cultural studies was the establishment of "sovereign ideology" in the texts and questioning the dominant position of the texts in the process of reception. The attitude that gives priority and a predictive character to the former in the relationship between the text and reader as a discourse has been fractured in cultural studies. The study by Hall et al. titled *"Policing the Crises"* questioned how the dominant ideology was constructed in the news texts. In his later writings, Hall mentioned the need to use the notion of "sovereign ideology" to elucidate the fundamental concerns of a critical approach (İnal, 1996: 91).

In the ensuing period, Morley's (1980, 1981) current affairs magazine, *Nationwide*, has revealed how audience readings or decoding studies were separated along political lines in their interpretations as a function of socio-economic or labour issues (Livingstone, 1991: 5). In this way, by following *The Nationwide Audience* study and the encoding-decoding model developed by Stuart Hall; David Morley tried to investigate the argument that the class position would determine the way in which the audience decoded the television programs (Smith, 2007: 234).

By making a fundamental distinction between encoders and decoders in the production of media texts, Hall (1973; 1980) states that the encoding of media texts depends on professional norms and procedures, institutional relations and technical equipment. The reception of the audience on this axis depends on cultural and political orientations, relations with broader frames of power and access to massively produced technology (Stevenson, 2008: 77). According to Hall (1999:

59-61), media texts have multi-purposes and can be read in three different ways. dominant/preferred, negotiated or oppositional readings, respectively. Dominant reading is the interpretation of the text according to prevailing ideology; that way the text is interpreted by the decoder as proposed by the sender. Negotiated reading includes a compromise between the coded message and the viewer's comment; some codes are rejected while some codes are accepted during the reception process. In oppositional reading, the viewer rejects all codes.

In negotiated reading, the person fractures the totality of the message and re-establishes it an alternative reference frame with the code he/she prefers. One of the most important political moments is the point where events that are normally interpreted and decoded in a negotiated manner are read critical. Here, sense making or meaning-meaning policy, i.e. the struggle within the discourse, begins (Hall, 2005: 97).

RESEARCH QUESTION

The Dove commercial, which is an uprising against the standardization of especially women on the basis of body-based discourses developed on the axis of consumption culture, has been circulated in the media and social media with the slogan *"Mybeauty# beyondnumbers"*. This one-minute commercial was broadcasted with the following slogans: *"we oppose the pressure of numbers on women. Let's break the rules of beauty with Dove! # beyondnumbers"*. The commercial film, broadcasted by adopting a discourse in the form of "rebellion" in a medium where consumer culture alienates individuals to everything such as labour and the body by commodifying all human areas including the body, encodes that women should rebel against the oppression disguised in numbers. By encoding the media texts presented in the form of dialogues in the commercial, this study analysed how the two groups of women and men interviewed by the in-depth interview technique received by encoded media texts in the commercial.

METHOD

The present study utilized the Perception Analysis method, explained in detail in the literature section, to analyse the codes generated by the consumption ideology in regards to women. In-depth interviews were conducted at different times in order to determine how these codes would be analysed by two separate groups of women and men. It is encoded in the texts of the commercial that the determinations about women are shaped around numbers but the numbers imposed by the system to be happy, successful or beautiful are insignificant. Again in the commercial, the actual insignificance of the numbers assessed in the framework of a universal definition such as size, height, weight and generalizations are emphasized by the following words:

- *34: the number of my tattoos, not my size*
- *90, 60, 90: not my measurements, my visas*
- *9: not the kilos I have lost, the months I spent with my daughter*
- *9,: not my score of 10, but my favourite rhythm*
- *92: not my "likes "but my friends who are with me on my happiest day*
- *26: not my age, the age I feel*
- *170: not my height, the songs in my repertory*
- *35:, it's not where my beauty comes from, it is the number of cities I have visited.*

The questions that were formed within the framework of these dialogues were first asked to the male group consisting of 9 university students. The questions were prepared from general to specific. The male participants were coded as M1, M2, M3, M 4, M5,… M9. Also, the group of 10 women was coded as F1, F 2, F 3, F 4,…., F 10.

FINDINGS AND INTERPRETATION

Interview Results from the First Group

The groups of men and women, the participants of this study, watched the one-minute Dove commercial separately and then the interview questions were asked. Initially, a general question was asked to the male participants, who were the first group that was interviewed: *"Do you believe that numbers are important in the perception of beauty?"*. The answers to this question are listed below. Five of the male participants stated that the numbers did not have any significance while four participants said that the numbers were important. In particular, M9 responded that numbers were important in terms of body weight from the male point of view and *(excess weight)* was not preferable. When the answers were checked, it was determined that the commercial broadcasted with the message that "numbers are not important" was decoded in the dominant reading approach by 5 participants while 4 participants preferred oppositional reading.

M1: Numbers don't matter; I think this way in my own life as well.
M2: I think the numbers don't matter.

M3: Numbers are important; we cannot escape from the reality. I think that numbers are important and inevitable.

M4: I don't think numbers are important. Information, knowledge and character-related situations can make women or men more attractive.

M5: I think numbers are important. Numbers are important to achieve something perfect.

M6: In my opinion, everyone can have any measurement or weigh as much as they like, as a matter of fact, people are created differently. Certain body measurements are being imposed on to put people in a mold.

M7: Number are not important; only certain groups want them to be important. Molds are imposed, but what is really important are the ideas of people.

M8: Numbers are important in terms of aesthetics.

M9: I think numbers are absolutely important. I cannot be with a lady who weighs 120 kilos, so I think numbers are important from a male perspective.

Immediately following these responses, the participants were asked another question: *"Do you think that women are pressured under various judgements and expectations to fit into expected molds?"*. All participants stated that they thought women were under pressure. However, M3 and M4 thought that men were under pressure as well as women:

M3: I think women are under pressure but men are under pressure too. Just like there is an ideal woman in our minds, likewise women have an ideal man in their minds and they are looking for him. Men are under pressure as a result of the efforts to become the ideal man.

M4: Men also under pressure in terms of beauty, muscular male profile is on the spotlight.

The participants were then asked *"Is the thing that is natural also beautiful"?* Seven of the participants stated that the natural was not beautiful, one participant mentioned it may change (according to what is discussed) while the other participant stated that the natural was rarely beautiful. In this context, generally, the men interviewed in the study believed that beauty was shaped by various factors. The response of M9 can be given here as an example: *"It is natural, it has a single eyebrow and it is not beautiful, so, the answer is no"*.

The participants who acknowledge the importance of numbers in the perception of beauty in general was asked the following question: *"Do you think that the importance of numbers can change?"*. This question was utilized to determine how the participants received the codes in the commercial stating that numbers were actually insignificant and women may defuse and neutralize the numbers by not paying any attention to them. Based on the main message in the commercial, i.e. the insignificance of numbers and the participants' responses, it can be argued that M2, M4, M5 and M8 were involved in oppositional reading while M1, M3, M6, M7 and M9 were involved in negotiated reading. In this context, it was observed that none of the participants preferred the dominant reading style.

M1: These taboos will break down if someone paves the way.
M2: I believe this perception cannot be changed. It is adopted in society and everyone has accepted it.
M3: This perception is a matter of mind-set. It can be changed; I believe that anything is possible.
M4: I think that perception cannot be ameliorated.
M5: I think it can't be changed. In order for the system to continue, it is necessary to put people into a certain mold. If people go out of these patterns, the system cannot continue.
M6: I'm undecided.
M7: It changes if the system changes.
M8: It will not change.
M9: I think it will not change, but I'm always seeing overweight women's fashion shows while I'm surfing on Instagram, maybe this can be a turning point.

Afterwards, the participants were asked the following question: *"Does the commercial you have watched represent a sincere belief or is it a marketing strategy"*? All the participants preferred oppositional reading at this point and read that the messages produced by Dove in the commercial were a marketing strategy. Immediately after this question, they were asked *"whether they believed in the sincerity of the brands that support women's movements?"*. Again, all male participants expressed their opinion that they did not believe the viewpoint advocated in the commercial and that this was a marketing strategy.

Interview Results for the Second Group

The second group in the study was asked the following question: *"Do you believe that women are pressured under various judgements and expectations to fit into expected molds?"*. All 10 participants in the interview expressed their belief that women were pressured by various molds. In addition to this question, the women participants were asked another question: *"Do you believe that men are pressured under various judgements and expectations to fit into expected molds?"*. Nine of the participants agreed that men were under pressure as well. After receiving a common answer to these questions that showed that women and men felt similar pressures, the participants were asked *"whether women or men were under more pressure?"*. Oneparticipant stated that there was more pressure on woman, while another participant said there was no pressure on men. The remaining 8 participants stated that both gender were under similar pressures.

The following question was asked to determine women's beliefs on beauty: *"Is the thing that is natural also beautiful?"* It was determined that 9 of the women participants found being natural to be beautiful. In this context, it is possible to argue that the codes in the commercial were basically suitable for dominant reading. Noting that the natural is not always beautiful, F5 replied: *"The natural is not always beautiful in a person. For example, nose jobs are a gift from God for some people, I mean, no one here can hide this; is that wrong? I believe there is such a thing"*.

Afterwards, the female participants were directed the same question that was directed to men: *"Do you think that the importance of numbers can change?"*. Five of the participants answered that the importance of numbers would not change by making oppositional reading. Via dominant reading, the remaining 5 participants responded by saying that the importance of the figures would be ignored in time and decoded the messages given in commercial accurately.

F1: I don't think the importance of numbers will change in my own opinion. I think not because, for example, 90 60 90 is a modelling concept now. But after Kim Kardashian, women with slim waists and large hips have emerged. These numbers may change somehow, but the molds will not change.

F2: I also don't think it can change, in fact, I don't think it will be over either. It may change too of course, 90-60-90 may be perhaps 100-80-100. But the numbers will continue to be important in any case.

F3: I believe it can be overcome. I mean, there is already a women's struggle in society now. But more time is necessary.

F4: So I also think it is possible to change with time. Because the more women try to make their voices heard, the more support they receive from each other and it continues to grow.

F5: I say it will not change. Because these numbers, whether they increase or change as you say, I would not know. At a time even the measurements for Barbie dolls were gradually expanded. But no one could take the numbers away. I mean, I don't think it's going to change, because changing it will be like the rain on somebody's parade. Those who impose this are already creating a market from this issue. So I also don't believe it will change.

F6: I say not.

F7: For example, in modelling; people who are outside certain measurements in terms of body size can also take part in modelling. Hence it can change.

F8: How numbers are perceived is changing gradually. Now, women's boyfriends are moving away from the thought that "I can't love you because of your weight" to the thought that "I can embrace you more because the places on your body that I have to love are also increasing". These expressions show us that the perception is changing.

F9: I think that will not change but it will rise or fall within the same numbers. But the numbers will always be important.

F10: Difficult, but of course it may.

Following this, as in the previous interview, the participants were asked *"whether the commercial they have watched represented a sincere belief or was it a marketing strategy"?* While 8 of the participants interpreted the commercial as a marketing strategy, one of them stated that although it was marketing in the commercial, it had sincerity. Another participant found the commercial completely sincere:

F2: Dove had slogans like "your most beautiful attire is your skin". For instance, compared to them, this commercial feels really sincere. Because there is a criticism in it. Such as "why do you put us into certain stereotypes?"... I thought the commercial supported this discourse. I think it's sincerest than the others. Of course marketing value is higher but it is a little more sincere.

F1: I don't think there is marketing in the commercial. Because from the beginning to the end of the commercial, there is no product promotion such as a woman's wavy hair or, how can I say it, it is not a commercial for hair emphasizing that the hair smells very good just someone is passing by... I mean, it doesn't start like a commercial for hair, and as a matter of fact, I guess there was a bank commercial before just like that, so you can't understand at first in the beginning that it is a commercial. Since it was not imposed later in the commercial that Dove shampoo will help your hair better this way or that way, I believe it is not fully a marketing strategy.

The female participants were asked *"whether they found the companies that support the women's movement sincere"*. In line with the previous question, 9 participants stated that they did not find these companies sincere, while E2 also responded with a similar answer that the companies had positive aspects for women's movements: *"Of course the aim is marketing, but there is also sincerity since it aims to support a specific target group"*.

FUTURE RESEARCH DIRECTIONS

Working with samples from different age groups and including a third and mixed group composed of male and female participants in the study may direct the researchers, who will do research following this line of study, to different findings.

CONCLUSION

This study, which conducted a reception analysis of the Dove commercial, broadcasted as a rebellion against the standardisation of women who bourgeon in the consumption culture, aimed to determine the participants' views about beauty and how they read the code in the commercial that beauty was not related to numbers.

As a result of in-depth interviews conducted with two separate groups of women and men, it was observed that 4 of the male participants had an oppositional reading of the commercial by accepting that the importance given to numbers would not change in terms of beauty. The other 5 male participants had negotiated reading. No negotiated reading was found in women. While half of the women interviewed in the study had oppositional reading, the other half had dominant reading. In this context, it was observed that while almost half of the interviewed men had no perception that the numbers would change, the remaining participants voiced the possibility that the importance of the numbers could change.

On the other hand, while only 2 of the male participants thought that men were under pressure, it is noteworthy that the answers of 9 of the women in the study expressed that men were under pressure as much as women. It was observed that women defined this pressure by citing physical structures such as the body and muscles, especially in the axis of visual elements. In this context, the fact that men did not feel under pressure while women described them as pressured shows that the discourses on the standardization of the male body were not taken into consideration by the male participants in the study.

Both groups interviewed in the study were asked "whether the natural thing was also beautiful". While 9 of the women interviewed in the present study found the natural to be beautiful, 7 of the males stated that the natural was not beautiful. In this context, an extensive difference was found in the perceptions of men and women on beauty. It is clear that women's job is quite hard in social life where both genders form their own existence with the perceptions of the opposite sex. As stated in the literature section of the study, the female body, which is the dearie of modernity, has become a passivized commodity under the supervision of the male gaze.

Some of the women who have been under such types of pressure demonstrated a tendency to dominantly read the messages given in the commercial and provided answers that stated that the body needs to be beautiful and should be liked without having to go through various filters. Furthermore, the idea that men who are given the right to rank women's beauty have strict beliefs about beauty was supported by the finding that the male participants tended to have oppositional reading for the messages given in the commercial. In today's society where there are several women organizations, the belief that women are more hopeful for the future was supported by the female participants in the study with their dominant reading of the codes in the commercial they watched.

REFERENCES

Adorno, W. T., & Horkheimer, M. (1996). Kültür Sanayii, Kitlelerin Aldatılması Olarak Aydınlanma. In Aydınlanmanın diyalektiği. Felsefi fragmanlar II (pp. 7-62). İstanbul, Turkey: Kabalcı Yayınevi.

Akdoğan, H. (2004). *Medyada Kadın*. İstanbul, Turkey: Ceylan Yayınları.

Akmeşe, Z. (2012). *Popüler Dergilerde Kadın İmgesinin Nesneleştirilerek Dönüşümü*. Dokuz Eylül Üniversitesi Uluslararası Kadın Konferansı Bildiriler Kitabı.

Baudrillard, J. (2001). *Baştan Çıkarma Üzerine*. İstanbul, Turkey: Ayrıntı.

Baudrillard, J. (2004). *Tüketim Toplumu*. İstanbul, Turkey: Ayrıntı Yayınları.

Çabuklu, Y. (2004). *Toplumsalın Sınırında Beden*. İstanbul, Turkey: Kanat Yayınları.

Çakar Mengü, S., & Mengü, M. (2009). Birmingham Okulu. Metin Çözümlemeleri, 343-363.

Cash, T. F. (1990). The Psychology of Physical Appearance: Aesthetics, Attributes and Images. In T. F. Cash, & T. Pruzinsky (Eds.), Body Images. New York, NY: Guilford.

Chaney, D. (1999). *Yaşam Tarzları*. Ankara, Turkey: Dost Kitabevi.

Coward, R. (1993). *Kadınlık Arzuları-Günümüzde Kadın Cinselliği*. İstanbul, Turkey: Ayrıntı Yayınları.

Dolu, Ş. (1993). *Medya ve Tüketim Çılgınlığı*. İstanbul, Turkey: Düşünen Adam Yayınları.

Fiske, J. (1999). *Popüler Kültürü Anlamak*. Ankara, Turkey: Ark Yayınları.

Hall, S. (2005). *Kodlama, Kodaçımlama*. Ankara, Turkey: Medya ve İzleyici Bitmeyen Tartışma, Vadi Yayınları.

İnal, M. A. (1996). *Haberi Okumak*. İstanbul, Turkey: Temuçin Yayınları.

Livingstone, S. (1991). Audience Reception: The Role Of The Viewer in Retelling Romantic Drama. In J. Curran, & M. Gurevitch (Eds.), Mass Media and Society. London, UK: LSE Research Online.

Livingstone, S. (1998). Relationships between media and audiences: Prospects for future audience reception studies. In T. Liebes, & J. Curran (Eds.), *Media, Ritual and Identity: Essays in Honor of Elihu Katz*. London, UK: Routledge.

Miller, G. (2009). *Tüketimin Evrimi*. İstanbul, Turkey: Alfa Yayınları.

Morley, D. (2005). *Sarkaçlar ve Tuzaklar*. Ankara, Turkey: Vadi.

Öztürk, A. (2012). Eril Bedenselleşme: Hegemonik Erkek Bedenin İnşası. *Felsefe ve Sosyal Bilimler Dergisi, 13*, 39–53.

Satar, B. (2015). *Popüler Kültür ve Tekrarlanan İmajlar*. İstanbul, Turkey: Kozmos Yayınları.

Smith, P. (2007). *Kültürel Kuram, Selime Güzelsarı*. Ankara, Turkey: Ütopya Yayınları.

Storey, J. (2000). *Popüler Kültür Çalışmaları-Kuramlar ve Metotlar*. İstanbul, Turkey: Babil Yayınları.

Taşkaya, M. (2009). *Beden Politikaları ve Reklamda Kadın, 2*. İstanbul, Turkey: Uluslararası Suç ve Ceza Film Festivali.

Topçuoğlu, N. M. (1995). *Basında Reklam ve Tüketim Olgusu*. Konya: Vadi Yayınları.

Wood, H. (2006). The mediated conversational floor: an interactive approach to audience reception analysis. Media, Culture & Society, 29(1), 75–103. doi:10.1177/0163443706072000

ADDITIONAL READING

Köse, H. (2010). *Medya ve Tüketim Sosyolojisi*. Ayraç Yayınları.

Lindlof, T. R. (1991). The Qualitative Study of Media Audiences. *Journal of Broadcasting & Electronic Media, 35*(1), 23–42. doi:10.1080/08838159109364100

Şeker, T. (2009). 5 N 1 K Haber Programının Alımlama Analizi. *Selçuk İletişim Dergisi, 5*(4), 105–117.

Simmel, G. (2006). *Modern Kültürde Çatışma*. İstanbul: İletişim Yayınları.

Wicks, R. H., & Drew, D. G. (1991). Learning from news: Effects of Message Consistency and Medium on Lecall and Inference Making. *The Journalism Quarterly*, 68(1/2), 155–164. doi:10.1177/107769909106800116

Yanıklar, C. (2006). *Tüketimin Sosyolojisi*. İstanbul: Birey Yayınları.

KEY TERMS AND DEFINITION

Commodity: Commodity is the beginning of Karl Marx's comprehensive study of the Capital. Commodity is clearly mentioned here as "the most basic cell of society."

Consumption Culture: It refers to a culture where consumers desire, pursue and strive to obtain goods and services for non-utilitarian purposes such as seeking status, seeking a to create a difference between them and the others and seeking innovation.

Culture: Culture is the set of moral and material values that makes a society different from other societies, that continues from the past by changes, that ensures order in the society which it has provides an identity and a sense of solidarity and unity.

Culture Industry: The claim that culture itself is an industry and that culture products have become commodities is the source of the concept of culture industry.

Mass Culture: Mass culture emerged in the years following the industrial revolution. The concept of mass culture defines all the power, behaviors, mythos, and phenomena which are difficult to resist and which are produced by industrial techniques and spread to a very large masses. Mass culture products are standard cultural products produced and transmitted by mass media only for the mass market.

ENDNOTE

[1] http://bugraderci.blogspot.com/2012/11/radyonun-gucu-orson-wellesin-sunumuyla.html, Date of Access: 10.04.2019

Chapter 8
Gender Representation in SMS Jokes

Yasmeen Sultana
Sindh Madressatul Islam University, Pakistan

Naima Saeed
University of Karachi, Pakistan

Tansif Ur Rehman
University of Karachi, Pakistan

ABSTRACT

This research aims to investigate how language is used in a new mode of communication such as SMS jokes portraying different roles of human gender. A distinct form of ideology is constructed in SMS jokes by using certain expressions which criticize the roles of both the genders in a humorous way which helps in reinforcing the already existing stereotypes about them. The study adopted the qualitative research method and purposive sampling technique was used for the selection of SMS jokes. Through this sampling technique, 30 different gender-biased SMS jokes were selected which were received on the cell phone numbers of researchers. It is believed that only the female gender becomes the target of ridiculous humor, but this study proves that the attitudes associated with both male and female are humiliating. The findings of research reveal that jokes play a pivotal role in constructing the overall image of both the genders. The language which is used in portrayal of both male and female gender is highly subjective, derogatory, abusive, and prejudiced.

DOI: 10.4018/978-1-7998-0128-3.ch008

INTRODUCTION

The study highlights some of the unique features related to SMS jokes which have not been identified yet. Since there is no such study available related to this specific topic of gender representation in jokes. That is the reason, many people are unaware of it and they take it for granted. People unconsciously forward these gender biased SMS jokes through their cell phones regardless of their implications on each gender and the roles assigned to them by society.

Although, it is a small-scale research, it accumulates sufficient data according to which the respective findings can be generalized and lead towards a result related to the representation of both the genders in SMS jokes as well as the language used to portray their individual roles. It also highlights the increasing use of new media, i.e. cell phone, which is meant for communication significantly, but also has been used for diverse purposes in contemporary era.

BACKGROUND

Though this aspect of jokes has not been yet fully explored, there are not enough researches available specifically on it in the Pakistani context. People daily encounter with different kinds of SMS jokes in which whatever is said is taken as granted or considered as humor. Jokes are very common and have become an integral part of routine life in Pakistan.

The respective researchers have tried to explore this unexplored genre with the help of some existing benchmark studies on the field. Therefore, it has been a challenging task to conduct such research and to provide guidance and awareness to the people about this medium of discourse.

RATIONALE AND SIGNIFICANCE OF THE RESEARCH

This research provides awareness to people in order to judge and see things critically with different and broad perspectives under the umbrella of language, gender, and the role of media. They are able to think about the already existing beliefs and stereotypes against both males and females and start questioning to check whether they are true or just making a false claim. It also helps them to assess things more objectively.

Therefore, in this way, they can evaluate the implied meanings of these kinds of gender biased SMS jokes by paying extra attention to the words used for humiliating both the genders which they have previously ignored.

RESEARCH QUESTIONS

1. How is gender portrayed in SMS jokes?
2. Which specific roles of gender (both males and females) are mostly the target of humor or criticism through jokes?
3. To what extent jokes play a significant role in shaping the already existing beliefs, i.e. stereotypes regarding both the genders?

LITERATURE REVIEW

Language is an effective tool for communication. Humans need language to express ideas, feelings, and emotions. Language plays a vital role in human society as is serves as the predominant means of communication. "Every cultural pattern and every single act of social behavior involves communication either in an explicit or implicit sense" (Sapir, 1921). It is only through language that effective communication takes place. By altering the word sequence in a respective sentence, an individual can surely modify its meaning and can divert it to another dimension as well, i.e. by even making it meaningless.

Similarly, jokes are smart and skillful use of language in which the speaker deliberately uses words in a way which creates humor. This makes it different from the other genres of discourse. According to Oxford Advanced Learner's Dictionary, a joke is something that an individual says for causing laughter as well as amusement, usually a short story with a funny punch line.

Lakoff (1975) as well as Tannen (1990) are few of the pioneers regarding language and gender research. In their view, the positions of the two genders are unchangeable as well as fixed. According to their perspective, women can only comply with the imposed roles.

Judith Butler's (1990) work proved to be a radical change in the field of gender studies. From philosophy of language, she used John Langshaw Austin's term 'performativity' and argued against the traditional feminists. She opined that gender should not be understood as either 'being' or 'having', but should be understood as 'doing'.

Throughout history, the notion of gender has been constructed and reconstructed with regards to class, sexuality, religion, race, ethnicity, politics, culture, etc. Now, it is almost impossible to separate which has been produced as well as maintained.

In contemporary era, sociocultural as well as politico-economical transition has to an extent facilitated performing gender roles in new and inconceivable modes. Still, the dilemma lies in the very fact that stereotypes encompassing gender influence human's delicate minds.

Even though the traditional stereotypes are not only found as significantly thriving, but in addition, encouraged by specific groupings (Tang and Hall, 1995). Recent work towards the analysis of linguistic stereotypes has revealed that a style could possibly be considerably less associated with a gender of the speaker and a lot more with an occupation (Cameron, 2000).

Generally, the mass media continuously exhibit the two genders in stereotyped ways, in which it impedes the respective expectations of pertinent prospects. Usually, males are depicted as being energetic, ambitious, strong, sexually dominant, as well as predominantly detached with regards to associations. In keeping view of the social perceptions of gender, the depiction of females are usually in the form of sex objects, who happen to be youthful, slim, gorgeous, submissive, highly dependent as well as often amateurish and even idiotic (Wildgen and Heusden, 2009).

Feminine characters spend most of their energies to enhance their physical appearance as well as looking after their family members. Due to the fact that mass media pervade individuals' lives, the modes misrepresent the respective genders may perhaps disrupt the contour of precisely how humans understand themselves as well as the things they apprehend as being a standard and acceptable for women and men in any society.

STEREOTYPICAL PORTRAYALS OF MALES IN MEDIA

Doyle (1989) is of the view that, children's television generally exhibits adult males as being hostile, eminent, as well as involved in thrilling pursuits from which they get incentives from other individuals for their 'masculine' achievements.

According to McCauley, Thangavelu, and Rozin (1988), numerous males on prime-time television are shown as self-reliant, hostile, as well as in charge. Television programming for most ages disproportionately shows males as being sincere, positive, proficient, potent, as well as in high-status jobs.

Boyer (1986) is of the view that, gentleness in males that has been apparent in the 1970s has ebbed, as developed male figures are redrawn to be a little more resilient as well as distanced from other individuals.

Highly grossing films like, John Wick, Logan, Thor, Spider man, Dunkirk, etc., exhibits the stereotype of extreme masculinity. Mass media, subsequently fortify the previous social ideals of masculinity. Males are shown in the form of tough, sexually aggressive, self-reliant, unafraid, hostile, completely in charge of all their feelings, and absolutely in no way 'feminine'.

Males are seldom depicted as performing their household chores (Brown & Campbell, 1986). Men and boys are rarely presented looking after each other. Males are also represented as being incompetent and uninterested regarding household work, i.e. cooking, homemaking, and child care (Doyle, 1989).

Media often exhibits male characters as incompetent imbecile, who are usually clumsy when it comes to taking care of children or doing some kitchen work. In children's books when someone is shown taking care of a child, it is usually the mother. This promotes a negative stereotype of males as either being devolved and uncaring family member.

STEREOTYPICAL PORTRAYAL OF FEMALES IN MEDIA

Cultural stereotypes are often observed when it comes to the media images of girls as well as women as they are underrepresented. Women are shown to be thin, young, passive, and dependent on men (Davis, 1990). Females in news shows are expected to be younger, attractive, as well as they talk less than their male counterparts (Craft, 1988; Sanders and Rock, 1988).

Mattel introduced a talking Barbie in 1992. It used to say, "Math class is tough", i.e. reinforcement of the stereotype that females are very inconvenient when it comes to Mathematics. According to Feldman and Brown (1984); Woodman (1991), even in children's programs, females are depicted to watch the males do different things. Music Television (MTV), an American satellite and cable television channel, mostly focused on females satisfying the male's fantasies regarding sex (Pareles, 1990 and Texier, 1990). The cultural image of women depicted in the media is often as peripherals, sexual objects, and dependent.

Usually, media portrays women as either totally good or bad. The characteristics of a good woman are, caring, engaged in domestic chores, and being pretty. Their roles are of victims, loyal, assistants, and martyrs. It is quite rare that females departing from traditional roles are shown as positive figures. Even this is done by making their career lives of low significance.

The bad image of women is in the form of witch, sex symbol, and an evil planner; often represented as cold, aggressive as well as mean. But, according to Wood (1984), the future role of women portrayed in the media will be less biased and stereotypes will also have a smaller role. But, still after 34 years women role is more or less the same as it existed during the last three to for decades.

NATURE OF THE STUDY

Since, the respective research was exploratory in nature, it comes under the qualitative research paradigm. The research questions do not demand for causal inference. So, the aim was to collect data and analyze it critically.

SAMPLING PLAN AND DATA COLLECTION

Purposive sampling technique was used for the selection of SMS jokes. Because, it focuses on a specific characteristic and feature. It helps in gathering the relevant information as well as avoids wasting time taking samples that have nothing to do with the research topic.

Therefore, through this technique, 30 gender biased SMS jokes were selected that were received on the cell phones of three respective researchers, i.e. 10 messages from each researcher's cell phone were selected. Although, it is a small-scale research, it accumulates sufficient data in order to judge the use of language and the portrayal of both the genders in these SMS jokes. The respective content reveals how language plays its role in order to reinforce the already existing stereotypes against the roles assigned to both males as well as females in a humorous and in an indirect way and how they are further exploited for this purpose.

DATA

1. Caution! If your wife uses two Sims, save her both numbers under one name "Wife". Never save them as "Wife 1" and "Wife 2" (Message from a hospitalized husband).
2. Maths and women are the two most complicated things in this world, but Maths at least has logic!
3. The wedding speech of a girl to her in-laws: "My dear new family, I thank you for welcoming me in this new house. Firstly, I must tell you that my presence here shouldn't change your daily life routines. Those who used to wash clothes, keep on doing it. Those who cook must keep cooking. Those who clean must keep cleaning. I'll not disturb anybody's routine. So far as I'm concerned, I'm here only to eat bun, have fun and control your son, any questions?"
4. A wife does better investigation and research than FBI or CIA.
5. **Wife:** How would you describe me?
   Husband: ABCDEFGHIJK.
   Wife: What does that mean?

Husband: Adorable, Beautiful, Cute, Delightful, Elegant, Fashionable, Gorgeous, and Hot.
Wife: Aw, thank you, but what about IJK?
Husband: I'm Just Kidding!

6. Have you ever noticed that a woman's "I'll be ready in 5 minutes" and a man's "I'll be home in 5 minutes" are exactly the same?
7. **Friend:** Aren't you wearing your wedding ring on the wrong finger?
   Poor Husband: Yes, I am, I married a wrong woman.
8. Joke about the first three years of marriage. In the first year, the husband speaks and the wife listens. In the second year, the wife speaks and the husband listens. And in the third year, they both speak and the neighbors listen.
9. What are the three quickest ways of spreading a rumor? Telegram, telephone, tell a woman.
10. A man is 32 years old and he is still single. One day a friend asked, "Why aren't you married? Can't you find a woman who will be a good wife?" He replied, "Actually, I've found many women I wanted to marry, but when I bring them home to meet my parents, my mother doesn't like them." His friend thinks for a moment and says, "I've got the perfect solution, just find a girl who's just like your mother." A few months later, they meet again and his friend asks, "Did you find the perfect girl? Did your mother like her?" With a frown face, he answers, "Yes, I found the perfect girl. She was just like my mother. You were right; my mother liked her very much." Then his friend says, "Then what's the problem?" He replied, "My father doesn't like her."
11. *Kisi ne ek shaadi shuda aadmi se pucha: "Aap shaadi se pehle kia karte the?" aadmi ki aankho me aanso aagaye aur bola: "Jo mera dil karta tha".*
12. Somebody asks a married person, "What do you do before marriage?" The person's eyes got wet and he replied, "Whatever my heart wished".
13. **Husband:** *Shaadi se pehle duaa ki thi, yaa Allah acha pakaane vaali bivi dena. Ghalti ho gaye, dua me khana bolna bhul gaya".*
    Husband: I prayed before marriage, O'God, give me a wife who cooks well. Mistakenly, I had forgotten to add food in the prayer.
14. **Shohar:** *Mene apne dost ko aaj khaane pe bulaaya he.*
    Bivi: *Tum pagal to nahi ho gaye? Ghar pura ganda para he, bartan bhi saaf nahi aur me kuch paka bhi nahi skti.*
    Shohar: *Ye sab dikhane ke liye hi to bula raha hu, kyuke vo bevakuf aj kal shadi krne ka soch raha he.*
    Husband: Today I have invited a friend for dinner.
    Wife: Are you mad? The house is totally messed up, dishes are unclean and I cannot cook anything.

Gender Representation in SMS Jokes

Husband: Basically, I am inviting him to show all this, because that fool is thinking for marriage these days

15. **Wife call par:** *Window ka lock nahi khul raha he.*
    Husband: Aisa karo thora oil garam krke us pe dal do.
    Wife: Kiya us se lock khul jaayega?
    Husband: Try to karo (15 minutes baad husband ne wife ko dobara call ki) tumne try kiya?
    Wife: Haan kiya, par ab to laptop hi off ho gaya he.
    Husband: Jaahil ki bachchi window to bataati konsi he...
    Wife on call: I could not open the lock of window.
    Husband: Pour some oil on it after heating.
    Wife: So the lock will get open?
    Husband: Try at least (After 15 minutes, husband calls wife) Have you tried?
    Wife: Yes, I have, but now the laptop has switched off.
    Husband: You daughter of an uninformed man. At least you should have told me about the window...)

16. **Boy:** *Viber use karti ho?*
    Girl: Uf! ye uneducated larkey bhi na... dear Viber nahi, viper hota he aur me kabhi kabhi use karti hun jab paani ziada ho warna pocha hi lagati hun.
    Boy: Hahahaha bas kar pagli rulaye gi kia!
    (**Boy:** Do you use Viber?
    Girl: Oh! these uneducated boys... dear its viper not viber and I use it when there is enough water otherwise I just mob.
    Boy: (with a laugh) just stop here you will make me cry!)

17. *Larkiyo ki shopping, khareedna kuch nahi hota bas... oye ye dekho, wow vo to dekho, ye kiya he, vo kiya he, ye kitne ka he? ye to bohot mehenga he, ye dukaan hi mehengi he, bhaai ye 7000 vaala 2000 me dena he to baat karo, varna ham jaarahe he (paas 1000 bhi nahi hote), chalo chalo us dukaan pe chalte he, paanch ghante lagaati hen phir chips kha ke aur dupatta peeko karva ke vaapis aajati hen.*
    (Shopping of girls, they do not purchase anything just say, hey look at it, wow look that, what is this, what is that, how much this costs? It is too expensive, this shop is really expensive, brother if you can give this one of Rs. 7000 in Rs. 2000 then we stay otherwise we are leaving (they do not have even Rs. 1000 with them), let's go to that shop, spend five hours then have chips and get peeko on *dupatta (stawl)* and return home)

18. *Larkiyon ki ajeeb aadat, tayyaar hone ke liye parlor jana he, aur parlor jane ke liye bhi tayyaar hona he.*
    (A weird habit of girls, they go parlor to get ready, and they get ready for going to parlor)

19. **Question:** *Ek aurat ek ghante mai chalees rotiyaa bana sakti he to do auraten mil ke ek ghante me kitni rotiya bana lengi? Answer: Ek bhi nahi, sirf baaten banayenge aur rotiya tanduur se ayengee.*
    (**Question:** If a woman makes forty loafs in an hour then how many loafs can be made by two women? Answer: None. They will gossip and loafs will ordered from the hotel)
20. *Female mai 'male' aata he, why? 'She' mai 'he' aata he, why? 'Woman' mai 'man' aata hai, why? Kyunke, mardon ki to purani aadat he aurton me ghusne ki.*
    (Why there is 'male' in 'female'? Why there is 'he' in 'she'? Why there is 'man' in 'woman? Because, it is an old habit of males to intrude into females)
21. **Boy:** *Kahan per ho?*
    Girl: Mai apne papa ki BMW mai club jaa rahi hun, abhi driver mujhe club mai chor dega, uske baad mall me shopping ke liye jaaongi, tab tumhen call karti hun, tum kahan per ho?
    Boy: Jis rickshaw mai tum ho iske left side mai latka hua hun, tum kirayaa mat dena, mene de diya he.
    (**Boy:** Where are you?
    Girl: I am going to club in my papa's BMW, driver will drop me at the club, then I will go to mall for shopping, from there I will call you, where are you?
    Boy: I am hanging on the left side of the same rickshaw you are in. Do not give the fare, I have already paid for you)
22. **Women:** *Meri paau ki ungli coffee table se takra gae he.*
    Ambulance Operator: (hastey huay) aur iske liye aap ambulance bulaana chahti hen?
    Women: Nahin, ambulance to mere shohar ke liye hai, usey hassna to nahi chaahiye thaa na.
    (**Women:** My little toe hit with the coffee table.
    Ambulance Operator: (with a laugh) For this reason you have called for an ambulance?
    Women: No, ambulance is for my husband, he should not have laughed)
23. **Son:** *Mjhe shaadi nahin karni mujhe sab aurton se dar lagta he.*
    Father: Kar le beta, phir ek hi se dar lagega baqi sab achi lagne lagengi.
    (**Son:** I do not want to marry, I have gynophobia.
    Father: do it son, then you will be only afraid of the one you married and you will start liking other women)
24. **Fauji:** *Sare dushman hum se darte hen aur hum bivi se.*
    Mochi: Mai juuton ki marrammat karta hun aur bivi meri.
    Teacher: Mai college mai lecture deta hun aur ghar mai sirf suntaa hun.
    Officer: Mai office mai boss hun aur ghar mai nokar.

Gender Representation in SMS Jokes

Judge: Mai court mai feslay sunataa hun aur ghar mai khud insaaf ka talabgaar hun. Feslaa aap ke haath mai hai, kunwaare raho, khush raho. No wife, easy life! Note: jo shaadi ker chuke hain vo sabar karen, jinki nahin hui vo shukar karen.
(**Soldier:** Enemies are afraid of us and we afraid of our wives.
Cobbler: I repair shoes and my wife repairs me.
Teacher: I give lecture in college and receives at home.
Officer: I am the boss in office and servant in my home.
Judge: I sentence in court and I am seeking for justice at home. Now! the decision is in your hand, be happy being a bachelor. No wife, easy life! Note: Those who are already married, have patience, those who are bachelor, be grateful)

25. **Wife:** *Aap ki birthday ke liye itna mehnga suit khareeda hai k bas.*
    Husband: Bohat bohat shukria, acha dekhao to sahi.
    Wife: Mai abhi pehen ke aati hun.
    (**Wife:** I have purchased a very expensive suit for you birthday.
    Husband: Thank you so much, let me see it.
    Wife: I will be back soon wearing it)

26. **Ghusseli bivi:** *Dekh lena tumhen to dozakh mai bhi jaga nahin mile gi.*
    Shohar: Naa miley, mai har jaga tumhare saath jana bhi nahin chahta.
    (**Angry wife:** You will see, you would not even get a place in hell.
    Husband: It's alright, I do not want to go everywhere with you)

27. **Bivi:** *Mujhe bukhaar ho raha hai.*
    Shohar: Mai to shopping pe jaane ka soch raha tha.
    Bivi: Mazaaq kar rahi thee.
    Shohar: Mai bhi mazaaq kar raha tha, chal roti paka!
    (**Wife:** I am suffering from fever.
    Husband: I was thinking to go for shopping.
    Wife: I was kidding.
    Husband: I was also kidding, go and make loaves!)

28. **Girl:** *Mai kesi lag rahi hun aaj? abhi beauty parlor se aayi hun.*
    Boy: To? band tha kia???
    (**Girl:** How am I looking today? Just came from the beauty parlor.
    Boy: So? was it close???)

29. **Girl:** *Agar paise darakht pe ugte to kia hota?*
    Boy: To larkiyan bandaron se bhi set hojatin.
    (**Girl:** What would have happened if money starts growing on trees?
    Boy: Then girls would have even settled down with the monkeys)

30. **Beta:** *Papa, aesi bivi ko kia kehte hen jo gori ho, khubsurat ho, samajhdaar ho, shohar ki izzat kare aur kabhi jhagra na kare?*
    Baap: Veham, kehte hen beta, vehem.

149

(**Man:** Father, what we call a wife who is fair, beautiful, intelligent, give respect to her husband and never quarrel?
Father: Ilusion, son, illusion)

31. **Beta:** *Mard kise kehte hen?*
    Baap: Us powerful insaan ko jo ghar pe hukumat karta hai.
    Beta: Bara ho kar mai bhi ammi ki tarah mard banunga.
    (**Son:** To who do we call a man?
    Father: A person who is powerful and governs the house.
    Son: When I will grow up, I will become a man like my mother)

FINDINGS

In these jokes, the beautiful relationship of husband and wife is the target of humor. Husbands are portrayed as unassertive, wretch, as well as innocent characters, always shown unsatisfied with their married lives and ever complaining about it. These jokes are highlighting the stereotypical role of a husband who is always obeying the commands of his wife and known as hen-pecked because of which they usually become the target of criticism and their self-esteem is also being challenged by the society.

Whereas, the wives are shown as more powerful, dominating, commanding, and authoritative figures. They are presented as rude, work-shy, cruel, bellicose as well as cunning by nature. Craftiness and wickedness are also associated with females, especially with the wives. As, these are considered their reliable tools for dealing with their husbands and in-laws.

Nowadays, it is a common assumption that all wives are treating their husbands in a negative way and they are considered as devils. Through these kinds of gender biased jokes, they are projecting the negative image of both husband and wife, and also humiliating their relationship of marriage that is the physical, psychological, as well as emotional bonding along with love and compassion based companionship.

On the other hand, in the cross-gender conversation, the male is presented as sane, confident, and more intelligent. While, the female is shown as less intelligent, non-practical, and naive. It emphasizes on the already existing stereotype that women have no sense and they lack certainty (Lakoff, 1975).

Cameron's (2000) view also support the claim that women's language has lack of influence as well as obsequiousness. Therefore, by employing the respective stereotype, they are trying to portray female identity as a weak and marginal figure of the society.

In the Pakistani context, an ideal woman according to the stereotypical male perception includes, being supportive, obsequious as well as emotional. They want to see them as obedient wives to their husbands as they were used to be. Females are shown as talking about materialistic things; they are senseless, dependent on male and always asking for confirmation of their work from others to get satisfaction. Because, they lack surety as well. They are usually careless and cannot live without gossiping.

In a few jokes, females are dehumanized and compared with inanimate things. Whereas, males are shown as eccentric and seducers, who are always behind females. These characteristics of both the genders that are being criticized through jokes are not really the true or accurate picture of these genders. It is mostly the over generalization of their social roles and attitudes towards each other.

Researchers want to show through this small scale research that there are not only females who use to become the target of criticism in jokes as well as in other genres of discourse. But, males are also criticized and humiliated equally through these types of gender biased jokes. The ideology behind humiliating cross-gender relations is to reinforce the already existing stereotypes and penetrate them in to the minds of everyone in the society through the bombardment of gender biased SMS jokes.

After receiving these prejudiced jokes, one may start thinking about their counterpart in the same way as it is defined in jokes. They become less tolerable for each other and start using offensive language for each other's gender if they get hurt. Therefore, jokes although taken as a lighter part of discourse carry a very loaded and influential place in the society. They are used as a weapon to integrate different ideologies related to different races, ethnic groups, languages, as well as genders.

SOLUTIONS AND RECOMMENDATIONS

1. Government of Pakistan should take strong initiatives for the betterment of women, because they are usually the target of humor in the Pakistani context.
2. For the socioeconomic upheaval of women, Pakistani politicians and scholars must strive.
3. The significant role of females in the progress of Pakistan should be portrayed by electronic as well as print media.
4. Full participation of women in all spheres of social life should be ensured by the Government of Pakistan by providing them with equal opportunities.
5. Due to socioeconomic discrimination, females are mostly considered suitable for domestic work only. They must be given proper economic facilities and job securities. This will help in minimizing gender discrimination in Pakistan.
6. Civil society groups as well as NGOs should raise awareness about sociocultural and religious norms.

7. Religious scholars must play their vital role in guiding people to abstain from any hatred or prejudice against opposite sex.
8. Pakistan Electronic Media Regulatory Authority (PEMRA) should strictly regulate the content being broadcast.
9. The sanctity of the social roles of husband and wife should not be the target of SMS jokes.
10. People should abstain from forwarding gender biased jokes.
11. In Pakistan there is a dire need to make education gender sensitive.
12. Individuals should report gender biased jokes to respective authorities.

FUTURE RESEARCH AND DIRECTIONS

Further researches can be conducted on the following encompassing themes:

1. The increasing trend of gender bias humor in Pakistan.
2. The impact of gender bias jokes on self-esteem.
3. Freedom of speech and humiliation.
4. Strategies for the promotion of equity based social roles in contemporary era.

CONCLUSION

The problems related to the understandings of implied meanings of jokes vary from person to person. Because, everyone has its own perception of looking at things which may be influenced by some social or cultural practices. Therefore, these respective findings are purely based upon how they are portrayed and how they are perceived by the society. To an extent, it can aware the masses about the over exploitation of media, its influencing power and reach, and also gives them a critical eye to see gender biased SMS jokes objectively and not to ignore the use of language in these jokes in defining the characteristics of both males and females.

REFERENCES

Boyer, P. J. (1986, Feb. 16). TV turns to the hard-boiled male. *New York Times*.

Brown, J. D., & Campbell, K. (1986). Race and gender in music videos: The same beat but a different drummer. *Journal of Communication, 36*(1), 94–106. doi:10.1111/j.1460-2466.1986.tb03041.x

Butler, J. (1990). *Gender trouble: Feminism and the subversion of identity*. New York, NY: Routledge.

Cameron, D. (2000). Styling the worker: Gender and the commodification of language in the globalized service economy. *Journal of Sociolinguistics, 4*(3), 323–347. doi:10.1111/1467-9481.00119

Craft, C. (1988). *Too old, too ugly, and not deferential to men. An anchor woman's courageous baffle against sex discrimination*. Rockland, CA: Prima.

Davis, D. M. (1990). Portrayals of women in prune-tune network television: Some demographic characteristics. *Sex Roles, 5*(23), 325–332. doi:10.1007/BF00290052

Doyle, J. A. (1989). *The male experience* (2nd ed.). New York, NY: McGraw-Hill

Feldman, N. S., & Brown, E. (1984). *Male vs. female differences in control strategies: What children learn from Saturday morning television*. Paper presented at the meeting of the Eastern Psychology Association, Baltimore, MD.

Lakoff, R. (1975). Extract from language and women's place. In D. *Cameron (Ed.), The feminist critique of language: A reader*. London, UK: Routledge.

Mattel offers trade-m for "Teen Talk" Barbie. (1992, Oct. 18). *Raleigh News and Observer*.

McCauley, C., Thangavelu, K., & Rozin, P. (1988). Sex stereotyping of occupation in relation to television representation and census facts. *Basic and Applied Social Psychology, 9*(3), 197–212. doi:10.120715324834basp0903_3

Oxford Advanced Learner's Dictionary. (n.d.). Retrieved from https://www.oxfordlearnersdictionaries.com/definition/english/joke_1?q=joke

Pareles, J. (1990, Oct. 21). The women who talk back in rap. *New York Times*.

Sanders, M., & Rock, M. (1988). *Waiting for prime time: The women of television news*. Urbana, IL: University of Illinois Press.

Sapir, E. (1921). *Language: An introduction to the study of speech*. New York, NY: Harcourt Brace.

Tang, S. H., & Hall, V. C. (1995). The over justification effect: A meta-analysis. *Applied Cognitive Psychology, 9*(5), 365–404. doi:10.1002/acp.2350090502

Tannen, D. (1990). *You just don't understand: Women and men in conversation*. New York, NY: Ballantine Books.

Texier, C. (1990, April 22). Have women surrendered in MTV's battle of the sexes? *New York Times.*

Wildgen, W., & Heusden, B. (2009). *Metarepresentation, self-organization and art.* New York, NY: Peter Lang.

Wood, J. T. (1984). *Who cares: Women, cure, and culture.* Carbondale, IL: Southern Illinois University Press.

Woodman, S. (1991). How super are heros? *Health, 40,* 49, 82.

ADDITIONAL READING

Attardo, S. (2009). Humor research: Vol. I. *Linguistic theories of humor.* Berlin: Mouton de Gruyter. doi:10.1515/9783110219029

Bandura, A. (2007). Reflections on an agentic theory of human behavior. *Tidsskrift for Norsk Norsk Psykologforening., 10,* 995–1004.

Downes, D. M., & Rock, P. (2011). *Understanding deviance: A guide to the sociology of crime and rule-breaking.* Oxford, UK: Oxford University Press. doi:10.1093/he/9780199569830.001.0001

Dunbar, N. E., Banas, J. A., Rodriguez, D., Liu, S. J., & Abra, G. (2012). Humor use in power-differentiated interactions. *Humor: International Journal of Humor Research, 25*(4), 469–489. doi:10.1515/humor-2012-0025

Gilbert, J. R. (2004). *Performing marginality: humor, gender, and cultural critique.* Detroit, MI: Wayne State University Press.

Greengross, G., & Miller, G. (2011). Humor ability reveals intelligence, predicts mating success, and is higher in males. *Intelligence, 39*(4), 188–192. doi:10.1016/j.intell.2011.03.006

Holmes, J. (2006). Sharing a laugh: Pragmatic aspects of humor and gender in the 86 workplace. *Journal of Pragmatics, 38*(1), 26–50. doi:10.1016/j.pragma.2005.06.007

Hurley, M. M., Dennett, D. C., & Adams, R. B. (2011). *Inside Jokes: Using Humor to Reverse-engineer the Mind.* MIT Press. doi:10.7551/mitpress/9027.001.0001

Isajiw, W. W. (2013). *Causation and functionalism in sociology.* Routledge. doi:10.4324/9781315888699

Kotthoff, H. (2006). Gender and humor: The state of the art. *Journal of Pragmatics, 38*(1), 4–25. doi:10.1016/j.pragma.2005.06.003

McGhee, P. E. (1979). *Humor, its origin and development.* San Francisco: W. H. Freeman.

Mickes, L., Walker, D. E., Parris, J. L., Mankoff, R., & Christenfeld, N. J. S. (2011). Who's funny: Gender stereotypes, humor production, and memory bias. *Psychonomic Bulletin & Review, 19*(1), 108–112. doi:10.375813423-011-0161-2 PMID:22037918

Rozek, C. G. (2015). *The gender divide in humor: How people rate the competence, influence, and funniness of men and women by the jokes they tell and how they tell them.* BA Thesis. Wellesley, MA: Wellesley College.

Smith-Lovin, L., & Robinson, D. T. (2001). Getting a laugh: Gender, status, and humor in task discussions. *Social Forces, 80*(1), 123–158. doi:10.1353of.2001.0085

Van Herk, G. (2012). *What is sociolinguistics.* Chichester, West Sussex, UK: Wiley Blackwell.

KEY TERMS AND DEFINITIONS

Gender Bias: A preference or prejudice toward one gender over the other.

Gender Representation: Representation of gender in society.

Gender Roles: Behaviors, values, and attitudes that a society considers appropriate for both male and female.

Ideology: A system of ideas and ideals.

Jokes: A thing that someone says to cause amusement or laughter.

Prejudice: Preconceived opinion that is not based on reason or actual experience.

SMS: A text message.

Stereotypes: A widely held but oversimplified ideas regarding a particular person or thing.

Section 2
Gender and Diversity Representation in Film Studies

Chapter 9
Man, Masculinity, and Violence in Turkish Cinema After 2000:
The Case of Kenan Imirzalioglu

Gökhan Gültekin
Sivas Cumhuriyet University, Turkey

ABSTRACT

The purpose of this study is to trace the relationship between male, masculinity, and violence in Turkish films after 2000. For this purpose, action, adventure, political, and drama films featuring Kenan İmirzalıoğlu, the pioneering anti-hero of male violence in popular Turkish films between 2000-2010 were focused. Thus, the sample of the study was composed of Deli Yürek: Bumerang Cehennemi (2001), Yazı Tura (2004), Kabadayı (2007), and Ejder Kapanı (2010) films. In all of these films Yusuf, Cevher, Devran, and Celal acted by İmirzalıoğlu use intense violence in the name of honor, power, and virility. Starting from such observation, the study has endeavored to make an interpretation on appearance of the relationship among man, masculinity, and violence based on the type, orientation, perspective and purpose of violence in the films, included the sample since the 2000s. In pursuit of such meaning first, it will be useful to mention the relationship among violence, man, and masculinity.

INTRODUCTION

Human beings have witnessed violence throughout history and have encountered numerous acts of violence such as murders, injuries, fights, looting, rape, and hunting. Violence has always been present since the murdering of Abel, the first child of Adam and Eve, by his brother Cain (Akıncı, 2013: 21). At the present time, violence has a more complex structure.

DOI: 10.4018/978-1-7998-0128-3.ch009

Today's science and technology age has instilled people a tremendous tendency to violence along with rationalism and materialism (Jung, 2011: 38). More precisely, 'civilization' has also served for the naturalization of violence (Eagleton, 2012: 202). Especially from the late 1950s, this naturalness has become thoroughly more apparent, violence and wildness have gradually increased (Demirbaş, 2012: 272). The fact that violence is now rather a tool of political and ideological goals is one of the main reasons for this increase (Dönmezer, 1994: 211). Despite all these changes, what has remained constant since Cain is that violence is always male-dominated.

In patriarchal societies, men are equipped with power, violence, governing and honor codes. When the man thinks that his power or honor is damaged, he does not neglect to resort violence through his power. Therefore, the films coming out of the society cannot remain indifferent to this character of man in real life. The situation is not very different in Turkey. The male characters of Turkish films are generally designed with the intense power and violence for the continuation of their power and honor in accordance with the patriarchal structure. Even a man can sometimes resort to violence to prove his adequacy and virility. It is possible to see that such characters who use violence for their honor, virility and power are concentrated in Turkish films especially after 2000. Many male characters resort to physical, psychological, sexual, verbal or economic violence for the sake of power, governing, honor and masculinity. Depending on all of these, the purpose of this study is to trace the relationship between male, masculinity, and violence in Turkish films after 2000. For this purpose, action, adventure, political and drama films featuring Kenan İmirzalıoğlu, the pioneering anti-hero of male violence in popular Turkish films between 2000-2010 were focused. Thus, the sample of the study was composed of *Deli Yürek: Bumerang Cehennemi* (2001), *Yazı Tura* (2004), *Kabadayı* (2007) and *Ejder Kapanı* (2010) films. In all of these films Yusuf, Cevher, Devran and Celal acted by İmirzalıoğlu use intense violence in the name of honor, power, and virility. Starting from such observation, the study has endeavored to make an interpretation on appearance of the relationship among man, masculinity, and violence based on the type, orientation, perspective and purpose of violence in the films, included the sample since the 2000s. In pursuit of such meaning first, it will be useful to mention the relationship among violence, man, and masculinity.

VIOLENCE, MAN, AND MASCULINITY

In the Classical Anglo-Saxon sense, violence is defined as 'causing physical injury of somebody' (Riches, 1989: 14; Rougier, 1989: 71). It can be said that the concept has passed from Arabic to Turkish in the meanings of 'toughness', 'brute force', and, 'rude behavior'. Today, its lexical meaning is 'using brute force, rude behavior, and, toughness towards those with opposite attitude or opinion' (Ünsal, 1996: 29).

Violence should not only be associated with physical aggression or power. As stressed by Marvin (1989: 153), violence is present in bullfighting; but the matadors do not appear in an aggressive mood against bulls. Matador uses violence in a very comfortable manner for entertainment purposes. In other words, there is no need for pure aggression in the emergence of violence; aesthetic and cold-blooded behaviors may also include violence. Again, violence does not need to be physical; it can be emotional or verbal. Thus, it is more meaningful to define violence as follows: Violence is the observed activity of the organism from the outside and requires the physical, psychological or social damage of the target.

Violence is not evaluated in the same way in societies with different cultural codes. While violence is condemned as a goal in some cultures, violence can be regarded as legitimate as a tool (Corbin, 1989: 44). For example, while violence is a privileged behavior in Dobu culture, it can be punished in Pueblos culture (Foucault, 2013: 74). Similarly, in some cities, regions or tribes of the countries such as Columbia, Italy and Mexico, the use of violence is an acceptable situation (Wolfgang and Ferracuti, 2010: 275-281).

Spierenburg (2010: 17) sees violence as 'impulsive' and 'designed' in the first axis and as 'ritual' and 'instrumental' in the second axis. While impulsive violence is an instant action that develops without a design, the intelligence of the perpetrator comes to the forefront and violence becomes controlled in the designed violence. The ritual violence in the second axis is an action made mostly for honor and by the individual for his own behalf; whereas, instrumental violence is the action made by an individual for gaining another thing, not for honor. Again, Spierenburg emphasizes that acts of violence can be transformed into a transitional structure between axes. Therefore, violence can not only be instrumental and impulsive, but also be ritual and designed.

It can be asserted that violence can occur not only in physical aspect but also emotional, verbal, sexual or economic aspects (Solmuş, 2012: 252). Violence can be moral as well as material. While material violence is related to distorting, damaging or destroying, moral violence emphasizes suppression or change of ideas (Corbin, 1989: 44).

As it can be seen, violence can be evaluated under different categories. In this respect, Gümüş addresses violence in four categories as follows (2006: 31):

1. In terms of intention-will (defense, struggle for life-living, destructiveness);
2. In terms of acceptance and application level (individual, organized);
3. In terms of armament level (with and without tools);
4. At the action and destructiveness level (counteraction, nutrition-hunting-use).

Regardless of the type, the power in the patriarchal world is male-dominated and man has the rightfulness to commit violence on his own. Moreover, violence is often a prerequisite for masculinity that is expected from the male in line with social conventions. For example, as cited by Wood (2004: 24), the only way for a man from the sub-class in Medieval England to prove himself is to show physical power and violence.

As in men, it is also possible to see violence acts in women. Arendt (1994: 51) even stresses that everyone has the right to resort to violence when it is necessary. Nevertheless, this has not been possible since people started hunting and gathering. The fact that hunting from these two vital duties was 'male-specific' has been an indicator for the fact that violence would spread with male dominance throughout history. In the same plane, the nature was identified with women and culture was identified with men, which paved the way for patriarchy (Pepper, 1996: 106).

While strengthening the men's power, patriarchy has excluded the women by putting them into the background (Warren, 1994: 181). Thus, male supremacy has been adopted in institutions such as school, family, religion, state and popular culture within the patriarchal social structure. Similarly, women have either been banned or accepted only as guests in many 'male places' such as coffee house, stadium, mine, hippodrome, barracks and mosque (Özbay, 2013: 186; 192). This can also be observed from the films coming out of the popular culture as a social field. In these films, women are mostly either secondary or remain objects to satisfy the desire of men. Violence sometimes takes place under women's sovereignty in the films along with the definitions such as 'masculine', 'tomboy' or 'man' but the issue to be evaluated in the study is the violence of inborn male characters. In addition, it may be helpful to support the issue with some examples from the primary characters and films that have influenced this process before examining the relationship among violence, male and masculinity in Turkish films after 2000.

PIONEERS OF MALE VIOLENCE IN TURKISH CINEMA

The man is equipped with various codes in terms of the cultural values of his society. According to the understanding of the patriarchal society, men are powerful, protective, and dominating (Baudrillard, 1997: 150). Accordingly, men are often characterized by codes of violence, power, and ruling in films produced in societies where patriarchalism is dominant. This situation is the same in Turkish cinema which is also patriarchal. The male characters of Turkish films usually pursue to maintain their manhood in the triangle of power, violence and honor. Men who do not comply with this pattern are either excluded or killed in a short time and taken out of the film story.

For the men of Turkish cinema, especially the film *Kanun Namına* shot in 1952 can be accepted as the cornerstone. Ayhan Işık, the brunette, dark-brave Turkish man of the film, gave a clue of how the male characters after him will be with his hard and rebellious attitudes (Özgüç, 1990: 49-56). Men who come after him are usually equipped with codes such as 'strong', 'respectable', 'tough' and, 'godfather'. Male characters such as Hayati Hamzaoğlu, Erol Taş, and Ahmet Tarık Tekçe who were not allowed to have this type of codes are bad men (Uluyağcı, 2001: 35). Cüneyt Arkın, Kadir İnanır, Orhan Gencebay or Kartal Tibet were seen as both strong and good men. The common point of all these good and bad men is that they are all equipped with violence. They were able to commit physical, psychological, economic or sexual violence against their wives, lovers, family members, each other, animals or nature.

In the period following the 1960 revolution, men were generally presented as people protecting and caring women and those who are bossy in the family (Abisel, 1994: 126-128). This responsibility has also made it necessary for men to be exposed to or commit violence for their honor. Eşref from *Namus Uğruna* (1960), Mehmet from *Acı Hayat* (1962), Osman from *Aşk ve İntikam* (1965), Haydar from *Aslan Yürekli Kabadayı* (1967) or Tarık from *Aç Kurtlar* (1969) are just a few of such men who are strongly intertwined for honor and revenge.

Male violence in the 1960s continued in the 1970s. Especially the film *Bir Teselli Ver* (1971) in which the singer Orhan Gencebay played the starring role led the familiarity with the type of arabesque film. The fatalism and fate intensified with this type paved the way for the domination of violence and sex elements to the films (Özgüç, 1990: 96-97). Again, in the same years, gradually increasing social concern in Turkey led men to be presented in different ways as orphan, father or heroes in the films (Arslan, 2005: 20). These codes continued to show violence as necessary and male-specific. As the primary violence perpetrators, men such as Cüneyt Arkın, Yılmaz Güney and Kadir İnanır in particular have appeared in many films including *Vurguncular* (1971), *Çaresizler* (1973) or *Silahlara Veda* (1976).

In the 1980s, when Turkish cinema entered a period of stagnation, the men who got out of traditional Turkish codes began to be transformed more than ever in terms of appearance and behavior. The men of cinema looked much more emotional, well-groomed and feminine at that time (Uluyağcı, 2001: 37). For example, Kadir İnanır was not a macho, but could be shown as a kind-hearted man in the film *Küçüğüm* (1987) (Onaran, 1995: 280). However, it was not possible to isolate the man from violence. Films such as *Destan* (1980), *Ölümsüz* (1982), *Damga* (1984), *Yılanların Öcü* (1985), *Umutsuzlar* (1986), *İnsan Avcıları* (1987) clearly revealed male violence.

The rise of liberalism since the 1990s has created a social structure suitable for mafia along with easy money earning, unemployment, poverty, and rapid urbanization. Mafia has increased crime and violence actions and caused gangs, money laundering, murder, injury, fraud etc. As stated by Özbay (2013: 189), the phrase 'every Turk is born a soldier' becoming gradually widespread in Turkish politics in the same years emphasized masculinity and served for legitimizing different forms of violence. Again, more involvement of women in the social life led men to become pessimist. The movement of cinema which was expected to be fed by all these social changes did not delay and pessimist men started to use violence more intensively. In this respect, *Tatar Ramazan* released in 1990 can be said to be an important example for the relationship of men and masculinity with violence in future films. The physical violence committed by Tatar Ramazan for the sake of never losing the masculinity was able to acquire a much more psychological and sexual appearance in *Berlin in Berlin* (1993).

The pessimistic view in Turkey in the 1990s left male characters in the films to use all forms of violence (physical, psychological, verbal, sexual, economic) in order to prove his honor, power and masculinity. As a matter of fact, it is possible to see the situation in Turkish films after the second half of the 1990s. This type of pessimistic men who cannot cope with his problems is powerless, failed, have lost his authority and cannot have self-fulfillment are found in the films such as *Eşkıya* (1996), *Nihavend Mucize* (1997), *Ağır Roman* (1997), *Her Şey Çok Güzel Olacak* (1998), and *Gemide* (1998) (Oktan, 2008: 158). All these men in the 1990s can suppress their pessimism by committing violence. Among the films acting from violence and masculinity, especially *Eşkıya* has an important place in terms of reaching 2.5 million audiences.

Eşkıya presented an effective recipe including crime, violence, action and drama to the subsequent popular films. Again, the admiration to Baran acted by Şener Şen over violence and virility can be thought to pave the way for anti-hero men who would gradually become intense in popular films. Therefore, it is possible to observe that the anti-heroes in the popular Turkish films have increased after the 2000s. What to do in accordance with the purpose of the study from this point of view is to try to make an interpretation from 'violence, man, and masculinity' in recent Turkish films.

ON VIOLENCE AND MASCULINITY IN TURKISH CINEMA AFTER 2000

Turkish cinema after 2000 has adopted a structure in which men and masculinity have been glorified more and more and nationalism has been all around (Büyükdüvenci and Öztürk, 2007: 49). In this structure, men such as Kenan İmirzalıoğlu, Necati Şaşmaz, Mehmet Akif Alakurt, Şener Şen, Erkan Petekkaya, Musa Uzunlar, and Haluk Piyes have appeared as perpetrators of violence in many films and TV series. All these men have become an anti-hero with the legitimacy of the acts of violence and they have been perceived as 'good men' at heart despite their actions. According to Süalp (2009: 140), anti-heroes, who have been considered worthy of society since the 2000s, are in fact composed of assailants, crime bosses or rapists.

When it is carefully examined, it is understood that the characters heavily equipped with power, ruling and masculinity after the 2000s generally use physical violence in the films. Accordingly, various studies have been conducted on the violence phenomenon in Turkish cinema after 2000. Although the approaches are different, nearly all studies have included men as the perpetrator of physical violence and women who are their victims. For example, in his study focusing on the violence phenomena in Turkish films, Yaşartürk (2012: 14; 24) focused on the causes of male violence against women in the family and if it is legalized or not through the films of *İtiraf* (2001), *Gönül Yarası* (2004), *Banyo* (2005), *İki Çizgi* (2008), *Vicdan* (2008), *Üç Maymun* (2008), *Sıcak* (2008) and *Geriye Kalan* (2011). The main conclusion of this study which was observed to briefly include the story of the films and domestic violence was that women in the films were exposed to psychological and physical violence in the family by their husbands, children or lovers. Again, Pişkin (2011: 583-590) emphasizes that Turkish cinema has intensified heroic men who have committed violence since the 2000s. According to her, violence is observed especially in male characters who are equipped with the 'nationalism' code. However, it is understood that Piskin's study has superficially mentioned the appearance of violence in the cinema through various films.

As exemplified above, it is very difficult to find findings on the orientation, types, time and places of violence especially in the studies on violence in Turkish films. More importantly, numerous studies have focused only on physical male violence. Therefore, in the present study, an interpretation was set on the relationship among man, masculinity and violence in the films after 2000 and it was thought that such deficiencies should be eliminated. In the light of all these, answers to the following questions considered to reveal the relationship among man, masculinity and violence in a more elucidative way were sought in the study.

- What type or types of violence do men utilize to prove his power and ruling status?
- Who or what is exposed to violence?
- Which one from instrumental, impulsive, purposeful, ritual or designed violence types serves to preserve honor, masculinity and power of men?
- Do the time and places where the male violence is perpetrated have an effect on man's power and ruling status?
- Is the violence perpetrator (actor) capable of pushing his masculinity on the person exposed to violence (victim) or observer (witness)?

Within the scope of these questions, the population of the study consisted of popular Turkish films released after the 2000s. From this population, action, adventure, political and drama films hosting Kenan İmirzalıoğlu as the leading anti-hero of male violence were focused. Comedy genre, combining violence with humor, and historical films emphasizing collective violence were excluded from the study. As a result of all these, the sample of the study was composed of *Deli Yürek: Bumerang Cehennemi* (2001), *Yazı Tura* (2004), *Kabadayı* (2007) and *Ejder Kapanı* (2010) films. Starting from these films, how the relationship among man, masculinity and violence gained an appearance in Turkish cinema after 2000 was tried to be interpreted through Yusuf, Cevher, Devran and Celal acted by İmirzalıoğlu.

Honor, Violence, and Masculinity Cycle:
Deli Yürek: Bumerang Cehennemi

In the early 2000s, Kenan İmirzalıoğlu first appeared as Yusuf in the film *Deli Yürek: Bumerang Cehennemi* (2001). Yusuf who has become a hero with *Deli Yürek* series returns this time in Diyarbakır to reveal his manhood, violence and power. It is seen that this political themed film which focuses on the struggle of Yusuf with the terrorist organizations and their supporters revolves around violence, masculinity, and honor.

Yusuf, who aggrandizes his masculinity with his physical appearance and his Zeybek dance at the wedding scenes at the beginning of the film proves his age by intensifying his acts of violence as the story continues.

Yusuf are not very impressed by the armed member of the organization who threatens him to leave Diyarbakır. The main thing that brings him into action is the time when he learns that Zeynep he accepts as his honor has been kidnapped by the organization to Mardin. Yusuf, who immediately goes to Mardin beat the man who is following him until he is put to sleep. When he finds Zeynep and sees her tied, he increases the violence dosage to the higher level. First, he applies verbal violence to Abdi and other two people: "I don't mean to hunt down the coyote, but find the bitch ahead of you. Raise your hands!" When he sees that this discourse is not effective, he kills two members of the organization who want to shoot him. He threatens Abdi to tell him where Doğan is by hitting his head with a gun.

When Yusuf finds Doğan, he shoots him in the legs after a short chase. Yusuf, who aims to make Doğan speak, does not continue his physical violence any more. He realizes that Hasan will shoot him with a sniper gun while he is trying to make Doğan speak and draws Doğan in front of him. After this moment when Doğan is shot to death, Yusuf attempts to justify his own violence. Such a meaning is hidden in his conversation with Bozo. After Bozo fired a gun in the mouth of two people from the Hezbollah terrorist organization, Yusuf says with frustration: "Are you a psychopath or a soldier? This is the brutality." Bozo's answer is clear: 'Whoever eating the bread of this country and betraying will be absolutely shot from where he eats bread one day." Thus, the perception that a soldier whose honor is the homeland and his masculinity will be accepted with all kinds of violence in the name of honor will pass onto Yusuf.

Yusuf who attributes a meaning to the brutality of Bozo goes to colonel Şeref who does work with the terrorists. His purpose is to find Hasan. When Şeref says that he does not know Hasan, Yusuf's verbal violence comes into play: "I know you've been expelled from the army due to your dishonor." Yusuf, who keeps the physical violence towards Şeref at the end of the film, leaves the place.

Yusuf who learns from Bozo that there is no Hasan but he is actually American David intends to complete his actions. Despite all the warning of Bozo, he takes Zeynep and goes to the storage of Şeref's company. This place, where the trade between David and Şeref is made, becomes the main place where Yusuf proves his power and manhood by protecting his honor. Yusuf knocks a man first for this; but he is immediately captured by someone else. Violence acts of Yusuf who is handcuffed by the men of Şeref and David increases after Zeynep is handcuffed. When Şeref would kill them, Yusuf removes his thumb from the joint and saves himself from the handcuff. When he puts his finger back into place, the orientation of violence is against Şeref and his men. Yusuf succeeds in taking the weapon, he gave to Zeynep, from her bag and headbutts to Şeref. Şeref's four men sees him and try to reach their weapons but he acts faster than them. He still doesn't want to kill Şeref with the thought that he is a Turkish soldier and he tells him to do this: "Take this gun and shoot your head. Think of your honor at least when you die". This suicide order is rejected when Şeref extends the gun to Yusuf. Yusuf, who does not trust his virility, is prepared. Yusuf, who does not allow such an unjustified violence, turns his back and shoots him. While all these are happening, there is only one person who moves away from the scene and whom Yusuf has to kill; David. The acceptance of Yusuf's masculinity by the audience also depends on David's most violent murder. Indeed, Yusuf does not leave this expectation unrequited. He manages to catch David on the road and pulls a bazooka out of the bag given to him by Bozo. Yusuf, who asks Zeynep to hold the steering wheel, steps out of the car's sunroof and pushes the trigger. While David blows up with fearful looks, Yusuf sits down smiling at Zeynep who is staring astonishedly behind them and strokes her cheek. Thus, the film ends with the music that supports the virility and courage of Yusuf who proves his power by saving both his country and his own honor.

Two Sides of Man and Masculinity: *Yazı Tura*

Yazı Tura (2004), focusing on the lives of Rıdvan and Cevher, who are fighting with terrorists in the Southeastern region, upon completion of their military service contains violence, drama, honor and masculinity codes heavily. Rıdvan and Cevher, who cannot survive the trauma experienced in the military, resort to all forms of violence in order to protect their honor and masculinity. The film, which does not allow Rıdvan to possess his masculinity and honor, leaves a large space for Kenan İmirzalıoğlu to glorify the masculinity of Cevher. The only thing Cevher needs to enter from this area is the dominance of violence. In response to Rıdvan, who represents the pessimistic and passive side of the man, Cevher shows the true face of masculinity that is expected from patriarchalism with the codes of courage, power and violence.

Cevher exhibits his manhood first on Muhittin who does not give him all money. When he goes to Muhittin's store, he first applies psychological violence to one of Muhittin's men who does not allow him to enter: "I will give you a piece of my bloody mind, I will talk and walk out." When the man tries to respond, Cevher uses physical violence by punching the man down. When he enters, he continues violence with the same order but much more intensely towards Muhittin. Cevher says Muhittin who tells that he will give the money the next day; "Don't be bitch, you also told me on the phone that you will pay the next week". When Muhittin makes a big mistake by saying "Now, I am saying that I am going to give it tomorrow", Cevher takes his knife and cut a pinch of Muhittin's hair along with the skin.

Although the physical violence of Cevher is always against men, Nazan as a woman is the only one exposed to his psychological violence. One day, Cevher asks Nazan, who is laying naked beside him to use heroin. Words of Nazan who has never used heroin offends Cevher: "Would you say Please?" What Cevher now needs to do to ensure his manhood and his power over the Nazan is simple: By pushing her head down and saying "take it". The masculinity of Cevher who proves his power over the woman with this move is blessed with confrontation with his stepbrother Teoman from another mother.

The film, which incorporates August 17 into its story, forms a bond between Cevher and Teoman after the earthquake. Cevher, whose father gets injured in the earthquake, meets Teoman from Greece and another mother. He tries to stay away from his brother Teoman, whose image he cannot associate with masculinity; but he cannot continue that. The night before Teoman returns to Athens, he goes to a bar in Tarlabaşı and calls Cevher. Cevher who goes to Teoman determines the time, place and person for the violence: "What are you doing here, they will cut you at this time." Teoman has no place in such manly place. Teoman has already been exposed to violence as a man. Teoman, who settled in Athens with his mother Tasula, was raped by his old upstairs neighbor when he was 8 years old: "I always went to him, sat on his lap, leaned my head on his chest. One day, he raped me. I don't know, I was child. (…) I am gay, you are a man." These words reveal that sexual violence of another man is the thing removing Teoman from his masculinity. Teoman's next action is directed to Cevher's masculinity which he would never allow. Words of Teoman who takes a lipstick from the next table and kisses Cevher's lips, are also an attack on the virility of Cevher: "We now look like each other, don't we?" Despite all this, Cevher did not commit violence to Teoman. On the contrary, Cevher's violence will not be directed to Teoman, but against other men who attack Teoman.

While Cevher walks on the streets crying after leaving the bar, Teoman walks around drunkenly. After a while, Teoman witnesses male violence against the transvestite he sees on the road. This violence which is first verbal and then becomes physical is directed to Teoman who wants to stop the fight. There is one more person witnessing this fight; Cevher. Cevher, who witnesses the beating of his older brother from the window of Zeyyat's shop, could not hold himself. Cevher who goes to the fight place starts to beat three men attacking Teoman. In the continuation of this physical violence, he cuts the throat of one of the men with the knife he takes out of his pocket. He also cuts off the ear of the man lying still on the floor. After these acts of violence, he surrenders to the police surrounding him and the film ends.

Man Ruling Violence for His Masculinity: *Kabadayı*

Kabadayı is the only film removing Kenan İmirzalıoğlu from anti-heroism between 2000 and 2010. For the first time in this film, İmirzalıoğlu is designed to be placed on the bad side of the male character scale. Devran who is acted by him is a ruthless and vicious violent perpetrator who consumes all life in true sense and thinks only of his own desires and happiness. In order to regain Karaca he sees as a kind of his honor, he yells, threatens, beats, and kills. The only thing he forgot is that an anti-hero who would fill his void would definitely be involved in the story. Such a gap is filled with Şener Şen, the Baran of the film *Eşkıya*, which has a great impact on the spreading of anti-heroes in Turkish cinema. Ali Osman, acted by Şener Şen, is the only person who will stop Devran. Devran cannot escape from being killed by Ali Osman even though he has dominated violence throughout the entire story.

Devran is ready to commit all kinds of violence to take his ex-love Karaca from Murat. In fact, it is observed that Devran uses physical, psychological, verbal and sexual violence. Throughout the story, Teoman, Ali Osman, Murat, Karaca, Sürmeli, Patron, Mustafa, Shadow chief, two men of shadow chief, his own man, Settar, Battal, Dursun, Beyto and Haco are exposed to Devran's violence. All of these violence acts of Devran are related to his attempt to prove his manhood and power to Karaca.

The first move that leads the Devran to violence acts comes from Karaca. One day, Karaca goes to Devran. Before she starts to talk, Devran rubs the roe tattoo on his arm saying that "This normally ruins manhood but this is love." This line shows the importance given by Devran to his manhood. Then he harasses Karaca. The expression "Don't touch Murat" of Karaca who prevents the sexual violence by not allowing him annoys Devran: "I will hurt him. I will dress that gay with a dress. Is that fag bag a man?" Karaca says to Devran who values manhood so much; "Masculinity cannot be achieved by trusting your men and then threatening someone. It will never be with the size of penis. Even with that, don't compare yourself with Murat, you are far behind him." These last words Karaca is saying by mocking and smiling intensify the violence acts of Devran. Devran first threatens Teoman by using verbal violence: "Listen to me, clown. That bar won't open tonight." In the next step, he starts irreversibly physical violence acts.

Devran kills Teoman, who does not listen to him and opens the bar that night. He also kills his own man who accidentally kills Karaca instead of Murat. When he learns that Karaca is kidnapped from the hospital the next morning, he beats his own men to reveal how honor, power and masculinity are important to him: "You destroyed my reputation. They took my girl in front of your eyes. You have no honor (…) I will put a bullet on all of your heads." This unrequited verbal violence is valid for everyone. In fact, when he threatens Ali Osman who takes Karaca under his protection, he sees this response: "If I kill you right here, I know I will not suffer a prick of conscience, because I will forget my swear (…) I will never remember how I pull the trigger and how your miserable brain is scattered." Despite this, the desire to get back Karaca does not prevent Devran from keeping its path.

Devran sets fire to the shops of Beyto, Haco, Dursun and Battal, the old tough friends of Ali Osman. While they are witnessing the sabotage with the incoming calls, Devran begins psychological violence: "(...)You didn't know me. Who is Devran, what is his power, what is his courage, what can he do, where can he reach? (…) Where is Ali Osman?" It is understood that the old tough guys, who talk about masculinity, could not withstand this pressure and betrays Ali Osman in a short time.

Devran who goes to Sürmeli on the next day shoots him in the head. This attitude of Sürmeli, who is a homosexual, takes away the masculinity of the tough friends who betrays Ali Osman. This has been approved by words of Ali Osman who go to them: "There was no courage, bravery, manhood (…) Four of you cannot be one Sürmeli." Devran proves his power and manhood by bringing down the tough guys and takes the reign of violence until he is killed by Ali Osman.

Why Devran cares so much about masculinity is understood when he kills the Boss. The Devran grew up in the orphanage and was raped repeatedly by an officer there. In order to regain his manhood, he kills that officer first. Then, he seems to get accustomed to prove his manhood through violence. What he says before killing the shadow chief while looking at the photographs of himself that the organization had is an indicator of why he tries to prove his masculinity through violence: "You turned a lion-like man into a monkey (…) I've been living in a hell for years thinking that these photos will be published in a newspaper. I have become paranoid, psychopath."

Devran who kills the shadow chief and two of his men meets with Murat for Karaca in the warehouse which is the last violence space of the film. He mentions about a game in which they will shoot at the same time with the guns having single bullet. The survivor will have Karaca. Devran who does not leave masculinity and violence asks his question: "Do you dare to play this game for the girl you love?" This psychological pressure intensifies when Devran puts his weapon on Murat's head and presses the trigger. He also pushes Murat to do the same thing: "Be a man, pull the trigger." Murat cannot stand and presses the trigger several times. Once it is realized that the gun has no bullet, Devran is now decided to kill him. Ali Osman comes there when he presses the trigger slowly to fire the only bullet he put inside with a smile. After he shoots three of Devran's men, he is also shot by Devran; but he does not die yet. Ali Osman who slaps Devran's face for a long time and leaves his face in blood finally kills him and dies by falling down in bloods. The last thing Devran does before he dies is to send a kiss to Karaca by smiling.

A Man Stuck with Violence and Revenge: *Ejder Kapanı*

As in *Deli Yürek: Bumerang Cehennemi* (2001) and *Yazı Tura* (2004) *Ejder Kapanı* (2010) also begins with the scenes of soldiers fighting with terrorists in the Southeastern Region. Young sister of Ensar who is one of these soldiers is raped which is the main basis point of the film. From this aspect, a feeling that you will watch a revenge film is given at the beginning. Indeed, in order to meet such an expectation, the *Ejder Kapanı* (2010) focuses on physical violence for the sake of honor and revenge. Ensar's sister Hazal falls into a mental hospital due to the rape and hangs herself there. To avenge his sister, Ensar is determined to kill first the one who raped his sister and then all the perverts who has released from prison with amnesty. Although this goal leads to associate the murders with Ensar, it is later understood that the acts of violence are carried out by the superintendent Celal. Therefore, the film would leave a large area for Celal, not for Ensar especially for the sake of honor and revenge. Ensar is only allowed to shoot big brother of Huseyin who rapes his sister and one of his men.

Celal refers not only to physical violence but also to intense psychological violence. He makes this clear during an interrogation he makes: "Look, I'll go to your wife. I show my badge. I'll go to your home. I say that I will search the house. I sleep with your wife. (…) Do you want me to get you out of here? I tide your hands and mouth. Then, we go to your house. And I will sleep with your wife in front of your eyes." The suspect who is exposed to such intense psychological and verbal violence has nothing much to say: "I killed." In the morning of this interrogation, intense psychological and physical violence carried out by Celal but directing the doubts to Ensar is witnessed.

The first person to be exposed to physical violence is a school's janitor Müslüm. Müslüm, who he is a criminal pedophile, works in the school somehow as a janitor. Without giving a clue about who is the killer, Müslüm is seen hanging on the flagpole in blood. There are also traces of physical violence in his room; blood is everywhere. Again, Ezo's discourse reveals the degree of this designed violence: "Sir, the victim's penis was cut and taken." The legitimization of such an action is ensured when Abbas takes Muslim's phone. It is seen that his phone contains half-naked photos of the girls in the school. The response that is possible to be given by the audience is also given by Abbas: "I will… his bloodline …"

Murders continue after the murdering of the Muslim. When four more torture-filled murders are committed, Abbas's opinion is now clear: "He tortures before he kills. This man either suffered a great trauma in his youth or was subjected to intense violence." It is revealed at the end of the story that this judgment is not true.

Murders are becoming increasingly frequent. Istanbul Police Headquarters, Homicide Department keeps receiving DVDs including torture videos consecutively. The torture videos in this DVDs are accompanied by the discourses of the victims about the information of where their graves will be. Celal, who comes to Ezo one day as the researches continue, starts joking with her. In this joke, Ezo hits Celal 's shoulder. Celal's reaction is to slap her smiling. Ezo smiles despite all these slaps. Thus, Celal's slaps containing physical violence is transformed into a symbol of ordinary masculinity. Ezo, who gives opportunity to this violence and even smiles at it, glorifies Celal's masculinity by having sexual intercourse in the later days. During the intercourse, Celal's ambition and Ezo's reactions like "what are you doing, easy", now open a way for the doubts to gather on Celal. As a matter of fact, as the images and discourses about the Abbas' researches are added into the loving scenes of Ezo and Celal, the audience solves the event in parallel with Abbas.

All the torture and murder acts in the film are actually performed by Celal. Celal leaves 15 bodies he hangs, burns or strangles. The places where he buries the bodies are designed to form a dragon picture on the map of Istanbul. When Abbas, who solves this incident, goes to Celal's house, he finds Ezo, who has no clue. At the time, Celal sets out to kill the child of an undersecretary who is one of the architects of the law that includes the forgiveness of rapists. He actually shot the kid before; but he learns from Ezo that the child is not dead. Thus, the revenge will be completed and the necessary message will be sent to justice.

When Abbas goes to Celal's house, he finds not only Ezo but also crime reporter Hasan. Hasan, whose hands and feet are chained and mouth is covered with tape, speaks after Abbas removes the band: "He made me watch all of them brother, all of his tortures. He had me recorded all his tortures and he killed them all brother." It is understood that Hasan's witnessing all of these physical violence acts psychologically destroys him. Hasan cries when he tells his experiences. Abbas, who also has this information, goes behind Celal.

Celal and Abbas are met in the darkness of the night in a warehouse which is the last violence space of the film. When Abbas asks Ensar, everything is revealed clearly. Ensar is killed without taking his revenge and Celal witnesses it. Celal first hits the person who killed Ensar. Until the last moment, the person who is defined as commando by everyone is held responsible for the murders. According to Abbas, the commando was Ensar until he learned all the events. The real thing is that all these acts of violence are carried out by Celal. Celal promises Ensar on his lap to get revenge; because his own sister was also raped. Celal's actions receive support from the people who learn the news: "We are all commandos. Turkey is proud of you." At that time, Celal is explaining the reasons for the murders to Abbas: "Did anyone give you a 4 year-old kid raped on the train tracks? Then looking at the eyes of that kid, have you draw the picture of that suspect? (…) When I was killing fucknuggets, I thought not only Ensar's sister but also my sister." Nevertheless, what Celal did is too heavy to be accepted by Abbas and Ezo. When they leave Celal, there is only one thing that needs to be done. To direct violence to himself. Celal does the same; fires the gun to his head. The film leaves no opportunity to witness to this suicide. Audience witnesses nothing but a single gunshot and Celal lying on the ground in blood.

FUTURE RESEARCH AND DIRECTIONS

In this study, post-2000 popular Turkish cinema is focused on in order to manifest the characteristics of the relationships between males, masculinity and violence. Thus, unlike previous studies, new findings have been reached about the types, orientation, causes and purpose of perpetration of male violence. In particular, the physical aspect of male violence highlighted in many studies and the perception that it is used against women is broken and it is shown that violence can also be psychological, verbal and sexual. On the other hand, observing that the character intensifies physical violence when his codes of manhood, honor and power are challenged shall also present insights for future studies. Moving from this point, future studies can examine the relationship between male-specific codes and violence in more detail. They may explore how the changes that occur over time in these codes are reflected into the violence tendency of the film characters. Again, it can be argued that a study on the violence of female characters in the world cinema at macro level or in the Turkish cinema at the micro level will make a great contribution to the literature.

CONCLUSION

Yusuf, Cevher, Devran and Celal, acted by Kenan İmirzalıoğlu, make sense of how valuable violence is for men and masculinity. All these characters commit all forms of violence for honor, power, ruling and masculinity. Especially to physical violence. Yusuf for Zeynep and homeland he knows as his honor, Cevher for his brother, Celal for Ensar perpetrate intense violence. Devran, on the other hand, use violence only for himself. Devran, who is separated from the others with this aspect, is removed from anti-heroism and cannot have the support to justify his actions. The violent acts of heroized Yusuf and Celal are justified somehow. Yusuf's violence is legitimate for the sake of the country. In the clearest way, this legitimation is performed by his own words he says to Bozo as "Are you a psychopath or a soldier? This is savagery." Celal's violence is legitimized by the people of the Turks themselves: "Turkey is proud of you." However, in general terms, it is understood that Yusuf, who only uses violence for his homeland, is forgiven. Cevher is captured by the police, the Devran is killed, and Celal commits suicide. In other words, characters who use violence for personal purposes are definitely punished.

All violent acts of Yusuf are directed to men. Cevher, Devran and Celal apply psychological and mild physical violence also to women. In this respect, it can be emphasized that the woman is designed with weakness and fear even though it cannot be said that she is exposed to severe violence. Woman's impotence gains meaning with the power and violence of man. While Zeynep needs the courage of her fiancée Yusuf, Nazan is an object to suppress the desires of Cevher when it is desired. Again, while Ezo is so weak that she can be slapped and slept by Celal who has had a short-term relationship with her, Karaca is a girl who is threatened, hit, cursed, and touched by her old lover Devran. Therefore, in the world of Yusuf, Cevher, Celal or Devran, where masculinity and violence have been intensively injected, women are never prioritized.

In a world full of masculinity and violence where women are excluded, homosexual men are not definitely allowed. Teoman is beaten and excluded or Sürmeli is killed, which is the clearest proof of this situation. Thus, while it is planned to put more emphasis on masculinity, ideological meaning is produced for the superiority of men.

The male violence in the films included in the sample can be instrumental, impulsive, purposeful, ritual or designed. Yusuf's violence is not a purpose but is an instrumental violence committed in the name of his fiancée Zeynep and the country which are his honor. In this aspect, it can be said that instrumental violence serves for defending honor. Unlike Yusuf, Cevher's violence is impulsive. This non-designed and reactive act of violence supports Cevher to prove his power, courage and manhood. In Devran and Celal characters, the situation is different. It cannot be said that the violence acts conducted by Celal in a designed way have an effect on his masculinity. His violence takes place for revenge. Devran's violence is instrumental and designed and it is only for proving himself. Devran, whose everything is masculinity and manhood, can never tolerate the actions and discourses he thinks to hurt his masculinity and he responds harshly.

It cannot be asserted that the time and places of the violence acts of the characters other than Devran are related with their masculinities. In general, the violence takes place in dark and solitary warehouses. The psychological violence scene in which Devran threatens the old tough guys serves for the sublimation of masculinity in a specific way. In such a case, witnessing should be considered to affect masculinity.

All witnesses or victims, except for Ali Osman who opposes Devran, accept the power of Yusuf, Cevher and Celal, who in some way are the perpetrators of violence. If these men are opposed, the intensity of violence increases and violence becomes a severe punishment. Hence, for all these men, violence is considered one of the symbols of masculinity.

It is necessary to think that it is possible to find numerous characters similar to the men mentioned here in Turkish cinema after 2000. If the man in fact perpetrates the violence, he will usually do so for honor, power, ruling or revenge. The male does not hesitate to resort to all kinds of violence if these social codes he needs to have are damaged because providing the continuity of his masculinity depends on these basic codes.

REFERENCES

Abisel, N. (1994). Popüler Yerli Filmlerde Kadının Kadına Sunuluşu "Aşk Mabudesi". In N. Abisel (Ed.), Türk Sineması Üzerine Yazılar. Ankara, Turkey: İmge.

Akıncı, S. F. (2013). *Kriminoloji*. İstanbul, Turkey: Beta.

Arendt, H. (1994). *İnsanlık Durumu* (B. S. Şener, Trans.). İstanbul, Turkey: İletişim.

Arslan, T. U. (2005). *Bu Kabuslar Neden Cemil?* İstanbul, Turkey: Metis.

Baudrillard, J. (1997). *Tüketim Toplumu* (H. Deliceçaylı, & F. Keskin, Trans.). İstanbul, Turkey: Ayrıntı.

Büyükdüvenci, S., & Öztürk, S. R. (2007). Yeni Türk Sinemasında Estetik Arayışı. *Felsefe Dünyası Dergisi*, (46), 45-49.

Corbin, J. (1989). İspanya'da Ayaklanmalar: Casasviejas 1933 ve Madrid 1981. In D. Riches (Ed.), Antropolojik Açıdan Şiddet (D. Hattatoğlu, Trans.). İstanbul, Turkey: Ayrıntı.

Demirbaş, T. (2012). *Kriminoloji*. Ankara, Turkey: Seçkin.

Dönmezer, S. (1994). *Kriminoloji*. İstanbul, Turkey: Beta.

Eagleton, T. (2012). *Tatlı Şiddet: Trajik Kavramı* (K. Tunca, Trans.). İstanbul, Turkey: Ayrıntı.

Foucault, M. (2013). *Akıl Hastalığı ve Psikoloji* (E. Bayoğlu, Trans.). İstanbul, Turkey: Ayrıntı.

Gümüş, A. (2006). *Şiddet Türleri. Toplumsal Bir Sorun Olarak Şiddet Sempozyumu*. Ankara, Turkey: Eğitim-Sen.

Jung, G. C. (2011). *Dört Arketip* (İ. Kırımlı, Trans.). İstanbul, Turkey: Sayfa.

Marvin, G. (1989). İspanyol Boğa Güreşinde Şeref, Haysiyet ve Şiddet Sorunu. D. Riches (Ed.), Antropolojik Açıdan Şiddet (D. Hattatoğlu, Trans.). İstanbul, Turkey: Ayrıntı.

Onaran, A. Ş. (1995). *Türk Sineması II*. İstanbul, Turkey: Kitle.

Özbay, C. (2013). Türkiye'de Hegemonik Erkekliği Aramak. In C. Özge Özmen (Ed.), Toplumsal Cinsiyet (p. 63). İstanbul, Turkey: Doğu Batı.

Özgüç, A. (1990). *Türk Sinemasında İlkler*. İstanbul, Turkey: Yılmaz.

Pepper, D. (1996). *Modern Environmentalism: An Introduction*. London, UK: Routledge.

Pişkin, G. (2011). *Hızlı ve Dengesiz Değişime Tepki Olarak Sinemada Şiddet: Türkiye Örneği: 1980-2006*. ICANAS Kongresi Bildiri Kitabı.

Riches, D. (1989). Şiddetin Anlamı (D. Hattatoğlu, Trans.). In D. Riches (Ed.), Antropolojik Açıdan Şiddet. İstanbul, Turkey: Ayrıntı.

Rougier, C. E. (1989). 'Le Mal Court': Başsız Bir Toplumda Görünen ve Görünmeyen Şiddet: Kamerun'daki Mkakolar (D. Hattatoğlu, Trans.). In D. Riches (Ed.), Antropolojik Açıdan Şiddet. İstanbul, Turkey: Ayrıntı.

Solmuş, T. (2012). *Sinemada Psikoloji: Anormal Davranışlar*. İstanbul, Turkey: Doruk.

Spierenburg, P. (2010). *Cinayetin Tarihi: Ortaçağ'dan Günümüze Avrupa'da Bireysel Şiddet* (Y. Yavuz, Trans.). İstanbul, Turkey: İletişim.

Süalp, A. T. Z. (2009). Yabanıl, Dışarlıklı ve Lümpen "Hiçlik" Kutsamaları Seyrelmiş Toplumsallık ve Yükselen Faşizan Hallerin "Post"lar Zamanı. In D. Derman, (Ed.), Türk Film Araştırmalarında Yeni Yönelimler 8: Sinema ve Politika. İstanbul, Turkey: Bağlam.

Uluyağcı, C. (2001). Sinemada Erkek İmgesi: Farklı Sinemalarda Aynı Bakış. *Kurgu Dergisi*, (18), 29-39.

Ünsal, A. (1996). Genişletilmiş Bir Şiddet Tipolojisi. In Ö. Solok (Ed.), Şiddet. Cogito (pp. 6-7). İstanbul, Turkey: Yapı Kredi.

Warren, K. (1994). *Ecological Feminism*. London, UK: Routledge.

Wolfgang, M., & Ferracuti, F. (2010). *The Subculture of Violence*. Taylor & Francis E-Library.

Wood, J. C. (2004). *Violance and Crime in Nineteenth-Century England*. Taylor & Francis E-Library. doi:10.4324/9780203391181

Yaşartürk, G. (2012). Domestic Space and Violence in Turkish Cinema: My Violence is Because of My Love. *Fe Dergi*, *4*(1), 14–27. doi:10.1501/Fe0001_0000000060

ADDITIONAL READING

Arendt, H. (1997). *Şiddet Üzerine* (B. Peker, Trans.). İstanbul: İletişim.

Atayman, V. (2004). *Şiddetin Mitolojisi*. İstanbul: Donkişot.

Erkanı, E. (2013). Sinemasal Şiddet. *Sanat ve Tasarım Dergisi*, *1*(4), 15–21.

Fromm, E. (1990). *Sevginin ve Şiddetin Kaynağı* (Y. Salman & N. İçten, Trans.). İstanbul: Payel.

Fromm, E. (2011). *İnsandaki Yıkıcılığın Kökenleri 1* (Ş. Alpagut, Trans.). İstanbul: Payel.

Grant, K. B. (2011). *Shadows of Doubt: Negotiations of Masculinity in American Genre Films*. Detroit: Wayne State University.

Güçhan, G. (1992). *Toplumsal Değişme ve Türk Sineması*. Ankara: İmge.

Heidensohn, F., & Silvestri, M. (1994). Gender and Crime. (Edit.: M. Maguire; R. Morgan; R. Reiner). The Oxford Hanbook of Criminology. Oxford: Oxford University.

Lorenz, K. (2005). *On Aggression* (M. K. Wilson, Trans.). Taylor & Francis E-Library.

Mead, M. (1975). *Male and Female*. New York: William Marrow.

Oakley, Ann (1985). *Sex, Gender and Society*. Hants: Gower.

Oktan, A. (2008). Türk Sinemasında Hegemonik Erkeklikten Erkeklik Krizine: Yazı-Tura ve Erkeklik Bunalımının Sınırları. *Selçuk İletişim Dergisi, 5*(2), 152–166.

Segal, L. (1992). *Ağır Çekim: Değişen Erkeklikler Değişen Erkekler* (V. Ersoy, Trans.). İstanbul: Ayrıntı.

Wiener, J. M. (2004). *Men of Blood*. New York: Cambridge University. doi:10.1017/CBO9780511511547

Yücel, V. (2014). *Kahramanın Yolculuğu: Mitik Erkeklik ve Suç Draması*. İstanbul: Bilgi Üniversitesi.

Yüksel, E. (2013). *2000'ler Türkiye Sinemasında Erkeklik Krizi ve Erkek Kimliğinin İnşası. Yayınlanmamış Doktora Tezi*. Ankara: Ankara Üniversitesi Sosyal Bilimler Enstitüsü.

KEY TERMS AND DEFINITIONS

Gender: Socially constructed definition of women and men. Gender is determined by the conception of tasks, functions and roles attributed to women and men in society and in public and private life.

Honor: The quality of knowing and doing what is morally right. A man's honor is generally his wife, mother or daughter's chastity or her reputation for being chaste.

Masculinity: Set of attributes, behaviors, and roles associated with boys and men.

Patriarchy: Social system in which men hold primary power and predominate in roles of political leadership, moral authority, social privilege and control of property.

Revenge: Form of justice enacted in the absence or defiance of the norms of formal law and jurisprudence. Inflict hurt or harm on someone for an injury or wrong done to oneself.

Sexuality: Identification of individuals in relation to their biological sex.

Violence: The intentional use of physical force or power, threatened or actual, against oneself, another person, or against a group or community, that either results in or has a high likelihood of resulting in injury, death, psychological harm, maldevelopment or deprivation.

Chapter 10

Rehabilitating Hegemonic Masculinity With the Bodies of Aging Action Heroes

Kelvin Ke
Shelton College International, Singapore

ABSTRACT

The aging action hero has become an important figure in post-millennial action cinema. Its significance can be seen in how aging heroes can be seen in such franchises like The Expendables (2009 – 2013), Taken (2008 – 2014), The Fast and the Furious (2001 – 2017), Mission Impossible (1995 – 2018), and James Bond (2006 – 2015). In the following chapter, it is argued that the aging action hero and the aging male body is significant because they provide an opportunity to rehabilitate the tropes of hegemonic masculinity and the indestructible male body by emphasizing the benefits of the aging male body and where male toxicity is replaced by wisdom and maturity; egocentricity is replaced by allocentrism. As a result, the presence of the aging hero shows the dynamism of action cinema in offering different and alternative visions of heroism and heroes.

BACKGROUND

The aging hero has become an important figure in post-millennial action films (Boyle & Brayton, 2012). This is significant because the idea of heroic masculinity tends to be associated with an image of young or matured men as its personification and not with aging or middle-aged men (Gates, 2010). If nothing else, the stories of Hercules and Achilles suggest that youthfulness, virility and physical prowess

DOI: 10.4018/978-1-7998-0128-3.ch010

all play a role in shaping our ideas about heroic masculinity. Therefore, it can be jarring to see middle-aged or greying actors continuing to play the role of a virile and vigorous action hero. But then again, it should not come as a surprise because (a) action films tend to generate a lot of money at the box office, and (b) men generally have a longer time span as leading men (Terry, Butler & Armond, 2011, p. 145). But more importantly, so long as the actor continues to be bankable at the box office, their positions as action heroes remain secure. But put aside the idea that the studio executives and Hollywood filmmakers are a capricious bunch of people who are only interested in profit and money, it may occur to the viewer that under the right and appropriate conditions, that casting older actors and allowing them to explore the issue of ageing can ameliorate some of the negative tendencies of action cinema; particularly the toxic representation of maleness and masculinity of action heroes. That is because the heroic figure "requires us to recognize, for example, that the hero is inherently an overcoded image: he bears meanings about justice, morality, and law, and about being a man, in the same layered iconography" (Sparks, 1996, p. 354).

So while it is an oft-repeated claim that Hollywood is a young person's game (Jermyn, 2012), the reception and box office records of big-budget action franchises such as *The Expendables* (2009 – 2013), *Taken* (2008 – 2014), *The Fast and The Furious* (2001 – 2017), *Mission Impossible* (1995 – 2018) and Daniel Craig's *James Bond* (2006 – 2015) strongly suggest that audiences are not only attracted to action films, but that they do not mind that men of a certain age continue to play action heroes. But while some may conclude that the reason older male actors continue to be cast in blockbuster films is because of sexism and ageism (Erigha, 2015), such a perspective may overlook the benefits of such a phenomenon. While gender inequality does exist in Hollywood and it is an important issue, it is perhaps timely to pull back and adopt a more conciliatory tone in looking at the positive aspects of the aging action hero and how aging engender certain positives changes in the genre.

But what are these changes? Firstly, the issue of age gives filmmakers and actors, if they so choose to embrace it, an opportunity to critically examine the myths of the action hero. Second, it allows the older actor to re-examine some of the assumptions of his younger action persona. Third, it gives the viewer an opportunity to watch and experience the development of both the actor and his action persona as they age on screen. While wider cultural pressures might be the cause of such changes, the reality is that the leading men of Hollywood like Tom Cruise, Vin Diesel, Sylvester Stallone, Liam Neeson, and Daniel Craig are also growing older in real life. And while some actors are not able to maintain their relevance and currency with audiences, it does not mean that age cannot be used in a productive way to advance the narrative of the male action hero (King, 2010).

Indeed, growing older does not have to be a death sentence for an actor if, and it is usually a big if, he is willing to not only acknowledge his age but to also allow his persona to be carried along with it and incorporate the benefits, and negatives, of aging. And if an aging actor can allow these things to happen, the gradual change in persona may allow for a deeper and richer understanding of the action hero archetype. But because Hollywood and popular culture tend to favour the idea of wanting their stars to be young and youthful looking, most actors tend to be careful of showing too much of their real age for fear of being seen as someone who is in decline or fading (Peberdy, 2011). Indeed, it should be clear that the action hero archetype and its emphasis on youthful maleness and masculinity are as much trapped by cultural factors as it is by industrial demands.

But the increased presence of the aging hero shows that film ales and actors are slowly realising that age does not have to be a career-stopper but it can be used to enhance both the image of themselves as aging actors and the image of action heroes as being necessarily the domain of younger actors. But while some might attribute the presence of the aging hero in post-millennial action cinema as part of a generic cycle, it is argued that it may be hard to see how filmmakers and actors going back to the kind of action heroes that the world had lived in the eighties and nineties.

However, it is because the eighties hardbody actors and action films were so popular that it continues to hold such outsized influence in thinking of maleness, masculinity and manhood that film and gender scholars are generally critical of the genre (Tasker, 1993). Indeed, in the context of action cinema, film and gender scholars have used the lens of hegemonic masculinity to examine the representation of men and masculinity in the genre (Messner, 2007). And one of the main criticisms against the genre is that action films and action heroes engender and promote a type of maleness and masculinity that is hegemonic and toxic (Boulware, 2016).

HEGEMONIC MASCULINITY AND ACTION HEROES

Hegemonic masculinity can be defined as a practice that legitimizes men's dominant position in society and justifies the subordination of women, and other marginalized ways of being a man (Connell, 2005, p. 77). This behaviour and way of being can be understood as comprising both "hegemony over women" and "hegemony over subordinate masculinities" (Demetrious, 2001, p. 341). The concept refers to the representation of a type of dominant masculinity that embodies normative behavioural ideals in a culture in a particular period (Connell & Messerschmidt, 2005). However, it is suggested that "the crucial difference between hegemonic masculinity and other masculinities is not the control of women, but the control of men and the representation of this as "universal social advancement," to paraphrase Gramsci." (Donaldson, 1993, p. 655).

In the context of cinema, the Hardbody action hero archetype represents such a version of this type of masculinity on the big screen. The archetype is usually an authoritative figure (i.e. a police officer, soldier or secret agent) that is not bounded by inconvenient rules that obstructs his pursuit of criminals and/or justice. And as a sign of his dominance and independence, he does not easily relinquish his authority to other men (i.e. to his supervisor, working partners and especially his enemies), nor does he easily enter into a mutually respectful relationship (i.e. romance or marriage), or is someone who is generally sensitive or concerned with the well-being of others. Furthermore, the Hardbody hero, having emerged during the eighties under President Ronald Reagan, the archetype is associated with a sense of being representative of the political and ideological climate of that era — particularly in terms of mythologizing American heroism and maleness through cinema.

The Hardbody hero with his hardened and indestructible male body is thus a cinematic representation to project an image of male strength, power, and dominance in films. But while film and gender scholars have pointed out the toxic and antisocial aspects of the action archetype and genre (Kareithi, 2014, p. 27), it is argued in this article that it is perhaps more prudent to watch the changes and developments that have taken place over the past thirty years to appreciate the growth, maturity, and indeed, the rehabilitation of some of the toxic and antisocial aspects of the action hero and action film.

To that end, the following article is a textual analysis that examines the development of the action hero over the past thirty years, particular in terms of seeing how the archetype and genre have changed with the ever-increasing presence of the aging action hero at the turn of the twenty-first century. Indeed, it is contended that the figure of the aging action hero does not only ameliorate the toxic and antisocial traits and behaviours of the action hero archetype but it also replaces them with the virtues of temperance, prudence, and allocentrism. The following argues for the significance of the aging action hero in rehabilitating the negative and toxic qualities of masculinity.

THE HARDBODY FILM GENRE

The Hardbody film is a genre that does not hide its pleasure or relish in producing cinematic violence for the screen. And the hard-bodied hero is the conduit in which such violence is conducted upon and conducted through the male body. To be sure, the hardbody film genre can be defined as a group of films that consists of those (usually very violent) Hollywood action films made chiefly between the eighties and early nineties that feature a central male hero as the lone protagonist charged with "saving the day." The genre is so named precisely because of its tendency to fetishize the display and visualization of the "actor's hard and sculpted muscularity and/or its athletic skills and physical prowess" (Ayers, 2008, p. 42). Susan Jeffords suggested that the hard body hero "stand not only for a type of national character — heroic, aggressive, and determined — but for the nation itself." (Jeffords, 1994, p. 25). And because the genre gained popularity in America under President Ronald Reagan, the hardness, indestructibility and self-righteousness of the hard bodied hero represent - to a certain extent – a renewed swagger and confidence of a national character. Thus the muscular and violent hard bodied hero can be seen as a kind of surrogate and champion of national desires.

While race plays an important role in shaping the hardbody archetype and it is hard not to agree with the view that there is a problem with a narrative that needs a white heterosexual male to save the world (Cammarota, 2011), the discussion of race is outside the scope of this article. But that does not mean that it is not recognised that Hollywood action cinema usually focused on white actors who, for the most part, are cast as the leading men in hardbody films. Whilst not strictly in the tradition of the blue-eyed, blond hair variant, the actors that have come to be closely associated with the genre tend to be European in descent or American in nationality. So while it is acknowledged that race and nationality play important roles in shaping the construction of a cinematic action hero, it is also argued that examining the development of both the archetype and genre outside of race can also prove productive and insightful.

Indeed, it is contended that action heroes can be a translatable construct. By adopting such a perspective, it helps to shift the focus from seeing the hardbody action hero as a symbol of American or Western construction to seeing how the construct can be inhabited by different actors of different races. Examples would be Jackie Chan or Denzel Washington. As race and nationality are such emotive and contentious issues, they will require a different and more expansive platform that can be afforded in this article. Thus the following will only focus on the qualities and changes in the hardbody archetype as such. However, future research may revisit these issues in relation to action cinema. So having left aside the issue of race, we can focus on a set of traits and behaviours that underpin the hardbody hero. And what are left are the motifs of (a) the indestructible body, (b) a volatile and violent temperament, and (c) an egocentric view of the world in relation to the self.

The theme of the indestructible body has to be the most important trope in the hardbody action genre. Indeed, actors playing hard bodied have to be physically fit, powerful and imposing. Therefore it is not surprising to see why actors like Sylvester Stallone, Chuck Norris, Arnold Schwarzenegger, Steven Seagal, Dolph Lundgren and Jean Claude Van Damme have come to represent the archetypal hard bodied hero. But at the same time, the cinematic personas of hardbody actors are also highly dependent upon their image and ability to fight in real life (e.g. Steven Seagal is an Aikido grand master; Chuck Norris is a karate champion, and even Arnold Schwarzenegger was a world champion in bodybuilding). But while there is a difference between fighting in real life and fighting on the screen, it is clear that the actors deliberately fuse reality with fiction. By doing so, it makes it easier for the viewer to suspend their disbelief when they are watching the actors fight and kill in the films. Hence, people enjoy watching Schwarzenegger play the role of an indestructible cyborg in James Cameron's *The Terminator* (1984) or as an unrelenting soldier who single-handedly defeats a group of space aliens in John McTiernan's *Predator* (1987).

Indeed, Lisa Purse argued that it is better to see that"[action] body is constructed as spectacle" (Purse, 2011, p. 39). And as such, it is clear that the physical size of the actor is an important element in conveying ideas of male power and strength. Indeed, the size of the hardbody is often a mark of superiority in the genre. But as important as the muscled body may be to the archetype, it is not enough to just have a muscular and imposing body. Indeed, it is the ability and capacity to do violence to others that distinguish the hard bodied hero from everyone else. Pick one hardbody action film from the eighties that starred Schwarzenegger, Stallone, or even Van Damme, and one would definitely find a scene where the actors would torture or kill a bad guy without feeling much remorse for their deaths. Corollary to that, the hero is also imbued with a "cheat code" that provides all sort of immunity from harm. An extreme example is the action persona adopted by Steven Seagal; a persona in which hard-core fans would know that the actor is infamous for never softening his image as an indestructible hero or allowing himself to be visibly bullied or hurt by other men.

But this idea of an immortal and invincible is not something that is particularly unique about the genre. Indeed, the idea of a seemingly all-powerful and indestructible hero can be traced all the way back to any of the classical mythology and legends of Western civilization such as Hercules or Zeus. Much like comic book heroes or mythological Gods, the hardbody action hero possesses not only incredible strength and power but also possesses an indestructible body. But unlike superheroes that are marked by an innate desire to do good, the hardbody hero lacks compassion or empathy in understanding the consequences of their violent behaviour. Indeed, the egocentrism of the hardbody action hero is precisely why critics have pointed out that the archetype projects not only a misrepresentation of maleness and masculinity but that the entire genre celebrates such a configuration over other forms of maleness and masculinities. As a result, film and gender scholars see the hardbody hero is a symbol and figure of a type of maleness and masculinity that is hegemonic and toxic. Hence, the bad reputation of action cinema.

But the Hardbody action hero is not a monolithic ideal (Ayers, 2008). There are different shades to the archetype. Drew Ayers differentiates the genre into three sub-cycles. (60) They are; (1) Developing Hardbody, (2) Repressed Hardbody, (3) Fully-Formed Hardbody. But the Hardbody can be further broken down into the following types: (1) The Technical Body (personified by the bodies of martial artists like Steven Seagal, Jean Claude Van Damme, Dolph Lundgren and Chuck Norris, and (2) The Resilient Body (personified by Bruce Willis, Arnold Schwarzenegger and Sylvester Stallone). But the Hardbody genre can add one more sub-cycle to its list and that is the aging hardbody hero. But the aging hardbody hero can be divided into two other subgenres: (i) the matured hardbody, and (ii) the greying hardbody.

The matured hardbody is similar to the fully-formed hardbody except that the former places more emphasis on cultivating and maintaining social and romantic relationships in their lives. And because their actions have an impact on the well-being of their family and friends, the motivations that drive them are not based on their physicality or lethality but on how they are able to prevent the bad guys from doing harm to others without much collateral damage to the world. Hence, their heroism comes from believing in a higher purpose than simply trying to show off their bodies, skills, or ability to kill. But rather their heroism stems from the fact that they are responsible for the well-being of others and their loved ones, and that they themselves do not necessarily believe in killing for the sake of it but in the service of either the community or society. But most of all, their heroism stems from the fact that they want to prevent harm from happening to their loved ones.

The concept of arête and excellence come into play in thinking about the conception and configuration of the cinematic action hero. Arête refers to Greek ideas about the physical and moral excellence of a person. And the process of growing up and growing older is the process in which one reaches or strides towards arête. Now, it may be that action heroes do not perform any other functions other than entertainment. But it does not mean that it has to be seen in such a manner. After all, millions if not billions of people watch action films. And if action films and heroes are simply crude entertainment, then the work and concern of film and gender scholars on the negative effects of action cinema on maleness and masculinity would not have engendered so much traction and discourse. So how might the figure of the aging action hero add to the conversation?

THE AGING ACTION HERO

In Adam McKay's buddy cop comedy *The Other Guys* (2010), the tropes of action cinema are taken to an absurd level by exposing the central conceits of action heroes. And that is the idea that that action heroes are indestructible and infallible; which in turn allows them to be as obnoxious and dismissive of other people; both men and women. In an extremely funny but surreal rooftop scene, two stereotypical police officers played by Dwayne Johnson and Samuel L. Jackson chases after a gang of robbers to the rooftop of a tall building. Believing in their invincibility and intoxicated by their masculinity, the two characters decide to continue their pursuit of the robbers by jumping off the rooftop without any apparent safety harnesses or parachutes with the implication being that they are indestructible hard bodies.

But as they dramatically jumped off the building in slow motion, along with a loud heavy metal soundtrack playing in the background with the lyrics "there goes my hero, watch him as he goes", hope is offered to the viewer that the two characters may actually survive the fall. But just as they are about to land, the soundtrack abruptly cuts off as we watch our two heroes die all because of their hubris and arrogance. As funny as the scene may be, it also exposes an underlying conceit in the action hero genre and that is the idea that action heroes are indestructible and immortal characters. Instead, the scene points out that the idea of a cinematic action hero is not necessarily representative of real characters or people.

Rather, the idea of an action hero is merely the manifestation of a cinematic imaginary about what a hero should be and look like. Since action heroes are cinematic imaginaries, it stands to reason that it can be reconfigured within boundaries of heroism. From being seen as merely an infantile and egocentric figure, the incorporation of aging allows the hardbody hero to mature and develop other areas of his character. At the same time, mortality has allowed the hero to explore his bodily vulnerability as a person. But importantly, it has allowed him to understand the importance of friendships and relationships.

Take for instance Denzel Washington's *Equalizer* (2014 - 2018) films or Liam Neeson's *Taken* films (2008 - 2014). Whilst the two series acknowledge the lack of power and mobility of their actors, they also take the trouble to emphasise their technical, mental, and physical acuity and efficiency. This is manifested by the characters' knowledge and expertise in combat, weapons, explosives and counter-terrorism. The perceived decline of their aging bodies is thus replaced with the emphasis on acquired skills and experience. But despite Rebecca Measey's argument that patriarchal control is reinforced in films where older male stars still play the leading man, the films make clear the price that heroes have to pay for their status. Instead of reaping the rewards of their heroism with fame and glory, the lives of aging action hero are either filled with a sense of loneliness - particularly in terms of romantic relationships - or consumed by the demands of having to save the world on a regular basis. In other words, their work has become their life. Furthermore, the accomplishments and skills of the aging action hero are not recognised by anyone except by a select group of colleagues and friends.

The ostentatiousness of the action hero in the eighties has been replaced by anonymity for the post-millennial aging action hero. But what is important in this reconfiguration of the post-millennial action hero is that ideas about heroism have shifted away from being just about the male body to become about the cultivation and maturity of his character. No longer is heroism just about physical strength. Indeed, heroism is about sacrificing personal ambitions in the service for the greater good. And prizing qualities such as tenacity, determination and resilience over vanity and personal glory.

Daniel Craig's run as James Bond is another example of how aging is explored and developed in action cinema by emphasizing tenacity and resilience (Dodds, 2014). Despite his constant injuries and diminishing physical abilities, the character nonetheless chose to continue his work not because of a desire to be a hero but because of an innate sense of loyalty and duty to his country. Even when Bond's relevance and effectiveness as an action hero are questioned in both Sam Mendes' *Skyfall* (2012) and *Spectre* (2015) because of his age, the superspy rose to the challenge in both cases by using his knowledge and experience to defeat his enemies. But these qualities of duty, tenacity and resilience are not only found in Daniel Craig's James Bond. Rather, they are also fundamental to the reconfiguration of the post-millennial aging action hero.

These defining traits of the post-millennial hero — and who else could be more representative than the granddaddy of super spies — are not only about the male body (its toughness and technicality) but they are also about innate qualities of self-sacrifice, mental resilience and tenacity. As a result, the aging of Daniel Craig's Bond reconfigures the decline and decay themes of aging and replaced them with an emphasis on experience and wisdom of a stable, dependent and resolute old hand. This positive attitude towards aging action heroes is best summed up in a scene in *Skyfall* whereby M (played by Judi Dench) recites a passage from Lord Tennyson's *Ulysses*

We are not now that strength which in old days
Moved earth and heaven; that which we are, we are;
One equal temper of heroic hearts,
Made weak by time and fate, but strong in will
To strife, to seek, to find, and not to yield

But not everyone is convinced that aging helps in maturing the action hero for the better. Instead Rebecca Measey argued that "[a]t a time when aging beyond the middle years is said to challenge male power and weaken patriarchal control, it is the very toughness of the hard body, rather than any moral, cultural or financial power that has allowed the aging male to remain heroic and hegemonic." (Measey, 2015,

p. 519). So while the ravages of time (e.g. crow's feet, wrinkled skin and baldness) may show on the face and body, the essential core power and toughness of the action body remains untouched by time. Thus the onset of aging does not negate the so-called toughness of the male body — particularly in terms of the actor's strength and power. Commenting on the *Die Hard* series (1988 - 2013), Measey argued that "the aging action hero maintains his assertive, authoritative and omnipresent position in Hollywood based on his continued physical dominance" (Measey, 2015, p. 519)

This view is supported by Lisa-Nike Bühring who argued that the continuing reproduction of aging actions stars as fit and capable "[s]upport a view of aging and masculinity which is deeply rooted in the western socio-cultural and political system of neoliberalism and which can be summarized as follows: as long as one is productive one is valuable to society." (Bühring, 2017, p. 56). But it can also be argued that such "geri-action" films perpetuate the idea that heterosexual males - albeit older and greyer ones - continue to be highly desired forms of maleness and masculinity. So while geri-action films are cognizant of the physical decline of the actor as well as his waning star power, they nonetheless showcase the body of the aging action star - albeit in a reluctant manner (even by veiling it). But the continuing presence of the greying action hero does not necessarily mean that they are the same character as when they were younger. Instead, it is clear that the geri-action films mark a narrative shift from "a lone hero to intergenerational, international star collectives." (Donnar, 2016).

Indeed, the heterosexual aging male hero has to share his duties, however reluctantly, with other, usually younger heterosexual male characters in their films. But while these younger versions exhibit the same kind of hubris and arrogance that they themselves were guilty of displaying in their youth, it is significant to note that the older characters recognize both the limitation and damage of such qualities in their lives. And these regrets or introspection are the results of years of living a life of violence and aggression. Hence, they become mentors or older brothers to younger versions of themselves as a result of growing older and wiser over the years.

RE-CONFIGURING ACTION HEROES INTO MATURE BODIES

It is important to remember that genres can shift and change over time (Neale, 2005). They are not necessarily fixed and stable but are malleable and dynamic. Likewise, the same goes for the action film and action hero. So while film genres go through different cycles and iterations over different periods of time, it is also possible to see that the archetypes that can found in them also adapt and change according to the socio-historical environment of the times. Indeed, it is possible to claim that the hard-bodied heroes of the eighties and early nineties are anachronisms of a time past long ago. And that the concept of the hard-bodied hero has to change and adapt to the times too. Hence, the development of the aging action hero which actually already started in the eighties when the hardbody genre was reaching its apotheosis in cinema.

Take the *Lethal Weapon* film series (1987 - 1998) as an example. Roger Murtaugh (played by Danny Glover), a soon to be retired police officer, finds out that he has to work with a new partner in Martin Riggs (played by Mel Gibson) — an ex-Marine harbours suicidal thoughts after the death of his beloved wife. Despite having different personalities and lifestyles, the two of them nonetheless developed a friendship that only grew stronger over the course of the film series. While the physical outlook of Martin Riggs does not necessarily fit alongside the stereotypical hard bodied action heroes, the character nonetheless exhibits two characteristics that are commonly found in the hardbody archetype. The first is the resilience and endurance motif of the male body. And the second is the technical and tactical expertise of the character. Indeed, Riggs is repeatedly subjected to all forms of beatings and torture throughout the films. But he usually triumphs not just because his body is able to sustain and endure the damage done to his body, but that he is also highly skilled with weapons, martial arts, and other related skill sets.

Indeed, the character's hardiness is shown in a scene in the third *Lethal Weapon* film when he enthusiastically shows off his battle scars to Cole (played by Rene Russo). Whilst the scene plays off as a quirky romantic scene between two competitive characters, it also showed that Riggs not only can take the damage but that he is also proud of having the scars as evidence of his sacrifice for the greater good. But perhaps the scene that best represents the tough and hard body theme is the electroshock torture scene in the first film. Riggs' endurance is so impressive that it prompted a henchman to remark that "nobody can take that". But what is significant about Riggs is not the existence of the hard body motif but the act of pairing it with the idea of the hard-bodied hero forming and developing friendships and relationships. Indeed, it is Riggs' friendship with Murtaugh - and not his indestructibility or machismo - that changed Riggs from being a blunt instrument to become an emotionally developed and mature character. Rather than weakening the resolve of the hard bodied hero, the series showed that friendships and relationships not only give significance to the actions and deeds of the hero but that they have become the impetus that drives the hero in his mission to serve and protect both the world and his loved ones. Indeed, Riggs' transformation as a relatively isolated and suicidal person at the beginning of the franchise to become a husband and father to his wife and child showed that ideas about the hard bodied action hero, even in the eighties and nineties, have started to realise the positive effects of aging on the development of the genre.

While *Lethal Weapon*'s themes of family and friends are not necessarily unique in of themselves, they are unique within the tradition and conventions of the action film genre. By orienting attention onto the importance of friends and family, the stakes become higher for the hero because his success or failure in saving the world has an immediate and direct impact upon the safety and well-being of his loved ones. Indeed, the legacy of *Lethal Weapon* cannot be underestimated because its influence can be found even in modern-day action films. Take Dominic Toretto (played by Vin Diesel) in *The Fast and Furious* series. He starts out as a character who lives "a quarter mile at a time" to become a character who understands that "the most important thing in life will always be the people is in this room right here, right now" are his friends who have become part of his extended family. His identity as an action hero has shifted from playing the role of a rebellious loner to become head and paterfamilias of a close-knit group of friends and family.

Rather like Bryan Mills (played by Liam Neeson) in the *Taken* films, the aging action hero - in the course of saving his wife and daughter - is forced to take down a gang of human traffickers. The impetus of his heroism stems not merely from a vague sense of serving justice but comes from a deep and emotional core of protecting his loved ones. And like Barney Ross (played by Sylvester Stallone) in *The Expendables* films, the things that are precious to the aging action hero is not only his sense of good and justice but his relationships, indeed his love, for his family and friends: qualities that not only expand the repertoire of action heroes but also humanizes the action hero archetype. Indeed, it is important to understand that having family and friends does not necessarily mean that aging heroes are weakened or softened by their presence in their lives. Instead, their motivations become more than just trying to do the right thing or saving the world for the sake of it. Rather it is about protecting their friends and loved ones from harm. But that does not mean that the hard-bodied action hero is necessarily weak or incapable of violence and aggression.

Take Keanu Reeves' *John Wick* (2014 - 2019) films as an example. In the series, Reeves plays a retired assassin who only wants to retire in peace. But he is repeatedly forced to return to a world super assassins and killers. But despite his combat skills and indestructible body, Wick is humanized as a character and action hero not because he is motivated by a desire to rid the world of bad guys. But that he is simply taking revenge for his loved ones (which includes the death of his puppy). While some might argue that love and marriage may have "feminized" the character, it is argued that they are in fact key motivators. Firstly, it was the prospect of having a normal marriage and life outside the criminal world that drove Wick to strike a bargain with his employer that he will be free to leave the organisation in exchange of one last hit job. Secondly, the death of his dog destroyed all hopes of a normal life. Thus Wick is driven to avenge not only his loss but to destroy the external forces that threaten his hopes of a normal life. While violent in of itself, Wick's actions are relatable because they are motivated by loss, suffering and grief. Another example is Denzel Washington's character in Antoine Fuqua's *The Equalizer* (2014). The character is an ex-black ops agent who lives a quiet life working in a home repair despot whilst mourning the death of his wife. But he is forced to take down a Russian mob after they threatened and hurt his friends. Or consider Liam Neeson's character in Pierre Morel's *Taken* (2008) he is forced to take down a human trafficking syndicate after his daughter was kidnapped by them. In all the above cases, the trigger was not to save the world or to be a hero. Rather, their involvement is due to external forces acting upon them to do something. And in all of those cases, they kill to protect someone close or dear to them. And not because of some vague notion of saving the world or to show others that they want to dominate or oppress them. Instead, all of them seek a quiet life after living a life of violence during their younger days.

This transition from being a hard-bodied hero to becoming an aging hero can also be clearly seen in the *Fast and Furious* film series. While many might not remember that Vin Diesel's character started off as an antagonist at the beginning of the series, most would not deny that his character has become a central figure in the series. Indeed, his character started off as a young and reckless racer/robber in the first film but slowly turns into a mature and responsible character over the course of the series. At the beginning of the series, the character embodies the heroic ideal of the rebel who lives by his own code. But by the end of the series, the character is not only married but bears the responsibility of being a father to a young child. Indeed, in the *Mission Impossible* film series, the evolution of Ethan Hunt (played by Tom Cruise) is another example of how the impetuous nature of youth, including violence and aggression, is tempered and moderated by the passing of time. While Ethan Hunt started out as a young man who is unburdened by relationships or personal attachments, his marriage and friendships in his later years give weight and significance to his actions. Hence, in Christopher McQuarrie's *Mission: Impossible - Fallout* (2018), Ethan Hunt's mission to defuse a nuclear bomb is made more significant precisely because the lives of his loved ones and friends are at stake in the film. This is significant because the spectacle of the body is deemphasised insofar as heroism is located within the individual. And the actions of the aging hero become more than simply the actions of someone who wants to dominate or subjugate others. Instead, the aging hero is pressed into service to save, rescue, and preserve the lives of others. By doing so, the configuration and actions of aging action heroes and their aging bodies repudiate not only the wanton violence of the hard body archetype in the eighties, but it also rehabilitates the tropes of hegemonic masculinity and the indestructible male body in post-millennial action cinema.

FUTURE RESEARCH AND DIRECTION

The issue and development of the aging action hero is a topic that has room to incorporate different perspectives and intersections. While the focus in this article is to understand how the aging action hero rehabilitates some of the hegemonic and toxic representations of maleness and masculinity, it is hoped that future research can incorporate the issue of race, nationality, ethnicity, and even different conceptions of what constitute heroic masculinity in different cultures and contexts. Additionally, it may prove useful to intersect the traditions of non-western cinemas with Hollywood and Western ideas of heroism. Indeed, more can be done to understand and unpack the potential in seeing the action hero not as symbols of hegemonic or toxic masculinity but as a cinematic construction that may engender more productive and constructive ways of reproducing masculinities on the big screen (Motley, 2004).

CONCLUSION

Although the figure of the aging action hero is increasingly the centre of attention in post-millennial action cinema, it should not be seen to be an isolated development in film history (Lennard, 2014). Rather, it is a development that has been going on since the eighties. Indeed, the hard-bodied hero and the aging hero are not separate entities but are entities that exist on the same continuum. But aging heroes do differ from their predecessors in significant ways. Firstly, they see the value of love and friendships in their lives. Secondly, they are people who have experienced loss in their lives and are now determined not to go through that again. Third, and as a result of the second, the aging action hero is cognizant of the realities of time and their aging bodies.

While some critics may argue that action cinema does not affirm the human condition (Bushman & Anderson, 2009), as the genre produces a kind of maleness and masculinity that is often violent and aggressive, it does not mean that its conception of what constitutes an action hero cannot or does not change over time. Indeed, it has been contended that a shift of emphasis has occurred regarding the traits and behaviours of action heroes. The career of Clint Eastwood and his efforts in playing with his action persona is perhaps the most useful in seeing that age is not a barrier to innovations or an obstacle in showing us different shades of what it means to be a cinematic hero. Perhaps one of the greatest feats that Eastwood has engendered in his career is to take the concept of being an action hero and turn it on its head by forcing his characters to deal with the consequences of living a violent life (Kupfer, 2008). Known for playing The Man with No Name in Sergio Leone's spaghetti westerns, Clint Eastwood's subversion is perhaps crystallised in his self-directed film *Unforgiven* (1992) whereby his character William Munny is made to confront his violent past and nature as an infamous gunslinger and killer. But instead of living the good and glorious life, or indeed, death, William Munny is shown living out a prosaic and anonymous life on the frontier.

But more importantly, Clint Eastwood's incorporation of age into his action persona provides a useful reference for using age as a way to create new and interesting stories and characters. Indeed, as Clint Eastwood grows older, his action characters do not so much use violence to solve problems but to understand that violence is often not the solution. Indeed, while the character of William Munny is compelled to avenge Ned's death in *Unforgiven*, the character of boxing trainer Frankie Dunn, in another Clint Eastwood directed film *Million Dollar Baby* (2004), is reluctant for Maggie, his student and surrogate daughter, to go into professional boxing because he knows the consequences of living a life of violence - albeit in professional boxing. Indeed, in both cases, Munny and Dunn suffer the consequences of living in a world that revolves around violence and aggression; the former bearing the wounds of being a cold-blooded murderer, the latter bearing the wounds of losing someone he loved. In both cases, Clint Eastwood showed that suffering and pain can only result from living in a world of violence.

The figure of the aging action hero is thus an exciting and critical configuration of both action heroes and action cinema (Saxton & Cole, 2013). That is because it allows filmmakers and actors to not only advance the static idea of the hardbody action hero. But it also allows them to incorporate age and maturity to rehabilitate the idea that that the archetype and genre are fixated with celebrating and promoting a type of masculinity that sees aggression, bullying and dominance as important signifiers of maleness and masculinity. Instead, it has been argued that the presence of the aging action hero provides an opportunity to see that age and growing old can engender maturity and wisdom in men. And that the heterosexual male hero is not necessarily fixed within a static model of maleness and masculinity. Rather, it is possible to see that the male action hero is as dynamic, malleable, and adaptable as any other archetypes and characters in cinema. And the development of the aging action heroes offers an opportunity to not only rehabilitate ideas of hegemonic masculinity but also offer new and different ideas of about the preferred type of maleness and masculinity in action cinema (Holt & Thompson, 2004).

REFERENCES

Ayers, D. (2008). Bodies, bullets, and bad guys: Elements of the hardbody film. *Film Criticism, 32*(3), 41–67.

Boulware, T. (2016). "Who Killed the World": Building a Feminist Utopia from the Ashes of Toxic Masculinity in Mad Max: Fury Road. *Mise-en-scène: The Journal of Film & Visual Narration, 1*(1).

Boyle, E., & Brayton, S. (2012). Ageing masculinities and "muscle work" in Hollywood action film: An analysis of The Expendables. *Men and Masculinities, 15*(5), 468–485. doi:10.1177/1097184X12454854

Bühring, L. N. (2017). Declining to Decline: Aged Tough Guys in 'The Expendables' and 'The Expendables 2'. *Journal of Extreme Anthropology, 1*(3), 41–60. doi:10.5617/jea.4528

Bushman, B. J., & Anderson, C. A. (2009). Comfortably numb: Desensitizing effects of violent media on helping others. *Psychological Science, 20*(3), 273–277. doi:10.1111/j.1467-9280.2009.02287.x PMID:19207695

Cammarota, J. (2011). Blindsided by the avatar: White saviors and allies out of Hollywood and in education. *Review of Education, Pedagogy & Cultural Studies, 33*(3), 242–259. doi:10.1080/10714413.2011.585287

Connell, R. W. (2005). *Masculinities.* Cambridge, UK: Polity.

Connell, R. W., & Messerschmidt, J. W. (2005). Hegemonic masculinity: Rethinking the concept. *Gender & Society, 19*(6), 829–859. doi:10.1177/0891243205278639

Demetriou, D. Z. (2001). Connell's concept of hegemonic masculinity: A critique. *Theory and Society, 30*(3), 337–361. doi:10.1023/A:1017596718715

Dodds, K. (2014). Shaking and stirring James Bond: Age, gender, and resilience in Skyfall (2012). *The Journal of Popular Film and Television, 42*(3), 116–130. doi:10.1080/01956051.2013.858026

Donaldson, M. (1993). What is hegemonic masculinity? *Theory and Society, 22*(5), 643–657. doi:10.1007/BF00993540

Donnar, G. (2016). Narratives of cultural and professional redundancy: Ageing action stardom and the 'geri-action' film. *Communication, Politics & Culture, 49*(1), 1.

Erigha, M. (2015). Race, Gender, Hollywood: Representation in Cultural Production and Digital Media's Potential for Change. *Sociology Compass, 9*(1), 78–89. doi:10.1111oc4.12237

Feasey, R. (2015). Mature masculinity and the ageing action hero. *Groniek, 44*(190).

Funnell, L. (2011). "I know where you keep your gun": Daniel Craig as the Bond–Bond girl hybrid in Casino Royale. *Journal of Popular Culture, 44*(3), 455–472. doi:10.1111/j.1540-5931.2011.00843.x

Gates, P. (2010). Acting his age? The resurrection of the 80s action heroes and their aging stars. *Quarterly Review of Film and Video, 27*(4), 276–289. doi:10.1080/10509200802371113

Holt, D. B., & Thompson, C. J. (2004). Man-of-action heroes: The pursuit of heroic masculinity in everyday consumption. *The Journal of Consumer Research, 31*(2), 425–440. doi:10.1086/422120

Jeffords, S. (1994). Hard bodies: Hollywood masculinity in the Reagan era. New Brunswick, NJ: Rutgers University Press.

Jermyn, D. (2012). 'Get a life, ladies. Your old one is not coming back': ageing, ageism and the lifespan of female celebrity. *Celebrity Studies, 3*(1), 1-12.

Kareithi, P. J. (2014). *Hegemonic masculinity in media contents.* A. Montiel (Ed.).

King, N. (2010). Old cops: Occupational aging in a film genre. In *Staging Age* (pp. 57–81). New York, NY: Palgrave Macmillan. doi:10.1057/9780230110052_4

Kupfer, J. H. (2008). The Seductive and Subversive Meta-Narrative of Unforgiven. *Journal of Film and Video, 60*(3/4), 103–114. doi:10.1353/jfv.0.0015

Lennard, D. (2014). Too old for this shit?: On ageing tough guys. In *Ageing, Popular Culture and Contemporary Feminism* (pp. 93–107). London, UK: Palgrave Macmillan. doi:10.1057/9781137376534_7

Messner, M. A. (2007). The masculinity of the governator: Muscle and compassion in American politics. *Gender & Society, 21*(4), 461–480. doi:10.1177/0891243207303166

Motley, C. (2004). "It's a Hell of a Thing to Kill a Man": Western Manhood in Clint Eastwood's Unforgiven. *Americana: The Journal of American Popular Culture, 3,* 14.

Neale, S. (2005). *Genre and Hollywood.* Routledge. doi:10.4324/9780203980781

Peberdy, D. (2011). Aging Men: Viagra, Retiring Boomers and Jack Nicholson. In *Masculinity and Film Performance* (pp. 146–168). London, UK: Palgrave Macmillan. doi:10.1057/9780230308701_6

Purse, L. (2011). *Contemporary action cinema.* Edinburgh, UK: Edinburgh University Press. doi:10.3366/edinburgh/9780748638178.001.0001

Saxton, B., & Cole, T. R. (2013). No country for old men: A search for masculinity in later life. *International Journal of Ageing and Later Life*, *7*(2), 97–116. doi:10.3384/ijal.1652-8670.1272a5

Sparks, R. (1996). Masculinity And Heroism In The Hollywood 'blockbuster' The Culture Industry and Contemporary Images of Crime and Law Enforcement. *British Journal of Criminology*, *36*(3), 348–360. doi:10.1093/oxfordjournals.bjc.a014099

Tasker, Y. (1993). Masculinity, the body, and the voice in contemporary action cinema. *Screening the male: Exploring masculinities in Hollywood cinema*, 230.

ADDITIONAL READING

Bordwell, D. (2006). *The way Hollywood tells it: Story and style in modern movies*. Univ of California Press.

Campbell, J. (2008). *The hero with a thousand faces* (Vol. 17). New World Library.

Campbell, J., & Moyers, B. (2011). *The power of myth*. Anchor.

Kolker, R. (2015). *Film, form, and culture*. Routledge. doi:10.4324/9781315728025

Moore, R. L., & Gillette, D. (1991). *King, warrior, magician, lover*. San Francisco: HarperCollins.

KEY TERMS AND DEFINITIONS

Archetype: It refers to a very typical example of a certain person or thing. In Jungian theory, it refers to a primitive mental image inherited from the earliest human ancestors, and supposed to be present in the collective unconscious. It can refer to a recurrent symbol or motif in literature, art, or mythology.

Genre: It refers to a classification system that categories films into groups which are usually categorized based on stylistic criteria, subject matter, themes, or even on the basis of actors or directors.

Hardbody Film: It is an action genre that was popular during the eighties and early nineties. It can be defined as a group of action films that usually feature a central male hero as the lone protagonist that has a tendency to fetishize the display and visualization of the actor's muscularity and deadly skills.

Hegemonic Masculinity: It refers to a practice that legitimizes the dominant position of a certain type of men in society and justifies the subordination of both men and women in accordance to a certain standard that may include sanctions against those who do not conform or adhere to said standards.

Heroic Masculinity: It refers to an ideology and a set of ideas regarding what constitutes a hero in a given society and culture. These include qualities or attributes that are regarded by cultures as characteristics of heroic men.

Persona: In Jungian theory, it refers to the mask or appearance one presents to the wider world.

Trope: It refers to a figurative or metaphorical use of a word or expression. In creative works, it is used to describe recurring literary and rhetorical devices, motifs and clichés.

White Savior Narrative: It refers to a cinematic trope that portrays the need for white characters to either rescue or assist non-white characters when they meet with problems.

Chapter 11
Gender Construction in Transmedial Narration:
Star Wars Transmedia and Fandom

Işıl Tombul
Independent Researcher, Turkey

ABSTRACT

Transmedia is a narrative that allows a message to meet with the user in different media. With media convergence, a story has become available in different media, and this has also led to the expansion of the market. Star Wars has an important transmedia and a wide fandom. Because the film is on the concept of power, the construction of power shows itself in this area with masculine symbolism. In the post-Disney period, the female characters are prominent, but the films protect the masculine narrative. The aim of this study is to examine the construction of gender in the transmedial narrative in Star Wars films together with the discussions in fandom. For this purpose, gender construction in the transmedial narrative are analyzed by case study.

INTRODUCTION

Transmedia storytelling is a narrative of the new digital era. With the technological revolution, transmedia story telling has emerged due to the obsolescence of the old media with the new media and the digitalism between the different media. The narratives now show multi-layered, variable, transitive, participatory features in accordance with the characteristics of the digital era. The transmedial narrative is now seen as a voluntary factor when it refers to the direction of the narrative.

DOI: 10.4018/978-1-7998-0128-3.ch011

The narrative is now moving on a ground where the variable, multiple, interactive, open-ended, consumer-generated. With the inclusion of the consumer, the issues that now appear as social inequality have begun to break. However, no matter how much the technology changes, the innovations that come to the social sphere can be used as an aid to the continuity and construction of the old values in the society, even though it is said that they change the society and provide more democratic and more egalitarian presentations. Because social values do not change as quickly as technology. The inequalities that exist in the field of society sometimes reconstructs themselves in this narrative. For this purpose, in this study, heroism and masculinity carried out in transmedial narrative through Star Wars will be examined.

The Star Wars film series created by George Lucas has a complex chronology. The story takes place in a distant galaxy. The film has broken records of revenue and has won Oscar in many branches. Lucas finished the screenplay for the Star Wars series in 1973, but the Hollywood producers asked him to start with the sixth series in the nine chapters. Then the film went down to six main parts. The fourth episode of this film was released on May 25, 1977 (NTV, 2018).

In 1999, the second trilogy began. Today, the third trilogy began in 2015 with the Force Awakens and continued with Last Jedi in 2017. When we look at Star Wars products, a character evolves from hero to villain. Star Wars is a cult piece that has been admiring the past generations since the first period. The film belongs to a particular fandom culture with an important fan base that has ceased to belong to a particular company. However, the film was criticized in terms of masculinity. In the film, masculinity which is built in intergalaxcies is built between the media today by tansmedia.

Transmedia Storytelling

Transmedia is primarily; used in commercials such as spin off, adaptations, merchandising, marketing, in the writings of Marsh Kinder and Mary Celeste Kearney. Kinder used this term to describe the relationship between children in the media market, movies, TVs, games and toys. The motivation behind this is linked to Hollywood's economic systems. In order to become a transcendent content system, the product has to rise suddenly, its success becomes a media event that dramatically accelerates the growth curve of the commercial success of the system. For instance, while toys are produced that allow audience to explore the false world of television or a cinematic upper system with imagination, they also teach children to be consumers to desire objects (Evans, 2011: 20-21).

Chenu et al. (2014) states that the term was produced in 2003 and that in 2006 H. Jenkins was widely accepted by writing articles. In a new media environment, Jenkins used the word transmedia to characterize both the emerging audience practices and the media industry strategies to better meet the expectations of this new kind of audience. At that time, the fictional universe of The Matrix was analyzed as a case study that allowed it to reflect these new cultural practices into action. According to Jenkins, what the Wachowski brothers had accomplished was to create a dense and complex story world that uses the power and aesthetics of the new network culture. They strategically distributed the media texts to the multimedia platforms so that the audience could reconstruct the entire narrative and understand what they had experienced in films, games and comics. This spread was made possible by the process of media convergence and the unification between media industries.

Transmedia storytelling technique, that especially with the Internet itself began to show more clearly, is possible to see beforehand. Even Mittell (2014: 253-254) says that the Bible scenes or narrative coverage like Frankenstein or Sherlock Holmes consider pictures that revive iconic 19th century characters that transcend any environment. With the development of technology over time, the proliferation of digital forms such as online video, blogs, computer games, DVDs, social networks and alternative reality games (ARG) has led to different transmedia techniques. One of the places where transmedia products show itself effectively is television. Evans (2011: 20-24), who has been working on this subject, gives an example of the Doctor Who series on the BBC since 1963. Doctor Who has survived to the present day by adapting to the changing media. After Dr. Who started in 1963; by-product texts, novel, BBC radio games etc. presented as new stories. This presents a non-audiovisual form of interaction that allows audiences to create their own stories. These by-products have expanded the Dr. Who world in a non-television form. In addition, the audience's attention was kept alive. Television content is not only transformed to transmedia storytelling, but also into digital interfaces as a whole. If the audience wants, it can consume the text on the broadcast. However, the audience has the option of monitoring these contents over other platforms with advantages or disadvantages. This point leads us to the issue of transmedia engagement. Transmedia engagement includes two processes that are related to the television industry and the audience's actual behavior. Audiences can switch between media by watching content on television, computer, mobile phone (Evans, 2011: 40). Schwab's predictions for interactive televisions in 1996 can be adapted to the Internet today. Schwab (1996) explains that shopping will be done without going out, touching the screen will connect with different geographic groups, and issues such as politics, career and communication will change. The transmedial narrative appears in these facilities offered by the internet.

Evans (2011: 19-20) says that the naming of the transmedia is actually wrong, because all the applications that can be described as transmedia involve telling stories on multiple platforms. Multiple communication platforms are used in the multimedia field. On the other hand, there is no relationship between these platforms. Transmedia storytelling is used in different platforms and there is a mutual relationship between these platforms. In Transmedia storytelling strategy, there is a dual relationship between the main product and the by-products. Developments in different channels affect the whole story. For example, the history of characters of a particular novel can be described in comics; gaps in comics can be discovered in online games (Gürel & Tığlı, 2014: 43-44).

In ideal transmedia storytelling, every medium does the best. An extended story can be introduced in a film, television, novel and comics; can be explored through the game or experienced as an amusement park. You don't have to watch the movie to enjoy the game (Jenkins, 2006a: 96). There are strong economic reasons behind Transmedia storytelling. Media convergence makes the flow of content inevitable on multiple media platforms. Combining entertainment and marketing, strong emotional ties are created and additional sales are made (Jenkins, 2006a: 104). Transmedia narratives have been developed for a wide range of applications such as entertainment, education, marketing, advertising, organizational change and activism (von Stackelberg, 2011).

Transmedia storytelling is often associated with major entertainment franchises, but beyond the entertainment business model, it has serious implications for education, defense, organizational management, marketing and brand awareness (Rutledge, 2011). Consumers do not assimilate content in a rational manner. Rather, they establishes an emotional relationship with the brand. Telling stories about a brand is a important way to build this link and create your own audiences. Different from the traditional system that is independent of the whole, each object creates transmedia merchandising, new contents and new information, which are integrated into the main narrative (Muñoz, 2016). Narrative fluency includes uninterrupted focus (Rutledge, 2015: 10).

First, transmedia storytelling provides a clear message that attracts attention to every level of the brain. Second, it uses different media distribution channels to reach and interact with different audience segments. Third, it creates mutual reinforcement channels with the mass. While a traditional marketing level places the brand and consumer in opposite positions, a transmedia story model invites the audience to join the world of the story and positions a brand and audience together. The linking of the brand through the story changes consumer perception and allows consumers to create their own understanding of the brand in a social context (Buckner & Rutledge, 2011). A single medium does not satisfy the audience and the stories are told through multiple media. Transmedial narrative gave the audience the ability to customize, personalize and respond (Pratten, 2011: 3).

Transmedial Narration

Transmedial narratology is often used as an umbrella term for narrative applications that focus on media other than literary texts (Thon, 2016: 14). The center of transmedia storytelling is consistency (Harvey, 2014: 279). "Canon", "Apocrypha" and "Fanon" stages of the story world are important. In the definition of Jenkins, Canon is a group of text that fans accept as a part of the media franchise, and bind to speculation (Jenkins, 2006a: 281). Apocrypha includes expanded world and by-products from different dimensions of the main story. Because of the parallels with Canon, the boundaries of Apocrypha are sometimes unclear. It contains alternative stories where different dimensions of the main story are presented. To preserve the property of Apocrypha, by-products must be produced by the creators of the story world. Fanon contains products that are produced by fans of the original product and are independent of the producer (Emet & Tığlı, 2014: 48-49). Klastrup & Tosca (2004) suggests a definition for transmedial worlds:

Transmedial worlds are abstract content systems from which a repertoire of fictional stories and characters can be actualized or derived across a variety of media forms. What characterises a transmedial world is that audience and designers share a mental image of the "worldness" (a number of distinguishing features of its universe). The idea of a specific world's worldness mostly originates from the first version of the world presented, but can be elaborated and changed over time. Quite often the world has a cult (fan) following across media as well. Subjects interacting with the transmedial world in any of its actualizations (for example a book, a film, a game...) can recognize the world by its abstract properties.

The transmedial worlds are mental structures shared by designers / creators of the world and the audience / participants. Experiences in this world; mythos, topos, ethos are informed in three different dimensions. Mythos is the founding story of the world. The background, which adds meaning to the present state of the world, includes myths and mythical characters and gods of creation. Topos is the place of the world in both space and geography. It shows how the spaces change and how the events developed. Ethos tells the morals of characters. If any of these categories is broken, the masses will react negatively. A mistake about a character that does not conform to a particular ethic as defined by the invention of a new place that disrupts the original topos, or in the realization of urtext, will cause confusion in the fan community (Klastrup & Tosca, 2014: 296-297). Looking at the Star Wars example, mythos is the creation of mythos star wars galaxies in here. When we look at topos, Star Wars Galaxies have been identified as "galaxy far, far away". When we look at Ethos, the basic ethical decision is whether The Dark Side or The Light Side (Klastrup & Tosca, 2004).

Storyworld is a wider concept than the fictional world because it includes both real and fictional stories. Components of story worlds are existents, setting, physical laws, social rules and values, events, mental events. *The existents* components contains the characters and objects required for the story. *Setting*; represents the space in which the existents exist. *Physical laws* are the principles that determine what events happen in the story. *Social rules and values* indicate the obligations of the characters. *Events* are the causes of state changes. *Mental events* are the reaction of characters to events (Ryan, 2014: 33-36).

Various elements of a transmedial system can expand a story world through changes and transpositions (see Ryan, 2013). In attempts to make a project more intense, realistic and accessible, practitioners select the media used by the characters. Real-world communication is represented through works in the media, and so thought is needed to represent a fictional world through similar media. This accessibility means that what the characters use in the fictional world can also be used by real-world people. In other words, similarity, beyond a presentation in the fiction, becomes a real object to be carried to a media. For example a dress has the same characteristics as the fictional and real world. Here, the artifacts have the same features as the real world works, and therefore they work to make the fictional world accessible in the real world. These are the objects of the fictional world in the real world (Done, 2009: 282-286).

Transmedia storytelling is based on extensions. Extensions can be used as tools to create an opinion about the characters and the motifs that direct them: to enrich the world of fiction and build bridges between events; to add a sense of reality to the world of fiction; to combine the world of fiction with the real world. A character in a story can be shown in all channels where the story is told, and characters may even appear as guests in different stories of the same producer. The story grows with new information presented each time, and consumers are involved. Not only the information is disseminated here, but in addition to the information, roles and tasks are presented to enable the story to be placed in the daily life of consumers. Another important feature of the texts of transmedual storytelling is that they are designed to leave missing points. Texts with missing points to be explained later are created. These shortcomings encourage the creation of new stories to explain the gaps (Gürel & Tığlı, 2014: 39-40). When Star Wars was printed, the novel's timeline was expanded with events that could not take place in the movie trilogy, or the stories around the secondary characters about the curious-looking aliens in the background of the original film were rearranged, as in the fairy tales of the Cantina series (Jenkins, 2003).

Writing is an important concept because it is about creativity and innovation as well as control and power. This makes authorship one of the most vital processes in modern media and culture. Some fans add new characters to the mix and create a fan movie or fiction that transforms other characters and events that already exist. To do so is to challenge Lucasfilm and Lucas' idea of having a monopoly in the magic world (Gray & Johnson, 2013: 4).In the above mentioned extension processes, there are not only construction companies but also fans have an important function in the creation process. Especially the Star Wars Expanded Universe concept is an important example. Apart from the producer company, many writers and fans have been involved in this process.

Star Wars Transmedia, Fandom and Gender

Since 1977, Star Wars has become a wide transmedial franchise spread across a variety of platforms, including novels, magazines, comics, video games, radio games and more. Luke Skywalker's heroic journey could have attained a natural outcome by defeating the Empire, but the world of Star Wars lived for a new wave of future adventures (Freeman, 2017: 62). Star Wars has expanded through print fiction. The novels of prequels are linked to other transmedia Star Wars texts (van Parys, 2017: 84). Star Wars movies has a transmedial narrative that spans many areas such as the book, toy, computer games, video games (see Hall, 2017: 87), exhibition (see Pett, 2016: 165), museum (see Herrera et.al., 2017: 156-167), customizable card game (see Lee, 2017), lego set (see Wolf, 2017), radio drama (see Webster, 2017). As Geraghty (2017: 117) indicates that Star Wars is a commercial supersystem of transmedia intertextuality. Star Wars is the best example of both contemporary transmedia storytelling and media franchising. Story and brand spread across multiple media platforms and textual commodities as the battle of good and evil.

The most important issue that distinguishes Star Wars from many works is the size of its fan base which lasts through generations. Jenkins says how central the toys are in the Star Wars transmedia system, but this is underestimated. They play a major role in Star Wars and in many contemporary media series. They are evocative objects that shape their imagination. They are authoring tools that give the recipient the right to rewrite and extend the story they see on the screen. Action figures show the background details of a fictional world and be as important as the hero's epic. New life is given as it becomes part of the fan's personal mythology. The expansion of Star Wars can first be read as the Skywalker epic, based on Hero's Journey and expanding outward over time and space. The second is to read Star Wars as a world where many different sections can be discovered in the background details (Jenkins & Hassler-Forest, 2017: 18-19).

Characters are transformed and reconstructed to serve the transmedia storyworld as the multimedia franchise grows and expands (Geraghty, 2017: 128). A narrative universe is based on the creation of narrative space. The represented space brings audiences to new content and expands the story with new stories. If we look at the

Star Wars example, the space represented in the galaxy has a number of familiar planets and characters. Each new franchise entry has expanded this area by offering new locations and characters added to the franchise's main story. There are also narrative areas outside the galaxy, such as those mentioned or implied in various texts, which have not yet been shown to the audience (Mejeur, 2017: 199-200). The process from 1977 to 1983 was the period in which the classic trilogy was produced. In this first stage, the Star Wars mythology was created in a laborious way, not just in the developed films. Transmedia storytelling was applied to novels, the comics, film, television movies, animated cartoons, radio adaptation, video game platforms etc. The second stage appears from the mid-1980s to the end of the 1990s. The third phase starts from the prequel trilogy (1999-2005) and continues until 2012 when Disney acquired the Star Wars. The fourth stage and the present period begin with the return of the franchise to the main cultural entity in the Disney era (Guynes, 2017: 13-14). As Lomax (2017: 47-48) says "...the expansive transmedia history of the Star Wars franchise demonstrates the need and potential to conceive of transmedia texts not as either entirely auteur-driven or team-based, but as a site of dialogical relations between singular notions of authorship and collaborative creative practices."

In an article he wrote in 2003, Jenkins says that we are entering a convergence era of media. Everything about the structure of the modern entertainment industry has been designed with the idea of building and developing entertainment franchises. Young consumers become knowledge hunters, enjoy watching character backgrounds and plot points, linking different texts within the same franchise. In addition, computers did not cancel the other media, but the computer owners consume more television, movies, CDs, and related media. The concept of the active audience was a controversial concept before the two decades, but today it is accepted by all. New technologies enable the average consumer to archive, annotate, appropriately, and recirculate media content. Institutions, such as law, religion, education, advertising, politics, and practices are redefined by a growing recognation (Jenkins, 2006b: 1). There is a consumer who describes what, when and how the media consumes. Because the audience is not only a media consumer but also a media producer, publisher, journalist and critic. However, the interactive viewer is not autonomous, it still works with the major media industries (Jenkins, 2006b: 135).

Leavenworth (2014: 215) points out that although academic interest in fan events has increased, there is still a tendency to see the relationship between production and consumption hierarchically and that fan products need to be included in the meaning-making process. The relationship between the fans and the producers. In extreme cases, the producers try to keep fan activities under control. Transmedia manufacturers' intentions are to allow audiences to interact and participate in production processes, but often this interaction and participation is not really interactive or participatory. Instead, it can be seen as a partial participation in which producers have real power. They are the producers who decide what to interact and how and when to use it. Therefore, the power and control of the production process is in the hands of producers, just like the traditional ways of culture and media production (Ross, 2012: 62). If we look at the museum example, the canon concept is important in museums. Visitors agree to transfer all their image rights to Lucasfilm before they can access their avatars and personal biographies. If they do not change their avatars or remove the trademark, they can share their avatars online, thus contributing to the promotional income of the exhibition through social media. In the practices arranged in the controlled space of the museum, visitors are invited to participate in the expansion of a universe; however, this participation is limited to the canon and unapproved extensions are legally restricted. In short, fans and visitors are determined by the canon vision of Lucas. On the other hand, the museum is a separate area to examine the relationship between producers and consumers and unequal power relations (Herrera et.al., 2017: 156-167). Butler (2017: 187-188) discusses the Star Wars audience in Marxist terms and analyzes the audiences as Laborer-watchers. Laborers sell labor for the value of use that can be exploited by capitalists to produce capital derived from commodity values. For example, the wage earned by the labor sold allows the laborer to consume a fun, like Star Wars, to spend his free time. This special consumption action converts them into laborer-watchers. This also subject them to ads. As laborer-watchers, audiences are sold to advertisers. Laborer-watchers are alienated and commodified.

Star Wars features both sci-fi and western genres. Therefore, it is a film that targets the male audience. The characters in Star Wars are predominantly male. There is a masculine and malicious system. Fighting with the spirit of cowboys and knights, swords, weapons, masculinity, war, the desire to provide justice, the good versus the evil, and so on. All this attracts an area of the film's sci-fi-western mix.

Star Wars, the relationship with feminist discourse in the past 40 years, constantly changing the transmedia concession and the political movement has changed constantly shaped by the changes. One thing that is increasingly apparent is that Star Wars tends to follow mainstream policies. However, fans have used their relationship with Star Wars to expand the boundaries of the story world and constantly transform it with real-world influence (Bruin-Molé, 2017: 240). As Jenkins (2013: xiii-xiv) says we must admit that fandom has its own traditions, values and norms that emerge through collective action and decisions. The transition from distribution to circulation signaled a movement towards a more participatory cultural model. People are now shaping, sharing, remixing media content in a way that has not been previously imagined, not as consumers of preconfigured messages (Jenkins et al. 2013: 2). There are also expectations that some videos about vidding are political in terms of gender and race, and some of them are fun in their relationship with the original material. Every reason that creates fanvids speaks in a subculture meaningfully.

For example, a group of queers in the multicultural utopian community wanted to change the core text of Star Trek by including gay, lesbian, bisexual and transgender characters (Jenkins, 2013: xxxii). San Diego Comic-Con, the Cartoon Fair, is an important intersection between Hollywood and the fan community. This is shaped by male-centered fan traditions, norms, and most of the participants are men. For this reason, when Hollywood talks about fans or when news media writes annual fandom story, usually men are generally encountered (Jenkins, 2013: xvii).

It can easily be said that fan base of Star Wars is made up of mainly men. Most of the Star Wars items in the commercial area are for direct male consumption. The fact that there is only one female main character in the trilogy is not enough evidence to say that the film is directed towards women. But the interesting thing is that despite all this male world, Star Wars has a large fan base, including women. Once a man-oriented science-fiction film, the work has turned into a cultural phenomenon with fans of all races and genders. Over the years, the number of female fans has grown exponentially. The reason for this is that the increasing social acceptance of science fiction and comic book culture is considered to be too much nerdy for women, especially ten years ago. The rapid increase in female Star Wars fans is supported, especially by franchises outside the film. Because such a large demography in the commercial field could not be ignored. However, despite all this, the films are still male-centered (Pianka, 2013: 32-33).

In the Star Wars series, Hollywood tried to stop the fan fiction. They encouraged the work of fan video producers, but also limited what they could do, and tried to collaborate with the players to create a multiplayer game to better match the fantasies of the players. Home movies didn't threaten Hollywood as long as they stayed at home. Production of fans peaked with the Web (Jenkins, 2006a: 134-136). When the Phantom Menace was released, the Internet was also becoming more popular. Hundreds of amateur Star Wars films have been collected on web pages. Some of these films attempted to replicate the digital effects of Star Wars using the resources of home computers; others parodied Star Wars. Jenkins says for the videos of male and female fans (Jenkins & Hassler-Forest, 2017: 24):

Parody certainly has always been popular with male fans, and male fans produced the bulk of these amateur Star Wars films, at least the ones visible through the official competitions. Some have argued that male fan preference for parody suggests an attempt to downplay their emotional investment in the media properties, to hold it at arm's length, to demonstrate their emotional superiority over the media that fuels their creative response. But these fan parodies also took shape precisely because it was a legally permitted space in which fan filmmakers could work. If we look carefully, though, the rules of the Star Wars fan competition rejected other emerging forms of fan media production, which might make their own claims on the character or narrative development, something like the 'shipping that emerges from female-centered fandom, and in particular the kinds of re-use of found footage and the exploration of the emotional lives of characters that characterizes vidding as a particularly female response to Star Wars.

There has always been a tension between the culture and the superstructure that influences culture, which is meaningful within the communities. Fans operate outside intellectual property, heteronormative and patriarchal assumptions. Within the classical forms of cosmopolitanism, people embrace the high culture of art, such as music, art, poetry, food, wine, international cinema and escape from the parochialism of their local cultures. Young people interact with popular media from all over the world (Jenkins, 2013: xxxviii).

Lucasfilm tried to control Star Wars fan broadcasts. In the feminist fanzine Slaysu, C. A. Siebert claims the right to produce underground art that challenges patriarchal assumptions. Siebert claims that Lucasfilm wants the fans to enjoy the universe of the Star Wars because of their men's war. But Siebert says he does not want to be a man and refuses to pretend to be the idealistic fool's ideal of others (cited in Jenkins, 1992: 31-32). Star Wars fans are often emphasized as men. But the emphasis on the concept of the fan is on women (Jenkins,1992:15):

Significantly, if the comic fan and the psychotic fan are usually portrayed as masculine, although frequently as de-gendered, asexual, or impotent, the eroticized fan is almost always female (the shrieking woman on the cover of the Vermorels' book); the feminine side of fandom is manifested in the images of screaming teenage girls who try to tear the clothes off the Beatles or who faint at the touch of one of Elvis's sweat-drenched scarfs, or the groupie servicing the stars backstage after the concert in rockamentaries and porn videos. Not only are these women unable to maintain critical distance from the image, they want to take it inside themselves, to obtain "total intimacy" with it. Yet, these representations push this process one step further: the female spectator herself becomes an erotic spectacle for mundane male spectators while her abandonment of any distance from the image becomes an invitation for the viewer's own erotic fantasies.

In Fandom, there are toxic fan practices, which Urbnaski (2017: 255) calls "... like gatekeeping to only allow in "true" fans, hurling heavily gendered insults, and creating an unwelcoming environment for anyone who does not identify as white, cis-gendered, straight, and male, also appear at real-life events". Brooker states that he did not consider racist fans as an important group in the interview. Some of them may be young, immature people who do not have the right ideas and try to provoke a reaction. They can use hashtags only to draw attention and feel as part of a group (Brooker & Hassler-Forest, 2017: 292).

The feminist reading in Star Wars is based on the old Leia character. But Leia's feminist reading is very controversial. On the other hand, it is also possible to see Leia's feminist readings among the fans. Later, Padme's damsel posture as in melodramas was another point of discussion. When we come to the present day, the characters Rey, Jyn and Finn have brought about significant changes in terms of gender and race. These changes, however, had to find a place in the trade context in the transmedial narrative, especially after the start of the Disney process. Therefore, it is not easy to think that these changes are optimistic. As Bruin-Molé (2017: 227) says that a transmedia franchise's feminist policy is much more complex because open-ended story worlds are always subject to new readings, additions, and changes (2017: 228-229):

When discussing a popular storyworld's engagement with feminism, however, there are three factors to consider. The first is indeed representational and asks whether a storyworld contains engaging, fully realized female characters. The second is paratextual, pertaining to advertising, merchandise, and reception. Transmedia marketing often extends beyond the corporate control of Lucasfilm, but it still has a powerful impact on the way the Star Wars brand is consumed and interpreted. Finally, we must also acknowledge industrial and political factors of who is allowed to add to the story and feels entitled to claim it as their own. These factors are often invisible to average consumers and may not even be acknowledged by the storyworld's creators, but they are important if a transmedia franchise like Star Wars is going to inspire sustained, real-world change.

For many fans, Princess Leia was a strong role model for gender equality, but she would have been forced to pursue the 40-year-old Star Wars fandom alone. The most well-known of the numerous female characters in the Expanded Universe texts are the Mara Jade, which appeared in the first Timothy Zahn's novel Heir to the Empire (1991). Mara was followed by many popular female characters such as Jila and Jan Ors, Ysanne Isard and Qwi Xux, such as Bastila Shan and Jaina Solo. Ahsoka in Clone Wars, like Mara, has collected followers. However, it does not seem appropriate to evaluate these characters in feminism. Like Padme, most of these female characters take their place in the story of the male character. These trends in the Expanded Universe strengthen women's single-use status and secondary status within the franchise. Thus, many factors indicate that the Star Wars galaxy is patriarchal. There are many women political leaders in Star Wars, but these individuals have rarely managed to overthrow the patriarchal traditions and policies of the galaxy while they stand against male-dominated systems. Married women take the surname of their husbands and the children receive the names of their fathers. Many of Star Wars' attempts to imagine a non-patriarchal society can be found in the franchise's non-canonical Expanded Universe stories. For example, in the online game The Old Republic (2011), there is matriarchy. In Courtship, published by Dave Bantam Spectra, women are divided because of their ideological approach, not because of their gender. But although it has matriarchal societies and strong female characters, the Courtship is ultimately unconvincing as a feminist narrative. Luke, Han and Isolder are the true heroes of the story. Feminism becomes synonymous with female dominated because the exotic dressings of the Witches resemble the sexualized Amazon warriors of science fiction of the 1950s. The novel exoticizes and objectifies female characters (Bruin-Molé, 2017: 229-233)

The world of transmedia wars in the Disney era has created a change in the Star Wars world-building model and franchise (Guynes, 2017: 154). However, this situation leads us to a reading of power because there is basically a "force". After the Star Wars was sold to Disney, female fans' complaints had to be taken into consideration to expand the market. For this reason, the concept of power here should not be left behind by the beautiful appearance of female heroes and should be examined. One of the most striking areas is the action figure toys.

Toys are material objects containing the dominant ideas of the society in which they exist. Toys serve not only as physical works that are shaped by ideologies but also as an important tool for the transfer of cultural norms and beliefs between generations (Sweet, 2013: 5). Sex-based toys can communicate specific heteronormative ideals to young consumers. Another concern with current Star Wars merchandising involves their industry's own attempts to feminist market (Bruin-Molé, 2017: 233-236).

Even though there is a change in female characters, this change is actually made according to the needs of the market and making a profit. On the other hand, since this marketing refers to certain representations, it causes transformation in feminist representations. Female representations are transformed in masculine areas with symbols of power such as weapons.

For example, when we look at action figures toys, male characters and female characters such as Leia, Rey and Jyn are noteworthy. Because the film is based on war and power, all transmedial narratives use power symbols, especially weapons and lightsaber. These icons show themselves clearly on action figures. Even when Force Awekans was released, a significant marketing was done by putting lightsaber filter on Facebook for use on profiles (see Suhas, 2015). The representations about Star Wars launches itself through these power icons.

The Star Wars transmedia is very wide and varied, like the Star Wars universe. Therefore, the content created by fandom and the transmedian products produced by the companies in the marketing field reveal an infinite number of creations today. Because of the masculine universe of the story, the masculine structure also manifests itself in these productions. As we look at the female figures, the feminine aspects of Leia's white dress and bikini were highlighted, while this changed in Rey and Jyn. In Rey and Jyn there is no representation in the dress and the colors of the clothes darkened. However, there is a look that looks like "sexless" in Rey, but Jyn is particularly mysterious and orientalist with the masculine look and the covering of your head. This orientalist repre In fact, Star Wars has a collage of pieces from many cultures: Cloaks reminiscent of medieval Europe, mysterious clothes reminiscent of Near East, fightings with lightsaber reminiscent of Far East. sentation can be seen in Leias's bikini scene which looks like belly dancer clothes. In addition, the weapons in the hands of women represent the phallic symbol, and they actually derive their strength from the masculine symbols. The differences in these weapons are also remarkable. For example, lightsaber is in Rey's hands. Leia and Jyn carry more weapons. These instruments, which are a very important phallic symbol, are in the hands of white male representations rather than women and black men. These instruments, which have a power representation, are in the hands of white males rather than women and black men.

CONCLUSION

Nowadays, culture is changing more quickly thanks to rapid circulation of knowledge. People are moving away from oppressive local cultures using media. For this reason, the communities created through the media and the fan communities on a subject open important cultural areas in this context. People tend to maintain their own culture in this area. There is therefore a tension between the superstructure trying to determine the culture and the subcultural forms. However, nowadays, while trying to determine the culture with great narratives, it is faced with a resistance within the fan culture. In other words, the producers cannot ignore the thoughts of the fans or the followers when they cannot act as they wish.

The universe of Star Wars is large and has a structure that is expanding day by day. After Disney's acquisition and thanks to fan culture, we can see that this universe is expanding and diversifying. Since Star Wars has a story based on power and power, it also comes with masculine narratives. Therefore, these masculine narratives find their place in the transmedial narrative. Even though the masculine narrative breaks after Disney's purchase, a manly structure still makes itself feel strong. Numerical scarcity of women and blacks, limits of power use, whether they are in a decision-making position or not. The topics are discussed. However, in general, it is not difficult to guess that this masculine structure will not disappear due to the fact that the story is based on power. Women will have to assume masculine roles in order to be in a position to decide in an environment of war.

FUTURE RESEARCH DIRECTIONS

Transmedia storytelling is a new digital language that has emerged through media convergence. With technological developments, it will show itself in different ways in the future. For this reason, this narrative structure needs to be studied in multidimensional context in the context of production, producer and consumer.

REFERENCES

Brooker, W., & Hassler-Forest, D. (2017). Afterword: "You'll Find I'm Full of Surprises" The Future of Star Wars. In S. Guynes, & D. Hassler-Forest (Eds.), Star Wars and the History of Transmedia Storytelling. Amsterdam, The Netherlands: Amsterdam University Press.

Bruin-Molé, M. (2017). Space Bitches, Witches, and Kick-Ass Princesses Star Wars and Popular Feminism. In S. Guynes & D. Hassler-Forest (Eds.), Star Wars and the History of Transmedia Storytelling. Amsterdam, The Netherlands: Amsterdam University Press.

Buckner, B., & Rutledge, P. (2011). *Transmedia Storytelling for Marketing and Branding: It's Not Entertainment, It's Survival.* Retrieved from http://www.kcommhtml.com/ima/2011_03/transmedia_storytelling

Butler, A. M. (2017). Invoking the Holy Trilogy Star Wars in the Askewniverse. In S. Guynes, & D. Hassler-Forest (Eds.), Star Wars and the History of Transmedia Storytelling. Amsterdam: Amsterdam University Press.

Chenu, C., German, R., Gressier-Soudan, E., Levillain, F., Astic, I., & Roirand, V. (2014, February). *Transmedia storytelling and cultural heritage interpretation: the CULTE project*. Museum and the Web Florence, Florence, Italy. Retrieved from https://mwf2014.museumsandtheweb.com/paper/transmedia-storytelling-and-cultural-heritage-interpretation-the-culte-project/

Done, C. (2009). *Transmedia Practice: Theorising the Practice of Expressing a Fictional World across Distinct Media and Environments* (Doctoral dissertation). School of Letters, Art and Media Department of Media and Communications Digital Cultures Program, University of Sydney, Australia.

Durkin, J. D. (2016). *Mediaite Interview: The Guy Who Was Nearly Arrested After Giving Ted Cruz That Lightsaber.* Retrieved from https://www.mediaite.com/online/mediaite-interview-the-guy-who-was-nearly-arrested-after-giving-ted-cruz-that-lightsaber/

Evans, E. (2011). *Transmedia Television: Audiences, New Media, and Daily Life.* New York, NY: Routledge. doi:10.4324/9780203819104

Freeman, M. (2017). From Sequel to Quasi-Novelization: Splinter of the Mind's Eye and the 1970s Culture of Transmedia Contingency. In S. Guynes, & D. Hassler-Forest (Eds.), Star Wars and the History of Transmedia Storytelling. Amsterdam, The Netherlands: Amsterdam University Press.

Geraghty, L. (2017). Transmedia Character Building Textual Crossovers in the Star Wars Universe. In S. Guynes, & D. Hassler-Forest (Eds.), Star Wars and the History of Transmedia Storytelling. Amsterdam, The Netherlands: Amsterdam University Press.

Gray, J., & Johnson, D. (2013) Introduction: The Problem of Media Authorship. In J. Gray, & D. Johnson (Eds.), A Companion to Media Authorship. Malden, MA: Wiley-Blackwell.

Gürel, E., & Tığlı, Ö. (2014). New World Created by Social Media: Transmedia Storytelling. *Journal of Media Critiques, 1,* 35-66.

Guynes, S. (2017). Publishing the New Jedi Order Media Industries Collaboration and the Franchise Novel. In S. Guynes, & D. Hassler-Forest (Eds.), Star Wars and the History of Transmedia Storytelling. Amsterdam, The Netherlands: Amsterdam University Press.

Hall, S. (2017). Franchising Empire Parker Brothers, Atari, and the Rise of LucasArts. In S. Guynes, & D. Hassler-Forest (Eds.), Star Wars and the History of Transmedia Storytelling. Amsterdam, The Netherlands: Amsterdam University Press.

Harvey, C. B. (2014). A Taxonomy of Transmedia Storytelling. In M.-L. Ryan, & J.-N. Thon (Eds.), Storyworlds across Media Toward a Media-Conscious Narratolog. London, UK: University of Nebraska Press. doi:10.2307/j.ctt1d9nkdg.17

Herrera, B. B., & Dominik, P. K. (2017). How Star Wars Became Museological Transmedia Storytelling in the Exhibition Space. In S. Guynes, & D. Hassler-Forest (Eds.), Star Wars and the History of Transmedia Storytelling. Amsterdam, The Netherlands: Amsterdam University Press.

Hoffmann, B. (2016). *Video Portrays Ted Cruz as Jedi Warrior From 'Star Wars'*. Retrieved from https://www.newsmax.com/headline/video-ted-cruz-jedi-warrior-star-wars/2016/01/04/id/708054/

Jenkins, H. (1992). *Textual Poachers Television Fans & Participatory Culture*. New York, NY: Routledge.

Jenkins, H. (2003). Transmedia Storytelling. *MIT Technology Review.* Retrieved from https://www.technologyreview.com/s/401760/transmedia-storytelling/

Jenkins, H. (2006a). *Convergence Culture: Where Old and New Media Collide*. New York, NY: New York University Press.

Jenkins, H. (2006b). *Fans, Bloggers, and Gamers: Exploring Participatory Culture*. New York, NY: New York University Press.

Jenkins, H. (2013). *Textual Poachers: Television Fans and Participatory Culture*. New York, NY: Routledge.

Jenkins, H., Ford, S., & Green, J. (2013). *Spreadable Media: Creating Value and Meaning in a Networked Culture*. New York, NY: New York University Press.

Jenkins, H., & Hassler-Forest, D. (2017). Foreword: "I Have a Bad Feeling About This" A Conversation about Star Wars and the History of Transmedia. In S. Guynes & D. Hassler-Forest (Eds.), Star Wars and the History of Transmedia Storytelling. Amsterdam, The Netherlands: Amsterdam University Press.

Klastrup, L., & Tosca, S. (2004). Transmedial Worlds— Rethinking Cyberworld Design. In *Proceedings of the 2004 International Conference on Cyberworlds*. Los Alamitos, CA: IEEE Computer Society. 10.1109/CW.2004.67

Klastrup, L., & Tosca, S. (2014). Game of Thrones: Transmedial Worlds, Fandom, and Social Gaming. In M.-L. Ryan, & J.-N. Thon (Eds.), Storyworlds across Media Toward a Media-Conscious Narratolog. London, UK: University of Nebraska Press.

Leavenworth, M. L. (2014). Transmedial Narration and Fan Fiction: The Storyworld of The Vampire Diaries. In M.-L. Ryan, & J.-N. Thon (Eds.), Storyworlds across Media Toward a Media-Conscious Narratolog. London, UK: University of Nebraska Press.

Lee, J. R. (2017). The Digitizing Force of Decipher's Star Wars Customizable Card Game. In S. Guynes, & D. Hassler-Forest (Eds.), Star Wars and the History of Transmedia Storytelling. Amsterdam, The Netherlands: Amsterdam University Press.

Lomax, T. (2017). "Thank the Maker!": George Lucas, Lucasfilm, and the Legends of Transtextual Authorship across the Star Wars Franchise Transmedia: Participatory Culture and Media Convergence. In S. Guynes, & D. Hassler-Forest (Eds.), Star Wars and the History of Transmedia Storytelling. Amsterdam, The Netherlands: Amsterdam University Press.

Mejeur, C. (2017). Chasing Wild Space Narrative Outsides and World-Building Frontiers in Knights of the Old Republic and The Old Republic. In S. Guynes, & D. Hassler-Forest (Eds.), Star Wars and the History of Transmedia Storytelling. Amsterdam, The Netherlands: Amsterdam University Press.

Mittell, J. (2014). Strategies of Storytelling on Transmedia Television. In M.-L. Ryan, & J.-N. Thon (Eds.), Storyworlds across Media Toward a Media- Conscious Narratolog. London, UK: University of Nebraska Press. doi:10.2307/j.ctt1d9nkdg.16

Muñoz, P. (2016). "Transmedia storytelling". *The Branded Content Marketing Association.* Retrieved from http://www.thebcma.info/transmedia-storytelling/

NTV. (2018). *Star Wars'ın dünü bugünü.* Retrieved from http://arsiv.ntv.com.tr/news/151333.asp

Pett, E. (2016). "Stay disconnected": Eventising Star Wars for transmedia audiences. *Participations, 13*(1), 152–169.

Pianka, J. P. (2013). *The Power Of The Force: Race, Gender, And Colonialism In The Star Wars Universe* (Master's thesis). Wesleyan University, Middletown, PA.

Pratten, R. (2011). Getting Started in Transmedia Storytelling. *Transmedia Storyteller.* Retrieved from http://www.tstoryteller.com/getting-started-in-transmedia-storytelling

Roos, C. (2012). *Producing Transmedia Stories - A study of producers, interactivity and prosumption* (Unpublished Master's Thesis). Malmö University.

Rutledge, P. (2011). *Transmedia Storytelling: Meaning Comes from the Ability to Share, Explore, and Discover.* Retrieved from http://www.pamelarutledge.com/2011/12/03/transmedia-storytelling-meaning-comes-from-the-ability-to-share-explore-and-discover/

Rutledge, P. (2015, March). *The Transmedia Trip: The Psychology of Creating Multi-Platform Narrative Engagement for Transmedia Migration*. Transmedia Storytelling Conference, Hanover, Germany. Retrieved from https://www.psychologytoday.com/sites/default/files/2017-01_-8_rutledge_transmedia_trip_.pdf

Ryan, M., & Kellner, D. (2010). *Politik Kamera: Çağdaş Hollywood Sinemasının İdeolojisi ve Politikası*. İstanbul, Turkey: Ayrıntı Publishing.

Ryan, M.-L. (2013). *Transmedial Storytelling and Transfictionality Poetics Today*, *34*(3), 361–388. doi:10.1215/03335372-2325250

Ryan, M.-L. (2014). Story/Worlds/Media: Tuning the Instruments of a Media-Conscious Narratology. In M.-L. Ryan, & J.-N. Thon (Eds.), *Storyworlds across Media Toward a Media-Conscious Narratolog*. London, UK: University of Nebraska Press.

Schwab, S. (1996). A Revolution in Television. In The Information Highway: An Overview. The San Diego, CA: Greenhaven Press.

Suhas, M. (2015). *There's A 'Star Wars' Lightsaber Facebook Filter That You Need In Your Life Right Now*. Retrieved from https://www.bustle.com/articles/129993-theres-a-star-wars-lightsaber-facebook-filter-that-you-need-in-your-life-right-now

Sweet, E. V. (2013). *Boy Builders and Pink Princesses: Gender, Toys, and Inequality over the Twentieth Century* (Doctoral dissertation). The University of California, Davis, CA.

Thon, J.-N. (2016). *Transmedial Narratology and Contemporary Media Culture*. University of Nebraska Press.

Urbanski, H. (2017). The Kiss Goodnight from a Galaxy Far, Far Away Experiencing Star Wars as a Fan-Scholar on Disney Property. In S. Guynes, & D. Hassler-Forest (Eds.), Star Wars and the History of Transmedia Storytelling. Amsterdam, The Netherlands: Amsterdam University Press.

von Stackelberg, P. (2011). *Creating Transmedia Narratives: The Structure and Design of Stories Told Across Multiple Media* (Unpublished Master's Thesis). School of Information Design and Technology, State University of New York Institute of Technology, Utica, NY.

Webster, J. W. (2017). Han Leia Shot First: Transmedia Storytelling and the National Public Radio Dramatization of Star Wars. In S. Guynes, & D. Hassler-Forest (Eds.), Star Wars and the History of Transmedia Storytelling. Amsterdam, The Netherlands: Amsterdam University Press.

Wolf, M. J. P. (2017). Adapting the Death Star into LEGO The Case of LEGO Set #10188. In S. Guynes, & D. Hassler-Forest (Eds.), Star Wars and the History of Transmedia Storytelling. Amsterdam, The Netherlands: Amsterdam University Press.

ADDITIONAL READING

Harvey, C. (2015). *Fantastic Transmedia: Narrative, Play, and Memory across Science Fiction and Fantasy Storyworlds*. Basingstoke: Palgrave Macmillan. doi:10.1057/9781137306043

Kaminski, M. (2012). Under the Influence of Akira Kurosawa: The Visual Style of George Lucas. In D. Brode & L. Deyneka (Eds.), *Myth, Media, and Culture in Star Wars: An Anthology* (pp. 83–99). Lanham, MD: The Scarecrow Press.

Knight, G. L. (2010). *Female Action Heroes: A Guide to Women in Comics, Video Games, Film, and Television*. Santa Barbara, CA: ABC-CLIO.

McVeigh, S. P. (2006). The Galactic Way of Warfare. In M. W. Kapell & J. S. Lawrence (Eds.), *Finding the Force of the Star Wars Franchise: Fans, Merchandise, and Critics* (pp. 35–58). New York: Peter Lang.

Reynolds, R. (1992). *Super Heroes: A Modern Mythology*. London: B.T. Batsford.

Scott, S. (2017). #Wheresrey?: Toys, Spoilers, and the Gender Politics of Franchise Paratexts. *Critical Studies in Media Communication*, *34*(2), 138–147. doi:10.1080/15295036.2017.1286023

KEY TERMS AND DEFINITIONS

Fan: Someone who admires someone or something, and likes that thing or anyone excessively.

Fandom: The name given to the community of fans in general.

Femininity: A series of roles, behaviors, and attributes generally associated with being a woman.

Gender: The definition of sexuality in the social process.

Masculinity: A series of roles, behaviors, and attributes generally associated with being a man.

Narration: A way of telling a series of events in such genres as novels, stories and fables.

Star Wars: Star Wars is the universe and brand of narrative created by George Lucas. There are products in film, comic, computer game, television, toy, etc. areas.

Transmedia: A narrative that allows a concept or a message to meet with the user in a complementary manner through different media.

Chapter 12
Overview of the Gay Characters in the New Cinema of Turkey

Özgür İpek
Sivas Cumhuriyet University, Turkey

ABSTRACT

Similar to the worldwide perceptions, gay characters in Turkish cinema are mostly perceived and used as elements of humor and comedy. They are also used as standards for measuring the masculinity of other male characters in some Turkish movies. And what about Today? What are the differences between the past and now? It is possible to say that Turkish cinema in 2000s involve more visible sexual identities apart from heteronormative understanding. This study will focus on the reflections and portrayals of only gay characters in New Turkish cinema.

INTRODUCTION

Popular films are under the influence of commonly accepted norms, rules, moral and ethic understandings in Turkey, just like in any other part of the world. Images presented to silver screen audiences are based on the idea of reflecting different realities in actual life such as femininity, masculinity, different sexual identities, male-dominance and situation of family in different societies. In other words, mainstream cinema or popular films are built on an understanding that reflects dominant social life, dominant viewpoints, life principles and dominant culture; what is perceived as 'different' in a society is rarely included in the movies framed with this understanding. Canonized, idealized value judgments are presented to the audience; social statues are reproduced in these films.

DOI: 10.4018/978-1-7998-0128-3.ch012

Overview of the Gay Characters in the New Cinema of Turkey

The issue of sexuality, like most of the other topics, is one of these value judgments and it is reproduced on the basis of the limitations of idealized society. Identities which are hidden or limited in social life –identities that are not completely, independently expressed in most of the traditional societies- are uploaded in the images in cinema. The productions of movie sector confirm these images and represent the so called 'normal' identities to the perceiver: The audience.

Popular movies are under the impact of dominant, traditional cultural structure that excludes all of the sexual identities other than heterosexuality; homosexuality (gay or lesbian), bisexuality and intersexuality are 'abnormal' according to the dominant understanding in the sector. Homosexual characters in movies since the beginning of cinematography have been mostly used as elements of comedy or humor. There are surely various films that reflect such characters through more casual dimensions; but even the modern cinema is full of examples that alienate different sexual identities or reflect them in a way that they are estranged or abnormalized. This attitude since the beginning of cinematography hasn't much changed. Individuals with different sexual identities are characterized and represented in films with problematic approaches in terms of individual and sexual characteristics.

Gay characters are mostly in the background, they are usually not presented at the center of the story in a film, and they are mostly separated from their original identities. These facts had been dominant especially until 1980s except for a few positive representations in films. Homosexual characters had been reflected in a quite problematic manner in the cinema for a very long time.

2000s is the main period that will be analyzed in this study; gay characters in Turkish movies of the period will be the main focus of analysis. Before analyzing the reflections in Turkey, it is necessary to mention similar characters in the world cinema. It will be possible to present and understand gay characters in Turkish movies and analyze the cinematography in the country only when the topic is firstly discussed in terms of its characteristics around the world.

Projections of Gay Characters in the Cinema

The first marks of gay identity in the cinema dates back to the end of 1800s. It is possible to say that gay characters were included in the movies during this very first period of cinema. The first movie with two gay characters is *The Gay Brothers* directed by William Dickson in 1895. The movie doesn't directly reflect a gay relationship; it implies the homosexual relationship in a more indirect manner. *The Gay Brothers* is the first movie with real-time voice records. It is only 18 seconds long and two male characters waltz intimately in a harmony. Another character plays violin in the background throughout the scene, and finally the fourth character enters the scene. It can be said that a humorous air is felt behind the representation of gay characters even in this very first example.

There has been a tendency to portray these characters in a humorous manner starting from *The Gay Brothers* until today. Although there are some movies with original narratives and characters –they will be mentioned in this study-, the reflections are usually stereotyped; these characters are mostly removed from their original contexts and popular movies that attract masses are produced within a limited perspective.

It is possible to say that male characters that represent the concept of hegemonic masculinity are included in most of the Hollywood studio films. Strong, self-confident, dominant male characters that look as if they can change the world are at the core of this concept. Hegemonic masculinity refers to the form of masculinity that works for having dominance over women and other male forms (Connell, 1987).

Serpil Sancar defines the notion of hegemonic masculinity as young, white, heterosexual, religious (within reason) male individuals who have full-time job and the ability to carry out active physical performance sufficient to be successful at a branch of sports (2009: 30).

Robert Hanke (1992) states that hegemonic masculinity, which is established as a form of dominance, casts gay identity away or destroys it symbolically and functions on the basis of this structure. Hollywood films, which are designed on the basis of this classical common structure, usually portray gay characters as negative examples of masculinity. This negative, faulty concept represented in movies clearly shows the viewpoint of dominant film producers in Hollywood.

Gays were firstly portrayed as humorous, deficient, insufficient individuals next to the dominant male characters around them. *The Soliers* (1923) is a significant example of this portrayal. The movie directed by Ralph Ceders is established on a humorous manner on the basis of different identities of characters; comic elements in the film are developed through the unique attitudes of characters.

One of the first homosexual themed popular cinema films is *Staircase* directed by Stanley Donen in 1969. The film tells the relationship between two male characters over years in a humorous manner. It doesn't deepen the identities of gay characters, rather prefers to create a type of humor over their sexual identities. There is a similar style in *Blacula*, directed by William Crain in 1972; homosexual characters are insulted because of their sexual identity and there is not a deep character representation in the film. *Dirty Harry*, directed by Don Siegel in 1971 similarly portrays gay characters as abnormal identities.

The film named *Cruising* directed by William Friedkin at the beginning of 1980s gives a completely different direction to the issue; a serial killer slaughtering gay characters is created in the film. The serial killer follows gays he sees and violently kills them. The movie aroused serious questions and discussions in the period it was broadcasted; while a group of people protested the movie, some others claimed that the protests are pointless as the movie basically portrays gay characters as normal people.

One of the representatives of relatively positive gay characters in mainstream movies is *Philadelphia* directed by Jonahan Demme in 1993. The film is one of the rare examples as it is not based on the conservative viewpoint dominating most of the films with gay characters. It is important to note that Demme produces a significant, unordinary movie in a period that homosexuality was a taboo that couldn't be easily discussed. Hollywood's studio system was a representative of this viewpoint in the period, which is why this movie was noteworthy and had an important place in the history of Hollywood movies with gay characters. The director boldly brings the issue to the question; *Philadelphia* directly reflects the hatred and marginalization directed towards this sexual tendency. The film takes a further step and claims that human beings should make effort to get know and understand homosexual characters. It is mentioned that if people give a chance to these individuals, take a step to know them, most of the problems will easily vanish. The movie surely has some positive dimensions, but it should be noted that there are some problematic elements in it. Firstly, the main character, acted by Tom Hanks, is put in the center although he is not heterosexual; he is shown as if he has the very same traditional, national and family values. The other problem in the film is that AIDS is presented as a disease that is only transmitted by direct sexual intercourse. Another mechanism of marginalization about these individuals is created through this perception.

Gus Van Sant's *My Own Private Idaho* (1991) is another significant homosexual themed movie in 1990s. The film is a loose adaptation of the play named *Henry IV* by Shakespeare. Two male prostitutes who earn their income by having sexual intercourse both with men and women are portrayed in the film; their adventure from Portland to Rome is full of travels and pursuits.

Gay characters have been portrayed as more 'normal' beings since 2000s; they are less ridiculed or used as the elements of humor. Ang Lee's *Brokeback Mountain* is undoubtedly one of the important examples; it is an award-winning movie broadcasted in 2005. Heath Ledger and Jake Gyllenhaal are the leading actors of the film adapted from the short story of E. Annie Proulx. The movie won Pulitzer Prize and it tells the story of two cowboys Ennis del Mar and Jack Twist who fell in love in 1963. The film should be perceived as a story of passionate love rather than a production with a homosexual theme. What makes this movie is special is that it presents love as a painful loneliness.

Ang Lee destroys the specific Western attitude which is built on hegemonic masculinity and creates a significant breaking point; the director succeeds in homosexualizing the sacred, valuable Western genre of American cinema.

Another production at the beginning of 2000s is *Le Fate Ignoranti* (2001) directed by Ferzan Özpetek. After her husband's death, a woman discovers that he had another life; she starts to have a new perspective both about life and herself as she learns the hidden truths of her husband's life.

Gus van Sant's *Milk* broadcasted in 2008 is another homosexual themed movie that should be mentioned. The life of Harvey Milk, which is full of challenges, is presented in the film. The film focuses on the political career of Harvey Milk; it starts with his travel from New York to San Francisco and ends with his death. The beginning of the movie is marked with the images of newspaper pieces that document the despotic attitude of America towards homosexuals especially during 1950s and 1960s; archive images of gay bar raids and arrests are presented to the audience. After these scenes, Harvey Milk's life as a political leader, his fight for identity and his values are the focuses of the film.

There have surely been positive developments in the sector in general as homosexual characters are now more important in today's movies and there is a bigger awareness about homosexual identities among audiences. Some important homosexual activists or leading figures are portrayed by the codes in popular films; but it should be noted that homosexual characters are changed while transforming them into movie characters. This can be interpreted as a way of adapting different sexual identities into mainstream understanding.

It can be said that movies that are not included in mainstream understanding –sometimes defined as art house or independent - give more importance to reflect different compositions and create original characters. Healthy and normal portrayals about homosexuality have recently increased mostly thanks to the movements for Rights and Freedoms, Queer activists, and pieces produced by thinkers such as Judith Butler and Michael Foucault. Gay, lesbian, bisexual or intersexual relationships that are beyond the heteronormative area are now reflected in a more normal manner in movies called Queer and New Queer cinema. Stories of these characters are now told to the audiences without making substantial changes.

A Single Man, directed by Tom Ford in 2009 is the adaptation of Christopher Isherwood's novel. George, a teacher acted by Colin Firth, loses his love Jim, who was the only human being that thoroughly understood him, in an accident. This loss is like the end of the world for George. He is a character that has lost the meaning of life and sensation of living after the unexpected death of his beloved. The sadness he deeply feels is reflected in the color palette of the film.

Andrew Haigh's *Weekend* (2011) tells the story of two homosexual males that are attracted to each other after a one night stand. The basic goal of Haigh who wants to separate the definition of love from labels such as 'heterosexual' or 'homosexual' love, attempts to emphasize the sexlessness of love.

Moonlight (2016) directed by Barry Jenkins, is a very interesting and original queer cinema example with its blue and black toned cinematography. The film presents the main character in three different time periods to the audience and tells the story of a black male character's journey of growth. The focus is on the harsh attitudes of the society against a black child who discovers his sexual identity and his effort for being accepted by that society. One of the most striking parts of the film is the existence of a secondary factor that causes the character to be estranged. He is not only a homosexual, but also a black character. Besides the difficulties faced by the main character, Jenkins reveals the drug traffic and criminal relations in schools. *Call Me By Your Name* directed by Luca Guadagnino in 2017 tells love and passion in combination with the elements in nature. Emotions reflected from two souls that intersect are sometimes in the blow of the wind, in the freshness of the water or in the sway of leaves.

Turkish Cinema and Gay Characters

Similar to the worldwide perceptions, gay characters in Turkish cinema are mostly perceived and used as elements of humor and comedy. They are also used as standards for measuring the masculinity of other male characters in some Turkish movies. On the other hand, there had been some homosexual characters dressed up as woman in Turkish cinema before the emergence of homosexual characters. *Leblebici Horhor* (Muhsin Ertuğrul, 1923), *Fıstık Gibi Maşallah* (Hulki Saner, 1964), *Avanta Kemal* (Cevat Okçugil, 1964), *Yalancının Mumu* (Sırrı Gültekin, 1965) and *Kibar Haydut* (Yılmaz Atadeniz, 1966) are some of these examples; leading male actors dress up as woman and find a way to overcome the difficulties they face (Özgüç, 1988).

Gay characters in various films such as *Mahalleye Gelen Gelin* (Osman F. Seden, 1961) and *Yusuf ile Kenan* (Ömer Kavur, 1979) are derided and despised by the other characters in these movies. At the beginning of 1980s, *Beddua* (1980, Osman Seden) is broadcasted; the film is probably the first one focusing on homosexuality and it attempts to understand a gay character and bring him into society. Bülent Ersoy is the leading actor and sexual identity crisis of the character is presented to the audience. Although homosexuality is associated with the fact that the character was raped at a small age, the film takes a partially positive position about homosexuality. On the other hand, it can be said that *Beddua* is the first film that involves violence and cruel treatment towards homosexuality.

Acılar Paylaşılmaz, directed by Eser Zorlu in 1989 is another production that associates homosexuality with a concrete reason. The film tells the story of a lonely and unhappy homosexual male character who had to grow without his father and the father who wants him stop being homosexual. We start to see more positive homosexual profiles in films by 1990s; the first example of these films is *Dönersen Islık Çal* directed by Orhan Oğuz in 1992. There is a trans-woman and a dwarf in the film; relationship of these two characters who are alienated from the society is the focus of the film. *Gece, Melek ve Bizim Çocuklar*, broadcasted in 1993 is a film that tells the story of trans-women. Prostitution is told in this important film directed by Atıf Yılmaz. Trans-women are sometimes attacked by customers or policemen, which is reflected to the audience who feel like observing the incidents while watching scenes. There are more gay characters in the silver screen during 1990s in Turkey. *İstanbul Kanatlarımın Altında* (1996) and *Ağır Roman* (1997) directed by Mustafa Altıoklar and *Hamam* (1997) directed by Ferzan Özpetek are some of these movies. *Hamam* tells the story of an Italian and a Turkish man who are attracted to each other.

Kutluğ Ataman's film *Lola+Bilidikid* (1999) is another film telling the efforts of a homosexual for proving his existence in a society. The film is a Turkish-German co-production. The main character Murat experiences violence at the hands of his family and meets transvestite Lola and her lover Bili. The director's purpose is to attract the attention to homophobia in Germany and Turkey; masculinity and patriarchy are the other issues that are discussed in the film.

A Glimpse to New Cinema of Turkey

It is possible to say that Turkish cinema in 2000s involve more visible sexual identities apart from heteronormative understanding. In this respect, there are LGBTI characters in various films such as *Cahil Periler* (Ferzan Özpetek, 2001), *9* (Ümit Ünal, 2002), *Yazı Tura* (Uğur Yücel, 2004), *Kabadayı* (Ömer Vargı, 2007), *Güneşi Gördüm* (Mahsun Kırmızıgül, 2009), *Teslimiyet* (Emre Yalgı, 2010), *Zenne* (Caner Alper and Mehmet Binay, 2011) and *Nar* (Ümit Ünal, 2011). On the other hand, there are significant documentaries broadcasted in the same period; these documentaries help general society see and understand the problems of these so-called unusual characters in daily life. *Benim Çocuğum* (My Child, 2013) by Can Candan and *Mr. Gay Syria* (2017) by Ayşe Toprak are especially important productions. The documentary by Can Candan tells the experiences of parents that have a homosexual child. Ayşe Toprak's documentary reflects the struggle of two Syrian gay refugees.

There are various feature-length fictional works telling the stories of gay characters in this period. *Anlat İstanbul* (2005) is original both in terms of character creation and scenario. The film is built on the adaptation of Grimm tales to the life in İstanbul and involves five different stories. The part named '*Cinderella*' tells the story of a trans-individual who has to prostitute because of a mobster. A gay character helps this trans-character, who wants to escape from İstanbul with her lover.

Zenne (2011) involves three gay characters and it is important as it reflects the intolerance towards 'the different'; the film is based on telling the story of a gay character who comes from one of the most traditionalist and intolerant part of the country. The film tells the life of Ahmet Yıldız who was killed by his father on July 15, 2008 as he was a homosexual. Ahmet's is the first case of honor killing involving a gay character; this type of murder is a custom in Turkey where men or women are killed by their family because of various reasons such as relationship outside marriage.

Yazı Tura is different from the other examples as a gay brother in the film is accepted by his family and protected towards the end of the story. Privacy, public sphere, good-bad, traditional-modern, hegemonic masculinity-homosexuality are the basic components of the film which ends with the glorification of family. In this respect, Cevher, the main character which symbolizes hegemonic masculinity, rejects his brother at the beginning of the story. Towards the end, audience sees that this hegemonic character protects his brother at the expense of committing a crime. *Güneşi Gördüm*, directed by Mahsun Kırmızıgül, focuses on issues such as Kurdish people, migration and homosexuality. Kadri's family has to migrate to İstanbul because of war; after a while, he enters a group of trans-individuals. Family members don't give him the chance to be happy.

Teslimiyet, directed by Emre Yalgın shows the world of trans-women. Yüksel says that the film presents the city as a dangerous place for trans-individuals. The city encodes them as violent figures that disturb social peace; they are portrayed as immoral, perverted, dangerous beings. The film questions the hegemonic spatial organization that justifies exclusion of these individuals. According to the scenario, real violent side of the society is made of individuals who own the masculine dominance codes (2016: 143). Trans-individuals are located in the violent, insecure parts of the city throughout the film; they are isolated from the city life. Insecurity in the city is combined with insecure bodies.

Popular comedy movies involve jokes about homosexual elements in addition to the other elements of humor. For instance, *GORA* (2004) directed by Cem Yılmaz and *Recep İvedik* (2008) directed by Togan Gökbakar are some of the Turkish movie examples in which homosexual characters are used as humor elements. On the other hand, *Kolpaçino: Bomba* (2011) has a sexist attitude and involves a group of men wandering in female clothes.

Aile Arasında, directed by Gülse Birsel brings a new perspective to Turkish cinema; the first Turkish trans-woman actress Ayta Sözeri is one of the important characters of the movie. Behice (acted by Ayta Sözeri) is defined as a graceful figure in this family comedy; she is never extreme, always dignified in her manners. She is a kind of a problem-solver, rational character in the family. It can be said that the elements of rationalism is represented by Behice. The common understanding of humor in many popular movies is turned upside-down with this character created by Gülse Birsel; trans-individuals gain actual identity through this characterization.

CONCLUSION

It can be seen that the understanding of humor produced through gay characters has still been used in modern Turkish cinema. Comedies such as *Recep İvedik, GORA* and *Kolpaçino* produce elements of humor by using the concept of homosexuality. Although it can be said that homosexual characters have been portrayed more realistically since 1980s, cinema has still been exploiting these images today. It is believed that productions like *Aile Arasında* will make positive contributions to analyzing and understanding these individuals. On the other hand, films like *Zenne, Teslimiyet, Anlat İstanbul, Güneşi Gördüm* and *Yazı Tura* are important as they attempt to ensure a positive perception in society, to accept and normalize homosexual individuals in life.

FUTURE RESEARCH AND DIRECTIONS

This study focuses on the reflections and portrayals of only gay characters in Turkish cinema. A new and more comprehensive study that involves all of the LGBTI individuals will make more important contributions to the literature. Documentaries about LGBTI members in Turkey, their living conditions in the country should be carefully researched and analyzed in order to extend the scope of analyses.

REFERENCES

Connell, R. (1987). *Gender and Power: Society, the Person, and Sexual Politics.* Cambridge, UK: Polity Press.

Hanke, R. (1992). Redesigning Man: Hegemonic Masculinity in Transition. In S. Craig, & S. Publications (Eds.), *Men, Masculinity and the Media.* London, UK. doi:10.4135/9781483326023.n13

Özgüç, A. (1988). *Türk Sinemasında Cinselliğin Tarihi.* İstanbul, Turkey: Broy Yayınları.

Sancar, S. (2009). Erkeklik: İmkansız İktidar. İstanbul: Metis Yayınları.

Ulusay, N. (2011). Yeni Queer Sinema. Fe Journal: Feminist Critique, 3, 1-15.

Yüksel, E. (2016). Güneşi Gördüm ve Teslimiyet Filmlerinde Trans Kimliklerin Mekânsal Örgütlenmesi ve Sınırlılıkları. Fe Journal: Feminist Critique, 8(2), 138-148.

ADDITIONAL READING

Türkölmez, E. (1993). Zenne: Niyet Neydi Akıbet Ne oldu. In H. Abelove, M. A. Barale, & D. M. Halperin (Eds.), *Altyazı Aylık Sinema Dergisi içinde, İstanbul, Şubat 2012. Rubin, Gayle: Thinking Sex: Notes for a Radical Theory of the Politics of Sexuality, in The Lesbian and Gay Studies Reader*. New York: Routledge.

Yüksel, E. (2018). Carol'da Eşcinsel Arzu ve Mutluluk Vaadi. In *Perdeyi Aralamak: Filmlerde Anlatı ve Eleştiri*. İstanbul: Ayrıntı Yayınları.

KEY TERMS AND DEFINITIONS

Cinema: Is a term first coined by the academic B. Ruby Rich in *Sight & Sound* magazine in 1992 to define and describe a movement in queer-themed independent filmmaking in the early 1990s. The term developed from use of the word *queer* in academic writing in the 1980s and 1990s as an inclusive way of describing gay, lesbian, bisexual and transgender identity and experience, and also defining a form of sexuality that was fluid and subversive of traditional understandings of sexuality.

Queer: An identity used to be vague or non-specific about a person's sexual orientation, identifying with the LGBT community as a whole. Also a description of people's non-heterosexual sexual orientations in a non-specific and unbiased manner.

Queer Theory: Is a field of critical theory that emerged in the early 1990s out of the fields of queer studies and women's studies.

Zenne: Is the term which is basically refers to a man dancer who looks like a woman. Zenne plays like women in women's outfits at weddings and festivals in the traditional nomadic Turkish tradition.

Chapter 13
Thinking About the Concept of Social Gender With a Film:
The Analysis of the Film *Tersine Dünya* With Judith Butler's Concept of Subject – Discussing the Fact of Social Gender That Is Presented in the Narrative of the Film

Berceste Gülçin Özdemir
İstanbul University, Turkey

ABSTRACT

The concept of social gender is an interdisciplinary matter of debate and is still questioned today. Making sense of this concept is understood by the ongoing codes in the social order. However, the fact that men are still positioned as dominating women in the contrast of the public sphere/private sphere prevents the making sense of the concept of gender. This study questions the concept of social gender through the female characters and male characters presented in the film Tersine Dünya (1993) within the framework of Judith Butler's thoughts regarding the notion of the subject. The thoughts of feminist film theorists also bring the strategies of representation of female characters up for discussion. Butler's thoughts and the discourses of feminist film theorists will enable both making sense of social gender and a more concrete understanding of the concept of the subject. The possibility of deconstruction of patriarchal codes by using classical narrative cinema conventions is also brought up for discussion in the examined film.

DOI: 10.4018/978-1-7998-0128-3.ch013

INTRODUCTION

Everything presented in the cinema has the power to change the world of spectators. The worldwide spectator prefers to watch mainstream movies. The number of spectators of art films is less than the number of spectators of mainstream films because art films put their audience in an intense process of thinking and do not approve the existing codes. Although the film Tersine Dünya is a mainstream film in Turkish Cinema, it raises many questions that the spectator will query because the film is important in terms of discussing the concept of social gender in Turkish Cinema. For centuries, feminist theorists have discussed the position of women and men in the differentiation of the public sphere and private sphere, and they offer strategies for the change of the male-dominated order. The public space without equality of opportunity also causes inequality of social order. In the public sphere where the discourse of men is considered more important, women are secondary. That is why they are the subordinate ones. These realities are presented to spectators through films. However, the presentation of realities reinforces the continuation of existing rules. It is also necessary to present a world where female characters and male characters are equal in terms of representation strategies in the films and understanding of gender codes in the social order. The spectators are trying to understand life through the films they watch continuously. However, if the films that provide the unknown facts about social gender are produced and if the possibility of a world, where there is equality of opportunity between women and men, is shown then the points of view of individuals on the codes in life will change.

BACKGROUND

In the film examined in the study, female characters and male characters act outside the rules and discourses of social order. Women replace men in the public sphere and men do their jobs by replacing women in the private sphere. The position of women and men in public and private spheres changes in this film. The roles attributed to women and the roles attributed to men are reversed. Likewise, the name of the film Tersine Dünya also embodies this perception. The issues 'what would life be like in a world inside out?' and 'how would the patriarchal realities that have been learned in terms of social gender show changes?' are shown in the film. Female characters are presented as strong ones in the public sphere, while male characters are the ones who live in the private space. In the study, the representation mechanism of the characters presented in the film narrative will be discussed in the context of the concept of social gender. The framework of this discussion will be examined in the context of feminist theorist Judith Butler's interpretation of the concept of "subjectivity". Within this direction, the ways that the female characters and male characters are presented to the spectator in public and private spaces in the film narrative will be examined. The representations of the characters in the public sphere and in the private sphere make it visible how they reveal their subjectivity in these spaces. The effect of the representation of female and male characters, who are presented with a different approach from the patriarchal point of view, in public and private spheres on their state of being "subjects" becomes important in this context. Butler's ideas about social gender and her ideas about subjectivity are important not only in terms of feminist theories but also in terms of film theories because the fact that these issues are opened up for discussion leads also to the differentiation of the representations of the characters. Classical narrative cinema iterates the discourses of social order. Contemporary narrative cinema, on the other hand, dislocates the codes of social order. The film cannot be described as an example of contemporary narrative cinema. However, it is more important that the representation strategies of the characters are against the social order because the characters of classical narrative cinema reinforce the patriarchal point of view and those who watch these films are individuals who do not question this point of view. On the other hand, the spectators who watch the films of the modern narrative cinema prefer to watch the movies focused on thinking. The film process that continues with question marks is not preferred by the people of popular culture. Such a vicious circle repeats the accustomedness of the social order. For this reason, it is very important to present social gender perception differently than the known codes in a film to be watched by the popular culture. Unusual characters and an unconventional world lead the spectators to question that there may be other lives and other perspectives. In the chapter Subjects of Sex/Gender/Desire in her book Gender Trouble (1999), Butler discusses the status of women as the subject of feminism. In this context, firstly, social gender will be explained. How the female characters and male characters are presented in the classical narrative cinema will be discussed. The issue of how these presentations are determined will be questioned. It is important how the films that are presented with a patriarchal perspective are perceived from the point of view of the spectators. For this reason, the importance of the films that break this male-dominated view will be addressed. The question 'how a representation mechanism should be followed in the films in order to break the male-dominated view' will be considered in order to break the male-dominated view. The ideas of feminist theorists and the ideas of feminist film theorists will, therefore, be included. Butler's interpretation of the concept of the subject will be explained, and the film will then be examined by the concept of subject that Butler interpreted from a feminist perspective. How female characters are presented as subjects in the public sphere will be examined and the contribution of female characters to feminist film theories will be explained. Male characters, on the other hand, will be questioned about their presentations in the private sphere and their subjectivity. The discussion of the subjectivities of the characters and how these characters are presented in the public sphere and in the private sphere allow for the change of the perception of social gender. The presentation of social gender in films is very important because spectators make sense of what they see. Just like books change people's lives, movies change people's lives as well. The film is very important for the understanding of social gender in terms of Turkish Cinema with the presentations of characters in public and private spheres. Women, who take part in the codes of social discourse, femininity, male, masculinity, subject, object, object of desire, being a man, the subject of which gender belongs to where, the roles assigned to the sexes, the imputations attributed to the sexes – all these realities are re-thought through the film. In this thinking process, Butler's discourses make it possible for the reader to interpret the film from a feminist perspective. The film, which allows for the presentation of social gender beyond stereotypes, will pave the way for the change of these judgments. The film makes it possible that other lives, other genders and other choices can exist. The film shows that the rules taught to individuals can be changed and that women are also subjects. Women, whose subjectivities are not seen in the public sphere, are made visible by this film. This presentation reveals that the public sphere is also the right of women. The rights granted to all mankind in the Declaration of Human Rights should also be granted to women. The debate on how to assume women as a subject in the public sphere in a world where they are not assumed as a subject yet is important but sad. The production of movies in which social gender is questioned in mainstream cinema will help to break down male domination and the existing discourses. Thus, the production and review of films from a feminist point of view have become important as well. Feminist theories are necessary not only for women but also for men to perceive the world. This study will try to make sense of the content of the concept of subject and will make people rethink the representations of the characters in the public and private spheres.

What Is the Concept of Social Gender?

There are many definitions of the concept of social gender. However, the most important detail for this concept, which is defined by different approaches, is that the content of the concept is shaped by patriarchal codes. While Ivan Illich defines the concept of social gender in his work *Gender* (1982), he refers to the Oxford Dictionary and defines the concept as follows: "one of three grammatical kinds, corresponding more or less to distinctions of sex (or the absence of sex) into which nouns are discriminated according to the nature of the modifications they require in words syntactically associated with them" (Illich, 1996: 13). The meaning of the concept of gender, which played a role in the emergence of the concept of social gender, also has to be reviewed. Illich states that sex is derived from Sexus in Latin; grammatically this word must be accompanied by the words masculine (virile) or feminine (muliebre). The new meaning of modern "gender" (sex) without social gender is also stated to be clearly manifested in terms such as "sexuality" (Illich, 1996: 26). Gordon Marshall explains the concept of social gender in the Dictionary of Sociology as well as the concept of gender: According to Ann Oakley, who introduced this term into sociology, while "gender" refers to the distinction between biological masculinity and femininity, "social gender" refers to the parallel and socially unequal separation between masculinity and femininity. Therefore, social gender draws attention to the socially established aspects of the differences between women and men. However, the scope of this term has expanded not only to the individual identity and personality but also to the cultural ideals and stereotypes of masculinity and femininity on the symbolic level, and to include the division of labor in institutions and organizations on the structural level (Marshall, 2005: 98). Both Illich and Marshall's gender and social gender explanations underline how concepts are shaped by cultural codes. In a social order in which women remain secondary behind men, explanations about gender and discourses of science also use masculine language. In this context, the masculine point of view that has infiltrated even the science should be pointed out. In her book *Reflections on Gender and Science* (1995), Evelyn Fox Keller makes an introduction to her book with a discussion on how science is presented to people as a masculine project (Keller, 2007: 9-15). Keller argues that attributing science to men is not the right approach. Keller questions the fact that women entering science-related professions doing science will cause some changes and argues that the nature of science stems from the idea of masculinity (Keller, 2007: 27). A revision of Keller's thoughts reveals the fact that the possibilities offered to women in the public sphere are not determined under equal conditions with men. One of the most important reasons for this state is that the patriarchal codes that exist in the concept of social gender have continued for hundreds of years. Even in history writing, a masculine language was created and references to historical milestones were attributed to men. This situation is not only valid for the science of history; the grounds attributed to men in all branches of science have pushed women into the background. Keller stated that when George Simmel was conveying his thoughts, he said that objectivity itself was an ideal that was identified with masculinity for a long time in history (Keller, 2007: 102). Sonya O. Rose criticizes social gender historiography. Rose indicates that social gender historians are interested in the differences between women and men, changes in time in the context of the nature of their relationships, and the diversity of a single society that the society exhibited in a certain period in the past (Rose, 2018: 16). However, according to Joan Scott, it has never been enough for women historians to prove that women have a history

(Scott, 2007: 7) because it has been very difficult to find the names of women in historical analyses. The carriers of many important historical moments that take place in the public sphere are still described as men all the time.

Judith Butler's Concept of Subjectivity

In her book *Gender Trouble* (1999), Judith Butler addresses various question marks in feminist theories in her discussions about gender, social gender, desire, and body politics. Her book begins with the chapter "Women as the Subject of Feminism". Butler indicates that women constitute the subject that is targeted for political representation and opened up the concept of representation. Butler mentions that representation is a political process that aims to provide political visibility and legitimacy to women, therefore suggests that the development of a language that can represent women is deemed necessary for feminist theory (Butler, 2012: 43). Butler's introduction to women's subjectivity does not only draw attention to the importance of political representation but also shows the possibility that women may be prepared for some natural struggles. In this context, revealing the differences between the concepts of gender and social gender brings out the patriarchal indicators loaded on social gender. Both the thoughts of Butler and the feminist theoreticians' inquiries about these two concepts provide the making sense of these concepts without making sense of subjectivity.

Butler points out that the distinction between gender and social gender was initially used to object to the expression "biology is fate" and emphasizes that social gender is culturally constructed. She expresses making more concrete sense of these two concepts by the following sentences: "if we pull the gender-social gender distinction to the logical extreme, we conclude with the proposition that there is a fundamental discontinuity between sexed bodies" (Butler, 2012: 50). Butler states that only the man is a 'person' and there is no social gender other than the feminine, and cites the opinions of Monique Wittig from her work *The Point of View: Universal or Particular?* (1983): "gender is the linguistic index of the political opposition between the sexes. Gender is used here in the singular because indeed there are not two genders. There is only one: the feminine, the 'masculine' not being a gender. For the masculine is not the masculine but the general" (Butler, 2012: 70). In accordance with Wittig's thoughts, Butler states that women can assume the status of a universal subject (Butler, 2012: 70). Butler gives reference to Luce Irigaray, who is one of the important representatives of feminist theory, indicates that Irigaray refers to women as "sex" which is not "one" and tries to show the paradoxical position of women in their discourse of identity. According to Irigaray, the female gender is not "deficient" or "the other" that defines the subject in its masculinity and that defines it negatively because the female gender is neither "deficient" nor "the other" but it is just implicit in the phallocentric scheme (Butler, 2012: 56-57). In the context of the opinions of both Irigaray and Wittig, Butler's question of the concept of gender would make a clearer understanding of the concept: "What is gender? Is it natural, anatomical, chromosomal or hormonal?" (Butler, 2012: 51). Under all these thoughts and question marks, the existence of the implicit patriarchal codes that exist within the concept of gender comes to light again. The social order, which labels a set of patterns and rules to the sexes, marginalizes the non-men and ignores the existence of women. The ongoing social order in the world is based on the name and gender of 'male'. For this reason, the basis of the source of the patriarchal indicators loaded on social gender seems to depend on the fate of individuals that they cannot choose by birth. Due to this irrational and non-equitable perspective, feminist theorists open the expression "biology is fate" up for discussion consistently.

Butler indicates that the various definitions and explanations about the meaning of social gender contain disagreements in their own rights. Butler details this issue a little more and questions, whether the discursive construction of the term social gender, gender, women or woman, or men or man to be discussed, is more fundamental. For these reasons, she suggests that identity categories should be reconsidered in the context of radical social gender asymmetry (Butler, 2012: 58). The ambiguity in the definitions and explanations of women or about women, of course, makes it possible to argue the concept of subjectivity. The subjectivity of a marginalized existence is not visible in the social order. The representation of what is defined with a man's name is not a direct representation. Butler mentions that in order to be represented, principally the requirements of being a subject should be fulfilled (Butler, 2012: 44). According to Butler, legal power also produces what she claims to represent. Therefore, it is not enough to question how women can be represented in language and politics. The feminist criticism should also understand how the "women" category, which is the subject of feminism, is produced and restricted by the power structures that will save the category (Butler, 2012: 45). Butler's thought must be reconsidered and it is important in this context to understand the form of the creation of the category of "women". Butler's concept of the subject and this sentence for representation conveys the subject to a deeper level: "the argument I will bring forward can be paradoxical, but perhaps "representation" will become a meaningful thing for feminism when the subject "women" is not assumed in any way (Butler, 2012: 50). This thought of Butler can be interpreted in very different ways from many different perspectives. However, Butler's point here is to point out that the subject "women" will lead to debates when assumed and will allow for questioning in different ways. Butler's opinion can be interpreted as follows: when we assume gender and the concepts that belong to gender in representation policies, assertions are produced with masculine codes even though everything related to these concepts in politics and language may become questionable and this state will not be meaningful with regard to feminism.

Feminism and Film

Understanding and analyzing the relationship between feminism and film narratives are important in terms of feminist film theories and practice. Feminism kept important movements, which made feminist film theories develop, alive in history. The representations with a feminist perspective presented in the film narratives can be seen as a result of these feminist movements. The film analyzed can be read as a presentation of a feminist perspective. The film, which was analyzed within the framework of the concept of subjectivity, enables the discussion of the representations of female characters and brings up again the issues discussed by feminist film theories regarding these representations. The presentation of the concept of subjectivity in the context of representation of female characters raises the question of the status of women as subjects and also opens the codes of the social order related to this subject up for discussion. In this context, film analysis helps to reverse the construction of patriarchal discourses. Feminist representation of the presentation of female and male characters in the public sphere/private sphere is an important step in contributing to both feminist film theories and feminist film practice.

DISCUSSING THE FACT OF SOCIAL GENDER THAT IS PRESENTED IN THE NARRATIVE OF THE FILM

The Story of the Film

The film narrative presents the lives of female characters and male characters in a different world that is against the discourses of the social order. The female characters are the ones who live in the public sphere, while the male characters are those who live in their private spheres. Women are independent and free characters who work in the public sphere, independent of the private sphere, who can go out at night, live their sexuality freely, be with different people from their spouses and do not deal with home activities. Male characters, on the other hand, are presented as victimized and desperate personalities, besieged in their private sphere, preparing food, doing the cleaning, taking care of children, eating together with other men while talking about problems and being obliged to allow their wives to cheat on them. All codes for social order have been replaced by this film.

Figure 1. From Tersine Dünya.

The Analysis of the Film 'Tersine Dünya' in the Context of Judith Butler's Concept of Subject

The dominance in the public sphere in the contrast that has been going on for hundreds of years between the public sphere and private sphere is attributed to men. Women belong to the private area, they are located there and they experience life there. In the film, the codes of the public sphere-private sphere opposition are reversed and this reversal ideology is embodied by calling the narrative of the film 'Tersine Dünya'. The name of the film also shows the proof of the functioning of the social order in the world. Likewise, the world is a world that operates under the domination of men and reveals its functionality in that way. With the destruction of the discourses of the patriarchal world, the whole order begins to function in a different way 'Tersine Dünya' provides an example not only for Turkish Cinema but also for world cinema in which the concept of social gender can be discussed substantially. The film provides the re-questioning of the division of labor about genders, the order about the functioning of the daily life and the coded opinions about men and women.

Patriarchal societies emerged with the disappearance of the matriarchal societies centuries ago. The domination of the balances of power such as wars and economic domination has led to the emergence of patriarchal societies. With increasing patriarchal discourse, women were forced to remain secondary and had no say in many issues. At the beginning of the 1900s, women founded organizations and took various actions in order to have the right to vote and had the right to vote over the years and in the following years they were able to declare their candidacy for elections. Women were victims in terms of civil law as well and they were unable to divorce from their husbands and had no right to work even in European countries. The feminist movements that emerged all over the world have enabled women to have rights in many areas and not to be under the domination of men. As the years passed, women, who could not divorce from their spouses, who were not entitled to work, and who could not vote, have been able to obtain their rights which must have existed since the beginning. Even in the 21st century, the issues of women being deprived of some of the rights that they should have and feeling the male domination on them remain on the agenda. This is proof of how much patriarchal codes are internalized around the world. The social order condemns women to their private sphere and allows them to experience life to a small extent. The most important proof of this is understood from the discourse of women working in the field of cinema in recent years. In the 71st Cannes Film Festival (2018), the filmmaker women issued a press statement and indicated that they did not receive equal pay in the films they acted with men and they shared the harassment scandals that occurred behind the camera with the public opinion. The situations to which the strongest actresses of the public space are exposed are the most important proof of male domination in the social order.

In the film 'Tersine Dünya', the female characters have replaced men's positions in this order. Women, who are seen at every stage of the public sphere, are those who govern society and have power in the government. Guards wandering around the street at night, prison guards and warden at the prison, the police chief and policewomen, the factory owner, the accountant, secretary, and the grocery store owner are female characters in this film. The male characters, on the other hand, are the ones who sit at home, do housekeeping, cook, take care of children, shop, make neighboring visits, gossip, tell each other fortunes, shot their eyes to their wife's cheating, and tightly attached to their private space. In the film, no character is preceded by any other character because since the message that the film intends to present is the existence of the inequality in the social order, the plot and the scenes are planned accordingly. The film, which uses the conventions of the classical narrative cinema, proceeds along a straight line of narrative. The film presents a representation strategy in accordance with the ideology of the contemporary narrative cinema and uses the codes of the classical narrative cinema in terms of cinematography. This state is very important for making sense of the concept of social gender because the spectators of the contemporary narrative cinema are already aware of many things since they are familiar with high cultural products. However, classical narrative cinema spectators enjoy watching the codes of popular culture over and over again. This film narrative is therefore important in terms of deconstructing the codes of popular culture. The questioning of popular culture codes dominated by the patriarchal point of view can allow the spectators of this culture to think about a number of issues and enable the change of the existing social order. A review of Butler's thoughts regarding the concept of the subject in the previous part recalls the issue of how the subject is inherent in politics and language. The language used in the works that use the codes of popular culture belongs to the sovereigns in the social order. Therefore, men are the subjects whose subjectivity is spoken and discussed. In this film, female characters are the ones whose subjectivity is presented in each section of the public space. The female characters who are the dominant power in the public sphere, whose discourses are valid, who protect and follow the laws, and who control the social order are represented as subjects and deconstruct the patriarchal cinematic codes. Even some of the sayings in the social order are presented in the lines in a way that emphasizes the subjectivity of women. In the film, many sayings that confirm women being of secondary importance next to men are turned upside down. The sentences that are used for the male characters are "it would be better if he didn't give the come-up-and-see-me-sometime-look", "you can just leave him with the army", "as a man, I am all alone", "doctors and engineers wanted to marry me in the past but I am still single", "who will take care of the honor of this man?", "being secluded is the fate of men", and "short hair, short intelligence" and these sentences are both used by the male characters to express themselves and are said by the female characters to the male characters. In all of these sentences, there are expressions that enable many inferences about how men should behave in the social order, who decides their honor, and how they are worthless by being secondary to women. As Butler stated, language is an important issue in terms of the representation of subjects. In particular, the language used in the representation strategies in the field of cinema helps the spectators to reinforce existing codes or opens the way to discuss the existing ideologies. The language used in this film is a masculine language. The plot is presented with the help of masculine codes and the desperation of male characters and it reveals how sexist discourses related to masculinity are. The film, which is presented with the strategies of the form of the classical narrative cinema, suggests the ideological structure of the classical cinema in terms of content. Female characters in the film are not victimized, desperate, deceived, violent, low in intelligence, or penalized; the ones who are presented under all these characterizations are the male characters. Male characters, whose subjectivity is controversial, are presented with character representations that are reversed as those who hold the domination of the existing social order. Butler expresses her thoughts with example sentences from Wittig and Irigaray and Butler's discourses reveal that everything that belongs to gender and social gender is created by the patriarchal order, so everything related to these concepts must be uncovered and questioned again. By asking a very clear and brief question as "what is gender?" Butler, in fact, does what the film does to the spectators. The film leaves the spectator alone with the questioning of all these concepts and likewise, Butler may reconsider the meaning of this concept that societies have adopted by internalizing the patriarchal perspective. While Butler asks "is it natural, anatomical, chromosomal or hormonal?" (Butler, 2012: 51) about gender, she makes people think 'who named gender? According to what was gender named?' or 'According to what are people qualified? Why are they qualified in certain patterns?' The film focuses on how the phallocentric discourses of gender are constructed. Many ethical issues such as 'Why should the party that holds the power insult the other party? Why should the party that holds the power of domination overwhelm the helpless in every field? Does the fact that the power is in the hands of individuals have to make them cruel?' are opened up for discussion with the film. Butler mentions that in order to achieve representation, it is first necessary to fulfill the necessities of being a subject (Butler, 2012: 44). While the female characters who hold power in the public sphere exist in this film with their subjectivity, the male characters cannot even reach the representation because their ego is taken away from them and it is the social order and its discourses that form the basis for it. The film addresses the rights that inhere the fact of being an individual by showing 'what would happen when the discourses of women in the public sphere are valid and there was a system in which men are secondary to women and occasionally denigrated?'

Scott indicates that the phallus is the only indicative and that it is foreseeable to construct the social gender of the subject and embodies her thoughts with the discourses of film theorist Teresa de Lauretis. According to De Lauretis, if we need to think about the construction of subjectivity in social and historical contexts, it is necessary to emphasize that there will be no way to make these contexts clear with the terms that Lacan suggests because social reality (material, economic and interpersonal relations that are historical) has been placed outside the subject (Scott, 2007: 29- 30). In the film, the discourses of social reality are deconstructed and the subject is shifted. While the subjects within social realities were men, the film presents the subject as female characters. However, while the female characters are presented as subjects, the masculinity of the language used in the film shows the language that "influential" people should use and represents the female characters in a masculine way. Women, who elaborate their care, makeup and care about their beauty, become masculine by the language they use, even if they do not forget their femininity. Leonore Davidoff states that the subject may be an actor who takes action and who has the ability to take initiative but that actor may need a subject who is dependent on the authority and on whom acts are done (Davidoff, 2012: 202). Parallel to Davidoff's thoughts, in order to be the subject, the subject has to dominate "the other party". Female characters provide a new look at the criticisms that indicate that they dominate the male characters and become the subject with the narrative content which has not been presented before. Susan Hekman, on the other hand, questions the philosophical system that reduces the subject to "phallic me" with the discourses of Jacques Derrida and argues that the only alternative that can be put forth is the deconstruction of this philosophical system which gives power to men (Hekman, 2016: 117). The film has altered the subject by subtracting the subject from the "phallic me". The subject is not the one that is described as non-

Figure 2. From Tersine Dünya.

male or "the other", whereas the female characters are represented by their existence in the public sphere and the ones who experience their femininity. Irigaray was taken as reference by also Hekman as a theorist who fed Butler's ideas. According to Irigaray, since women cannot be subjects, they will not be able to be active and autonomous subjects who make history like men either (Hekman, 2016: 139). For this reason, it is possible to state that subjects taking an active role in history, which is one of the conditions that has enabled the autonomy of subjects, is embodied in the roles given to the female characters by the film because, the female characters are not only those who hold the public space, but they also prove their subjectivity as the ones who maintain the functionality of power. From the point of view of Julia Kristeva, subjects are the product of discourse; they do not exist in the given sense, they are not producers but they are produced (Hekman, 2016: 145). In this context, female characters are the subject of film discourse and the director adopts a narrative strategy that breaks the pleasure of the male-dominated gaze as the person who produces the discourses of the film.

In her book, *Technologies of Gender: Essays on Theory, Film, and Fiction (Theories of Representation and Difference)* (1987), De Lauretis presents the multiple debates on social gender to the reader. De Lauretis makes an introduction to her book by questioning the meaning of the concept of social gender and draws attention to the close relationship between representation and social gender. According to De Lauretis, social gender is a representation and the questionings about "the entity" that constitutes the classes in this relationship come to light as well (De Lauretis, 1987: 4). The gender-centered social gender system is based on a socio-cultural construction. The construction of social gender concretely demonstrates the process of its representation, as well as its production (De Lauretis, 1987: 5). In the context of De Lauretis's ideas, the female characters of the film question the gender-centered social gender system based on the socio-cultural construction. De Lauretis, who tries to explain the subject of feminism, describes all the inherent essences of women as well as the making sense of the female subject and details them under the definition of the technology of gender. De Lauretis makes facts such as nature, mother, mystery, evil incarnate, object of masculine desire and knowledge, proper womanhood, femininity and concepts such as women, real, historical beings and social subjects reconsidered in social relations (De Lauretis, 1987: 10). De Lauretis also raises questions about how women's representation is performed when producing social gender-specific discourses in films and reveals new questions in terms of feminist film theory and feminist film criticism. On the other hand, in her work *Feminist Film Studies: Writing the Woman Into Cinema*, Janet McCabe states that feminist film theory and criticism contribute very seriously to the making sense of sexual difference and social gender (McCabe, 2004: 2). Mary Ann Doane, Patricia Mellencamp, and Linda Williams are among the theorists who have contributed to feminist film studies by discussing 'images of women' in the context of their film work. Feminist film criticism primarily addresses social attitudes, opinions, cultural values and patriarchal myths (McCabe, 2004: 7). In the indicators presented to the spectators in the film, the representation of the characters can be discussed through the concepts that McCabe states and the existing patriarchal order can be criticized while making inferences about the subjectivity of the characters. The film conveys the discourses that the patriarchal myths infiltrate into the social order by the female characters while making people question the subjectivity of women in real life. In her work *Recent Developments in Feminist Criticism*, Christine Gledhill interprets the debates in feminist film theory and criticism practice with reference to various theorists. Gledhill quotes some thoughts that Claire Johnston wrote in *Women's Cinema as Counter-Cinema* (1973) and the article *The Place of Women in the Cinema of Raoul Walsh* (1974) that Johnston co-wrote with Pam Cook and reveals again the arguments that women are not represented as women. Gledhill attributes the reason for it to the presentation of women's images through masculine discourses and questions how "real experiences" should be represented in films (Gledhill, 1978: 459). The questions that Gledhill opened for questioning years ago are still being discussed. However, although the content of the film examined in this study does not answer Gledhill's questions with a realistic representation mechanism, it is guiding to the breakdown of the masculine discourse in the social order. Referring to Doane in her work *Women's Pictures: Feminism and Cinema*, Annette Kuhn reminds the assertion that images of women are defined by various forms of subjectivity in a patriarchal way (Kuhn, 1994: 199). Kuhn points out that the images of the characters are linked to their subjectivity. The film is important for presenting female characters with their femininity because even though the film shows that they sometimes use masculine language in their discourses, it also shows the images of the female characters in which they behave in the way they feel like, and this shows an important clue to feminist film practice. When the issue of how subjectivity can be represented in terms of female characters in films is questioned in accordance with the ideas of various feminist film theorists, many subject titles are observed to emerge. What is important in this context is whether the director's narrative language is influenced by the discourses of the male-dominated social order or not and if so, how much it is influenced by them.

In her book *Women and Film: Both Sides of the Camera* (1983), Ann Kaplan discusses the discourses of all the theorists whose views are shared throughout the book with examples of films. The book starts with the chapter 'Is the Gaze Male?' and asserts claims by suggesting the breaking of the view that is based on male-dominated pleasure. The reality behind the fact that the subjectivity of female characters is able to win is the narrative strategies that play a role in breaking the masculine gaze. Kaplan shares with the reader how to present the subjectivity of female characters with many examples of films. Kaplan reminds that the ability of female characters to present their subjectivity in films through the body, through voice, through discourse, and through imagination includes the potential to break also the dominant male culture (Kaplan, 2001). Therefore, it is possible to state that all claims indicated by Butler about subjectivity coincide with the discourses of the feminist film theorists who are mentioned in the study because feminist film theorists also think that the ideology behind the representation of female characters in films is based on a male-dominated ideology and they argue that this point of view also directs cultural codes. In the context of Butler's thoughts, it is necessary to revise the structuring of law, language, culture, and representation or changes will start to emerge when the woman is perhaps not mentioned in a more radical discourse. This approach, which emphasizes Butler's paradoxical way of thinking, is quite radical, but it makes possible the emergence of the subjectivity of women when considered in philosophical contexts. The film approaches the feminist film practice with the language it presents in terms of the style and content of the narrative in revealing the subjectivity of female characters and once again reminds the spectators emphatically that women are "subjects".

FUTURE RESEARCH DIRECTIONS

The representation of social gender in film narratives is important for the discourses of social order. Therefore, the transformation of the male-dominated perspective that exists on the basis of the conventions of the classical narrative cinema is controversial. The feminist film theorists, who produce inquires about this issue, have created a variety of discussion fields to the scientists who study in this field of social sciences. In the 21st century, it is important to study in detail how social gender should be presented by media tools as well as to study in detail by which discourses it is coded by the society. The fact that the concept of the subject is still questioned in the present day presents a serious clue about the inability to make sense of the concept of social gender. The representation of social gender in cinema and how the discrimination occurs in films are among the subjects that appear in film criticisms and analyses. However, while how women and men should be represented in films in the public/private space contrast is questioned by film examples, different solution strategies should be suggested. These issues, which are discussed broadly in the academic literature, are not perceived in daily life by individuals with low levels of education. What is important is educating and raising awareness of the individuals who lack knowledge of these issues and concepts. One of the main pillars of this training may be films and the findings of field research can be made academically questionable again.

CONCLUSION

'Tersine Dünya' presents the social order to the spectator with a narrative content that reverses the codes of the existing social order. The narrative content of the film, which features the narrative structure of classical narrative cinema, is presented with the purpose of breaking the male-dominated gaze and is important for discussing the concept of subjectivity. While Butler's thoughts on the concept of the subject ensure that both the ideas about gender and the discrimination in social order against women are questioned, they also play a role in making the discourses of the film visible. The female characters' presentation without losing their femininity reveals their subjectivity. The female characters, who feel their femininity and dominate the public sphere, experience life freely. The male characters, on the other hand, are those who lose their subjectivity. In the history of Turkish Cinema, 'Tersine Dünya' is a film in which men and women change places in the social order. Feminist film theorists have questioned patriarchal codes that have been implicated in the concept of social gender and gender behind the presentation of female characters as subjects in films. For this reason, the film becomes important in terms of making gender-related questionings visible. The female characters, who are represented in different roles instead of the stereotyped female characters, provide a concrete example of alternative narrative languages while deconstructing the patriarchal indicators.

The film transforms the sentence "biology is fate" into "biology cannot be fate" and makes the spectators think about the wrong codes that exist in the male-dominated order. It is the judgment of the patriarchal order that the individual who works in the public sphere will have the freedom he wants at home and that he can crush his wife's rights while having this freedom. As men exist in the public sphere, they live in the social order as individuals who can cheat on their spouses, humiliate them, use violence, and misuse their homes as they wish. The film shows this state by replacing the male characters with the female characters. Representing the existing codes in the opposite way makes questionable concepts visible.

REFERENCES

Butler, J. (2012). *Cinsiyet Belası: Feminizm ve Kimliğin Alt Üst Edilmesi* (B. Ertür, Trans.). İstanbul, Turkey: Metis Yayınları.

Davidoff, L. (2012). *Feminist Tarihyazımında Sınıf ve Cinsiyet* (Z. Ateşer, & S. Somuncuoğlu, Trans.). İstanbul, Turkey: İletişim Yayınları.

De Lauretis, T. (1987). *Technologies of Gender: Essays on Theory, Film, and Fiction (Theories of Representation and Difference)*. Bloomington, IL: Indiana University Press. doi:10.1007/978-1-349-19737-8

Gledhill, C. (1978). Recent Developments in Feminist Criticism. *Quarterly Review of Film Studies*, *3*(4), 457–493. doi:10.1080/10509207809391419

Hekman, J. S. (2016). *Toplumsal Cinsiyet ve Bilgi: Postmodern Bir Feminizmin Öğeleri* (B. Balkız, & Ü. Tatlıcan, Trans.). İstanbul, Turkey: Say Yayınları.

Illıch, I. (1996). *Gender* (A. Fethi, Trans.). Ankara, Turkey: Ayraç Yayınları.

Kaplan, E. A. (2001). *Women & Film: Both Sides of the Camera*. London, UK: Routledge Taylor & Francis Group.

Keller, F. E. (2007). *Toplumsal Cinsiyet ve Bilim Üzerine Düşünceler*. İstanbul, Turkey: Metis Yayınları.

Kuhn, A. (1994). *Women's Pictures: Feminism and Cinema*. London, UK: Verso Publication.

Marshall, G. (2005). *Sosyoloji Sözlüğü* (O. Akınhay & D. Kömürcü, Trans.). Ankara, Turkey: Bilim ve Sanat Yayınları.

McCabe, J. (2004). *Feminist Film Studies: Writing the Woman Into Cinema*. London, UK: WallFlower Publication.

Rose, O. S. (2018). *Toplumsal Cinsiyet Tarihçiliği Nedir?* (F. B. Aydar, Trans.). İstanbul, Turkey: Can Yayınları.

Scott, W. J. (2007). *Toplumsal Cinsiyet: Faydalı Bir Tarihsel Analiz Kategorisi* (A. T. Kılıç, Trans.). İstanbul, Turkey: Agora Yayınları.

ADDITIONAL READING

Bacchi, C. (2001). Dealing with "Difference": Beyond "Multiple Subjectivities". In P. Bray & C. Bacchi (Eds.), *N*. Perth: University of Western Australia Press.

Beardsley, E. L. (1976). Referential Genderization. *The Philosophical Forum*, *5*, 285–293.

Bleier, R. (1984). *Science and Gender: A Critique of Biology and Its Theories on Women*. New York: Pergamon Press.

Bourdieu, P. (2001). *Masculine Domination* (R. Nice, Trans.). Stanford, CA: Stanford University Press.

Butler, J. (2019). *Against Proper Objects: Introduction*. Retrieved from http://www.sfu.ca/~decaste/OISE/page2/files/ButlerAgainstProper.pdf

Cooley, C. H. (1902). *Human Nature and The Social Order*. New York: Scribner's.

Cowan, S. (2005). Gender Is No Substitute For Sex: A Comparative Human Rights Analysis of The Legal Regulation of Sexual Identity. *Feminist Legal Studies*, *13*(1), 67–96. doi:10.100710691-005-1457-2

Doane, A. M. (1994). The Desire to Desire: The Woman's Film Of The 1940's. Bloomington, IN: Indiana University Press, no. 2/3, pp. 1–26.

Erens, P. (1990). *Issues in Feminist Film Criticism*. Bloomington and Indianapolis, IN: Indiana University Press.

Haraway, D. (1988). Situated Knowledges: The Science Question in Feminism and the Privilege of Partial Perspective. *Feminist Studies*, *14*(3), 575–599. doi:10.2307/3178066

Haraway, D. (1991). *A Cyborg Manifesto: Science, Technology and Socialist-Feminism in the Late Twentieth Century in Simians, Cyborgs, and Women: The Reinvention of Nature* (pp. 149–181). New York: Routledge.

Kimmel, M. (2000). *The Gendered Society*. Oxford, UK: Oxford University Press.

Mayne, J. (1990). *The Woman at the Keyhole: Feminism and Women's Cinema*. Bloomington: Indiana University Press.

Mazey, S. (2002). Gender Mainstreaming Strategies In The EU: Delivering On An Agenda? *Feminist Legal Studies*, *10*(3), 227–240. doi:10.1023/A:1021223828355

McMahon, M. (1995). *Engendering Motherhood: Identity and Self-Transformation in Women's Lives*. New York: Guilford Press.

McNay, L. (2000). *Gender and Agency: Reconguring the Subject in Feminist and Social Theory*. Cambridge: Polity Press.

Modleski, T. (1991). *Feminism without Women: Culture and Criticism in a "Postfeminist" Age*. New York: Routledge Publication.

Nicholson, J. L. (1987). Gender and History: The Limits of Social Theory in the Age of the Family. *Science and Society, 51*(3), 358–361.

Nicolson, P. (1996). *Gender, Power and Organisation*. London: Routledge Publication.

O'Connell, H. (1996). *Equality Postponed: Gender, Rights and Development*. Oxford, London: World View Publishing / One World Action.

Phillips, A. (1987). *Feminism and Equality*. Oxford: Blackwell.

Robson, A., & Robson, J. (Eds.). (1994). *Sexual Equality: Writings by John Stuart Mill, Harriet Taylor Mill and Helen Taylor*. Toronto: University of Toronto Press.

Rubin, G. (1975). In R. Reiter (Ed.), *The Traffic in Women: Notes on the 'Political Economy' of Sex in Toward an Anthropology of Women* (pp. 157–210). New York: Monthly Review Press.

Ryle, R. (2011). *Questioning Gender: A Sociological Exploration*. Thousand Oaks, CA: Pine Forge Press.

Scott, J. (1988). Deconstructing Equality-Versus-Difference: Or, The Uses of Poststructuralist Theory For Feminism. *Feminist Studies, 14*(1), 33–50. doi:10.2307/3177997

Skeggs, B. (1997). *Formations of Class and Gender*. London: Sage Publication.

Smith, A. R. (2010). *The Politics of Sexuality: A Documentary and Reference Guide (Documentary and Reference Guides)*. London, USA: Greenwood Publication.

Smith, S. (2008). *Gender Stereotypes: An Analysis of Popular Films and TV*. Geena Davis Institute on Gender in Media. Retrieved from http://www.thegeenadavisinstitute.org/downloads/GDIGM_Gender_Stereotypes.pdf

Thornton, M. (1986). Sex Equality Is Not Enough For Feminism. In C. Pateman & E. Gross (Eds.), *Feminist Challenges: Social and Political Theory*. Sydney, NSW: Allen and Unwin.

Verhaeghe, P. (2019). *Beyond Gender: From Subject to Drive*. New York: Other Press.

Walby, S. (1997). *Gender Transformations*. London: Routledge Press.

Walsh, M., & Gatens, M. (2004). *Twenty Years Since 'A Critique Of The Sex/Gender Distinction: A conversation with Moira Gatens*. Retrieved from https://www.tandfonline.com/doi/abs/10.1080/0816464042000226447

Weedon, C. (1999). *Feminism, Theory and the Politics of Difference*. Oxford: Blackwell Publishing.

KEY TERMS AND DEFINITIONS

Classical Narrative Cinema: The narrative structure that presents film narratives within the male-dominated view.

Female Characters: They are the ones who perform the representation of women's roles in film narratives.

Representation: Presenting an event, person or situation to the spectators with certain narrative strategies.

Sexuality: Identification of individuals in relation to their biological sex.

Social Gender: Social gender is a form of gender that is created within the frame of the social order discourses.

Subject: The state in which an individual can feel himself/herself with his/her own existence.

Subjectivity: It indicates that judgments can vary from person to person.

Chapter 14
Presentation of Female Character Subjectification in Iranian Cinema

Dilek Ulusal
Kırıkkale University, Turkey

ABSTRACT

Cinema is a social practice where myths about femininity and masculinity are produced, reproduced, and represented. Within this context, in cinema which produces feminine myths and forms female representations by reproducing them, feminist narratives are incontrovertible. In this study, female characters in political woman theme film Ten, directed in 2002 by Abbas Kiarostami who is recognized as one of the most successful directors of Modern Iranian Cinema, are examined in terms of feminist film theory. As a result of the study, it was observed that the director Kiarostami uplifted the identity of women by the narrative of the female characters he placed in the subject position of the film and tried to overthrow the established perception towards the women who were qualified as "the other" in Iranian society, through cinema.

INTRODUCTION

In a society, when male sovereignty comes to mind, first of all, it is the pressure of men on women. From a sociological point of view, this process has become an ideology and formed the patriarchal ideology in male-dominated societies. Patriarchal ideology is the ideology of male domination condemning women to serve men and to accept this role of service (Donovan, 1997: 273-274). Recently, inequality of women and men is one of the most mentioned topics in cinema. According to Lauretis (1984: 15-16), in cinema, which is a means of social representation, the relation of subjectivity, gender and sex differentiation with meaning and ideology is at the center of cinematic theory. Similarly, women who were excluded from the society after the Islamic Revolution in 1979 were excluded from the society by making cinema a means to serve the patriarchal ideology, the women either could not take part in the cinema or could just be an object serving the male subject. This situation ended with the moderate Islamist Muhammad Khatami elected as President in 1997. In the time of Khatami, who supported the art and artist, anti-Revolutionary directors established Modern Iranian Cinema. Anti-Revolutionary Directors, who have drawn women-themed political films within the modern Iranian Cinema, have attempted to glorify women's identity by destroying "the other" perception towards women in society. The aim of this study is to put forward the subjectified presentation of female characters in Modern Iranian Cinema via the film "Ten" by benefiting from feminist film theory.

Feminist analysis has become sharper and more powerful through the power of images that replace ideology (Smelik, 2008: 3- 4). Within this context, the necessity of handling the feminist and semiotic film theories together in the analysis becomes evident. Because images form the majority of narration in Iranian Cinema, feminist and semiotic film theories will be used to analyze the films to be examined.

GENDER AND POTENCY RELATIONSHIP

The concept of gender includes social and cultural norms that are determined and imposed by society in relation to masculinity and femininity. The reflection of this concept in society constitutes the roles assigned to men and women in that society (Yılmaz, 2007: 1). The role indicates the position of the person in the organized social structures, the responsibilities related to this position, the privileges and the rules that direct the interaction with people in other positions. Different roles given to women and men by society as; mother, father, teacher, soldier, are known as gender roles. Women and men are expected to maintain their lives by adhering to these rules determined by society (Dökmen, 2004: 16).

According to Connell (1998: 56), the notion of a socially crafted, previously learned scenario that was previously prepared for individual behavior could easily be adapted to gender. Connell supported that terms like "gender role", "men role" and "women role" became widespread in 1940s and starting from 1940s, gender role got into the central category of academic thinking and gender differences were listed under the title of "role" in literature. The most important names working on sexist roles in these years are the American Cultural Anthropologist Margaret Mead, the American sociologist Talcott Parsons and the French philosopher Simone de Beauvoir. Parsons has developed a functional theory of gender roles and the cultural contradictions surrounding them. Mead, on the other hand, was concerned with the emotional appearance of culture as a whole, and thus documented the ways in which different cultures approached sex and gender. But de Beauvoir, based the emergence of social roles on power. Thus, whereas Mead and Parsons shaped the gender role around tradition and communal stability view, de Beauvoir shaped that as ruling over women (Connell, 1998: 57-58).

According to Donovan (1997: 232), de Beauvoir's contribution to feminist theory is to make use of existentialist theory in order to explain the cultural and political status of woman. De Beauvoir supports that in a patriarchal culture, being a man or having a male status is set up as positive or norm, whereas being a woman or having a female status is set up as negative or abnormal, in other words "the other". Along with this, he says that because feminism acts in line with "Existentialism", the anatomy is not a destiny, and a person is bound to this world with his/her body. De Beauvoir points out that, it is easier for a male body to perform free creative activities because of having sexual activity without the fear of punishment, having no restrictive features like menstruation or getting pregnant, whereas a female body has restrictive activities because of menstruation or getting pregnant (As cited in Donovan, 1997: 233-234). In this context, as De Beauvoir has pointed out, it can be said that the gender-specific roles determined by the dominant ideology and culture in a society are also determined according to existential characteristics. But as we can infer from his words: "One is not born, but rather becomes, a woman" De Beauvoir argues that the status of women's "being the second sex" is more social, historical and cultural rather than existential. He criticizes this situation to the fullest, saying that this situation creates a certain female personality in everyday life. (Direk, 2009:12).

The more radical wing of the feminist movement, emphasizing the importance of power in gender relations, criticizes other feminist movements for their inadequacy (Connell, 1998:61). By focusing on the political side of the intersexual relations in her book "Sexual Politics" Kate Millett emphasizes that sexual politics is formed by relationships based on power, that is, systems in which a group of people is ruled by another (2018, 44-45). According to Millett (2018, 47):

The feature that has not been subject to examination in the social order, or even has not been realized, is that men see their sovereignty over women as an innate right. In this way, the "internal exploitation" system has emerged.

Presentation of Female Character Subjectification in Iranian Cinema

This order is more definite, more rigid and more durable than any racial division, class division. Although it seems that there is equality between women and men today, sexual sovereignty continues as the most common ideology of our culture and constitutes the concept of fundamental strength.

According to Foucault, sexuality is produced and used by various mechanisms in different ways and for different purposes. Foucault, who believes that sexuality is determined particularly according to power, argues that sex itself merely bases upon the claim that "the sexuality regulated by the bodies dominated by power and their materiality, power, energies, sensations and pleasures is the most speculative, the most ideal and the most intrinsic element."[1] Foucault describes the way people describe themselves as sexually freed individuals, in fact, that people fall into a tighter network of power rather than liberating sexually (Weeks, 2013: 59). Accordingly, it appears that Foucault also agrees with other feminist thinkers that gender-based determinations are power-based in societies.

Radical groups of women's liberation movements argue that women are oppressed because of the power of men over women, and that changing women's position primarily means opposing men's power in society and eventually destroying it (Connell, 1998: 61). In the same way, there has been a counter-reaction to the representation of women in cinema by radical feminist groups and feminist directors and as a result of this opposition, a feminist theory of cinema emerged.

RELATIONSHIP BETWEEN CINEMA, GENDER AND POWER

Feminist cinema is a cinema which demonstrates gender differences from a female perspective and displays a critical awareness of the asymmetrical power relationship between sexes (Öğüt, 2009: 203). But, in mainstream cinema, narratives for women are based upon stereotypes and the language of expression is language of masculine power. The ones out of this masculine power are seen as objects to be narrated upon (Yüksel, 2010: 88). Based on this information, it is necessary to say that mainstream cinema, which forms its rhetoric on masculine dominant language and makes women "objects" by presenting female characters mostly as bodies that address the sense of pleasure of men, has recently become popular and has created popular cinema. On top of that, Berktay also argues that a raunchy female image, which is presented as the women in popular cinema, is generally presented with her body and seduces the man (2005: 4). In this context, John Berger's interpretation of the role of gender in examining the history of art and visual culture "female body became the object of fetish of the male gaze" may also be valid for the cinema, the most important representation of visual culture.[2] However, in the New Wave and

Neorealist cinemas, which are known as art cinema and which generally deal with social realities, the women are not so underestimated as to be transformed into an object of consumption that exists only with her body. Even in such cinemas, sometimes women are removed from being the object of the film and placed in the position of the subject of the film, and thus, "the other" perception for women in cinema is tried to be eliminated. Similar situations are also present in feminist cinema. Feminist cinema opposes the representation of women in the form of nonhistorical objects, using a cinematic language that eliminates the dominant masculine view and stereotyped myths. The most important feature that distinguishes the films of women directors who do not accept the differences between the good girl and the bad girl based on social language hierarchy, and which question the way women are represented on the text or on the screen, is that they created a new perspective and language (Öğüt, 2009: 203- 204).

The filmmakers, who were annoyed by the fact that women were generally presented in their films in a way that appealed to the sense of pleasure of men, and who think that women are not involved as much as they should both as actresses and directors in cinema, developed a feminist theory of cinema in the 1970s For the first time in August 1972, women kicked up a row in the place where the Edinburgh Film Festival was held and succeeded. At the beginning of 1973 Claire Johnston was successful in screening of women's films at the National Film Theatre. In fact, at that time, the ideological reasons behind the feminist film production led to the emergence of feminist cinema theory. In this context it should be said that in the early periods of Feminist cinema theory sexuality and its presentation and its relations with the dominance of male power in a patriarchal society are determined as the main area of interest.[3]

Claire Johnston argued that the representation of women by traditional gender roles is ideologically based. Johnston, who writes articles on feminist film theory and practice, emphasizes in her writings that women are uniformized. Opposing restrictive traditions in cinema, Johnston proposes a movie as entertaining. Johnston also opposes classical cinema which sees a woman as an extension of male perception and criticizes the traditional roles for women in cinema. In this respect, she emphasizes the necessity of introducing a new concept of cinema that opposes the dominant cinema and its male-dominated base. She names the cinema as avant-garde, namely counter-cinema.[4] Laura Mulvey, one of the founders of feminist cinema, touches on the importance of male-dominated perspective in cinema in her article of "Visual Pleasure and Narrative Cinema". Mulvey argues that the pleasure that arises from Scopophilia, is a male-specific pleasure. She says that while women are exhibited to give pleasure to men who are the active controllers of the gaze they are also used as a threatening symbol of the fear of emasculation (As cited in: Öğüt, 2009: 204).

In this context, it can be said that in Mulvey's understanding of cinema, the woman is used to serve the man's sense of pleasure and that she adopts the notion of "the subject of pleasure" for the woman, besides, Mulvey approaches the inequality of woman-man in cinema based on Freud's psychoanalytic approach rather than Johnston's ideological approach.

FEMINIST NARRATION IN IRAN CINEMA

Cinema is a social practice where myths about femininity and masculinity are produced, reproduced and represented (Smelik, 2008: 1). In this context it is necessary to emphasize the importance of feminist narratives in the cinema which produces and reproduces feminine myths. Feminist theory against traditional patriarchal cinema criticizes traditional cinema (Aslantepe, 2010: 4). Contrary to the traditional concept of cinema which makes the structure of narration an effective and powerful masculine character, Feminist cinema has feminine dominance and female characters are the subject of the film. According to Teresa de Lauretis (1984:5), women in Western culture are fictionalized and represented as "the other" in cinema. These women are completely separated from the real women living under social and historical conditions. Smelik (2008:12), however, argues that it is not possible for the feminine subject to take part in this structure. According to Smelik (2008: 37), this fictionalized woman finds herself in a pointless absence that women cannot represent themselves and the woman is stuck in between the masculine representations and the womanhood reflected by the image that these representations produce. According to Peterson and Matthews, representation legitimizes dominant ideology in culture, and in any case is created by political motives. In the light of what has been said, it should be said that the feminist theory which is based on the representations of women in cinema, tries to produce statements on the fact that women should not be represented as the subject of desire, and paves the way for the birth of a new social subject belonging to women. Shortly, one of the most important innovations created by women's cinema is to refuse to fetishize women by making them objects. According to Öğüt (2009:204), Feminist cinema either avoids the fetishization of the feminine subject or deconstructs it with a critical approach. Öğüt argues that it is not possible to transform the female character into a fetishized image anymore when she becomes a subject or when she struggles to win her own agency and will (2009: 204).

After the Islamic Revolution in 1979, the modern cinema of the Pahlavi Period, which was also a great change in Iranian cinema, was destroyed and masculine domination was observed in cinema. In the post-revolutionary Iranian Cinema, the creation of Islamic cinema was encouraged in order to spread religious ideas in the period defined as the "First Republic". In this period, film production was brought under the control of the government and a very strict censorship law was designed (Dönmez-Colin, 2006: 57). And, in this period, the cinema was also used in the light of the Divine Cemal and Celal for revealing and expression of the inherent ingenuity of mankind (Aktaş, 2015: 84). During the First Republican Period, because government thought that showing the woman in a story or a play may cause the men get excited and get out of the way, the woman was almost never included in the cinema. If a female character is needed to be included in a film, she could only appear as an "obedient wife" or "an enduring mother". Because the law prohibits physical intimacy between men and women, love themed subjects have never been portrayed on the screen (Dönmez-Colin, 2006: 59). In this regard, in the early years of Revolution which is called First Republican Period, it should be said that women could only take position of "object" in the films as a side character (service character).

The cinema period after the Islamic Revolution, that Dönmez and Colin named 'First Republic' ended in 1997 when Muhammad Khatami was elected as President. Khatami, who came to power after the death of Ayatollah Khomeini, succeeded in changing the course of cinema in Iran. Khatami who always emphasized the idea of civilized society, believed that women who were marginalized from the social life after the Islamic Revolution, should be engaged in artistic activities (Aktaş, 2015: 105). Thus, in the Iranian cinema "First Republic" Period was over, and a new period of cinema called Social Cinema has begun. In the period of Social Cinema, documentary-style films which address social realities were made. During this period, the anti-revolutionary directors made women-themed political films by bringing the destructive effects of the Islamic revolution, especially on women, to the cinema. Thus, women who were in position of objects in the early ages of revolution were brought to the position of subjects of films by anti-evolutionary directors. It has been seen that anti-Revolutionary directors who think about changing the perception of women in the society by creating a new woman image in the cinema by creating women images based on women's grievances, use the spectral expression in designing this new woman because the effects of Islamic Revolution are still being practiced though being decreased.

PRESENTATION OF SUBJECTIFIED FEMALE CHARACTERS IN FILM "TEN"

Anti-revolutionary directors such as Abbas Kiarostami, who didn't get much of a place in cinema during the early years of the Islamic revolution in Iran in 1979, began to take an active part in cinema in 1997 with the election of moderate Islamist Muhammad Khatami, who supported the art and artist, as the President. Abbas Kiarostami's film "Ten", that he shot in 2002, is shown among women themed political films made in and after 1997 which is the period known as the period of social Cinema in Iran. As in the case of other women themed political films, in the film ten, director Kiarostami wanted to eliminate the perception of "the other" towards women in Iran, accompanied by the narration of female characters in position of subject and their stories. In the film "Ten", the situation is different. The film takes place in a car from beginning to end. The main character, in other words the subject of the film is a woman. The narration is based upon the story of this woman. Throughout the film, women who get in and out of the car are especially chosen by the director to support the story of the main female character. Dialogues between these characters and the main female character in the car throughout the film results from the director's desire to criticize masculine mentality that prevails in Iran governed by Sharia law. The only character (male) in the position of the object is Amin, the main female character's son.

The film begins with the female character taking her son Amin into the car. Amin blames her mother for divorcing her father. She explains herself to prove that she was right about the divorce by saying, "I was like a dead person when I was married to your father, I had to lie in the court to get divorced. Because in Iran, laws don't give women any right." In this scene, director Kiarostami, shows us that, as an object of the film, the son who questions and scolds his mother fearlessly is a "bad" character, and the mother who tries to prove her righteousness to her son, is a "good" character. Thus, through the speech of the mother character addressing to her son Amin, the director Kiarostami, tries to reintegrate the women who are alienated from the family and society back to society and uplift them by trying to put forward the reaction of the marginalized women against the order in Iran where the patriarchal society dominates the structure. Kiarostami supports the reaction of the woman in the subject position of the film through indicators like her modern style dressing, her make-up, her flashy accessories, her way of covering etc. The fact that the movie was filmed in a car, not in a house dictated as a place of women in the Iranian society, gives the car a metaphoric meaning. Kiarostami associates the car that he preferred as the main place of the film with the driver female character. He strengthens this relation in the company of other female characters who get in the female driver's car -including a prostitute- and their dialogues with the driver. In this context it can be said that main female character who is the car driver in the film and other female characters are the subjects of the film. Because when the stories of all female characters come together in the film, only a feminist narrative can be established. In this way, Kiarostami, through this feminist narrative he established in the film, price to bring women to a more combative, active, strong and free position in society by trying to change the perception towards women seen as passive, oppressed and marginalized in the society.

Especially in the conversations between the woman and the prostitute who the driver takes in her car, it is observed that the director tries to overthrow the perception of "the other" towards women in Iranian society. In these scenes in which we cannot see the face of the prostitute, her words become more riveting. In these scenes, the driver's questions and prostitute's answers to these questions are very important in terms of the "feminist narrative" that the director seeks to construct through the characters of the film. To the question of the driver woman, "how did you go astray?", the prostitute responses: "I had a normal life like other women who lived in Iran then. I was engaged. I went astray when my fiancé left me. Now I love my job, and I think it's too stupid to be stuck on a man." This answer by the prostitute can be interpreted as a feminist discourse that the director tries to compose through the woman characters who are the subjects of the film. Because in the words of the prostitute, there is the design of an individual who can stand on her own legs and who is fit into social life. In this context, it is seen that, Kiarostami acts in a way that Feminist cinema theorists opposes male-dominant view and woman's being stereotyped in cinema.

In the film, one of the most important indicators of the opposition to the patriarchal ideology that differentiates women in the Iranian society is the female character with shaved hair the main female character takes in her car. This female character who tells the driver woman that the man he loved got married to another woman, removes the headscarf and her shaved hair is seen. Director Kiarostami performs the reaction against the patriarchal order in İran with a metaphorical narrative he formed through the shaved hair of this female character subjectified in the film which he shot from a feminist point of view. When the story she tells and her shaved hair are associated, it seems to have a metaphorical meaning of "woman's reaction to man". The director wants to strengthen the feminist narrative infrastructure in the film with these metaphoric and semiotic narratives in the film and thus carries the film to a more artistic dimension.

FUTURE RESEARCH DIRECTIONS

This feminist study which is applied through the subjectified female characters of the film "Ten", which is shown among the women-themed political films, aims to become an academic work to guide researchers who will conduct future researches on gender and cinema. The patriarchal system, which is practiced with Islamic rules in the Middle East, known as the Islamic geography, assimilates women in society and this victimization experienced by women is carried to the cinema by feminist directors who criticize the system and advocate equality between women and men. This study is a gender-based study of female characters in Iranian cinema, which is included in Middle Eastern cinema. My suggestion to those who will conduct further studies on gender and cinema will be that they should study on Middle Eastern countries where the inequality of men and women is most common and on the cinemas of these countries.

CONCLUSION

In the period, known as "Social Cinema" period in Iran in 1997 and after, especially anti-Revolutionary filmmakers shot women-themed political films from a feminist point of view by taking the familial and social problems of women who experienced the destructive effects of the Revolution, to the scene. In this study, the female characters in the film Ten, which is shown among the women-themed political films in the modern Iranian Cinema, were examined in the light of the feminist and semiotic film theories. As a result of the study, it was seen that director Kiarostami tried to form a feminist narrative by breaking the established perception towards women who are seen as oppressed passive and marginalized and by placing the woman characters as the subject of the film in "Ten" and supported this narrative he tried to establish through subject female characters via metaphors and indicators. By this way, it is observed that Kiarostami acts with the approach adopted by the theoreticians who oppose the masculine dominated view, which monotype the woman in cinema, and accomplishes this through a feminist narrative that he constructs through the female characters that he subjects in his film.

REFERENCES

Aktaş, C. (2015). *Şarkın Şiiri İran Sineması*. İstanbul, Turkey: İz Yayıncılık.

Arslantepe, M. (2010). *Sinemada Feminist Teori: 3. Uluslararası Bir Bilim Kongresi Olarak Kadın: Edebiyat, Dil, Kültür ve Sanat Çalışmalarında Kadın Sempozyumu*. Konya, Turkey: Selçuk Üniversitesi.

Berktay, F. (2005). Meşum Kadınlar, Solucanlar, Maymunlar, Zehirli Sarmaşıklar. *Kadın Belleği Dergisi*, 1.

Connell, R. W. (1998). *Toplumsal Cinsiyet ve İktidar*. İstanbul, Turkey: Ayrıntı Yayınları.

Direk, Z. (2009). *Simone de Beauvoir: Abjeksiyon ve Eros Etiği: Cogito Düşünce Dergisi*. Yapı Kredi Yayınları.

Dökmen, Z. (2004). *Toplumsal Cinsiyet*. İstanbul, Turkey: Sistem Yayıncılık.

Dönmez-Colin, G. (2006). *Kadın, İslam Ve Sinema*. İstanbul, Turkey: Agorakitaplığı yayınları. Retrieved from http://www.sanatduvari.com http://www.2014hit.blogspot.com

Donovan, J. (1997). *Feminist Teori*. İstanbul, Turkey: İletişim Yayınları.

Lauretis, T. (1984). *Alice Doesn't: Feminism, Semiotics, Cinema*. Bloomington, IN: Indiana University Press. doi:10.1007/978-1-349-17495-9

Millett, K. (2018). *Cinsel Politika*. İstanbul, Turkey: Payel Yayınları.

Öğüt, H. (2009). *Kadın Filmleri ve Feminist Karşı Sinema: Cogito Düşünce Dergisi*. Yapı Kredi Yayınları.

Peterson, T. G., & Mathews, P. (2008). Sanat Tarihinin Feminist Eleştirisi: Sanat Cinsiyet Sanat Tarihi ve Feminist Eleştiri. İstanbul, Turkey: İletişim Yayınları.

Smelik, A. (2008). *Feminist Sinema ve Film Teorisi*. İstanbul, Turkey: Agora Kitaplığı.

Weeks, K. (2013). *Feminist Öznelerin Kuruluşu*. İstanbul, Turkey: Otonom Yayıncılık.

Whitham, G., & Pooke, G. (2018). *Çağdaş Sanatı Anlamak*. İstanbul, Turkey: Hayalperest Yayınları.

Yılmaz, A. (2007). Reklamlarda Toplumsal Cinsiyet Kavramı: 1960-1990 Yılları Arası Milliyet Gazetesi Reklamlarına Yönelik Bir İçerik Analizi. *Selçuk Üniversitesi İletişim Fakültesi Dergisi*, 4(4). Retrieved from http://www.acikerisim.selcuk.edu.tr

Young, M. I. (2009). *Yaşanan Bedene Karşı Toplumsal Cinsiyet: Toplumsal Yapı ve Öznellik üzerine Düşünceler: Cogito Düşünce Dergisi*. Yapı Kredi Yayınları.

Yüksel, S. D. (2010). Sinemada Ulusal Kimliğin Pekiştiricisi Olarak Kadınlar. *Selçuk İletişim Dergisi*, 6(3).

ADDITIONAL READING

Arber, S., Davidson, K., & Ginn, J. (2003). *Gender And Ageing*. Philadelphia: Open University Press.

KEY TERMS AND DEFINITIONS

Feminist Film Theory: It is a research method which focuses on inequality of women and men in the films and focuses on feminine discourse.

Gender: It is the social structure that determines the expectations, values, images, behaviors, roles, beliefs of men and women in a society.

Main Stream Cinema: Films that the cinema industry invests in and are shot for commercial purposes and appealing to all kinds of audiences. Popular topics are processed in main stream cinema. Its purpose is to achieve success at the box office and to provide the desired revenue from the films it offered as products.

Myth (Mythology): It is a folk story with an imaginative, allegorical narrative of gods, goddesses, the birth of the universe, spreading from generation to generation and transforming in time through the imagination of society. And another meaning is a person or an idealistic concept that has become a legend. The Feminine Myth is the set of roles assigned to the women in a society and made traditional in that society.

New Realistic Cinema: It is the cinema movement that emerged in Italy after World War II and pioneered the New Wave French Cinema. In New Realistic Cinema, social realistic issues are discussed as it has been in New Wave French Cinema.

New Wave Cinema: It is a cinema movement that emerged in 1950s in France and which was held up as an example by other countries' cinemas. The most important feature of this movement is that it shoots documentary-style films by taking social realistic issues in cinema.

Semiotic Film Theory: It is the theory that analyzes the implicit meanings imposed on the visual materials used in cinema, which builds its narrative on visuality.

ENDNOTES

[1] As cited in: Weeks, K. (2013). Feminist Öznelerin Kuruluşu, 58.
[2] Whitham, G., Pooke, G. (2018). *Çağdaş Sanatı Anlamak*. (1.Baskı), 67.
[3] http://www.sanatduvari.com
[4] http://www.2014hit.blogspot.com

Chapter 15
Gender in the Honky Tonk as a Space of Representation:
The Film *Dutturu Dunya*

Meltem Yılmaz Bilecen
https://orcid.org/0000-0002-3205-1027
Sivas Cumhuriyet University, Turkey

ABSTRACT

This study was prepared to investigate the gender roles in honky tonk organization, which has an important place in the bureaucratic structure of Ankara and can be considered as the place of representation against the representations of space, specifically in the film Dutturu Dunya. The film Dutturu Dunya was shot at a time when the new realism movement started in Turkish Cinema and found personality with Zeki Ökten. In the film, Ulus, Bakanlıklar mounted for the representation of the space and Hıdırlıktepe which is an extension of the representation space and described as the slum area are used as the main place. In the study, the gender roles are explained based on space fiction and dialogue of the film. It was seen as a result of the analysis that unlike the common opinion, not only the body and labor of woman working in honky tonk but also body and labor and labor exploitation of men were realized. The matter distinguishing male and female workers is that honky tonk is a place where woman goes astray but man somehow earns his living.

INTRODUCTION

People not only experience the space but also think and dream through it. Therefore, the space does not only shape the present social world (experienced and understood as a meaningful life condition), but also shapes other possible social worlds that can inspire action and express collective dreams. (Stavrides, 2010:11)

DOI: 10.4018/978-1-7998-0128-3.ch015

Gender in the Honky Tonk as a Space of Representation

After Ankara became the capital of the Republic, it is known that new missions are attributed to the city both socially and politically and these missions bring new openings to the people living in the capital, which has become the showcase of the Republic, for changing their understanding of entertainment as well as their work and home life. It is known that during the first years of the Republic, the ways of planned urbanization were sought with Lörcher and Jansen's Plans; on the other hand, places defined as places of memory by Pierre Nora (2006) began to be established in order to form the urban culture and entertainment sense and ballroom and theater halls were opened to transform the urban identity. It is expressed in the work of Yakup Kadri Karaosmanoğlu (2009:109) entitled "Ankara" presenting a section from the period when Ankara Palas, which was opened to host visitors coming to Ankara, hosted ball and similar events and was welcomed by the people of the city.

It can be said that the first periods of the republic, which included not only the efforts of building a city but also a nation defeated by the squatting and then to the habits of the population who were not urbanite but living in the city as well as their cultures they adapted to the city after the 1950s. Ankara which was the capital of the bureaucracy at that time was also the capital of honky tonks[1] when it comes to the 80s. Honky tonks whose content videos are viewed by million times in Youtube and the music type produced there are also listened by millions of people all over the country constitute an important unplanned part of Ankara. Honky tonks can be considered as a counter-position against the personality of the city, as well as the traditional one's transformation and emergence in a new area. It can even be asserted that the urban personality prevails over the personality of the city in spite of all the planning efforts. As stated by John Urry (1999), urban personality is shy, standoffish, and tired (1999,20). However, honky tonks removed the distance between a man, who had not seen any female body other than his wife and who had lived only in a place close to their family members, and the "female figure", allowed him to meet on common ground with the people whom he did know and who were not from the same location, brought him to the outside world and adapted a traditional entertainment type such as the drinking party with dancing girls (oturak alemi) performed only in fests or in weddings into daily life and removed him from the negative characteristics of the city for a while. Even though the role of women in honky tonks which can be asserted to serve as a therapy mechanism for men and is a masculine place is described as essential, ultimately, honky tonk is a place where the woman "falls".

In this study, Ankara Honky tonks which completely symbolize the social transformation with their location, presentation, content and entertainment concept contrasting with the bureaucratic and planned urban identity of Ankara were investigated through the honky tonk symbolic film "Dutturu Dunya" and the gender roles in honky tonk as a sector were tried to be identified over the film.

The main reason for the selection of this film is that the film which is still aired in national television channels today has been aired in many TV channels with different belonging structure and ideological orientation and it has been watched by many different audiences. For this reason, it serves for the spreading and acceptance of certain judgments about honky tonk.

The film "Dutturu Dunya" which was directed by Zeki Ökten in 1988, whose script was written by Umur Bugay, and whose starring characters were Kemal Sunal (Mehmet) and Jale Aylanç, becomes more meaningful when considering that Zeki Ökten is an important name of the New Reality Movement in Turkish Cinema (Yakın: 2009).

Main places of the film are the Hıdırlıktepe where Mehmet's house is located and which is very close to the historical city center Ulus which is one of the shantytowns of Ankara and formed through planning for the representation of space; Ulus Çankırı Street which is the most busy and also so-called "honky tonks region" of Ankara is the location, where the honky tonk that Mehmet works is located, and Bakanlıklar which is also shaped in the context of the representation of the place where Mehmet's brother-in-law works and Mehmet also fills lighter gas.

In the study, dialogues and location fiction in the honky tonk scenes in the film are discussed while analyzing the film and the dialogues are analyzed with discourse analysis. The fact that the cinema text whose visual aspect is prominent has visual and linguistic dimensions and as pointed out by Roland Barthes (2012:28), visual essence strengthens their meaning by supporting a linguistic statement and visual statement is in a structural renewal or substitution connection also brings a semiotic analysis.

The position of the women and men working in honky tonks, which is a masculine entertainment venue, and necessitating the continuity of honky tonk is discussed in the light of the indicators in the film.

I-Spatial Representation and Representative Space of Ankara

Although cities are tried to be shaped by urban planners and administrative powers systematically, each city is fed by the life practices of the people living in that city and patterned with the cultural life perception of these people. People sometimes shape the city and sometimes the city shapes human through laws, rules and plans. It can be asserted that there is a mutual and obligatory relationship between man and city. The definitions reported initially are melting the cities in a common pot and it can be said that the elements featuring the cities are the features that distinguish them from each other. Each city brings along its lifestyle and life perception.

Gender in the Honky Tonk as a Space of Representation

In the presentation of cities, symbols and judgments which are highlighted and suggesting how to perceive that city are produced. While these judgments are sometimes produced by the people living in these places, they are sometimes shaped by managerial powers. As seen in the conceptualization of the representation of space and representative space by Lefebvre (2014:63), while the representation of space is produced by the government, "representative spaces are dependent on the illegal and underground side of social life, as well. They represent mixed symbolism depending on art that cannot be probably defined as space code but as the code of the representative spaces". When this definition is examined in the context of Ankara, it is seen that Ankara underwent the process of restructuring as a result of the establishment of the Republic and the announcement of Ankara as the capital, Löcher (Cengizkan,2004)'s plans between 1924-1925 and Jansen's Plans in 1928 were applied (Şenyapılı,2004:63-68) and the representation of Ankara, the capital, was being prepared by means of these applications. When the honky tonks which are the subject of the study are examined from Ankara perspective at this point, honky tonk is a representative space. Since for people living Ankara, the honky tonks located on Talatpaşa Boulevard, Maltepe or Çankırı Streets are considered as the places that were quite ordinary, as if they were always there, if a woman did not work there then she could not have the possibility to hang around; they could be perceived as the places which were meaningless and interspersed and whose signs were hanging on the route selected to take a bus or to go to the shops or public institutions. In fact, the honky tonks located in Ankara have a unique place in its city history and culture.

While preparing a study on Honky tonk culture, perhaps the first thing to do is to define the honky tonk. In this way, the features that distinguish the Honky tonk from other places can be determined and it can be clarified what kind of space it is. The word Honky tonk has three different meanings according to Turkish Dictionary of Turkish Language Association;

1. Each of the structures of an organization or an institution, in a garden.
2. Independent exhibition area for products at a fair.
3. The public entertainment house that is open up to late night.

The honky tonk, which will be addressed in this study, has a similar meaning to the explanation in the third definition to the exclusion of the other two definitions, but it is not just about this definition. If the honky tonk is interpreted as it is in the third definition, it is not possible to see some elements mentioned therein.

The first problem is related to the entertainment included in the definition of honky tonk. The concept of entertainment, according to the Turkish Language Institution's current Turkish dictionary, means;

1. Having fun, debauchery:
2. Thing or someone helping to have joyful and cheerful time.

In these definitions, there is no gender discrimination related to the person to be entertained. However, since the entertainment area in question is honky tonk, in practice, the people who will have fun are separated from the gender perspective. Honky tonk is a place where men go for fun and women "fall" into and only work. In short, women are not the costumers of this space. In this respect, the production, distribution and marketing of entertainment for men is carried out. It is not possible to draw this meaning from the definition made.

When the entertainment concept in the space (especially when considering the city where the study was conducted) is examined as the thing helping to have joyful and pleasant time stated in the definition, it can be classified as music and alcohol and the people who serve people to have joyful and pleasant time are:

- **Hostesses:** Women providing benefit to their working place such as casinos, bars by eating and drinking with the customers.
- **Belly Dancers:** Women who perform a dance as a profession.
- **Players:** Women allowing men to join their dances they perform similar to folkloric dances of Ankara but not similar to folkloric dance in terms of the role taken or the playing type in the space.
- **Artists:** Can be classified as women and/or men singing song or playing any instrument in the space.

As it is seen in the classification, the entertainers are usually women and even some works are only specific to women. This situation also support that these places are the entertainment places for men which were determined at the beginning. As a result of these inferences, the definition of a honky tonk that does not appear in the dictionary appears. Honky tonk is a public entertainment house where men have fun and women work as a hostess, belly dancer, player, and artist.

Dutturu Dunya reveal the roles of other workers and women in honky tonk along with their positions based on the sections of the life of a male "artist", a projection of honky tonk.

I Honky Tonk of Düttürü Dünya

The film, which was directed by Zeki Ökten in 1988, whose script was written by Umur Bugay, and whose starring characters were Kemal Sunal (Mehmet) and Jale Aylanç (Mehmet's wife Gülsüm), was shot in Bakanlıklar along with two main locations in Ankara including a slum in Hıdırlıktepe and a honky tonk located in Ulus. This triplet is important places helping us to see the position of the representative space and representation of space in everyday life. Hıdırlıktepe is one of the locations where the slum settlements, which can be evaluated as a resistance to planned urbanization and surrounded around Ulus/"historical city center", first started. Ulus, where the honky tonk is located, is a place that hosts historical heritage of many civilizations (Ankara Castle, Augustus Temple, Column of Julian, Roman Bath, Hacı Bayram Mosque, Zincirli Mosque, Parliament I, Tashan, Suluhan, State Museum of Painting and Sculpture, The Museum of Independence ...), has gotten away from being a historical city and trade center, and includes Çankırı Street which is the longest honky tonk corridor of Ankara. Bakanlıklar is the place built by Jansen's Plan according to the values represented by Nazım City Plan and the Republic. This spatial division makes the film even more meaningful.

While the film Dutturu Dunya provides sections from the Ankara of that period through Mehmet's life, the film shot at real places provides an important source of data in the examination of honky tonks. Because, as Karadoğan stated, the most obvious difference of Ökten from many other directors in Turkish cinema is that he can approach to the events, people, communities and historical periods mentioned in his films with a sociological or sometimes anthropological perspective (Karadoğan,2007). In the film, a quite realistic approach to the problem of poverty and squatting around the city center which was settled in the 1980s was displayed.

The film is about the struggle for life of clarinet player Mehmet, his wife and their three children including one disabled child between the honky tonk in Ulus, where Mehmet works, and their shanty house that belongs to his brother-in-law and is about to be pulled down in Hıdırlıktepe neighborhood which is one of the poorest districts of Ankara

Honky tonk in the film "Dutturu Dunya" is a work place that provides and is even quite far from providing a family to make barely a living. Mehmet goes out from his house in Hıdırlıktepe every night and goes to the honky tonk and returns back to his house at dawn on foot on the way from Ulus Meydan route. It is seen that Mehmet who is trying to make a living for his family by playing clarinet in the honky tonk is proud of doing his job even though he does not earn good, his wife has to work as a cleaning lady in the houses in Çankaya and this work does not even give a shanty they can live in. Because he is an artist in his own eyes. For him, the honky tonk is a work place to turn an honest penny.

Spatial Fiction

The film begins with a scene where a group of men dancing in the honky tonk. The music of a song named as "Nar Ağacı Narsız Olur mu?" which is an Ankara folk song written by Zekeriya Bozdağ is heard at the background.[2] While some of the men dancing on the floor wear leather jackets, some wear fabric jacket. The constant elements in their cloths are shirt and fabric pants.

The purpose of "entertaining men" which is one of the basic functions of a honky tonk can be clearly seen in this scene. The answer to the question "when a man plays" go beyond wedding floor. Men who have not even danced their own weddings due to "toughness and dignity" have fun without the need of a special reason and on a place where they can determine the time they wish and they do not need a special outfit or care. The food and beverages on the table (specially presented candles, champagne glasses), their presentations, and women's dresses (evening dress) summarize a situation described by Piere Bourdieu (2015)'s work entitled as "Distinction". These elements, which once emphasized the exclusiveness of the privileged class, started to be used by the subclass and brought banality with it. Closure of women's clothing does not prevent the presentation of the female body as a commodity.

Scene 3: After this image, the camera turns to the scene and a blonde woman with bob haircut and outward blow dry is seen to be singing. She wears a yellow sequined evening dress. This woman has also chosen a dress that is quite closed and far from décollete. The dress looks rather sloppy and cheap. Without the sequins, the dress has no difference with the casual dress. Nevertheless, it can be understood from her dress that she is more elaborated than the male customer profile and she does not appear as an ordinary person there. Behind this scene, two men wearing black suit and white shirt and playing darbuka and clarinet are seen and it is understood from their acts that they enjoy playing. Then, two other men wearing the same dress and playing saz (a stringed instrument) and kanun behind them come on the screen. The orchestra plays on the back of the stage on an area framed by red fabric. Although they are in a honky tonk, the musicians are actually dressed appropriate for their missions and far from the state of general negligence, but they also have an ordinary appearance from its uniformity. The clothes carry their dignity and seriousness of being an artist.

Scene 4: A person entering the stage with a plate of torn flowers in his hand pours flowers from the head of the singing woman and it can be seen from her face that she is unhappy with the situation. Woman's act of not being satisfied with welcoming the action performed to appreciate or look nice to her has no meaning. Because the customer also pays extra money to the flowers and this provides a new input for the honky tonk. Flowers provide the continuation of a myth; Women are flowers and love flowers and flower is the ideal means for making a gesture to a woman.

Scene 7: Mehmet and his friend come out of the honky tonk at dawn. Honky tonk is located on the right at the beginning of a by-street which is connected to Çankırı Street. It has a ragged entrance decorated with posters which is below the road level. Mehmet and his friend walk straight from Çankırı Street to Ulus Square and they turn from the statue and walk towards their house. This scene of the film is again a valuable reference in terms of the representative space and representation of space.

Honky Tonk Scene

Scene 1: On the stage, the same woman is singing the song named "Mavi Gozler O Bicim" that was sung by Küçük Ceylan at that time. On the woman's neck, there are money banknotes added to each other. In this scene where honky tonk is more clearly seen, there are street lamps and flower motifs on the columns. In an area below the entry level, it is quite interesting to have used such patterns reminding of the street. The space that does not make any sense while passing in front of it creates its own street beneath the ground. The music playing in the background is like an arabesque version of a folk song. The rhythm is fast and it doesn't play a sad track in any scene. It is understood from the songs played here that the works of Mehmet who continuously writes sad songs have no place here. Ultimately, the honky tonk is an entertainment venue and the art to be performed here has to match the mission of the honky tonk.

Scene 2: Men and women have been sitting at some tables while women are just sitting at the other tables. A woman approaches to a table with the waitress and she meets the men at the table by extending her hands and then she sits at the table. While men are sitting side by side with women they just met, images such as the warmth between women and men and woman putting her hand on the man's shoulder and caressing his hair are reflected in the film scenes. In these scenes, the man has a more passive appearance; whereas, the woman presents an image who can communicate more comfortably and try to seduce the customer. Women are also dressed quite modest in this scene. Other than the belly dancer and the singer who comes to the stage in the 52nd minute, the shortest dresses of women in the honky tonk scenes are under their knees and their neck are quite closed even if they wear evening dresses. This causes the idea that the presence of a woman is adequate in order to exhibit sexual attraction in honky tonks.

With their appearance reflected on the frame of the film, the honky tonks of the 80s are rather bleak, uncared and sloppy. This uncared state is reflected both on the clothes of women working here and on the clothes of those coming here as an audience. Honky tonk is not a space where people wear the most elegant clothes and go to have fun with their most cared condition. Honky tonk is a space where men dance, drink, do not even pay attention to the voice of the singing person, and chat with the women working here, and the clichés such as soft lighting, red color, no design, etc., are mainly used.

Gender Positions in the Place

As mentioned earlier, honky tonk is not a space to which women go to have fun with themselves or with their spouse, boyfriends or relatives. This feature of the space also reflects on the film. It is also seen in the dialogue between Mehmet and the neighborhood guard. At the 11th minute of the film, a woman washes her clothes with the help of water she boiled using a boiler in front of her shanty house while Mehmet and his friend are walking in Hıdırlıktepe.

Mehmet's friend darbuka player Rifat: *(turn his head to the guard) Any news from your daughter?*
Guard: *She was last seen in Adana, she fell to a honky tonk.*
Mehmet: *Speak properly, we also work at honky tonk.*

While honky tonk is bread and butter for Mehmet and his working in a honky tonk is not found odd, there is an opposite situation for the woman. The woman is doing bad things here. In fact, although Mehmet's situation is not found odd by the guard, Mehmet's job is a problem for his wife. Gülsüm perceives Mehmet's job as understood from these lines "He smells like a raki, live it up with women until the morning". Mehmet, however, had drunk only a glass of raki at the breaks throughout the night and had no entertainment-related relationship with the women working there.

When it comes to the honky tonk scenes in the film, there are only women working as hostess, belly dancer or soloist in the venue. Hostess is the most money-making job here. This meaning can be drawn from the following dialogue between Serap and Mehmet.

Arif: *Customer ready, see Necip Bey, come on, you're good again. Serap is seen on the scene with a black dress and a red jacket worn on that dress, she has a cigarette in her hand, she walks slowly but confidently.*
Serap: *Is it too much for you?, let us work, we have sat to the point that we've started to collect dust.*
Mehmet: *You should be a woman in this country, Arif people are pouring money to them, the art is a lie.*
Serap: *Before hitting the table where the men are sitting, she hits on her buttocks to reply kindly to him.*

In fact, Serap is the soloist of the venue. From this point of view, it can be said that status of her work is higher than the other works performed in the club. But she does not do the hostess work for necessity. She even uses this to make a show to Mehmet. In spite of her old age, "being selected" is also a "pride" reason. When

Gender in the Honky Tonk as a Space of Representation

we look at the body language of the woman, it is seen that she does not comply with the gender-based roles of men and women and does not have any hesitation in contacting with the male body. Hostess work is symbolized as one of the most profitable lines of work at honky tonk in general terms. In another scene, when Mehmet could not get an advance from the owner of honky tonk, he wants to borrow money from another hostess at the venue which support the idea "hostesses earn a lot" shown in the other scene.

Mehtap: *Look at the prick, he will stuck us until the morning with a single drink. Am I the wailing wall here, he is drunk and telling his life, he is a truck driver, when he does, he dates with five girls...*
Mehmet: *Shush! easy, stop stop!*
Mehtap: *If you don't have any money, I'll order.*
Mehmet: *You are great lady Mehtap, don't think I am buttering up but I love you the most among them.*
Mehtap: *Hey beep beep, you only talk, you love but have you taken me to a dinner or have you bought any sh....t?*
Mehmet: *Just wait, once my songs hit the market, you will see the beep beep, I will pay you to stay in 5-star hotels. Have you listened to my last song, tears tears my friend, why they say men do not cry, don't make me suffer this pain any more... don't you think that it will be a hit haa?*
Mehtap: *I swear it is beautiful..*
Mehmet: *Hey Mehtap (says and he couldn't finish his talk), look the man is drunk since you did not care for him.*
Mehtap: *The bas....rd was already drunk......*
Mehmet: *Can you give me some money, I will pay back?*
Mehtap: *Are you broke?*
Mehmet: *You have no idea*
Mehtap: *How much?*
Mehmet: *300-400*
Mehtap: *Fu..... I swear on my son that I do not have that much.*
Mehmet: *Don't swear.*
Mehtap: *I had a 100, and my mother took it off. It is coal money, my boy is with her you know.*
Mehmet: *Don't tell me what his father does?*
Mehtap: *I queer his pitch, is he a man?*
Mehmet: *Okay, okay, I didn't ask. ...*

It is understood from these dialogues that although she earns more than Mehmet, she does not have much money anyway. The woman has to make a living for the house and is not alone as considered. She has a family. Although her mother does the care of the child, the necessary material needs are met by Mehtap. The rule that man brings money to the house which can be seen as a routine for regular familial relations during this period does not function in this family structure.

Another point that is remarkable in the dialogues is that women continuously use the slang and jargon and the masculine gesture, mimic, body movements are dominated on the woman along with the jargon used. Her speech forms are always open to fight and threatening. Placing hands on waist and challenging stand out especially in the scenes with Serap. The burden of working in a job that is seen as immoral by the public and clinging to life as a woman made them "masculine" in such a space established on their femininity.

Serap-Waiter- Mehmet Dialogue

Serap: *Didn't I tell you not to pour these shit on my head? (Serap's hands are on her waist while saying these words.)*
Waiter: *Leave the scene without saying anything.*
Şerif: *I am sorry.*
Serap: *Come on, what's up with this client, Serif brother?*
Mehmet: *The customer is the usual customer, but you are falling down*
Serap: *No way!*
Saz player: *It is midweek, don't sleep beep beep, there is a match on TV.*
Mehmet: *Cold comfort, you don't sleep baby cow, the honky tonk is full.*

As is seen in the dialogue, the soloist in the stage is responsible for gaining and keeping the customer. Service, space design, food and beverage options and presentation are not considered as a tool for retention, but the burden is collapsed on one person.

In another dialogue between Mehmet and Serap;

Serap: *Hey beep beep, what's up with that bluster.*
Mehmet: *What bluster, I guess you have a problem with your ears?*
Serap: *Don't deal with me, or else.*
Mehmet: *Or else, what?*
Serap: *I will tell Necip brother and he will get rid of you from here.*
Mehmet: *Girl, talk nicely or I will tear your mouth.*
Serap: *Tear it if it is easy.*
Şerif: *It is a shame Serap, stop it.*

Serap: *What I am gonna stop Serif brother, staying behind me making bluster, blow that pipe to you mother.*
Mehmet: *It is not called as pipe, learn and then come to the stage.*
Serap: *Who do you think you are, as if he went to the school for this job..*
Şerif: *Enough is enough!*
Mehmet: *I do not let anyone tell anything to my art!*
Serap: *I will sh.. your art, I can play that clarinet with my as...*
Waiter: *Mehmet brother*
Mehmet: *What....*
Waiter: *Your brother-in-law is waiting for you at the door ...*
Mehmet: *Hah, now we're up!*
Rıfat: *Wow, the man came and found you even here,*
Mehmet: *He finds me, he finds me even if I bury myself under the ground..*
Serap: *He does not know note or method, he thinks that he is a composer, the animal blow a few pipe in the military, that is it...*
Şerif: *That is enough my daughter!*
Serap: *Anyway..*

While Serap discusses in a very determined way, she sees herself in a superior position than Mehmet. That is why she threatens to fire him. While the soloist is the strongest woman position in this space, it also serves as superiority towards many men including waiter and musicians. Relationships are quite informal, the boss is referred to as a brother, there is no distance in the relations with employees and body contact is established without any gender discrimination. However, the other detail that should not be overlooked is the fact that the soloist is a valid money maker but not a guaranteed position. This situation can be seen from the Necip's dialogue first with Pervin and then with Serap in a day when Serap does not come to work.

Necip: *Pervin come on my daughter, undress.*
Pervin: *But Necip brother, what do I say, I do not know method or style...*
Necip: *My daughter, forget about the style or method now. What are they, let the customers clap and enjoy, come on girl says and take a tweak on her cheek.*

While Serap sees herself in a very strong position, in fact, she does not have an important place for Mr. Necip. Her place can be replaced; anyone who does not have any knowledge can do her job. Her work is nothing more than cheering up the customers. It is useful to underline that Mr. Necip call the women working for him as "my daughter" with a fatherly manner in his dialogues but he has no positive attitude attributed to father.

When examining the dialogue between Serap and Necip after the situation arisen

Serap-Necip Scene

Serap: *But, that is not right Necip abi?*
Necip: *What you did is not right too my daughter, if you are thinking your art, come on time.*
Pervin enters the stage with a red evening dress with decollete on the back and chest.
Serap: *Well, it suits you well, I wonder what will you sing with your crow like voice?*
Necip: *Shut it, don't encourage her, come on my daughter, ignore her now.*
Pervin: *Hahaha!*

Although it is known by everyone that Pervin cannot sing, she can take the stage instead of Serap. If Serap can do hostess work, Pervin can also do the soloist work. In short, there is no distinction between works or a caste. However, the soloist has a superior position than the musicians and waiters, no matter what. For Mr. Necip, none of them have a special place due to the work they do and if they don't make money, they can all be discarded.

In men, the situation is also not pleasant. A person working in a work branch can transfer to another work branch. For example, the old wrestler who have no work inside but works as the stander to take the coats of the guests may take the stage to wrestle with the chair when the soloist is late. For Honky tonk owner, each one is a mobile resource that can fill in the absence of each other. Their emotions and demands are of no importance, they are commodities as a wrestling chair. Even the position of the chair is more valuable than the men and women working here because the chair is a fixture. Although Mehmet positions himself as a clarinet player, his place is only a "beep beep" in the eyes of the other workers and of the owner.

CONCLUSION

While honky tonk which is a representative space is a spatial structure related to the underground of men and women, the non-moral burden in the discussion of legitimacy and illegality is placed on the shoulders of the woman. While the female body is fetishized, the perception of honky tonk, which transforms this fetish into a theatrical material, leads to the identification of women starting from the world of men. While the audience or men working at honky tonk undertaking an active role return to their role in daily life to a "family father" in their home as seen in Mehmet, women working in honky tonk continue their "blamable life" along with the necessity of taking all the cost of living alone on their shoulder. Ultimately, while the honky tonk is a space where the men earn their living and have fun, it is the place women fall in. In the film, the woman has also a family although it has an irregular structure. A useless husband and a money-grubbing parent are a must-have element in the story of a woman working in honky tonk. Because it is a prerequisite that there is nothing else to hold for falling into the honky tonk.

Regardless of their gender, people are a commodity for honky tonk owner. Their labor is worthless and alienated. The role of men working in the honky tonk is lesser evil. Their work is not respected in everyday life, but unlike women, they are not "dishonorable".

FUTURE RESEARCH DIRECTION

In this study, it was revealed that the labor of the honky tonk workers is devalued, alienated and ignored regardless of gender. Thus, the perception of honky tonks as a masculine entertainment place is broken and the roles of men are brought under question. Future studies can evaluate the roles of male customers of honky tonks and the ways they perceive the women working at these venues. In this way, different dimensions of honky tonks in terms of gender can be elicited

REFERENCES

Barthes, R. (2012). *Gösterge Bilimsel Serüven*. İstanbul, Turkey: Yapı Kredi Yayınları.

Bourdieu, P. (2015). *Ayrım*. İstanbul, Turkey: Heretik Yayınları.

Cengizkan, A. (2004). *Ankara'nın İlk Planı 1924-25 Lörcher Planı*. Ankara, Turkey: Arkadaş Yayınları.

Doğan, A. E. (2006). Mekân Üretimi Ve Gündelik Hayatın Birikimi Ve Emek Süreçleriyle İlişkisine Kayseri'den Bakmak, Praksis. *Cilt, 16*, 91–122.

Karadoğan, A. (2007). *Yoksul: Zeki Ökten*. Dipnot Yayınları.

Lefebvre, H. (2014). *Mekanın Üretimi*. İstanbul, Turkey: Sel Yayıncılık.

Nora, P. (2006). *Hafıza Mekanları*. Ankara, Turkey: Dost Kitabevi Yayınları.

Şenyapılı, T. (2004). *Barakadan Gecekonduya, Ankara'da Kentsel Mekânın Dönüşümü 1923-1960*. İstanbul, Turkey: İletişim Yayınları.

Stravdires, S. (2010). *Kentsel Heterotopya*. İstanbul, Turkey: Sel Yayıncılık.

Urry, J. (1999). *Mekanları Tüketmek*. İstanbul, Turkey: Ayrıntı Yayınları.

Yakın, O. (2009). 1980 Sonrası Yeni Gerçekçilik Örneği Olarak Düttürü Dünya. *Kebikeç*, (27), 331-350.

KEY TERMS AND DEFINITIONS

Gender: Gender roles shaped by social norms.

Honky Tonk: Honky tonk is a place where men go for fun and women "fall" into and only work. In short, women are not the costumers of this space. In this respect, the production, distribution and marketing of entertainment for men is carried out. It is not possible to draw this meaning from the definition made.

Men: Man laborers working in honky tonk. Waiter, musician, cloakroom attendant, barmen.

Women: Woman laborers working in honky tonk. Hostesses, belly dancers, players: artists.

ENDNOTES

[1] The Turkish word 'pavyon', which refers to a particular type of entertainment space, does not have a direct English equivalent. It has a specific seating layout with a stage. It is a space within which folkloric or belly dance music is performed live, men and women dance to this music together, and belly dancers and hostesses are to be found, as well as where its pricing system is quite expensive (especially for foreigners), and which is not illegal but is perceived by society as being illegal due to both its spatial organization form alongside gender roles.

[2] For more information see http://www.turkudostlari.net/turku_bilgileri.asp?turku=773

Chapter 16
Gender Is Political:
Evaluation of Gender in *Susuz Yaz* (*Dry Summer*) and *Yilanlarin Öcü* (*Revenge of the Snakes*) Films

Pelin Erdal Aytekin
https://orcid.org/0000-0002-1422-4860
Aydın Adnan Menderes University, Turkey

ABSTRACT

Studies on women identity in the context of gender yields significant results, especially when considering the practice of cinema. Mainstream cinema is an essential area of indicators for handling women's identity. Susuz Yaz and Yılanların Öcü films are two important films in which Metin Erksan dealt with the concept of property within his filmography. These two films, which address the concept of property through the ownership of land and water, also represented the social existence of women's identity with the rural lifestyle in particular, making the social structure in which women are perceived as property visible. In this context, the study evaluates the image of the woman in cinema on the concepts of body, property and rights. The method approach shaped its roots from the foundations of sociology, communication and cultural theories. The subject was presented by analyzing it within the perspective of interpretive social science. It was concluded that the debate on whose property the land and water are also raised the discussion of the property of women's identity.

DOI: 10.4018/978-1-7998-0128-3.ch016

INTRODUCTION

Deleuze (2003a, 2003b) emphasizes that each form of art is defined by the diversity of human thought. In this respect, he perceives cinema not only as a kind of storytelling and transfer of information but also as a state of the possibilities of imagination and thought converted into cinematic indicators. Thus, this whole process is also functionalized in the representation of a philosophy. This final and transformative approach, which Deleuze refers to in the specific concept of philosophy for cinema, is dealt with in this study in the specific context of gender discourse, property and cinema.

The intense relationship between the concept of gender and the concepts of power and authority also include the concept of property into this whole context, and the relation of property right with "power" (erk) makes the issue of where women's identity stands in this equation controversial. It should not be overlooked that the authority holding power also has a role in determining the boundaries and drawing the lines of gender. The view of women in the masculine world is quite decisive when entering into the gender-specific layers. It should be noted that the transition from hunter-gatherer to agricultural production was influential on the formation of gender patterns. Also, the ongoing traditional cultural system in the context of gender has been carried this kind of deeply internalized knowledge, and experience that is unable to verbalized from generation to generation (Aytekin and Rızvanoğlu, 2018). In these contexts, the article primarily discusses the changing position of women in the social field and especially in the field of production. Therefore, the transformation of the concept of property, and simultaneous change on this subject with the transition to patriarchal order is fundamental as one of the points that will form the center of the study.

While the transformation of women's identity within the economic production areas is the main subject of women's studies, the determinism of gender in this subject serves guidance. In this respect, the discussion will also focus on how authority and power affect the separation between sexes within the boundaries of gender. The study will discuss how the concept of property is transformed and what it is; how this concept can be evaluated under the headings of power and sovereign power, and then which point this subject corresponds to regarding separation between sexes. What is important here is to reveal the dominant and ideological structure that is effective in the formation of gender roles.

Based on the orientation of this whole conceptual framework, two critical examples of Turkish cinema, *Yılanların Öcü* (1962) and *Susuz Yaz* (1963) directed by Metin Erksan will be analyzed as samples. Both films offer important indicators for addressing the discussion both concerning placing the concept of property in the center and as films that make the property discussion through the representation of women. The role of cinema in revealing the representation of women is essential both regarding influencing large masses and as it is influenced mainly by the social dynamics. As Mulvey (1975) also points out, the view of mainstream cinema is masculine, and the representation of women's identity is shaped under this masculine view. Both *Yılanların Öcü* and *Susuz Yaz* films aim to show how this masculine view, in the context of the property concept, is represented under the influence of power and authority.

BACKGROUND

Transformation of Gender Into Property in the Context of Gender

Simone de Beauvoir (1993:34) has made a very generalist and assertive comment on the subject by saying "Sometimes, the world of women is compared with the world of men, but it must be noted once again that women have never established an autonomous and closed society; they are involved in a community of men and have a secondary position". Although he stated with this tendency, he seems to imply that the issue of power is transformed into a property right for man and that the masculine point of view has validity as a social pre-acceptance. Connell (1998:153), stating in a more descriptive framework that authority was in direct relation to gender as a legitimate order of power and that authority was acting on the same plane as "manhood", shows, again and again, the importance of gender in determining the network of relationships surrounding the woman. The social legitimacy of gender is in an intense network of relations with the concepts of power and property.

Before deepening the relationship between women and property in the specific concept of gender, it may be useful to address the issue in the context of gender: the concept of gender refers to a biological approach that enables differentiation of distinct physical characteristics. Thus, a wide variety of speculative and cultural hierarchical models and obligations are loaded on gender definitions. Connell (1998:255) summarizes the subject in the following way in his book *Gender and Power:*

A newborn has biological sex but has no gender yet. As the child grows up, society also places a set of sex-based rules, patterns and behavior models in front of the child. Certain factors or actors of socialization - especially family, media, groups of friends and schools - embody these expectations and models and prepare environments where the child can adopt them. This results in a gender identity that normally coincides with the social expectations of a particular sex.

More specifically, "gender roles are the tasks and activities attributed by a culture to a sex" (Kottak 2001:443). When talking about the biological origin of being a man and woman, Aksu Bora (2018:37) also adds that it is not possible to reduce gender to this origin. Sex has a structure that is established later on and formed by social context, which is called gender. The most critical factor that shapes the gender and increases the stratification among the sexes is the significant change experienced in the production rituals. Harari (2015:150) says that almost all known societies in history since the agricultural revolution have adopted various socio-political and imaginary hierarchies. The most dominant of these is the gender hierarchy, although biological differences may seem negligible in this sense. In hunter-gatherer communities, gender-related segregation is scarce, and there are two fundamental reasons for this; the state of war and trade not being found within the social structure as a primary motivation. In the hunter-gatherer groups, hierarchical segregation is scarce, and also aggression and competition are not among the accepted behaviours. The transition to agriculture and, in particular, the use of plow in agricultural production as a technique significantly changed the active role of women in production dynamics. Since the plowing has eliminated the task of weed collecting which was considered to be a women's task, all responsibility for livelihoods was taken over men so that there was an increase in gender stratification. As Kottak says, with the spread of plow agriculture, women have significantly moved away from production for the first time in human history. This situation "has counteracted the worthless domestic role of the women with the valuable non-domestic labour of the men" (2001:453). In this case, the most critical factor removing the woman from the production area has been related to the acquisition of "plus product"[1]. Processing of the soil in a shorter time and with less power than processing with anchors, sharp sticks and similar tools not only made it possible to obtain more products from larger soil parts compared to the previous ones but also resulted in an increase in the total food supply. Besides, the use of the animals' muscle strength increased production; thus, it provided a surplus product that would enable those not growing food products to benefit from the production. As McNeill (2004:51) said: "The invention of the plow significantly changed and diversified the texture of human life." However, it is not possible to state the same approach for the new transformation of female identity. The main reason why the emerging surplus product is seen as another development increasing women's shift in domestic organization. The primary function of women in the center of production was limited to domestic responsibilities, which were seen as a secondary function. At this point, the most important issue is that the productional segregation has reached a spatial limitation. Women were moved away from production spaces considered as common places and were restricted to a closed environment such as homes. Thus, they were moved away from the production processes where they could have had a voice; and therefore, degraded to a secondary position in the administrative processes. This new position of women in the patriarchal order as a property issue should be dealt with in detail as one of the central points of the study.

Fatmagül Berktay (2009:81) states that a structure emerged in the Mesopotamia region between 3500 and 3000 BC, which later turned into the city states, and simultaneously writing was discovered and that these developments caused rivalries between the states which led to military struggles; thus a male-dominated structure was formed. What is essential at this point, as stated earlier, has been to evolve into a social structure with more classes in which the property owner classes were formed with the increase in the rate of agricultural production to feed large human communities. Berktay (2009:81) explains the institutionalization of the patriarchal structure as follows:

The patriarchal family, which guaranteed the passage of property from father to son through inheritance and thus gave men the control of women's sexuality, was established, passed into laws and secured by the state. Within this framework, women's sexuality was identified as the property of men, firstly of the fathers and then the husbands, and the sexual "purity" of women (especially their virginity) became a bargainable economic value...

The patriarchal system's restriction of women's freedom and the positioning them within the places with certain boundaries such as homes suspended the active presence of women in the decision-making processes and left them to survive within the meanings imposed on women by gender. Therefore, it is meaningful to evaluate female identity in a property debate. The concept of property brings about a variety of discussions due to the forms of meaning it represents. In his book *The Old Society II*, Lewis Henry Morgan (1998) places the situation of property turning into private ownership in the stage where animal husbandry and agriculture, which he defines as middle barbarity, developed but iron had not yet begun. In this period, Morgan says that the relationship between man and land changed considerably. In this period, some of the land still in common use was distributed to cover administrative expenses, some to the construction of the temple in order to fulfill religious rituals, but a more significant part was distributed to communities residing in the same residential area to ensure their livelihood. Even though this situation has changed the concept of property substantially, the sale of land to other non-descendants, which was the real factor in shaping the concept of private property, was only possible in later periods. Morgan (1998:339) dates the period in which the concept of private property was apparently seen with the end of this period that began with the processing of iron, which he describes as the upper phase of the historic barbarism. However, especially the beginning of field agriculture created a significant change in the concept of property, the introduction of trade with the transition to the traditional agricultural order privatized the concept of property to a certain extent. This means that the transition of women from the production site into the houses and the privatization of the property occurred almost simultaneously.

Above all, it can be said that the patriarchal structure mostly left the woman outside the property in the countryside, and on the contrary, incorporated the rights and labor power of the women into the realm of property; thus women entered the property area of their "husbands' houses" after marriage. According to Stirling's (1966:121-131) evaluation in *Turkish Village*, while the patriarchal structure distributes the property of the land among the sons after the death of the father, the daughters are left out since they will already go outside the household and enter into another house's (family's) production mechanism.

Kin marriage or closed society marriage can be considered among the reasons for women's transformation into a property issue. Tillion (2006:135) explains this issue under the title "women are part of the property, just like fields." This title explains the close relationship between consanguineous marriages or, at best, in-village, endogamic marriages, and the concept of property, and also it can be said that this linkage takes control of the fact that the "property", which is chiefly of vital importance to the rural world, does not go to outsiders/foreigners.

In any case, the "family," as a social structure surrounding the women, is one of the most critical factors that determine their position. Bora (2018:40), saying that this is the main subject of the second wave feminist studies, states that it is not possible to talk about equality unless discrimination of this area is removed at the center of the critical discourse on women's social inclusion. From this perspective, the domestic organization and the patriarchal order which constitutes its mainframe make the position of woman in the common plane controversial.

Eugéne Enriquez (2004:217) states that the political or social authority, as quoted by Levi Strauss (1967:149), has a male-dominated representation:

Political authority or social authority on its own is always in the hands of men, and this superiority of the male is a constant quality whether by reconciling with a matrilineal or patrilineal lineage, as in most primitive societies, or whether by imposing on all dimensions of social life as it is observed in developed groups.

Amal Rassam (cited in Berktay 2009:16) states that the discussions on the social status of women should be read in the following three planes: "(a) social organization of power, (b) the nature of the ideological and institutional instruments that control the female body, (c) the sexual division of labor in society and roles." Due to the nature of the issue, the majority of the discussions under the heading of gender studies require progress through the concepts of gender-power-authority. The relationship between the dominant social perspective and the social dynamics of power at the point where sex has turned into gender and opened to codings in this context as well as the gender roles identified in this direction are shaped within a bunch of relationships that are difficult to separate from one another.

In this case, we can try to find answers to the following questions from the point also questioned by Kandiyoti (2015:197): "What are the social contexts and practices that play a key role in the production of gender stereotypes? How do the forms of power and domination among men play a role in the reproduction of patriarchy?" How do these acquired roles influence the way women's identity is placed in the social sphere? When we consider it under the heading of gender studies, it is not only about the social positioning of women at this point, but also about where the identity of men stands in this positioning, and with a full-scale approach, how both sexes are positioned in a social framework. Taking action to ask all these questions, cinema is at the point of representation which can provide firm answers to these questions. In this context, how the film narrative displays a network of indicators on the axis of women and property, and what the cultural equivalents of this network of indicators will be included in the study scope, and cinema will be examined as a sample area among the factors shaping gender. Based on this approach, a study will be conducted on the two important films representing the subject, *Yılanların Öcü* (1962) and *Susuz Yaz*(1963).

YILANLARIN ÖCÜ: PROPERTY OF LAND, PROPERTY OF WOMEN

Socialist feminists say that the coexistence between the two genders was broken down with the development of the concepts of paternity and private property, but their primary emphasis is on the development of women's oppression under the influence of capitalism after the industrial revolution. Socialist feminists suggest that women were more productive and respected in pre-capitalist societies. (Douglas 1995:47)

In her article *The State of Film and Media Feminism*, Anette Kuhn (2004:1223) aims to read the promises of the film regarding gender, to draw up footnotes on the content of the film, and to understand the connection between man and woman as a subject of gender when she talks about the extent to which gender affects the content of the films, and also the scope of feminist psychoanalytic theory that focuses on the rituals of women/men within the narrative of the film. Cinema can be seen as an essential medium of practice for the separation of gender codes.

It is possible to find the most obvious examples of a reading made in this context in Yeşilçam cinema. Yeşilçam cinema shows an important mainstream cinema feature where men and women can be read as stereotypes. In terms of the established patterns of gender, they have almost never stepped outside the dilemma of good and evil. Nilgün Abisel limited the representation of women in Turkish melodrama cinema to family institution and motherhood in her book *Türk Sineması Üzerine Yazılar*. Abisel (2005:296) therefore states that "the basic function of women as determined by the universal patriarchal lifestyle is also valid for these films". There are basically two leading roles in these films; those who act within the boundaries determined by gender and who go beyond it. Women who act in accordance with their role are those who are content with what they have by choosing marriage and raising children, those who are self-sacrificing by facing various struggles, who do not demand, but always accept the duty to fulfill the demands of men, who protect their chastity in any situation, and who exist only for the peace of their home.

On the contrary, women who violate the boundaries are those who are always condemned to remain out and to be unhappy, who always want more, who have stars in their eyes, and who will do whatever is necessary to achieve that. Although both *Yılanların Öcü* and *Susuz Yaz* show significant differences, they proceed in a similar line concerning the representation of women. While both films do not include a "bad woman" typage, "good-innocent women" have adopted a classic role pattern.

Kara Bayram's wife Hatce is one of the important characters representing this. In many scenes of the film, she is just called as "gelin" (bride) and sometimes as "kadın gelin" (woman bride). The visibility of woman in social dynamics is shaped by the family and motherhood she establishes through marriage. The bride exhibits an innocent, loyal and contentious appearance, as in the whole of Turkish cinema. Abisel (2005:298) describes the mother-bride women of Turkish cinema as follows: "being content with what they have, facing any difficulties, showing all kinds of sacrifices, being non-demanding on any subject, maintaining chastity and acting in accordance with the demands of men". In this respect, the bride of *Yılanların Öcü* film, Hatce, carries these characteristics. At the beginning of the film, she fulfilled her role as a mother who showed her austerity in response to Bayram's promises by saying "I want neither clothes nor anything else". She is more enthusiastic about what will be bought for her son rather than herself. Nevertheless, Erksan's women sometimes give hints about sexuality even if they are vague. Bayram and his wife going to the haystack one morning due to the presence of the mother in the house is one of the rare scenes in which the woman is shown as the one demanding sexuality. This situation brings Erksan's female characters out of melodrama cinema women to a certain extent. At this point, the woman appears as the one who demands sexuality. Except for that, she is the mother and lives her whole life around her children, working for the benefit of the family she has acquired through marriage. Attempting to take the laundry from the hands of her mother-in-law despite coming to a point where she might miscarry a baby is the most important indicator of this situation. In the film, the second woman character that goes beyond the classical women's character is Haceli's wife. She is brave and open enough to confess her love for Bayram to his mother. Moreover, she does not see a negative attitude towards this confession. In contrast, the mother feels sorry for Haceli's wife and recommends his son Bayram to be with her. The patterns established by Yeşilçam cinema are demolished at this point, but another factor that allows them to get out of the patterns is the treatment of women, especially their sexuality, as a property issue. Bayram has an affair with Haceli's wife as if he wants to take revenge from him. The loss of the area in front of their homes as a property issue is compensated by having Haceli's wife at this point. The battle over property is won through the possession of a woman. Nevertheless, Haceli's wife is not among the characters who are excluded in the film as she is honest and does not try to get what she wants. She appears as wanting to side with who is right. Nevertheless, she has to remain committed to the family she acquired through marriage. Connell says that such a female identity cannot have any expectations to have any power depending on natural conditions;"A womanhood which is organized as an adaptation to men's power and prioritizes submission, child raising and empathy as female virtues is not in a position to establish hegemony on other forms of femininity" (Connell, 1998:252). A female typology who accepts does not expect more and does not even demand to have power exhibits a de facto appearance despite the multidimensionality and complexity of gender approaches. This attitude towards Haceli's wife also confirms this approach. Haceli's brothers saying "don't interfere in such matters with your woman's mind" to his wife who disagreed at a point of dispute, and then "I would give you a nice beating if I were my brother" pins the passive position of the woman in terms of decision-making. Kandiyoti (2015:50) mentions two factors that determine the position of women in rural areas: childbirth and aging;

Regardless of the position of the woman in production, her contribution is mostly ignored, and the works that require expertise or that are related to the public sphere continues to be in the hands of men... In the above mentioned cases, women do not have any control over neither production nor reproduction; in either case, the product belongs directly to the paternity.

Therefore, childbearing is especially crucial for economic transformation in rural areas. The processing of the land as a property proceeds in direct proportion to the crowdedness of the family population. The crowdedness of the population means having more processed land. In this regard, keeping the land functional as a property proceeding through the paternity, and ensuring continuity between generations again proceeding through paternity, that is, the progression of lineage through the children women give birth to show a parallel development. Since the land ownership only progresses through men, the lineage also makes the female identity invisible by disabling the mother's role. The woman's position in the countryside mostly cannot go beyond this framework[2]. The bride of *Yılanların Öcü* film, Hatce, wants to go beyond this framework. She is pregnant with the fourth child, and reacts by saying "another child?" Bayram's answer, who says "The peasants need children, it is beyond your comprehension", shows the property-lineage relationship. Hatce still does not want children for the same reason, forty-five acres of arid field is not strong enough to feed this population. The size of the land acquired as a property and the size of the population must be directly proportional. Women also continue to be valued as an important part of the property that enables the continuation of the lineage.

Another factor influencing the position of women in rural areas is "aging", which is represented by the character Irazca Ana. Irazca Ana is one of the strongest characters of the film as well as in the Turkish cinema in many ways. Irazca Ana character goes beyond the patterns of Turkish cinema as a female character who starts the discussion on property, never holds back under any circumstances, and from whom male characters abstain in several points. The scene at the beginning of the film clarifies this. While Haceli is measuring the front of Bayram's house to build a house, he meets the fearless gaze of Irazca Ana and she says: "I do not mind Bayram, but his mother does not look nice at all." What brings this position to her is primarily due to the fact that she got old, and thus, left behind her "female" representation. Secondly, she has gained status as the mother of a son; thus the relationship she has found with a male figure gives her power. Irazca's relationship with his son Bayram carries characteristics of obedience in many aspects. And Bayram does not resist the will of his mother and adapts to her directions, and even allows her to organize the affair he will have with another woman. As a figure, she is an important driving force in his son's life. It is understood that Bayram is committed to his mother with a strong bond. This situation implies the Oedipus conflict[3]. Freud says that in the oedipal phase, the daughters move away from the mother, but for the sons, mother remains as an object of love. This stage of development, as suggested by Kandiyoti (2015:29), in many ways turns the mother-son relationship into a private one. The son is the future safeguard and guardian of the mother. She protects his son and his family as if protecting her own future. Irazca Ana almost never sleeps but always keeps guard. She is almost as invincible as a rock. She throws herself in front of the digger. She does not put her son forth but herself. Moreover, all the counter-movements against Haceli are planned by Irazca Ana. Irazca Ana fully impersonates the "mother" figure in the social representation.

The beating scene at the end of the film can be read along with the man's status of having "power". In parallel with the increase of wars together with the emergence of property issues the between the male communities, those who use and possess the physical power also hold the authority. Therefore, the women identity is weak and delicate in most of the films while the men are strong and dominant. Abisel (2005:325) argues that women's social weakness is reinforced by the addition of physical weakness; "the claim of physical weakness is the main basis for the rationalization of violence and surrender as a form of behavior that is appropriate to the given roles of women." Since having power will also bring together authority, gender segregation remain in the dilemma of the possessor and the possessed. For many years, Yeşilçam cinema has made numerous productions to reinforce this approach and at the same time attributed the way power and authority existed to those with physical power, namely, men. Male identity appears to be the representative of power and authority, especially in mainstream cinema.

In the whole film, property rights are discussed continuously. With the construction of a house in front of Bayram's house, the concept of shared property is also addressed. This is one of the reasons why Agali Dayı opposes this. When he says "the village will be narrowed", the owner of the property right is opened to discussion. Another property debate is Bayram's lamb. The lamb that will adorn the feast to be given for the arrival of the governor is Bayram's lamb. Mukhtar again takes the lamb and cuts it without consent or permission. Animals and lands are the two most important property subjects of the rural. It is how they maintain their livelihoods and thus it is vital for the households. In addition to these two issues, the film also discusses women's property. Irazca Ana, standing in front of Haceli says: "If you kill me, you go to prison. In that case, I cannot have your wife but Bayram will." The fact that the women are seen as a commodity and exchanged just like a property is reflected in a dialogue here, and valorized just like transferring a right. Nevertheless, the discussion of the right to property extends the issue beyond the separation of women and men. The situation is highly valued by the rural and the ruling segment. Teodor Shanin (1971) puts the feature of "being a pressured group" among the main characteristics of the village community. According to Shanin's approach, the ruling class is in a dominant position over the peasantry and peasants are located far from the rulers. We see this approach in many scenes of the film. Both the pressure and divergence that the Mukhtar builds on the peasant as the representative of the power, and the overthrowing of the Mukhtar and other will by the overwhelming power of the Governor, function as circles overlapping each other. In any case, however, the villagers are excluded from the center of decision and only left in the ruled position.

In this case, it would be inadequate to say that gender disparity is only between male and female. The subject also takes place between different forms of masculinity (roughly the classification of the ruler and the ruled). The representation of "hegemonic masculinity" by Connell's conceptualization describes this type of separation.

When evaluated under the titles of rule, power and gender, hegemonic masculinity is primarily related to women's identity and then to masculinity patterns. Connell (1998:249) describes hegemonic masculinity as follows;

Hegemonic masculinity can consistently accommodate the openings towards domesticism and the openings towards violence, the openings towards misogyny and the openings towards heterosexual attraction at the same time. Hegemonic masculinity is built in relation to women and subordinate masculinities.

This point constitutes an essential center of the study. There is no possibility of hegemonic femininity, but even if it exists, this is the acceptance of a dominant global male dominance from the time of the formation of femininity. Men can have the privilege of holding the power of masculinity through pressure on both women and other men. Thus, the power of the accepted ruling of men is only contributed to by obeying it, and an entire property debate can be made within this framework: Who does the property belong to? Who is the owner of power? As Connell (1998:245) said, the interaction between only different forms of masculinity is a critical part of the patriarchal social order and the woman can often take part in the side roles of this social structure. *Yılanların Öcü* film reads the discussion regarding the right to property in line with the gender-based segregation and also addresses the subject in the context of the ruler and the ruled, the power of the ruler-authority. The position of women in the countryside is always prone to be political. In particular, Irazca Ana's position in the film questions the place of women within "ruling" "power". While Irazca stands against the unjust rule of the man, the Governor, namely, the ruler who represents the state and more importantly the values of the republic stands by Irazca. There is a point here where the subject is idealized. While the rural authority - the Mukhtar - is seen as small, cunning and ignorant, the state itself, the republican values are exalted specifically by the Governor. In any case, the power is represented by a male figure and the representative of the state also finds value under this identity. The main issue here is that the positioning based on gender is political, and in the end, the woman, in the quest for right and justice, stands beside the "ruling power" and hopes for help from it.

As Nephan Saran (1984:162) underlines in his book *Köylerimiz*, "gender is a trait determining who the authority belongs to in the village households" and the authoritarian power is in the man and father. He has a say as the decision-maker and the lineage proceeds from father to son. While the preference is always made for the sons, women serve as a medium for the continuation of the lineage. The fact that the head of the household is the father also brings the consequence that father has absolute and unbreakable authority. The women's position always comes after the men. In this case, gender-related segregation should be considered as a feature emphasized all the time, especially in rural areas. *Yılanların Öcü* shows this entire social structuring. Authoritarian separation based on gender, and the power that is always possessed by the male or in some cases by the elderly woman - mother - where the elderly father passes away wholly coincide with the social structure represented by the film. The right to property also belongs to the authority owner and this right always proceeds through the male lineage as an element of the patriarchal structure. As Irazca Ana, Bayram and his family try to protect this property, they represent this right through the power of the man, as in the whole of the rural population..

SUSUZ YAZ: WHO OWNS THE WATER? WHO OWNS THE WOMEN?

The subject of seeing water resources as a property subject and sharing the resources fairly is, of course, the subject of all civilizations where agriculture is strengthened. William H. McNeill (2004), in his book *The History of the World*, dates the appearance of a specialization field in the distribution of water to the Sumerian civilization around the 3rd millennium BC. However, despite all this organization about the distribution of water, problems occurred between neighbouring cities and especially the construction of long irrigation canals, the opening of additional areas from the rivers to the water channels, the decrease of the water in the lower parts of the river and the growth of the discussions on this issue. McNeill (2004:43) seems to almost determine the main path of *Susuz Yaz* film while talking about "settling the disputes related to the rights on the water through peaceful means, and possibility of easily turning the question of rights into a problem of life and death in the least rainy years."

Susuz Yaz has a strong story as a film about the impossibility of owning water. Throughout the film, the subjects of whom the water actually belongs to, and whether the soil where it springs from or the destination it flows should be taken into consideration are discussed. At the beginning of the film, Osman (Abi) announces that he would not let the water down to the fields anymore, but only irrigate his own crop as it comes out of his own soil. The disagreements between his brother Hasan and himself appear here. While Osman argues "isn't the water ours?" Hasan responds by saying "it belongs to the earth". And, the villagers agree with Hasan. They say, "Water belongs to everyone, how can you own the flowing water". As one of the villagers says, they cannot comprehend the way Osman possesses the water which has been flowing from there since the Adam. Thus, the problem of belonging arises at the beginning of the film. Who owns the water? What about the property of women?

In a parallel narrative, the film also discusses who owns the woman and to whom her rights passes to. According to Osman, the brother must behave as soon as possible and marry Bahar. Osman says "behave so that someone else would not have it". The property debate about women arises from the fact that the brother must convince Bahar to marry him to sow the fields before the harvest time. Bahar refers to the impossibility of getting married before the harvest is collected. Her mother would not allow in any other way. Saran (1984:168) demonstrates the indisputable importance of the family in rural marriages and confirms the importance of the human population in the center of rural - agricultural - production by saying "marriage in rural areas is a social phenomenon that concerns families, rather than individuals, and controls the participation of new members in a family".

When an individual property becomes widespread, the rule of equal sharing between siblings may have helped to keep the younger siblings within the family. The need for human beings was also consistent with the traditional command structure based on the brother privilege, (Tillion 2006:128). This statement of Tillion is also one of the determinants of the relationship between Osman and Hasan. The sharing of water, which is the film's main subject of conflict, increases the tension of the conflict between the brothers. Although Hasan does not agree with Osman's idea, he cannot come against him as the necessity of rural structuring of the kinship roles, eventually Osman is the older brother, and he cannot oppose his decision as the younger brother, he says "I do not consent, but what can I do, you are my elder". Starting from the individualization period of the property, an appropriate kinship organization has occurred and has been organized in a way to support the economic structure in all aspects. Both the position of the brothers in the family and the importance of women in this structure - their place both regarding the continuity of the lineage and the multiplicity of population required for agricultural and animal production - is great. Osman refers to this subject when he says, "Our fields have grown, and of course the work has also grown, we need people to work". For these reasons, Bahar should come to the "husband's house" as soon as possible. Osman says that Bahar's economic production power should also be passed onto their family as they will pay a dowry for her.

Susuz Yaz is full of gender codes. In particular, the population requirement brought by way of agricultural production strengthens this separation. Osman says he wants a large number of children from Bahar and Hasan the night of their marriage. This demand should be interpreted as an indicator of power in the countryside while creating a hysterical feeling by saying "I want children, I want men, men". In particular, the high numbers of the male population means the increase of the people who will have the strength to work in the field. Engels (1990:12) states that this is the primary motivation of the mode of production which he bases on materialistic roots;

According to the materialist conception, the dominant factor in history is eventually the production and reproduction of material life. However, this production has a dual essence. On the one hand, the production of means of living, nutrition, clothing, sheltering objects and the tools they require; on the other hand, the production of people themselves, the reproduction of the species.

The increase of the population, the continuation of the lineage, is the most important element of the repeated reproduction of material life. Despite the importance of increasing the population required for the continuation of agricultural production, the existence of difficulties in the sharing of water and land makes the issue of property controversial. The discussion of "who owns the water" which is often repeated in the film, turns into the debate of "the population is growing, the land is growing, so how we will share the water". While one condition for ensuring the continuation of the production of material life is the increase of the population to work in production, the subject passes onto the distribution of resources with the increase of the population.

In this film, the peasant and the ruling power are also confronted. The villagers resort to the administration against Osman who cuts the water. First they go to the village Mukhtar, but Osman does not pay attention to him. He says "Let hem go to the court". The clerk writes, "Although there is a title and property problem..." Although the law has decided on the side of the villagers before, the decision is disrupted in favor of Osman. The question of who owns the water, which is the main subject of the film, is repeatedly debated in the film also by the official authorities.

Susuz Yaz film also discusses the women's duty area just like *Yılanların Öcü* film. Although women are an essential part of rural production, they are also an essential executive of the house order. All the domestic work is seen as the primary duty of women even though they work in the field. While Osman demands something almost always from Bahar, he expects to be looked after as part of his extended family. He says: "Bahar gelin, you go and prepare food for lunch, but make it a marvellous meal so that we understand there is a woman in the house". Aksu Bora (2018:60) says that, based on a feminist perspective in defining home work, the daily and repetitive nature of housework transforms women into a secondary species. Moreover, it is the duty of the woman to keep the clean and sheltered world of the home permanent, while the domestic work is integrated into the outside workforce within a natural process. The woman needs to be a part of the production in the outside world as well as being the executive of household affairs. The man does not think that he should take any responsibility at this point.

Especially the *Susuz Yaz* film opens up the identity of women through the representation of the body. In the Bahar Gelin's identity, the female body is monitored continuously, and a sexual desire is felt and followed. With this aspect, Erksan not only discussed the property issue in the film but also discussed the sexuality and the belonging of the female body. Laura Mulvey (1975) in her article *Visual Pleasure and Narrative Cinema*, describes how mainstream cinema encourages people to monitor the human body. A desire is created in the audience to look curiously. The audience feels similar to when a baby first meets the mirror - the sense of satisfaction felt in the process of recognizing oneself - watching the body reflect on the screen. What makes cinema attractive is the identification link established with the subject that appears in the screen. In this respect, cinema reflects the female body on the screen as an object of desire. This look is the male viewpoint, and the woman figure on the screen is watched with a "masculine viewpoint". In this context, the woman on the screen should have a visual appeal to create the motive for watching. Traditionally, the mainstream cinema uses the female body from this aspect. The center of the story is almost always male, and the woman is only secondary as the viewed. In Erksan's filmography, *Susuz Yaz* is one of the top films where the female body is most visible. As Mulvey put it, Bahar becomes visible both for the viewer and for the Osman character, in the body of a young and beautiful woman who is watched and monitored.

After Hasan takes the blame of his brother and goes into prison, the subject continues almost entirely on becoming Bahar's owner. Next, almost all the subsequent scenes were built on the escaping-chasing between Bahar and Osman. The subject of property changes direction here, and it turns into the dilemma of who owns water? Also, who owns Bahar? However, in the end, just like in *Yılanların Öcü* film, the good defeats the bad. For the good ones, a hopeful journey begins. In both films, Metin Erksan discusses property and the position of women in society. In both films, even if a woman is injured, she does not die. There is always hope for the future.

Susuz Yaz film also addresses the subject of property with a reading parallel to gender just like in *Yılanların Öcü* film. While the property is discussed in the central axis of the film, on the other hand, the place of the woman in the rural area and the position in which she is "owned" is discussed. It can be said that although the woman identity is in a position to be discussed in almost all social stratification, the rural area, where agricultural production is made, can be defined as a living space where the sense of dominance of women is more intense. Just like owning the soil or the water, the woman and her production practice is also owned. After marriage, the woman belongs to the male household, and she is expected to bring about the production of life - nutrition and sheltering needs - as well as the continuation of the lineage. As Saran (1984:168) says, "the new bride comes to the man's father's house as a rule and cannot leave this house unless it is deemed appropriate by the family. Setting up a separate household in rural areas is an exceptional situation." In this respect, the visibility of women in rural areas is quite low compared to urban areas, and the traditional structure maintains its functionality without making any concessions. *Yılanların Öcü* and*Susuz Yaz* films directed by Metin Erksan can be regarded as the most realistic representations of this structuring in the cinema.

FUTURE RESEARCH DIRECTIONS

Considering gender studies in the context of cinema reveals high quality outputs in terms of contributing to the literature. The social dynamics' representation power of cinema had functioned as an important narrative center in the representation of gender. This study deals with the representation of gender in cinema in the context of property; proceed through two films that allow the subject to be explained and reveals the patterns in which the woman is told. Further studies could be examining the representation of women in different narrative genres such as comedy, film-noir, crime & investigation and adaptations in terms of gender representation in films. At the same time, that could have been tried to understand the representation of men's place in the cinema narrative as a gender pattern.

CONCLUSION

The concept of gender, in contrast to the concept of sex, refers to the adoption of various social codes by the identities of men and women beyond the differences imposed by nature on these sexes. Beyond the sex gained at birth, they acquire patterns about being an individual, a woman, and a man because of some social categories. The separation between women and men became so visible that the role of women in the transition from hunter-gatherer to agricultural production has undergone a severe change and a transformation from the outside world to the domestic production has taken place. At the same time, this situation removed women from being in a decision maker position and left the power and authority entirely to the administration of the men.

The concept of property has also changed with the transition to agricultural production - plus product production, as in the transition to patriarchal order, and a significant difference has occurred in the concept of property with the introduction of the concept of private property. While the concept of private property has increased the importance of women in the production of material life while advancing through families and descendants, the progression of the lineage through the male household removed the visibility of the female identity.

While cinema was shaped as an essential area of representation of women's identity in this sense, especially mainstream cinema has put good-evil stereotypes on women and handled women's identity in this way. Turkish cinema constitutes an important example in terms of examining the place of female identity. Although Metin Erksan's cinema shows some differences from the mainstream Yeşilçam cinema, the films *Susuz Yaz* and *Yılanların Öcü*, in which the concept of property is seriously discussed, have added a secondary argument to this debate over the property of women's identity. *Yılanların Öcü* film reads the discussion about the owner of the right to property in line with the gender-based separation and also deals with the subject in the context of the ruler and the ruled as well as the power of the ruling. While *Susuz Yaz* film was discussing the property of the water, it started to discuss the identity of women with the dilemma of who owns the woman. It can be said that the representation of women in both films mainly did not go beyond traditional patterns, despite their importance concerning continuation of the lineage and the material life, they could not become a decision-maker and maintained their secondary role. Moreover, the "property of women" was added to the discussions regarding the property of land and water, and as the final point the emphasis on that women belong to the "husbands' house" is repeated.

Women's identity is one of the primary issues of almost all cultural studies, but also an efficient study field for the cinema area. Even though gender-based segregation was based on strong social dynamics, the change in production practices mobilized a significant transformation. Due to all these reasons, *Yılanların Öcü* and *Susuz Yaz* films gave a realistic direction to the subject in order to reveal where the identity of women within the Turkish cinema is visible and at which points there is a problem of representation as well as the change experienced. The aim here is to reveal the relation of women's identity with the concept of property through the representation of cinema, and the connection of this network of relations with the dominant ideology. Women's identity as a gender issue seems to need to be consistently and permanently examined, researched and interpreted.

REFERENCES

Abisel, N. (2005). *Türk Sineması Üzerine Yazılar*. Ankara, Turkey: Phoenix Yay.

Aytekin, B. A., & Rızvanoğlu, K. (2019). Creating learning bridges through participatory design and technology to achieve sustainability in local crafts. *International Journal of Technology and Design Education, 29*(3), 603–632. doi:10.100710798-018-9454-3

Berktay, F. (2009). *Tek Tanrılı Dinlerin Karşısında Kadın*. İstanbul, Turkey: Metis.

Bora, A. (2018). *Kadınların Sınıfı*. İstanbul, Turkey: İletişim.

Connell, R. W. (1998). *Toplumsal Cinsiyet ve İktidar* (C. Soydemir, Trans.). İstanbul, Turkey: Ayrıntı.

de Beauvoir, S. (1993). *Kadın* (B. Onaran, Trans.). İstanbul, Turkey: Payel.

Deleuze, G. (2003a). *Cinema 1: The Movement and Image*. Minneapolis, MN: University of Minnesota Press.

Deleuze, G. (2003b). *Cinema 2: The time-image*. Minneapolis, MN: University of Minnesota Press.

Douglas, C. A. (1995). *Sevgi ve Politika: Radikal Feminist ve Lezbiyen Teoriler*. İstanbul, Turkey: Kavram.

Engels, F. (1990). *Ailenin Özel Mülkiyetin ve Devletin Kökeni*, K. Somer (Trans.). Ankara, Turkey: Sol.

Enriquez, E. (2004). *Sürüden Devlete* (N. Tutal, Trans.). İstanbul, Turkey: Ayrıntı.

Freud, S. (1972). *Cinsiyet ve Psikanaliz*. Ankara, Turkey: Varlık.

Harari, Y. N. (2015). *Hayvanlardan Tanrılara Sapiens: İnsan Türünün Kısa Bir Tarihi* (E. Genç, Trans.). İstanbul, Turkey: Kolektif Kitap.

Kandiyoti, D. (2015). *Cariyeler, Bacılar, Yurttaşlar*. İstanbul, Turkey: Metis.

Kottak, C. P. (2001). *Antropoloji*. Ankara, Turkey: Ütopya.

Kuhn, A. (2004). The State of Film and Media Feminism. *Signs: Journal of Women in Culture and Society, 30*(1).

McNeill, W. H. (2004). *Dünya Tarihi* (A. Şenel, Trans.). Ankara, Turkey: İmge.

Morgan, L. H. (1998). *Eski Toplum II* (Ü. Oskay, Trans.). İstanbul, Turkey: Payel.

Mulvey, L. (1975, Autumn). Visual Pleasure and Narrative Cinema. *Screen, 16*(3), 6–18. doi:10.1093creen/16.3.6

Saran, N. (1984). *Köylerimiz*. İstanbul, Turkey: Edebiyat Fakültesi.

Şenel, A. (1996). *Siyasal Düşünceler Tarihi*. Ankara: Bilim ve Sanat.

Shanin, T. (1989). *Peasant and Peasants Societies*. Middlesex, UK: Penguin Books.

Stirling, P. (1966). *Turkish Village*. New York, NY: John Wiley & Sons

Tillion, G. (2006). *Harem ve Kuzenler* (Ş. Tekeli, & N. Sirman, Trans.). İstanbul, Turkey: Metis.

ADDITIONAL READING

Altındal, A. (2004). *Türkiye'de Kadın*. İstanbul: Alfa.

Dowling, C. (1994). *The Cindrella Complex: Women's Hidden Fear of Independence* (S. Budak, Trans.). Ankara: Öteki.

Paglia, C. (2001). *Sexual Personae: Art and Decadence from Nefertiti to Emily Dickinson. Yale*. Yale University Press.

Phillips, A. (1991). *Engendering Democracy. Basil*. Blacwell and Polity Press.

Russel, B. (2003). *Evlilik ve Ahlak* (E. Gürol, Trans.). İstanbul: Morpa Kültür.

KEY TERMS AND DEFINITIONS

Interpretive Social Science Approach: It is one of the social scientific research techniques in which the study type is based on the definition and interpretation of the contents.

Property: A quality or trait belonging and especially peculiar to an individual or thing and the exclusive right to possess, enjoy, and dispose of a thing. Ownership.

Susuz Yaz: The movie of Metin Erksan's (1963) which told property of water in the rurals.

Women's Identity: Female experience varies from the male model in the cultural context.

Yılanların Öcü: The movie of Metin Erksan's (1962) which told property relationships in the rurals.

ENDNOTES

[1] The surplus product "is an excess that is used by people who produce more than the consuming members of a community directly from the producers' work and who are not directly employed by producers" (Şenel 1996: 23).

[2] In the previous chapter, Stirling's researches in the book *Turkish Village* approach the subject from the same perspective.

[3] "Oedipus complex.... Because of the son's devotion to the mother and the hate of the father, the complex formed in the sub-conscious and carries the sex character" Sigmund Freud, Cinsiyet ve Psikanaliz, Ankara: Varlık Yayınları, 1972, p. 252.

Chapter 17
A Feminist Film:
Caramel

İkbal Bozkurt Avcı
Fırat Universtiy, Turkey

Derya Çetin
Bolu Abant Izzet Baysal University, Turkey

ABSTRACT

Feminist film theory evaluates films by some concepts such as subject positions, narrative closures, and fetishism. This theory suggests that the catharsis of popular films is in the service of the male audience. However, many feminist films centered on women are also made, which are outside the mainstream cinema and reach a considerable amount of viewers. This study aims to evaluate Caramel (Nadine Labaki, 2007) by the concepts of feminist film theory. The film expresses a country dominated by taboos through these five women.

INTRODUCTION

The idea that cinema is a suitable instrument for the camera to actually express woman's subjectivity has been uttered by many female directors since the early years of cinema. But the dawn of the feminist cinema theory dates back to 1960s (Hayward, 2000: 112). This is because the film theorists, generally having focused on the issues of classes and ideology until 1960s, only began to move to gender identity debates along with the rise of the second wave of feminism, one of the opposing cultural movements (Büker, 2010: 205; Özden, 2014: 191). The feminist film theory pursues the same political, theoretical and ideological goal as the feminist movement. According to this, the feminist film theory objects to the presentation of woman only as an image in cinema and placement of woman in a secondary position before man by undermining the sexist arrangements that run based on the patriarchal ideology. Along with this objection, possibility of a female cinema that opposes narratives that place man in the centre in film works has begun to be discussed. This study aims to evaluate Caramel (Nadine Labaki, 2007) by the concepts of the feminist film theory.

THE FEMINIST FILM THEORY AS A FEMINIST RESPONSE TO CINEMA

Nilüfer Timisi (2011: 162) classifies the evolution of the feminist film theory from its dawn to the present based on the dominant and critical approaches in social sciences. Timisi identifies as dominant/mainstream the first of these approaches that were popular in early 1970s. These film works, also called as Anglo-American, take the French surrealists and their texts' reinterpretation as their reference (Allen, 2004: 125). The theoretical foundation of these works that generally focus on the issues of gender and the representation of women in cinema is composed by the books of theorists such as Molly Haskell, Marjorie Rosen and Joan Mellen. Adopting a sociological and empirical attitude, these writers examine the historical position of women in films in a chronological order (Smelik, 2008: 2) and see as a problem that they are represented by negative stereotypes in their studies written based on Hollywood cinema. While the theoretical foundations of early feminist film works are laid by these writers, female film festivals are organized on one hand, and female directors such as Alica Guy-Blaché, Lois Weber, Anita Loos, Aziza Amir, Maria Landeta, Gilda de Abreu and Carmen Santos contribute to the feminist cinema by improving themselves in film production (Stam, 2000: 171-172). Thus, the mainstream feminist film works have gained significant theoretical and practical accumulation in terms of later examining film production processes and developing theories focused on viewer.

The second tradition that dominates the feminist film criticism is based on the arguments – especially of the Marxists such as Theodor Adorno and Louis Althusser – of the Frankfurt School of 1940s and 1950s. Besides, the feminist film theory is based on Freud's group psychology in explaining how cinema is managed by capital in order to create a compliant population (Allen, 2004: 125) and on the ideas of Lacan (Baudry, 1992: 310), who presents the conceptualization of "mirror stage" by rereading Freud in identification of viewer with its image seen on the scene (Büker, 2010: 207). The scenario of the feminist film theory based on Neo-Marxism, Freudian and Lacanian idea, semiotics and psychoanalysis has radically

A Feminist Film

changed according to the early feminist film theory. This is because while Marxist idea focuses on the ideological and economic side of film, the semiotic view points to the role of the fundamental cinematographic instruments such as the running of the camera and the use of fiction. Psychoanalysis allows theorists to approach film based on the conceptions of "subjectivity, visual pleasure and desire" (Öztürk, 2000: 86-87). In this direction, feminist film theorists have moved their interest from the criticism that contents of films are ideological to the cinematographic mechanism and instruments used in films to produce meaning. Now theorists have begun to think not that films reflect meanings like in early times, but that these meanings are built by film producers (Smelik, 2008: 3). So, theorists such as Pam Cook, Rosalind Coward, Annette Kuhn, Jacqueline Rose, Sandy Flitterman-Lewis, Elisabeth Cowie, Gertrud Koch, Parveen Adams, Teresa de Lauretis, Kaja Silverman and Judith Mayne have largely contributed to the feminist counter-cinema led by Claire Johnston and Laura Mulvey (Branigan & Buckland, 2014: 189).

Claire Johnston begins her text named *'Women's Cinema as Counter-Cinema'* in the book titled *'Notes on Women's Cinema'* (1973) edited by her with Panofsky's identification about two (the vamp and the angel at home) fundamental woman stereotypes in action in early years of cinema, that is, with the present woman myths in cinema (Johnston, 2006: 78). This is because the path to change cinema and create the women's cinema as the counter-cinema goes through understanding the ideological exercises in the dominant cinema practices. Therefore, the first thing to do is present the "effect" of woman's position on the process of building the meaning of film by determining "how" woman is presented. Well, how is woman presented in these films? Here come the questions of such as how woman is put in the frame, enlightened and dressed. Effect means how woman is positioned within the narrative (Hayward, 2000: 116). According to Johnston, woman in the cinema dominated by man is presented by what she represents for him. Explaining this sentence, Johnston (2006: 79) makes the matter clear as follows: "Although woman is largely focused on as theatrical in cinema, it is right to say that woman does not exist as woman, I think." Then the thing to do is create a women's cinema that exists both inside and outside of the mainstream cinema, but is not hierarchical, collectively produces films and also uses film both as a political weapon and a means of entertainment (Nelmes, 1998: 77). Johnston emphasizes that woman subjectivity in cinema is only possible with a counter-cinema that opposes the dominance of man and questions this dominance, that is, with women's cinema.

While the study of Claire Johnston proposing a Counter-Cinema is important to the feminist cinema, there is also the cult article of Laura Mulvey, the leader of the feminist film theory, undoubtedly a theorist and an activist like Johnston. Mulvey states that the article titled *'Visual Pleasure and Narrative Cinema'* first published in 1975 in 'Screen Journal' has four fundamental elements, which are Hollywood, psychoanalysis, feminism and avant-garde. Mulvey questions these four fundamental elements and tries to make sense of their relationship with each other while writing her article. Showdown of these four fundamental elements revealed two fundamental points in Mulvey's mind: Mulvey had the opportunity to examine Hollywood as a complicated cinema not by underrating it with a cinephile fascination, but by trying to understand it. Thus, she reached the idea that classical cinema both guaranteed the sex differences and visualized woman as a theatrical object. Secondly, she found that the Hollywood studio system has the narratives woman and desire in the centre as a material of entertainment (Kırel, 2012: 215-216). Based on these two fundamental points, Mulvey reaches a third point; Hollywood films constitute a system that offers materials suitable for psychoanalysis. Based on all these, Mulvey (2010: 211) attempts a showdown with the dominant cinema. In this showdown Mulvey points to the necessity to know how the mainstream cinema runs to avoid the traps of the male-dominant cinema. Therefore, Mulvey uses the psychoanalytical theory as a political weapon to show how patriarchal unconscious is built in films.

The writer, focusing on the relationship between the scene and the viewer, has developed "the theory of male gaze" (Smelik, 2008: 3). Mulvey, in this theory, focuses more on the look of the viewer than the characters' positions in the filmic narrative. This is because in the film, the female character becomes the object of the look of the male character by means of codes and agreements. This fact creates the viewer identified with the male character by opening the door for the woman to look (Hayward, 2000: 117). More simply, the classical narrative cinema is based on "the female body as a source of pleasure" and "the look of the male" in Mulvey's words (Bakır, 2008: 63). The writer, defining this process of look as scopophilia[1], states that this concept, adapted by her from Freud, is one of the pleasures taken from cinema. The concept of scopophilia means treating other people as objects and subjecting them to a curious look in psychoanalysis. In this direction, the visual pleasure taken by cinema means the departure of the viewer from what is being watched and the objectifying of what is being watched (Timisi, 2011: 168-169). Mulvey states that scopophilia in the dominant cinema is a structure that functions around activity and passivity shown by gender difference, and says that this double contrast is divided into genders.

Laura Mulvey, in the theory developed by her, has revealed the narrative and cinematic techniques that only grants the men the right to look in cinema. According to this, the male character directs his look towards the female character in the filmic narrative. The viewer in the cinema hall automatically and often unconsciously identifies with the male gaze. This is because the camera films not only from the male character's optical, but also libidinal look. Therefore, the cinematic look has three planes of camera, character and viewer, which objectifies and makes theatrical the female character. Scopophilia in the classical cinema makes sense of woman

A Feminist Film

with her being lookable (Mulvey, 1989 quo.; Smelik, 2008: 5). The writer states that the importance of the mirror stage, that is, the moment a child recognizes his image in the mirror, developed by Jacques Lacan, in establishing the ego is also quite important to his theory. According to Lacan, the mirror stage occurs when children's physical ambitions beat their own motor capacities and along with the joy of recognizing themselves finally caused by their assumption that their mirror images are more holistic and perfect than they experience in their bodies. Thus, the recognition is covered by wrong recognition. According to this, the recognized image is comprehended as the reflecting body of "ego". But the fact that it is wrongly comprehended as if it were superior causes him to reflect outside this body as the ideal ego. In this case, the alienated subject that again thinks about itself as another thing as an ego ideal opens the way of identifying with others in the future (Mulvey, 2010: 216). Thus, structurally, ego formation occurs with imaginative functions just as in cinema. Before Christian Metz, in his texts on cinema and psychoanalysis, has put forward this analogy, Mulvey has put forward that cinematic identifications are structured on the limit of gender difference. Presentation of the distorted image of the female character as passive and weak against the representation of the more perfect, more complete, stronger ideal ego of the male character in cinema creates a great contrast. Thus, the viewer is to identify with the male character rather than the female character in the film (Smelik, 2008: 5-6). In the patriarchal order, woman still takes the place of an indicator for the male other not as the producer, but the conveyor of the meaning, as surrounded by an order in which she could live to the end her fantasies and obsessions imposed by the man through linguistic instructions upon her dependent and quiet image (Mulvey, 2010: 212).

The narrative structure in the traditional cinema sets the male character as active and having power. The dramatic action that progresses based on it opens around the male character, and look is organized in this direction (Smelik, 2008: 4-5). According to Laura Mulvey (2010: 216), cinema films, in addition to satisfying the existing desire for pleasure-giving look, develops scopophilia within its own narcissistic aspect by going ahead more. At this point, two contrary aspects are revealed of the pleasure-giving structure of cinematic look: The first one is the scopophilic pleasure arising from use of another person as an object of sexual stimulation through looking, and the second stems from an identification with the visible image, developed through and seen with the establishment of narcissism and ego. In other words, the first is seen as a function of sexual motives, and the second of ego libido. This contrast between libido and ego has not only created a wonderful world of fantasies, but also developed a particular reflection of reality throughout the entire history of cinema. According to this, sexual motives and processes of identification have a meaning within the symbolic order where desire is expressed. This meaning expresses the act of castration within the order where language exists. So, the act of looking, which is pleasure-giving in terms of form, can be threatening in terms of contents. And this paradox is revealed by woman, only found in films as an image (Mulvey, 2010: 217-218). The female character, reminding man the lack of a penis with her look, is the source of deep fears. So, the traditional narrative cinema resolves this threat of castration through narrative structure or fetishism. Way of making unnoticeable the threat of castration in film narratives is find the female character guilty. This guilt is confirmed either through punishment or rescue. This guilt in cinema narrative finds its place in the story with two traditional ends deemed proper for woman: The female character either dies or gets married at the end of the narrative. So, the catharsis waits on the male viewer in both cases (Smelik, 2008: 6).

The writer, after drawing frame for the concept of scopophilia, presents how look is organized in cinema, and the decisiveness of the male look by discussing the phenomenon of look over gender. According to Mulvey (2010: 218), "The decisive male look conveys its own fantasy to the appropriately formed female figure. Women, in their traditionally exhibitionistic roles, are both the ones that are looked at and exhibited with their appearances encoded for strong visual and erotic effect, which give a message of lookability. Woman, exhibited as a sex object, is the leitmotif of erotic spectacle." The visual pleasure based on peeking makes the looker a subject, and the looked an object. This look of man involves both the viewer, and the characters of the film. The focus of the look of the male characters in cinema is the female character. Therefore, the female character cannot avoid the look of the male character in cinema (Mulvey, 1993: 116 quo.; Kabadayı, 2013: 100).

Thus, while in cinema the viewer is the subject of the male look/is active, the female body is positioned as the object of that look/as passive. So, the instrument of cinematograph produces two kinds of primary pleasures, which are voyeurism/peeking scopophilia and fetishism/fetishistic scopophilia (Arslan, 2009: 18). Voyeurism or peeking scopophilia is a result of "seeing and making sure of the private and forbidden one". This way of peeking associated with sadism is an active practice involving the erotic pleasure of looking at others as if they were objects. In fetishistic peeking, the highlighted figure is either replaced with the object of the fetish, or the threat of this figure is eliminated. To make the object relaxing once its threat has been eliminated, it is turned into a fetish (Timisi, 2011: 169).

Laura Mulvey, at the end of her theory based on Freud's and Lacan's ideas, states that there are three types of looks in cinema. First is "the look of the camera that films pro filmic events", the second is "the look of the viewer that has watched the finished product", and the third is "the characters on the illusion of the scene who look at each other". According to Mulvey, narrative film agreements refute the first two, and subject them to the third. Purpose of this conscious action is to prevent the detractive awareness of the viewer by eliminating the presence of the continuously interrupting camera (Mulvey, 2010: 228). Mulvey actually aims to

A Feminist Film

solve the filmic language codes of the Hollywood understanding of cinema and to develop an alternative approach by addressing the position and experience in the face of the film (Kırel, 2012: 235). Mulvey (2010: 229), in the last paragraph of her study for that, states that the only thing to do against the female image stolen and used in cinema is to abolish the classical type of film.

Susan Hayward (2000: 120), in her feminist film theory, mentions a third period from 1984 to the present. In this period, Laura Mulvey's text titled *'Visual Pleasure and Narrative Cinema'* was the focus of criticisms in addition to being a reference to many studies. The criticisms are about why Mulvey described the female viewer as male. Ann Kaplan (2010: 120), in her text titled *'Feminism and Film'*, based on Mulvey's article, investigates the possibility of the female look and what the female viewer meant, and emphasizes that woman in films does not have to be the object of the look. According to Kaplan, the female viewer has no desire for peeking, unlike the male viewer. The female viewer that passes the male positioning becomes able to be dominant and to be moved to the position of the subject of the look. Mary Ann Doane, in her text titled *Film and Masquerade: Theorizing the Female Spectator'* (1982), focuses on the conception of "look" through the female viewer, and discusses the negation of the female look. Doane says that peeking requires distance and that it is not possible in cinema for the female viewer. This is because what she views in the film is her own image. The female viewer only gets away from this situation when she uses a mask, and thus is able to make a difference between her image and herself. Ann Doane, putting forward that masking is not satisfying either, also states that over-identification for the female viewer could produce narcissism. Thus, Doane points out that the female viewer is what is consumed by the image rather than the consumer of the image (Saygılıgil, 2013: 158).

Teresa De Lauretis, in her study titled *'Alice Doesn't: Feminism, Semiotics, Cinema'* (1984), focuses on the relationship between the narrative structure and the female viewer. According to this, woman in the western culture is represented as the "other" differently from man. Here, woman is composed of a fiction or representation. That is, she is completely different from the real women who lived under social and historical conditions. Therefore, the female subject cannot find a place for herself within this structure. Woman is stuck between the male representations and the image of woman that has been produced by these representations. At this point, the cinema narrative is regarded as one of the ways of reproducing subjectivity. Every film, that is, story is founded on the subject's desire and the breakdown of this desire into socio-cultural codes. And the narrative structures are determined by the oedipal subject. The theorist treats this desire both as a way of emphasizing the socio-political economy that is the determinant of the dominance of men on women, and the emerging subjectivity of the gender differences (Smelik, 2008: 12). Kaja Silverman, another remarkable feminist theorist of the age, in her book titled *'The*

Threshold of the Visible World' (1996), based on Lacan's sentence that "the mirror stage resembles the threshold of the apparent world", states that the field of view is approached by passing through the mirror stage. Silverman believes that "look" has a transforming power. Eye, the organ for looking, is able to give neglected bodies the present of active love. For this reason, look has the potential to be able to associate the unimportant or unfamiliar one with the most personal and most important one (Saygılıgil, 2013: 159).

A FEMINIST FILM: CARAMEL

Story of the Film

The film tells the story of five women from different ages and locations, who come together in a hairdressing salon in Beirut. The main character, Layale, is portrayed by Nadine Labaki, who is also the director of the film. Layale is a young, single woman working in a middle-class barber shop. Layale, who lives with her family, has a relationship with a married man, Rabih. Nisrine, a Muslim young woman, is engaged and plans to marry soon. Rima is a young woman who likes women with a masculine appearance. Jamale is a widow elderly woman with abandoned children for another woman by her husband. Rose, who is also a tailor, is also an aunt of Layale. She lives with her sister Lili, whose mental health isn't seen very well because of her advanced age. In the film, the stories of five characters are told in parallel, and and except the Layale's story, all stories are about equal weight. Layale finds little interest in her married lover, then she's curious about her family. She secretly contact his family, suffers and eventually leaves his lover. On the other hand, Rose when she intends to have love with a man who is new to life and interested in herself, her sense of responsibility towards her sister outweighs and she finishes the relationship. Nisrine is worried about her wedding day because she is not a virgin and she relieves her concerns by going through a virginity operation. Jamale is the only character in the film who has never undergone a transformation. At the end of the movie, he continues to carry the unease he is given by the fear of aging. Feeling closeness to a beautiful woman who is a customer of the hairdresser, Rima finds the happiness when the woman corresponds to her.

Subjects and Hidden Subjects

In the women-centered film Caramel, at the beginning of the story, female characters are in a passive position to guide their own lives, while at the end of the film almost all become active and become strong subjects. In the beginning of the movie there are

A Feminist Film

two sounds that mobilize Layale, one is the horn playing in front of the hairdresser, and the other is the ringing of the mobile phone. No matter what she does, Layale immediately leaves her action when she hears these voices and acts according to the wish of the married man in her life. Layale seems happy to sit in the parked car in some secluded locations with her lover. One day, when Layale sees a photo of Rabih's wife and daughter by mixing the wallet he had dropped in the car, this state of pleasure begins to change. The event that actually transformed Layale is the fact that Rabih did not come to the celebration prepared for anniversaries. In order to spend a night together, Layale finds a hotel that can accept themselves without a marriage certificate. She cleans the dirty room with great effort. When Rabih declares that he cannot come up with a text message, she is disappointed. When her friends came to the hotel room to comfort her, Layale described her situation as follows:

I'm here like an idiot since the morning. I wiped the entire room from head to toe. I almost blew a wall-to-wall rug. And more importantly, I've been willing to replace prostitutes and didn't even bother to call me. Only one message; He couldn't get over his wife. All my life depends on a single horn sound. I'm waiting for the horn to hit. I can't look into my family's eyes, you know. I come home at night. 'Where were you?' they say. What can I say? I don't want to lie anymore. I'm telling myself he is leaving his wife. Not knowing who this woman is, she really is killing me out of curiosity. Who is this woman? And what kind of woman? I wonder how she smells. What kind of woman she is? Is she beautiful? More beautiful than me? What is she doing?

Then Layale transforms and leaves Rabih. Layale doesn't go out even though he comes to the front of shop and insists on the horn. Then Layale's phone starts ringing and she doesn't answer. This is where Layale has ceased to act in accordance with the desires of Rabih and began to act on her own desire. Layale doesn't care about the horn continues to work happily.

Speaking Women, Silent Men

At her book "The Acoustic Mirror" Kaja Silverman had moved the focus from the sight to the voice, and thus created the opportunity to approach to the female subject from a unique perspective within the framework of feminist film theory. Silverman asserts that the masculine subject is given the properties of being one and being complete in the cinema, not only by the image and the appearance, but also by the means of the recording and the usage of the voice (Cited by: Smelik, 2008: 15). One of the three male characters in the film, Rabih, is not fully visible in the film and his voice is not heard. In the scenes where they meet with Layale, his arm and his back is partially visible but his face never appears. Layale's voice is heard in telephone conversations, but Rabih's voice is not heard. Aside from this conscious choice, on the other hand, the second male character in the film, Youssef, also has a silent stance that does not express his own desires. Youssef is a young police officer who lives in the same neighborhood as Layane and is interested in Layane. He only expresses his interest in Layale in a speech he has made to himself alone. Youssef waits in a café across the shop and secretly watchs Layale. At the front of the window, Layale starts talking with Rabih on the telephone. Youssef, who watches her from afar, pretends to be talking to herself. The conversation between them is as follows:

L-Hello my love, Y-Hello my sunshine, L-You dropped your wallet that's why I call, Y-I am waiting for your call, I am waiting for one hour. Ask Joseph if you don't believe, L-Stop bullshit, when are you coming? Y-Not now, I am drinking my coffee and Joseph tell fortunes. He sees a chair and a very beautiful girl looking out of the window but who doesn't see me. One day instead of cutting the penalty to the woman parked in the wrong place, he realized that he liked her a lot.

In these words, Youssef explains his feelings for Layane to himself in a place that no one has heard. For the first time, Youssef, who is invisible to Layane throughout the film, becomes noticeable for Layane in the final wedding scene. While dancing in the ensemble, Layane looks at him in a different way than before, and approaches and starts dancing with him. Similarly, the third male character of the film, Charles, remained silent and instead of speaking directly to Rose, he left a note on the tailor's window asking for a date.

FUTURE RESEARCH AND DIRECTIONS

It is thought that some perspectives that are not covered by this study will open useful discussion areas for future studies. A psychoanalytic analysis of the symbols in the film can raise considerable questions. Director Nadine Labaki, interprets one character of film which named Jamale as follows: "A lot of women in my country are in this situation because this situation take an important palace in the seduction power of a Lebanese woman."[2] (Jamale is a woman who does not accept that she has had menopause.)

CONCLUSION

The narrative structure in the traditional cinema sets the male character as active and having power. The dramatic action that progresses based on it opens around the male character, and look is organized in this direction (Smelik, 2008: 4-5). Considering the characters of the film in terms of subject positions, it is seen that women are in the center, but whether they are strong subjects can be discussed. Layane is single woman, but as she herself testifies in the film, her whole life depends on a horn. When her lover hits the horn, she leaves everything she does and rushes to him. This is the man who has never seen his face and never heard his voice in the film that leads the course of the events. This passive position is also acceptable for other female characters of the film. Nisrine acts according to the oppressive environment of her and her fiancé's family. She ignores her own desires and acts according to their wishes. Similarly, Rose, in accordance with the needs of her family is giving up on her own desires. Jamale to be defeated her fear of aging and Rima doesn't make any attempts for the woman she likes. From these points of view, it can be said that women in the film exhibit a passive appearance even if they are at the center. However, in the second half of the film, almost all of the characters experience a change. They give a new direction to their lives according to their own desires. Thus, the passive posture they exhibit in the first half of the film changes and they becomes strong subjects.

REFERENCES

Allen, R. (2004). Psychoanalytic film theory. In T. Miller, & R. Stam (Eds.), *A Companion to Film Theory* (pp. 123–145). Blackwell Publishing.

Arslan, U. T. (2009). Aynanın sırları: psikanalitik film kuramı. *Kültür ve İletişim*, *12*(1), 9-38.

Bakır, B. (2008). *Sinema ve Psikanaliz*. İstanbul, Turkey: Hayalet Kitabevi.

Baudry, J.-L. (1992). Ideological effects of the basic cinematographic apparatus. In *G. Mast, M. Cohen, & L. Braudy (Eds.), Film Theory and Criticism: Introductory Readings* (pp. 302–312). New York, NY: Oxford University Press.

Branigan, E., & Buckland, W. (2014). *The Routledge Encyclopedia of Film Theory*. London, UK: Routledge.

Büker, S. (2010). Feminist ve psikanalitik eleştiriye giriş. In S. Büker, & Y. Gürhan Topçu (Eds.), *Sinema: Tarih/Kuram/Eleştiri* (pp. 205–210). İstanbul, Turkey: Kırmızı Kedi Yayınevi.

Eagleton, M. (2013). *Feminist Literary Critism*. New York, NY: Routledge.

Hayward, S. (2000). *Cinema Studies: The Key Concepts*. London, UK: Routledge.

Johnston, C. (2006). *Karşı-sinema olarak kadınların sineması* (Vol. 14). Sinemasal.

Kabadayı, L. (2013). *Film Eleştirisi: Kuramsal Çerçeve ve Sinemamızdan Örnek Çözümlemeler*. İstanbul, Turkey: Ayrıntı Yayınları.

Kaplan, E. A. (2000). *Feminism and Film*. Oxford, UK: Oxford University Press.

Kırel, S. (2012). *Kültürel Çalışmalar ve Sinema*. İstanbul, Turkey: Kırmızı Kedi Yayınevi.

Marshall, G. (1999). *Sosyoloji Sözlüğü*. Ankara, Turkey: Bilim ve Sanat.

Mulvey, L. (1975). Visual pleasure and narrative cinema. In Visual and Other Pleasures (pp. 14-26). London, UK: Macmillan.

Mulvey, L. (2010). Görsel haz ve anlatı sineması. In S. Büker, & Y. Gürhan Topçu (Eds.), Sinema: Tarih Kuram Eleştiri (pp. 211-229). İstanbul, Turkey: Kırmızı Kedi Yayınevi.

Nelmes, J. (1998, Winter). Sinemada cinsiyet ve cinselliğin sunumu. Sinemasal, 71-94.

Özden, Z. (2014). *Film Eleştirisi: Film Eleştirisinde Temel Yaklaşımlar ve Tür Filmi Eleştirisi*. Ankara, Turkey: İmge Kitabevi.

Öztürk, S. R. (2000). *Sinemada Kadın Olmak*. İstanbul, Turkey: Alan Yayıncılık.

Saygılıgil, F. (2013). Feminist film kuramı. In Z. Özarslan (Ed.), *Sinema Kuramları 2: Beyazperdeyi Aydınlatan Kuramlar* (pp. 143–165). İstanbul, Turkey: Su Yayınevi.

Smelik, A. (2008). *Feminist Sinema ve Film Teorisi ve Ayna Çatladı*. İstanbul, Turkey: Agora Kitaplığı.

Stam, R. (2000). *Film Theory: An Introduction*. Blackwell Publishing.

Timisi, N. (2011). Sinemaya feminist müdahale: Laura Mulvey'de psikanalitik seyirciden teknolojik seyirciye. In M. İri (Ed.), *Sinema Araştırmaları: Kuramlar, Kavramlar, Yaklaşımlar* (pp. 157–182). İstanbul, Turkey: Derin Yayınları.

ADDITIONAL READING

Butler, A. (2002). *Women's Cinema: The Contested Screen*. London: Wallflower.

Chaudhuri, S. (2007). *Feminist Film Theorists*. London, New York: Routledge.

Erens, P. (1990). *Issues in Feminist Film Criticism*. Indianapolis: Indiana University Press.

Haskell, M. (1974). *From Reverence to Rape: The Treatment of Women in the Movies*. New York: Holt.

Humm, M. (1997). *Feminism and Film*. Edinburgh: Edinburgh University Press.

Kaplan, E. A. (1983). *Women and Film: Both Sides of the Camera*. London, New York: Routledge. doi:10.4324/9780203328149

Kuhn, A. (1982). *Women's Pictures: Feminism and Cinema*. London, New York: Routledge.

Mulvey, L. (1989). *Visual and Other Pleasures*. Bloomington: Indiana University Press. doi:10.1007/978-1-349-19798-9

Penley, C. (1988). *Feminism and Film Theory*. London, New York: Routledge.

Tasker, Y. (2000). *Working Girls: Gender and Sexuality in Popular Cinema*. London, New York: Routledge.

Unterburger, A. (1998). *Women Filmmakers & Their Films*. Detroit: St. James Press.

Wright, E. (2000). *Lacan and Postfeminism*. London: Icon Books.

ENDNOTES

[1] The pleasure of looking at someone (Mulvey, 2010: 2014).
[2] For more information see http://www.chantierfilms.com/wp-content/uploads/BASIN-B%C3%9CLTEN%C4%B0_Caramel.pdf. Date of access 15.05.2019.

Compilation of References

Abadan-Unat, N. (1991). The impact of legal and educational reforms on Turkish women. In N. R. Keddie, & B. Baron (Eds.), *Women in Middle Eastern history* (pp. 177–194). New Haven, CT: Yale University Press.

Aberbach, D. (2003). The poetry of nationalism. *Nations and Nationalism*, *9*(2), 255–275. doi:10.1111/1469-8219.00085

Abisel, N. (1994). Popüler Yerli Filmlerde Kadının Kadına Sunuluşu "Aşk Mabudesi". In N. Abisel (Ed.), Türk Sineması Üzerine Yazılar. Ankara, Turkey: İmge.

Abisel, N. (2005). *Türk Sineması Üzerine Yazılar*. Ankara, Turkey: Phoenix Yay.

Adak, S. (2010). Construction of gendered identities in Turkish national memory: 'Our' women and 'other' women in the stories of Ömer Seyfeddin. *Çankaya University. Journal of the Humanities and Social Sciences*, *7*(1), 75–100.

Adorno, W. T., & Horkheimer, M. (1996). Kültür Sanayii, Kitlelerin Aldatılması Olarak Aydınlanma. In Aydınlanmanın diyalektiği. Felsefi fragmanlar II (pp. 7-62). İstanbul, Turkey: Kabalcı Yayınevi.

Akdoğan, H. (2004). *Medyada Kadın*. İstanbul, Turkey: Ceylan Yayınları.

Akgiş, Ö., & Karakaş, E., (2018). Bir Sosyal Ağ Olan Hemşehri Derneklerinin Yoksullukla Mücadeledeki Rolü Üzerine Uygulamalı Bir Araştırma. *Ege Coğrafya Dergisi*, *27*(1), 21–34.

Akıncı, S. F. (2013). *Kriminoloji*. İstanbul, Turkey: Beta.

Akmeşe, Z. (2012). *Popüler Dergilerde Kadın İmgesinin Nesneleştirilerek Dönüşümü*. Dokuz Eylül Üniversitesi Uluslararası Kadın Konferansı Bildiriler Kitabı.

Aktaş, C. (2015). *Şarkın Şiiri İran Sineması*. İstanbul, Turkey: İz Yayıncılık.

Alangu, T. (2015). *Billur Köşk Masalları*. İstanbul, Turkey: Yapı Kredi Yayınları.

Aliçavuşoğlu, E. (2012). Psikanaliz, Freud ve Sanat. *Sanat Tarihi Yıllığı*, (20), 1–16.

Allen, R. (2004). Psychoanalytic film theory. In T. Miller, & R. Stam (Eds.), *A Companion to Film Theory* (pp. 123–145). Blackwell Publishing.

Compilation of References

Altay, N., & Gümüş, N., (2010). Hemşehrilik ve İzmir'deki Hemşehri Dernekleri. *e-Journal of New World Sciences Academy, 5*(3), 231-239.

Althusser, L. (1994). *İdeoloji ve Devletin İdeolojik Aygıtları. Mahmut Özışık ve Yusuf Alp (çev.)*. İstanbul, Turkey: İletişim Yayınları.

Anthias, F., & Yuval-Davis, N. (1989). Introduction. In *N. Yuval-Davis, & F. Anthias (Eds.), Woman-Nation-State* (pp. 1–15). London, UK: Palgrave Macmillan. doi:10.1007/978-1-349-19865-8_1

Antmen, A. (2012). *Sanat / Cinsiyet: Sanat Tarihi ve Feminist Eleştiri*. İstanbul, Turkey: İletişim Yayınları.

Apak, K. H., & Kasap, F. (2014). Türk Televizyonlarındaki Gıda Reklamlarında Kadın ve Erkek İmgesi Üzerine Bir İnceleme. *Journal of International Social Research, 7*(34), 814–832.

Arat, Y. (1996). On gender and citizenship in Turkey. *Middle East Report (New York, N.Y.), 198*(198), 28–31. doi:10.2307/3012873

Arat, Y. (2000). From emancipation to liberation: The changing role of women in Turkey's public realm. *Journal of International Affairs, 54*(1), 107–126.

Arat, Y. (2001). Women's rights as human rights: The Turkish case. *Human Rights Review (Piscataway, N.J.), 3*(1), 27–34. doi:10.100712142-001-1003-9

Arat, Y. (2005). Women's challenge to citizenship in Turkey. In F. Birtek, & T. Dragonas (Eds.), *Citizenship and the nation-state in Greece and Turkey* (pp. 104–116). London, UK: Routledge. doi:10.4324/9780203311462_chapter_7

Arat, Z. (1998). Educating the daughters of the republic. In Z. F. Arat (Ed.), *Deconstructing images of Turkish woman* (pp. 175–181). New York, NY: St. Martin's Press.

Arendt, H. (1994). *İnsanlık Durumu* (B. S. Şener, Trans.). İstanbul, Turkey: İletişim.

Arslan, U. T. (2009). Aynanın sırları: psikanalitik film kuramı. *Kültür ve İletişim, 12*(1), 9-38.

Arslan, T. U. (2005). *Bu Kabuslar Neden Cemil?* İstanbul, Turkey: Metis.

Arslantepe, M. (2010). *Sinemada Feminist Teori: 3. Uluslararası Bir Bilim Kongresi Olarak Kadın: Edebiyat, Dil, Kültür ve Sanat Çalışmalarında Kadın Sempozyumu*. Konya, Turkey: Selçuk Üniversitesi.

Ayers, D. (2008). Bodies, bullets, and bad guys: Elements of the hardbody film. *Film Criticism, 32*(3), 41–67.

Aytekin, B. A., & Rızvanoğlu, K. (2019). Creating learning bridges through participatory design and technology to achieve sustainability in local crafts. *International Journal of Technology and Design Education, 29*(3), 603–632. doi:10.100710798-018-9454-3

Bakır, B. (2008). *Sinema ve Psikanaliz*. İstanbul, Turkey: Hayalet Kitabevi.

Barthes, R. (2012). *Gösterge Bilimsel Serüven*. İstanbul, Turkey: Yapı Kredi Yayınları.

Batı, U., & Baygül, Ş. B. (2006). Reklamlarda İdeal Kadın Bedeninin Sunumuna İlişkin Bir İçerik Analizi. *Journal of Communication Studies, 2*, 49–73.

Baudrillard, J. (2001). *Baştan Çıkarma Üzerine*. İstanbul, Turkey: Ayrıntı.

Baudrillard, J. (2004). *Tüketim Toplumu*. İstanbul, Turkey: Ayrıntı Yayınları.

Baudry, J.-L. (1992). Ideological effects of the basic cinematographic apparatus. In G. Mast, M. Cohen, & L. Braudy (Eds.), *Film Theory and Criticism: Introductory Readings* (pp. 302–312). New York, NY: Oxford University Press.

Becerikli Yıldırım, S. (2005). Çocuk Öykülerinde Toplumsal Cinsiyet Göstergeleri: Oya ile Kaya Örneği [Indicators of Gender in Children's Stories: Case of Oya and Kaya]. In *Uluslararası Çocuk ve İletişim Kongresi* (vol. 2). Istanbul, Turkey: İ. Ü. İletişim Fakültesi Yayınları.

Belsey, A., & Chadwick, R. (1998). Kod ve Etik. In A. Basley, & R. Chadwick (Eds.), *Medya ve Gazetecilikte Etik Sorunlar*. Ayrıntı Yayınları, Birinci Basım.

Berktay, F. (2005). Meşum Kadınlar, Solucanlar, Maymunlar, Zehirli Sarmaşıklar. *Kadın Belleği Dergisi*, 1.

Berktay, F. (2009). *Tek Tanrılı Dinlerin Karşısında Kadın*. İstanbul, Turkey: Metis.

Binark, M., & Gencel Bek, M. (2010). Eleştirel Medya Okuryazarlığı [Critical Media Literacy] (2nd ed.). Istanbul, Turkey: Kalkedon Yayınları.

Binark, M., & Gencel Bek, M. (2010). *Eleştirel Medya Okuryazarlığı: Kuramsal Yaklaşımlar ve Uygulamalar*. İstanbul, Turkey: Kalkedon Yayınevi.

Boland, E. (1987). The woman poet in a national tradition. *Studies: An Irish Quarterly Review, 76*(302), 148–158.

Bolay, S. H. (2004). *Felsefe Doktrinleri ve Terimleri Sözlüğü*. Ankara, Turkey: Akçağ Yayınları.

Bora, A. (2011). Kadınların Sınıfı: Ücretli Ev Emeği ve Kadın Öznelliğinin İnşası [Women's Class: Paid Domestic Labor and Building Women's Subjectivity]. Istanbul, Turkey: İletişim Yayınları.

Bora, A. (2018). *Kadınların Sınıfı*. İstanbul, Turkey: İletişim.

Bora, T. (2017). *Cereyanlar: Türkiye'de siyasi ideolojiler*. İstanbul, Turkey: İletişim.

Boulware, T. (2016). "Who Killed the World": Building a Feminist Utopia from the Ashes of Toxic Masculinity in Mad Max: Fury Road. *Mise-en-scène: The Journal of Film & Visual Narration, 1*(1).

Bourdieu, P. (1986). The Forms of Capital. In J. G. Richardson (Ed.), Handbook of theory and research for the sociology of education. New York, NY: Greenwood Press.

Bourdieu, P. (2015). *Ayrım*. İstanbul, Turkey: Heretik Yayınları.

Boyer, P. J. (1986, Feb. 16). TV turns to the hard-boiled male. *New York Times*.

Boyle, E., & Brayton, S. (2012). Ageing masculinities and "muscle work" in Hollywood action film: An analysis of The Expendables. *Men and Masculinities, 15*(5), 468–485. doi:10.1177/1097184X12454854

Branigan, E., & Buckland, W. (2014). *The Routledge Encyclopedia of Film Theory*. London, UK: Routledge.

Brooker, W., & Hassler-Forest, D. (2017). Afterword: "You'll Find I'm Full of Surprises" The Future of Star Wars. In S. Guynes, & D. Hassler-Forest (Eds.), Star Wars and the History of Transmedia Storytelling. Amsterdam, The Netherlands: Amsterdam University Press.

Brown, J. D., & Campbell, K. (1986). Race and gender in music videos: The same beat but a different drummer. *Journal of Communication, 36*(1), 94–106. doi:10.1111/j.1460-2466.1986.tb03041.x

Bruin-Molé, M. (2017). Space Bitches, Witches, and Kick-Ass Princesses Star Wars and Popular Feminism. In S. Guynes & D. Hassler-Forest (Eds.), Star Wars and the History of Transmedia Storytelling. Amsterdam, The Netherlands: Amsterdam University Press.

Buckner, B., & Rutledge, P. (2011). *Transmedia Storytelling for Marketing and Branding: It's Not Entertainment, It's Survival*. Retrieved from http://www.kcommhtml.com/ima/2011_03/transmedia_storytelling

Bühring, L. N. (2017). Declining to Decline: Aged Tough Guys in 'The Expendables' and 'The Expendables 2'. *Journal of Extreme Anthropology, 1*(3), 41–60. doi:10.5617/jea.4528

Büker, S. (2010). Feminist ve psikanalitik eleştiriye giriş. In S. Büker, & Y. Gürhan Topçu (Eds.), *Sinema: Tarih/Kuram/Eleştiri* (pp. 205–210). İstanbul, Turkey: Kırmızı Kedi Yayınevi.

Bushman, B. J., & Anderson, C. A. (2009). Comfortably numb: Desensitizing effects of violent media on helping others. *Psychological Science, 20*(3), 273–277. doi:10.1111/j.1467-9280.2009.02287.x PMID:19207695

Butler, A. M. (2017). Invoking the Holy Trilogy Star Wars in the Askewniverse. In S. Guynes, & D. Hassler-Forest (Eds.), Star Wars and the History of Transmedia Storytelling. Amsterdam: Amsterdam University Press.

Butler, J. (1990). *Gender trouble: Feminism and the subversion of identity*. New York, NY: Routledge.

Butler, J. (2009). *Toplumsal Cinsiyet Düzenlemeleri. Cogito: Feminizm [Gender Regulations. Cogito: Feminism]*. Istanbul, Turkey: YKY.

Butler, J. (2012). *Cinsiyet Belası: Feminizm ve Kimliğin Alt Üst Edilmesi* (B. Ertür, Trans.). İstanbul, Turkey: Metis Yayınları.

Butler, J. (2012). *Cinsiyet Belası: Feminizm ve Kimliğin Altüst Edilmesi*. İstanbul, Turkey: Metis Yayınları.

Butler, Ju. (2004). *Kırılgan Hayat Yasın ve Şiddet Gücü*. İstanbul, Turkey: Metis Yayınları.

Büyükdüvenci, S., & Öztürk, S. R. (2007). Yeni Türk Sinemasında Estetik Arayışı. *Felsefe Dünyası Dergisi*, (46), 45-49.

Çabuklu, Y. (2004). *Toplumsalın Sınırında Beden*. İstanbul, Turkey: Kanat Yayınları.

Çaha, Ö. (2010). *Sivil kadın Türkiye'de kadın ve sivil toplum (Genişletilmiş 2. Baskı)*. Ankara, Turkey: Savaş Yayınevi.

Çakar Mengü, S., & Mengü, M. (2009). Birmingham Okulu. Metin Çözümlemeleri, 343-363.

Cameron, D. (2000). Styling the worker: Gender and the commodification of language in the globalized service economy. *Journal of Sociolinguistics*, *4*(3), 323–347. doi:10.1111/1467-9481.00119

Cammarota, J. (2011). Blindsided by the avatar: White saviors and allies out of Hollywood and in education. *Review of Education, Pedagogy & Cultural Studies*, *33*(3), 242–259. doi:10.1080/10714413.2011.585287

Cankaya, Ö. (2003). *Bir Kitle İletişim Kurumunun Tarihi: TRT 1927-2000*. İstanbul, Turkey: Yapı Kredi Yayınları.

CarlsonT, ., & DjupsundG, . (2014). Taking Risks in Social Media Campaigning: The Early Adoption of Blogging by Candidates. *Scandinavian Political Studies*, *37*(1), 21–40. doi:10.1111/1467-9477.12011

Cash, T. F. (1990). The Psychology of Physical Appearance: Aesthetics, Attributes and Images. In T. F. Cash, & T. Pruzinsky (Eds.), Body Images. New York, NY: Guilford.

Cebeci, O. (2015). *Psikanalitik Edebiyat Kuramı*. İstanbul, Turkey: İthaki Yayınları.

Çelenk, S. (2005). *Televizyon, Temsil, Kültür*. Ankara, Turkey: Ütopya Yayınevi.

Cengizkan, A. (2004). *Ankara'nın İlk Planı 1924-25 Lörcher Planı*. Ankara, Turkey: Arkadaş Yayınları.

Chaney, D. (1999). *Yaşam Tarzları*. Ankara, Turkey: Dost Kitabevi.

Chein, I. (1981). Appendix: An introduction to sampling. In L. H. Kidder (Ed.), *Selltiz, Wrightsman, and Cook's research methods in social relations* (4th ed.; pp. 418–441). Austin, TX: Holt, Rinehart and Winston.

Chenu, C., German, R., Gressier-Soudan, E., Levillain, F., Astic, I., & Roirand, V. (2014, February). *Transmedia storytelling and cultural heritage interpretation: the CULTE project*. Museum and the Web Florence, Florence, Italy. Retrieved from https://mwf2014.museumsandtheweb.com/paper/transmedia-storytelling-and-cultural-heritage-interpretation-the-culte-project/

Connell, R. W. (2005). *Masculinities*. Cambridge, UK: Polity.

Compilation of References

Connell, R. (1987). *Gender and Power: Society, the Person, and Sexual Politics*. Cambridge, UK: Polity Press.

Connell, R. W. (1998). *Toplumsal Cinsiyet ve İktidar*. İstanbul, Turkey: Ayrıntı Yayınları.

Connell, R. W. (1998). *Toplumsal Cinsiyet ve İktidar: Toplum, Kişi ve Cinsel Politika* (C. Soydemir, Trans.). İstanbul, Turkey: Ayrıntı Yayınevi.

Connell, R. W., & Messerschmidt, J. W. (2005). Hegemonic masculinity: Rethinking the concept. *Gender & Society*, *19*(6), 829–859. doi:10.1177/0891243205278639

Corbin, J. (1989). İspanya'da Ayaklanmalar: Casasviejas 1933 ve Madrid 1981. In D. Riches (Ed.), Antropolojik Açıdan Şiddet (D. Hattatoğlu, Trans.). İstanbul, Turkey: Ayrıntı.

Corbin, J., & Strauss, A. (2015). *Basics of qualitative research: Techniques and procedures for developing grounded theory* (4th ed.). Thousand Oaks, CA: Sage.

Coward, R. (1993). *Kadınlık Arzuları-Günümüzde Kadın Cinselliği*. İstanbul, Turkey: Ayrıntı Yayınları.

Craft, C. (1988). *Too old, too ugly, and not deferential to men. An anchor woman's courageous baffle against sex discrimination*. Rockland, CA: Prima.

Davidoff, L. (2012). *Feminist Tarihyazımında Sınıf ve Cinsiyet* (Z. Ateşer, & S. Somuncuoğlu, Trans.). İstanbul, Turkey: İletişim Yayınları.

Davis, D. M. (1990). Portrayals of women in prune-tune network television: Some demographic characteristics. *Sex Roles*, *5*(23), 325–332. doi:10.1007/BF00290052

de Beauvoir, S. (1993). *Kadın* (B. Onaran, Trans.). İstanbul, Turkey: Payel.

De Lauretis, T. (1987). *Technologies of Gender: Essays on Theory, Film, and Fiction (Theories of Representation and Difference)*. Bloomington, IL: Indiana University Press. doi:10.1007/978-1-349-19737-8

Deleuze, G. (2003a). *Cinema 1: The Movement and Image*. Minneapolis, MN: University of Minnesota Press.

Deleuze, G. (2003b). *Cinema 2: The time-image*. Minneapolis, MN: University of Minnesota Press.

Demetriou, D. Z. (2001). Connell's concept of hegemonic masculinity: A critique. *Theory and Society*, *30*(3), 337–361. doi:10.1023/A:1017596718715

Direk, Z. (2009). *Simone de Beauvoir: Abjeksiyon ve Eros Etiği: Cogito Düşünce Dergisi*. Yapı Kredi Yayınları.

Dodds, K. (2014). Shaking and stirring James Bond: Age, gender, and resilience in Skyfall (2012). *The Journal of Popular Film and Television*, *42*(3), 116–130. doi:10.1080/01956051.2013.858026

Doğan, A. E. (2006). Mekân Üretimi Ve Gündelik Hayatın Birikimi Ve Emek Süreçleriyle İlişkisine Kayseri'den Bakmak, Praksis. *Cilt*, *16*, 91–122.

Dökmen, Z. (2004). *Toplumsal Cinsiyet*. İstanbul, Turkey: Sistem Yayıncılık.

Dolu, Ş. (1993). *Medya ve Tüketim Çılgınlığı*. İstanbul, Turkey: Düşünen Adam Yayınları.

Donaldson, M. (1993). What is hegemonic masculinity? *Theory and Society, 22*(5), 643–657. doi:10.1007/BF00993540

Done, C. (2009). *Transmedia Practice: Theorising the Practice of Expressing a Fictional World across Distinct Media and Environments* (Doctoral dissertation). School of Letters, Art and Media Department of Media and Communications Digital Cultures Program, University of Sydney, Australia.

Dönmez-Colin, G. (2006). *Kadın, İslam Ve Sinema*. İstanbul, Turkey: Agorakitaplığı yayınları. Retrieved from http://www.sanatduvari.com http://www.2014hit.blogspot.com

Donnar, G. (2016). Narratives of cultural and professional redundancy: Ageing action stardom and the 'geri-action' film. *Communication, Politics & Culture, 49*(1), 1.

Donovan, J. (1997). *Feminist Teori*. İstanbul, Turkey: İletişim Yayınları.

Douglas, C. A. (1995). *Sevgi ve Politika: Radikal Feminist ve Lezbiyen Teoriler*. İstanbul, Turkey: Kavram.

Doyle, J. A. (1989). *The male experience* (2nd ed.). New York, NY: McGraw-Hill

Dumanlı, D. (2011). Reklamlarda Toplumsal Cinsiyet Kavramı ve Kadın İmgesinin Kullanımı; Bir İçerik Analizi. *Yalova Üniversitesi Sosyal Bilimler Dergisi, 1*(2), 132–149.

Durakbaşa, A. (1998b) Cumhuriyet döneminde modern kadın ve erkek kimliklerinin oluşumu: Kemalist kadın kimliği ve 'münevver erkekler'. In A. B. Hacımirzaoğlu (Ed.), 75 Yılda kadınlar ve erkekler, "Bilanço 98" kitap dizisi (pp. 29–51). İstanbul, Turkey: Türkiye Ekonomik ve Toplumsal Tarih Vakfı.

Durakbaşa, A. (1998a). Kemalism as identity politics in Turkey. In Z. F. Arat (Ed.), *Deconstructing images of Turkish woman* (pp. 139–156). New York, NY: St. Martin's Press.

Durakbaşa, A. (2011). Türk modernleşmesinin kamusal alanı ve "kadın yurttaş". In S. Sancar (Ed.), *Birkaç arpa boyu… 21. yüzyıla girerken Türkiye'de feminist çalışmalar* (pp. 461–475). İstanbul, Turkey: Koç Üniversitesi Yayınları.

Durakbaşa, A., & İlyasoglu, A. (2001). Formation of gender identities in republican Turkey and Women's narratives as transmitters of 'herstory' of modernization. *Journal of Social History, 35*(1), 195–203. doi:10.1353/jsh.2001.0082 PMID:17600966

Dural, A. B., & Yas, S. (2007). Göç eden nüfusta grup içi tabakalaşma ve siyasetin yeniden şekillenmesi. *Akademik Fener*, 22-31.

Durkin, J. D. (2016). *Mediaite Interview: The Guy Who Was Nearly Arrested After Giving Ted Cruz That Lightsaber*. Retrieved from https://www.mediaite.com/online/mediaite-interview-the-guy-who-was-nearly-arrested-after-giving-ted-cruz-that-lightsaber/

Compilation of References

Eagleton, M. (2013). *Feminist Literary Critism.* New York, NY: Routledge.

Eagleton, T. (2012). *Tatlı Şiddet: Trajik Kavramı* (K. Tunca, Trans.). İstanbul, Turkey: Ayrıntı.

Ecevit, Y. (2003). Toplumsal Cinsiyetle Yoksulluk İlişkisi Nasıl Kurulabilir? Bu İlişki Nasıl Çalışılabilir? [How to Establish a Relationship between Gender and Poverty? How to Work on Such a Relationship?]. *C.Ü. Tıp Fakültesi Dergisi, 25*(4), 83-88.

Engels, F. (1990). *Ailenin Özel Mülkiyetin ve Devletin Kökeni*, K. Somer (Trans.). Ankara, Turkey: Sol.

Enriquez, E. (2004). *Sürüden Devlete* (N. Tutal, Trans.). İstanbul, Turkey: Ayrıntı.

Erigha, M. (2015). Race, Gender, Hollywood: Representation in Cultural Production and Digital Media's Potential for Change. *Sociology Compass, 9*(1), 78–89. doi:10.1111oc4.12237

Erken, J. (2018). Feminist Teori Işığında Muğla Masallarında Kadın Algısı. *Sosyal ve Beşeri Bilimler Araştırmaları Dergisi Kadın Çalışmaları Özel Sayısı, 19*(42), 163–186.

Evans, E. (2011). *Transmedia Television: Audiences, New Media, and Daily Life.* New York, NY: Routledge. doi:10.4324/9780203819104

Fay, B. (2001). *Çağdaş Sosyal Bilimler Felsefesi* (İ. Türkmen, Trans.). İstanbul, Turkey: Ayrıntı Yayınevi.

Feasey, R. (2015). Mature masculinity and the ageing action hero. *Groniek, 44*(190).

Feldman, N. S., & Brown, E. (1984). *Male vs. female differences in control strategies: What children learn from Saturday morning television.* Paper presented at the meeting of the Eastern Psychology Association, Baltimore, MD.

Fiske, J. (1999). *Popüler Kültürü Anlamak.* Ankara, Turkey: Ark Yayınları.

Fliche, B. (2005). The Hemşehrilik and the Village: The Stakes of an Association of Former Villagers in Ankara. *European Journal of Turkish Studies, 2.* Retrieved from http://ejts.revues.org/385

Foucault, M. (2006). *Sonsuza Giden Dil, çev. Işık Ergüden.* İstanbul, Turkey: Ayrıntı Yayınları.

Foucault, M. (2013). *Akıl Hastalığı ve Psikoloji* (E. Bayoğlu, Trans.). İstanbul, Turkey: Ayrıntı.

Freeman, M. (2017). From Sequel to Quasi-Novelization: Splinter of the Mind's Eye and the 1970s Culture of Transmedia Contingency. In S. Guynes, & D. Hassler-Forest (Eds.), Star Wars and the History of Transmedia Storytelling. Amsterdam, The Netherlands: Amsterdam University Press.

Freud, S. (1972). *Cinsiyet ve Psikanaliz.* Ankara, Turkey: Varlık.

Funnell, L. (2011). "I know where you keep your gun": Daniel Craig as the Bond–Bond girl hybrid in Casino Royale. *Journal of Popular Culture, 44*(3), 455–472. doi:10.1111/j.1540-5931.2011.00843.x

Gariper, C., & Ve Küçükcoşkun, Y. (2009). *Dionizyak Coşkunun İhtişam ve Sefaleti, Yakup Kadri'nin Nur Baba Romanına Psikanalitik Bir Yaklaşım*. İstanbul, Turkey: Akademik Kitaplar.

Gates, P. (2010). Acting his age? The resurrection of the 80s action heroes and their aging stars. *Quarterly Review of Film and Video*, 27(4), 276–289. doi:10.1080/10509200802371113

Gazetesi, G. (2019). Tarihli haberi. Retrieved from http://www.gunes.com/yasam/talihsiz-kadin-is-yerinde-dayak-yedi-961789

Geraghty, L. (2017). Transmedia Character Building Textual Crossovers in the Star Wars Universe. In S. Guynes, & D. Hassler-Forest (Eds.), Star Wars and the History of Transmedia Storytelling. Amsterdam, The Netherlands: Amsterdam University Press.

Geray, H. (2017). İletişim Alanından Örneklerle Toplumsal Araştırmalarda Nicel ve Nitel Yöntemlere Giriş [Introduction to Quantitative and Qualitative Methods in Social Researches with Examples from the Communication Field]. Ankara, Turkey: Ütopya Yayınevi.

Gezgin, İ. (2007). *Masalların Şifresi*. İstanbul, Turkey: Sel Yayıncılık.

Giddens, A. (2012). *Sociology* (6th ed.). Cambridge, UK: Polity Press.

Giddens, A. (2012). *Sosyoloji, (Prep. Cemal Güzel)*. İstanbul, Turkey: Kırmızı Yayınevi.

Gledhill, C. (1978). Recent Developments in Feminist Criticism. *Quarterly Review of Film Studies*, 3(4), 457–493. doi:10.1080/10509207809391419

Göngör, N. (2006). Göç Olgusu ve Arabesk. Aralık Uluslararası Göç Sempozyumu, Sistem Matbaacılık, İstanbul.

Gray, J., & Johnson, D. (2013) Introduction: The Problem of Media Authorship. In J. Gray, & D. Johnson (Eds.), A Companion to Media Authorship. Malden, MA: Wiley-Blackwell.

Gümüş, A. (2006). *Şiddet Türleri. Toplumsal Bir Sorun Olarak Şiddet Sempozyumu*. Ankara, Turkey: Eğitim-Sen.

Günaydın, B. (2011). *Çocuklara Yönelik Programlarda Toplumsal Cinsiyet Rollerinin Sunumu: TRT Çocuk ve Yumurcak TV* [Presentation of Gender Roles in Children's Programs]. Ankara, Turkey: Radyo ve Televizyon Üst Kurulu Uzmanlık Tezi.

Güneş. (2019). *Unfortunate Woman Beaten at Work*. Retrieved from http://www.gunes.com/yasam/talihsiz-kadin-is-yerinde-dayak-yedi-961789

Günindi Ersöz, A. (2016). *Toplumsal Cinsiyet Sosyolojisi*. Ankara, Turkey: Anı Yayınevi.

Gürel, E., & Tığlı, Ö. (2014). New World Created by Social Media: Transmedia Storytelling. *Journal of Media Critiques, 1*, 35-66.

Gürel, E., & Alem, J. (2010). Postmodern Bir Durum Komedisi Üzerine İçerik Analizi: Simpsonlar [Content Analysis on a Postmodern Sit-com: Simpsons]. *Uluslararası Sosyal Araştırmalar Dergisi*, 3(10), 332–347.

Guynes, S. (2017). Publishing the New Jedi Order Media Industries Collaboration and the Franchise Novel. In S. Guynes, & D. Hassler-Forest (Eds.), Star Wars and the History of Transmedia Storytelling. Amsterdam, The Netherlands: Amsterdam University Press.

Güzel, N. S. (2007). *Edebi Metin Çözümlemelerinde Dilbilim-Biçembilim-Kuram*. Manisa: Kendi yayını.

Haber Turk. (2007). *Homosexual Murder in Nisantasi*. Retrieved from https://www.haberturk.com/yasam/haber/38804-nisantasinda-escinsel-cinayeti

Haber Turk. (2019). *The Massage Parlor Raid: 6 Women, 11 Detainees*. Retrieved from https://www.haberturk.com/masaj-salonuna-baskin-6-si-kadin-11-gozalti-2452057#

haberturk.com. (2007). *Tarihli haberi*. Retrieved from https://www.haberturk.com/yasam/haber/38804-nisantasinda-escinsel-cinayeti

Haberturk.com. (n.d.). Retrieved from https://www.haberturk.com/masaj-salonuna-baskin-6-si-kadin-11-gozalti-2452057# Date

Hall, S. (2017). Franchising Empire Parker Brothers, Atari, and the Rise of LucasArts. In S. Guynes, & D. Hassler-Forest (Eds.), Star Wars and the History of Transmedia Storytelling. Amsterdam, The Netherlands: Amsterdam University Press.

Hall, S. (2005). *Kodlama, Kodaçımlama*. Ankara, Turkey: Medya ve İzleyici Bitmeyen Tartışma, Vadi Yayınları.

Hanke, R. (1992). Redesigning Man: Hegemonic Masculinity in Transition. In S. Craig, & S. Publications (Eds.), *Men, Masculinity and the Media*. London, UK. doi:10.4135/9781483326023.n13

Harari, Y. N. (2015). *Hayvanlardan Tanrılara Sapiens: İnsan Türünün Kısa Bir Tarihi* (E. Genç, Trans.). İstanbul, Turkey: Kolektif Kitap.

Harvey, C. B. (2014). A Taxonomy of Transmedia Storytelling. In M.-L. Ryan, & J.-N. Thon (Eds.), Storyworlds across Media Toward a Media-Conscious Narratolog. London, UK: University of Nebraska Press. doi:10.2307/j.ctt1d9nkdg.17

Hayward, S. (2000). *Cinema Studies: The Key Concepts*. London, UK: Routledge.

Haywood, I. (1994). Fathers and sons: Locating the absent mother in 1960s children's television series. *JSTOR*, 6(2), 195–201.

Hekman, J. S. (2016). *Toplumsal Cinsiyet ve Bilgi: Postmodern Bir Feminizmin Öğeleri* (B. Balkız, & Ü. Tatlıcan, Trans.). İstanbul, Turkey: Say Yayınları.

Herrera, B. B., & Dominik, P. K. (2017). How Star Wars Became Museological Transmedia Storytelling in the Exhibition Space. In S. Guynes, & D. Hassler-Forest (Eds.), Star Wars and the History of Transmedia Storytelling. Amsterdam, The Netherlands: Amsterdam University Press.

Hoffmann, B. (2016). *Video Portrays Ted Cruz as Jedi Warrior From 'Star Wars'*. Retrieved from https://www.newsmax.com/headline/video-ted-cruz-jedi-warrior-star-wars/2016/01/04/id/708054/

Holt, D. B., & Thompson, C. J. (2004). Man-of-action heroes: The pursuit of heroic masculinity in everyday consumption. *The Journal of Consumer Research, 31*(2), 425–440. doi:10.1086/422120

Honigmann, J. J. (1982). Sampling in ethnographic fieldwork. In R. G. Burgess (Ed.), *Field research: A sourcebook and field manual* (pp. 79–90). London, UK: Allen &Unwin.

Hooks, B. (2002). *Feminizm Herkes İçindir*. İstanbul, Turkey: Çitlenbik Yayınları.

Horrocks, R. (1994). *Masculinity in Crisis. Myths, Fantasies and Realities* (J. Campling, Ed.). New York, NY: St. Martin's Press. doi:10.1057/9780230372801

Humm, M. (2002). *Feminist Edebiyat Eleştirisi*. İstanbul, Turkey: Sal Yayınları.

Hürriyet Gazetesi. (2003). Retrieved from http://www.hurriyet.com.tr/gundem/muhabirin-is-kazasi-189230

Hürriyet Gazetesi. (2019). *Tarihli haberi*. Retrieved from http://www.hurriyet.com.tr/gundem/otel-odasindaki-sir-cinayet-cozuldu-41171221

Hürriyet News. (n.d.). *Reporter's Work Accident*. Retrieved from http://www.hurriyet.com.tr/gundem/muhabirin-is-kazasi-189230

Hürriyet. (2019). The Female Driver Scattered the Horrors! Retrieved from http://www.hurriyet.com.tr/gundem/kadin-surucu-dehset-sacti-tekme-tokat-saldirdi-41126752

Illıch, I. (1996). Gender, (Çev. Ahmet Fethi). Ankara, Turkey: Ayraç Yayınevi.

Illıch, I. (1996). *Gender* (A. Fethi, Trans.). Ankara, Turkey: Ayraç Yayınları.

İnal, M. A. (1996). *Haberi Okumak*. İstanbul, Turkey: Temuçin Yayınları.

İzmirli Olmak Sempozyum Kitabı. (2009). *İBB Ahmet Pirifltina Kent Arflivi ve Müzesi*. İzmir.

Jeffords, S. (1994). Hard bodies: Hollywood masculinity in the Reagan era. New Brunswick, NJ: Rutgers University Press.

Jenkins, H. (2003). Transmedia Storytelling. *MIT Technology Review*. Retrieved from https://www.technologyreview.com/s/401760/transmedia-storytelling/

Jenkins, H., & Hassler-Forest, D. (2017). Foreword: "I Have a Bad Feeling About This" A Conversation about Star Wars and the History of Transmedia. In S. Guynes & D. Hassler-Forest (Eds.), Star Wars and the History of Transmedia Storytelling. Amsterdam, The Netherlands: Amsterdam University Press.

Jenkins, H. (1992). *Textual Poachers Television Fans & Participatory Culture*. New York, NY: Routledge.

Compilation of References

Jenkins, H. (2006a). *Convergence Culture: Where Old and New Media Collide.* New York, NY: New York University Press.

Jenkins, H. (2006b). *Fans, Bloggers, and Gamers: Exploring Participatory Culture.* New York, NY: New York University Press.

Jenkins, H. (2013). *Textual Poachers: Television Fans and Participatory Culture.* New York, NY: Routledge.

Jenkins, H., Ford, S., & Green, J. (2013). *Spreadable Media: Creating Value and Meaning in a Networked Culture.* New York, NY: New York University Press.

Jensen, K. B. (2005). Sosyal Kaynak Olarak Haberler: Danimarka Televizyon Haberleri Hakkında Nitel Ampirik Bir Çalışma. In *Medya ve İzleyici Bitmeyen Tartışma.* Ankara, Turkey: Vadi Yayınları.

Jermyn, D. (2012). 'Get a life, ladies. Your old one is not coming back': ageing, ageism and the lifespan of female celebrity. *Celebrity Studies, 3*(1), 1-12.

Johnston, C. (2006). *Karşı-sinema olarak kadınların sineması* (Vol. 14). Sinemasal.

Jung, G. C. (2011). *Dört Arketip* (İ. Kırımlı, Trans.). İstanbul, Turkey: Sayfa.

Kabadayı, L. (2013). *Film Eleştirisi: Kuramsal Çerçeve ve Sinemamızdan Örnek Çözümlemeler.* İstanbul, Turkey: Ayrıntı Yayınları.

Kabadayı, L. (2014). *Film Eleştirisi.* İstanbul, Turkey: Ayrıntı Yayınları.

Kağıtçıbaşı, Ç., & Cemalcılar, Z. (2017). *Dünden Bugüne İnsan ve İnsanlar: Sosyal Psikolojiye Giriş [Person and Persons from Past to Today: Introduction to Social Psychology].* Evrim Yayınevi.

Kalaycı, N. (2015). Toplumsal cinsiyet eşitliği açısından bir çizgi film çözümlemesi: PEPEE [An Analysis of a Cartoon in terms of Gender Inequality: PEPEE]. *Eğitim ve Bilim, 40*(177), 243–270.

Kandiyoti, D. (2015). *Cariyeler, Bacılar, Yurttaşlar.* İstanbul, Turkey: Metis.

Kandiyoti, D., & Kandiyoti, D. (1987). Emancipated but unliberated? Reflections on the Turkish case. *Feminist Studies, 13*(2), 317–338. doi:10.2307/3177804

Kaplan, E. A. (2000). *Feminism and Film.* Oxford, UK: Oxford University Press.

Kaplan, E. A. (2001). *Women & Film: Both Sides of the Camera.* London, UK: Routledge Taylor & Francis Group.

Karadoğan, A. (2007). *Yoksul: Zeki Ökten.* Dipnot Yayınları.

Karakuş, G. (2018). *Nazan Bekiroğlu'nun Roman Ve Hikayelerinde Postmodernizm-Büyülü Gerçekçilik, Tasavvuf Ve Psikanalitik, Ordu Üniversitesi, Sosyal Bilimler Enstitüsü.* Ordu, Turkey: Yüksek Lisans Tezi.

Kareithi, P. J. (2014). *Hegemonic masculinity in media contents.* A. Montiel (Ed.).

Karpat, K. (1960). Social themes in contemporary Turkish literature. *The Middle East Journal*, *14*(1), 29–44.

Keller, F. E. (2007). *Toplumsal Cinsiyet ve Bilim Üzerine Düşünceler*. İstanbul, Turkey: Metis Yayınları.

Keloğlu-İşler, E. İ. (2014). Kültürel ekme kuramı bağlamında Türkiye üretimi çizgi filmler ve çocuk bilincinin inşası, İletişim ve Diploması Dergisi [Turkey-Made Cartoons and Creation of Children's Awareness in the context of Cultural Cultivation]. *Journal of Communication and Diplomacy*, *15*(2), 65-78.

KilicS, . (2009). Kamuoyu Oluşum Sürecinde Sosyal Hareketler ve Medya. *Niğde Üniversitesi İİBF Dergisi*, *2*(2), 150–167.

KilincÖ, ., & UztugF, . (2016). Televizyon Dizilerinde Yaşlılığın Temsili. *Sosyoloji Dergisi*, *36*(2), 477–506.

King, N. (2010). Old cops: Occupational aging in a film genre. In *Staging Age* (pp. 57–81). New York, NY: Palgrave Macmillan. doi:10.1057/9780230110052_4

Kırel, S. (2018). *Kültürel Çalışmalar ve Sinema*. İstanbul, Turkey: İthaki Yayınevi.

Kırtıl, G. A. (2003). Feminist Edebiyat Eleştirisi Açısından Sevim Burak. *Kadın Araştırmaları Dergisi*, *0*(8), 127–151.

Klastrup, L., & Tosca, S. (2014). Game of Thrones: Transmedial Worlds, Fandom, and Social Gaming. In M.-L. Ryan, & J.-N. Thon (Eds.), Storyworlds across Media Toward a Media-Conscious Narratolog. London, UK: University of Nebraska Press.

Klastrup, L., & Tosca, S. (2004). Transmedial Worlds— Rethinking Cyberworld Design. In *Proceedings of the 2004 International Conference on Cyberworlds*. Los Alamitos, CA: IEEE Computer Society. 10.1109/CW.2004.67

Korkmaz, R., & Özcan, T. (2007). 1950 sonrası. In T. S. Halman (Ed.), *Türk edebiyatı tarihi 4* (2nd ed., pp. 63–124). Ankara, Turkey: Kültür ve Turizm Bakanlığı Yayınları.

Kottak, C. P. (2001). *Antropoloji*. Ankara, Turkey: Ütopya.

Kozak, M., & Kizilirmak, I. (2006). Turistik Ürün Çeşitlendirmesi Kültür ve Turizm Müdürleri Görüşlerine Dayalı Bölgesel Yaklaşımlar. *Mustafa Kemal Üniversitesi Sosyal Bilimler Enstitüsü Dergisi*, *3*(5), 1–24.

Kuhn, A. (2004). The State of Film and Media Feminism. *Signs: Journal of Women in Culture and Society*, *30*(1).

Kuhn, A. (1994). *Women's Pictures: Feminism and Cinema*. London, UK: Verso Publication.

Kupfer, J. H. (2008). The Seductive and Subversive Meta-Narrative of Unforgiven. *Journal of Film and Video*, *60*(3/4), 103–114. doi:10.1353/jfv.0.0015

Compilation of References

Kurtoğlu, A. (2001). Hemşehrilik ve şehirde siyaset. İletişim Yayınları, İstanbul, Turkey.

Kurtoğlu, A. (2005). Mekansal Bir Olgu Olarak Hemşehrilik ve Bir Hemşehrilik Mekanı Olarak Dernekler. *Social Sciences on Contemporary Turkey*. Retrieved from https://www.researchgate.net/publication/30453637_Mekansal_Bir_Olgu_Olarak_Hemsehrilik_ve_Bir_Hemsehrilik_Mekani_Olarak_Dernekler

Kurtoğlu, A. (2012). Siyasal Örgütler ve Sivil Toplum Örgütleri Bağlamında Hemşehrilik ve Kollamacılık. *Ankara Üniversitesi SBF Dergisi, 67*(1), 141–169. doi:10.1501/SBFder_0000002241

Kuruoğlu, H. (2006). Türkiye'de Televizyon Haber Bültenlerinde Haber Öznesi Olarak Kadın", In D. İmançer (Ed.), *Medya ve Kadın* (pp. 237–271). Ankara, Turkey: Ebabil Yayınevi.

Lakoff, R. (1975). Extract from language and women's place. In D. *Cameron (Ed.), The feminist critique of language: A reader*. London, UK: Routledge.

Lauretis, T. (1984). *Alice Doesn't: Feminism, Semiotics, Cinema*. Bloomington, IN: Indiana University Press. doi:10.1007/978-1-349-17495-9

Leavenworth, M. L. (2014). Transmedial Narration and Fan Fiction: The Storyworld of The Vampire Diaries. In M.-L. Ryan, & J.-N. Thon (Eds.), Storyworlds across Media Toward a Media- Conscious Narratolog. London, UK: University of Nebraska Press.

Lee, J. R. (2017). The Digitizing Force of Decipher's Star Wars Customizable Card Game. In S. Guynes, & D. Hassler-Forest (Eds.), Star Wars and the History of Transmedia Storytelling. Amsterdam, The Netherlands: Amsterdam University Press.

Lefebvre, H. (2014). *Mekanın Üretimi*. İstanbul, Turkey: Sel Yayıncılık.

Lemish, D. (2013). I. Türkiye Çocuk ve Medya Kongresi Bildiriler Kitabı [Papers on the 1st Congress on Children and Media in Turkey]. *Cilt, 2*, 35-47.

Lennard, D. (2014). Too old for this shit?: On ageing tough guys. In *Ageing, Popular Culture and Contemporary Feminism* (pp. 93–107). London, UK: Palgrave Macmillan. doi:10.1057/9781137376534_7

Livingstone, S. (1991). Audience Reception: The Role Of The Viewer in Retelling Romantic Drama. In J. Curran, & M. Gurevitch (Eds.), Mass Media and Society. London, UK: LSE Research Online.

Livingstone, S. (1998). Relationships between media and audiences: Prospects for future audience reception studies. In T. Liebes, & J. Curran (Eds.), *Media, Ritual and Identity: Essays in Honor of Elihu Katz*. London, UK: Routledge.

Lloyd, G. (2015). Erkek Akıl Batı Felsefesinde 'Erkek' ve 'Kadın' [The Man of Reason: "Male" and "Female" in Western Philosophy] (2nd ed.). Istanbul, Turkey: Ayrıntı Yayınları.

Lomax, T. (2017). "Thank the Maker!": George Lucas, Lucasfilm, and the Legends of Transtextual Authorship across the Star Wars Franchise Transmedia: Participatory Culture and Media Convergence. In S. Guynes, & D. Hassler-Forest (Eds.), Star Wars and the History of Transmedia Storytelling. Amsterdam, The Netherlands: Amsterdam University Press.

Loon, N. M. V., Gummuluru, S., Sherwood, D. J., Marentes, R., Hall, C. B., & Dewhurst, S. (2019). Direct Series Analysis of Human Herpesvirus 6 (HHV-6) Series from Infants and Comparison of HHV-6 Series from Mother/Infant Pairs. *Oxford Journals Press,* 1017-1019.

Marshall, G. (1999). *Sosyoloji Sözlüğü.* Ankara, Turkey: Bilim ve Sanat.

Marshall, G. (2005). *Sosyoloji Sözlüğü* (O. Akınhay, & D. Kömürcü, Trans.). Ankara, Turkey: Bilim Sanat Yayınevi.

Marshall, G. (2005). *Sosyoloji Sözlüğü [Dictionary of Sociology].* Ankara, Turkey: Bilim ve Sanat.

Marvin, G. (1989). İspanyol Boğa Güreşinde Şeref, Haysiyet ve Şiddet Sorunu. D. Riches (Ed.), Antropolojik Açıdan Şiddet (D. Hattatoğlu, Trans.). İstanbul, Turkey: Ayrıntı.

Mathieu, N.-C. (1978). Man-culture and woman-nature? *Women's Studies International Quarterly, 1*(1), 55–65. doi:10.1016/S0148-0685(78)90362-7

Mattel offers trade-m for "Teen Talk" Barbie. (1992, Oct. 18). *Raleigh News and Observer.*

McCabe, J. (2004). *Feminist Film Studies: Writing the Woman Into Cinema.* London, UK: WallFlower Publication.

McCauley, C., Thangavelu, K., & Rozin, P. (1988). Sex stereotyping of occupation in relation to television representation and census facts. *Basic and Applied Social Psychology, 9*(3), 197–212. doi:10.120715324834basp0903_3

McNeill, W. H. (2004). *Dünya Tarihi* (A. Şenel, Trans.). Ankara, Turkey: İmge.

Mejeur, C. (2017). Chasing Wild Space Narrative Outsides and World-Building Frontiers in Knights of the Old Republic and The Old Republic. In S. Guynes, & D. Hassler-Forest (Eds.), Star Wars and the History of Transmedia Storytelling. Amsterdam, The Netherlands: Amsterdam University Press.

Merriam, S. B. (2009). *Qualitative research: A guide to design and implementation.* San Francisco, CA: Jossey-Bass.

Messner, M. A. (2007). The masculinity of the governator: Muscle and compassion in American politics. *Gender & Society, 21*(4), 461–480. doi:10.1177/0891243207303166

Michel, A. (1984). Feminizm. Yeni Yüzyıl Kitaplığı, Pres Universitaires De France Yayınları.

Miller, G. (2009). *Tüketimin Evrimi.* İstanbul, Turkey: Alfa Yayınları.

Millett, K. (2018). *Cinsel Politika.* İstanbul, Turkey: Payel Yayınları.

Compilation of References

Millward, A. A. (2011). Urbanisation viewed through a geostatistical lens applied to remote-sensing data. *Area, 43*(1), 53–66.

Mirza, A. (2016). Kenar Mahalleliğin Sinemadaki Yansımaları. *Abant Kültürel Araştırmalar Dergisi, 1*(2), 21–33.

Mittell, J. (2014). Strategies of Storytelling on Transmedia Television. In M.-L. Ryan, & J.-N. Thon (Eds.), Storyworlds across Media Toward a Media- Conscious Narratolog. London, UK: University of Nebraska Press. doi:10.2307/j.ctt1d9nkdg.16

Moran, B. (2002). *Edebiyat Kuramları ve Eleştiri*. İstanbul, Turkey: İletişim yayınları

Morgan, L. H. (1998). *Eski Toplum II* (Ü. Oskay, Trans.). İstanbul, Turkey: Payel.

Morley, D. (2005). *Sarkaçlar ve Tuzaklar*. Ankara, Turkey: Vadi.

Motley, C. (2004). "It's a Hell of a Thing to Kill a Man": Western Manhood in Clint Eastwood's Unforgiven. *Americana: The Journal of American Popular Culture, 3*, 14.

Muhammet, Ö. (2018). "Buralarda yabancı yok": Hemşehri derneklerinin kentlileşme üzerine etkisi, Ankara'daki Oflular örneği. *Türk Coğrafya Dergisi, 70*, 87–98.

Mulvey, L. (1975). Visual pleasure and narrative cinema. In Visual and Other Pleasures (pp. 14-26). London, UK: Macmillan.

Mulvey, L. (2010). Görsel haz ve anlatı sineması. In S. Büker, & Y. Gürhan Topçu (Eds.), Sinema: Tarih Kuram Eleştiri (pp. 211-229). İstanbul, Turkey: Kırmızı Kedi Yayınevi.

Mulvey, L. (1975, Autumn). Visual Pleasure and Narrative Cinema. *Screen, 16*(3), 6–18. doi:10.1093creen/16.3.6

Muñoz, P. (2016). "Transmedia storytelling". *The Branded Content Marketing Association*. Retrieved from http://www.thebcma.info/transmedia-storytelling/

Mutlu, E. (2004). *İletişim Sözlüğü*. Ankara, Turkey: Bilim ve Sanat.

Neale, S. (2005). *Genre and Hollywood*. Routledge. doi:10.4324/9780203980781

Necmettin, Ö., & Yavuz, K. (2008). Organize Suç Örgütlerinin Oluşumunda Hemşehrilik İlişkilerinin Rolü. *Polis Bilimleri Dergisi, 10*(4), 15–42.

Nelmes, J. (1998, Winter). Sinemada cinsiyet ve cinselliğin sunumu. Sinemasal, 71-94.

Nora, P. (2006). *Hafıza Mekanları*. Ankara, Turkey: Dost Kitabevi Yayınları.

NTV. (2018). *Star Wars'ın dünü bugünü*. Retrieved from http://arsiv.ntv.com.tr/news/151333.asp

Oakley, A. (1972). *Sex, Gender and Society*. New York, NY: Pantheon.

Öğüt, H. (2009). *Kadın Filmleri ve Feminist Karşı Sinema: Cogito Düşünce Dergisi*. Yapı Kredi Yayınları.

Ölçer, E. (2003). *Türkiye Masallarında Toplumsal Cinsiyet ve Mekân İlişkisi. Bilkent Üniversitesi Ekonomi ve Sosyal Bilimler Enstitüsü*. Ankara, Turkey: Yüksek Lisans Tezi.

Onaran, A. Ş. (1995). *Türk Sineması II*. İstanbul, Turkey: Kitle.

Onur, B. (2004). Gelişim Psikolojisi: Yetişkinlik, Yaşlılık, Ölüm [Developmental Psychology: Adulthood, Old Age, Death]. Ankara, Turkey: İmge Kitabevi.

Orr, D. (2008). The politics of poetry. *Poetry*, *192*(4), 409–418.

Ortner, S. B. (1972). Is female to male as nature is to culture? *Feminist Studies*, *1*(2), 5–31. doi:10.2307/3177638

Oskay, Ü. (2005). *İletişimin ABC'si*. İstanbul, Turkey: Der Yayınları.

Oxford Advanced Learner's Dictionary. (n.d.). Retrieved from https://www.oxfordlearnersdictionaries.com/definition/english/joke_1?q=joke

Özbay, C. (2013). Türkiye'de Hegemonik Erkekliği Aramak. In C. Özge Özmen (Ed.), Toplumsal Cinsiyet (p. 63). İstanbul, Turkey: Doğu Batı.

Özbay, F. (2014). Türkiye Aile Yapısı Araştırması İleri Analiz Raporu. Ankara: TC Aile ve Sosyal Politikalar Bakanlığı ve İPSOS.

Özdemir, B. G. (2017). Türk Sinemasında Özel Alan Kamusal Alan Karşıtlığında Anlatıda Mekan Ögesinin Kullanımı. IBAD Uluslararası Bilimsel Araştırmalar Dergisi, 108-118.

Özden, Z. (2014). *Film Eleştirisi: Film Eleştirisinde Temel Yaklaşımlar ve Tür Filmi Eleştirisi*. Ankara, Turkey: İmge Kitabevi.

Özgüç, A. (1988). *Türk Sinemasında Cinselliğin Tarihi*. İstanbul, Turkey: Broy Yayınları.

Özgüç, A. (1990). *Türk Sinemasında İlkler*. İstanbul, Turkey: Yılmaz.

Özgür, Ö. (2017). *Yayınlanan Kadın Programlarında Toplumsal Cinsiyet Rollerinin Sunumu*. Uluslararası Hakemli İletişim ve Edebiyat Araştırmaları Dergisi.

Öztürk, A. (2012). Eril Bedenselleşme: Hegemonik Erkek Bedenin İnşası. *Felsefe ve Sosyal Bilimler Dergisi*, *13*, 39–53.

Öztürk, S. R. (2000). *Sinemada Kadın Olmak*. İstanbul, Turkey: Alan Yayıncılık.

Pareles, J. (1990, Oct. 21). The women who talk back in rap. *New York Times*.

Patton, M. Q. (2002). *Qualitative research and evaluation methods* (3rd ed.). Thousand Oaks, CA: Sage.

Peberdy, D. (2011). Aging Men: Viagra, Retiring Boomers and Jack Nicholson. In *Masculinity and Film Performance* (pp. 146–168). London, UK: Palgrave Macmillan. doi:10.1057/9780230308701_6

Compilation of References

Pelin, A. (2018). Yerli Dizilerde Kadın Kimliğinin Temsili Üzerine Bir Örnek; "Yaprak Dökümü" Dizisi. *Erciyes İletişim Dergisi, 5*(4), 447–463. doi:10.17680/erciyesiletisim.371332

Pepper, D. (1996). *Modern Environmentalism: An Introduction.* London, UK: Routledge.

Peterson, T. G., & Mathews, P. (2008). Sanat Tarihinin Feminist Eleştirisi: Sanat Cinsiyet Sanat Tarihi ve Feminist Eleştiri. İstanbul, Turkey: İletişim Yayınları.

Pett, E. (2016). "Stay disconnected": Eventising Star Wars for transmedia audiences. *Participations, 13*(1), 152–169.

Pianka, J. P. (2013). *The Power Of The Force: Race, Gender, And Colonialism In The Star Wars Universe* (Master's thesis). Wesleyan University, Middletown, PA.

Pişkin, G. (2011). *Hızlı ve Dengesiz Değişime Tepki Olarak Sinemada Şiddet: Türkiye Örneği: 1980-2006.* ICANAS Kongresi Bildiri Kitabı.

Pratten, R. (2011). Getting Started in Transmedia Storytelling. *Transmedia Storyteller.* Retrieved from http://www.tstoryteller.com/getting-started-in-transmedia-storytelling

Pryzgoda, J., & Chrisler, J. C. (2000). Definitions of Gender and Sex: The subtleties of meaning. *Sex Roles, 43*(7-8), 553–569. doi:10.1023/A:1007123617636

Purse, L. (2011). *Contemporary action cinema.* Edinburgh, UK: Edinburgh University Press. doi:10.3366/edinburgh/9780748638178.001.0001

Reinharz, S. (1992). *Feminist methods in social research.* Oxford, UK: Oxford University Press.

Riches, D. (1989). Şiddetin Anlamı (D. Hattatoğlu, Trans.). In D. Riches (Ed.), Antropolojik Açıdan Şiddet. İstanbul, Turkey: Ayrıntı.

Romano, Y., & Penbecioğlu, M. (2009). From Poverty in Turns to New Poverty: A Scrutinize to Changing Dynamics of Urban Poverty in Turkey. *Toplum ve Demokrasi, 3*(5), 135-150.

Roos, C. (2012). *Producing Transmedia Stories - A study of producers, interactivity and prosumption* (Unpublished Master's Thesis). Malmö University.

Rose, O. S. (2018). *Toplumsal Cinsiyet Tarihçiliği Nedir?* (F. B. Aydar, Trans.). İstanbul, Turkey: Can Yayınları.

Rougier, C. E. (1989). 'Le Mal Court': Başsız Bir Toplumda Görünen ve Görünmeyen Şiddet: Kamerun'daki Mkakolar (D. Hattatoğlu, Trans.). In D. Riches (Ed.), Antropolojik Açıdan Şiddet. İstanbul, Turkey: Ayrıntı.

Rutledge, P. (2011). *Transmedia Storytelling: Meaning Comes from the Ability to Share, Explore, and Discover.* Retrieved from http://www.pamelarutledge.com/2011/12/03/transmedia-storytelling-meaning-comes-from-the-ability-to-share-explore-and-discover/

Rutledge, P. (2015, March). *The Transmedia Trip: The Psychology of Creating Multi-Platform Narrative Engagement for Transmedia Migration*. Transmedia Storytelling Conference, Hanover, Germany. Retrieved from https://www.psychologytoday.com/sites/default/files/2017-01_-8_rutledge_transmedia_trip_.pdf

Ryan, M.-L. (2014). Story/Worlds/Media: Tuning the Instruments of a Media-Conscious Narratology. In M.-L. Ryan, & J.-N. Thon (Eds.), *Storyworlds across Media Toward a Media-Conscious Narratolog*. London, UK: University of Nebraska Press.

Ryan, M., & Kellner, D. (2010). *Politik Kamera* (E. Özsayar, Trans.). İstanbul, Turkey: Ayrıntı Yayınevi.

Ryan, M., & Kellner, D. (2010). *Politik Kamera: Çağdaş Hollywood Sinemasının İdeolojisi ve Politikası*. İstanbul, Turkey: Ayrıntı Publishing.

Ryan, M.-L. (2013). *Transmedial Storytelling and Transfictionality Poetics Today*, *34*(3), 361–388. doi:10.1215/03335372-2325250

Sabbah, A. F. (1995). *İslam'ın Bilinçaltında Kadın*. İstanbul, Turkey: Ayrıntı Yayınları.

Saktanber, A. (1995). Türkiye'de Medyada Kadın: Serbest, Müsait Kadın veya İyi Eş, Fedakar Anne. In Ş. Tekeli (Ed.), *Kadın Bakış Açısından Kadınlar*. İstanbul, Turkey: İletişim Yayınları.

Saluk, R. G. (2018). Menzel'in Dilinden Billur Köşk Masalları. *Akademi Dil ve Edebiyat Dergisi*, *1*(2), 41–51. doi:10.34083/akaded.410063

Sancar, S. (2009). *Erkeklik: İmkansız İktidar*. İstanbul: Metis Yayınları.

Sanders, M., & Rock, M. (1988). *Waiting for prime time: The women of television news*. Urbana, IL: University of Illinois Press.

Sapir, E. (1921). *Language: An introduction to the study of speech*. New York, NY: Harcourt Brace.

Saran, N. (1984). *Köylerimiz*. İstanbul, Turkey: Edebiyat Fakültesi.

Sarı, A., & Ve Ercan, A. C. (2008). *Masalların Psikanalizi*. Erzurum, Turkey: Salkımsöğüt Yayınları.

Satar, B. (2015). *Popüler Kültür ve Tekrarlanan İmajlar*. İstanbul, Turkey: Kozmos Yayınları.

Saxton, B., & Cole, T. R. (2013). No country for old men: A search for masculinity in later life. *International Journal of Ageing and Later Life*, *7*(2), 97–116. doi:10.3384/ijal.1652-8670.1272a5

Saygılıgil, F. (2013). Feminist film kuramı. In Z. Özarslan (Ed.), *Sinema Kuramları 2: Beyazperdeyi Aydınlatan Kuramlar* (pp. 143–165). İstanbul, Turkey: Su Yayınevi.

Schroeder, K. (2007). *Popüler Feminizm, Türkiye ve Britanya'da Kadın Dergileri*. İstanbul, Turkey: Bağlam Yayınları.

Schwab, S. (1996). A Revolution in Television. In The Information Highway: An Overview. The San Diego, CA: Greenhaven Press.

Compilation of References

Scott, W. J. (2007). *Toplumsal Cinsiyet: Faydalı Bir Tarihsel Analiz Kategorisi* (A. T. Kılıç, Trans.). İstanbul, Turkey: Agora Yayınları.

Sekmen, M. (2017). Masallar ve 'Anlat İstanbul' Filminin Toplumsal Cinsiyet Eleştirisi. *Atatürk Üniversitesi Sosyal Bilimler Enstitüsü Dergisi, 21*(3), 827–845.

Şenel, A. (1996). *Siyasal Düşünceler Tarihi*. Ankara: Bilim ve Sanat.

Şenyapılı, T. (2004). *Barakadan Gecekonduya, Ankara'da Kentsel Mekânın Dönüşümü 1923-1960*. İstanbul, Turkey: İletişim Yayınları.

Serim, Ö. (2007). *Türk Televizyon Tarihi 1952-2006*. İstanbul, Turkey: Epsilon Yayınevi.

Sezer, M. Ö. (2017). *Masallar ve Toplumsal Cinsiyet*. İstanbul, Turkey: Kor Kitap.

Shanin, T. (1989). *Peasant and Peasants Societies*. Middlesex, UK: Penguin Books.

Shelley, P. B. (1840). *Essays, letters from abroad, Translations and fragments*. London, UK: Edward Moxon.

Showalter, E. (1996). Towards a Feminist Poetics. In P. Rice & P. Waugh (Eds.), Modern Literary Theory: A Reader. London, UK: Arnold.

Smelik, A. (2008). *Feminist Sinema ve Film Teorisi ve Ayna Çatladı*. İstanbul, Turkey: Agora Kitaplığı.

Smelik, A. (2008). *Feminist Sinema ve Film Teorisi*. İstanbul, Turkey: Agora Kitaplığı.

Smelik, A. (2008). *Feminist Sinema ve Film Teorisi: Ve Ayna Çatladı* (D. Koç, Trans.). İstanbul, Turkey: Agora Yayınevi.

Smith, P. (2007). *Kültürel Kuram, Selime Güzelsarı*. Ankara, Turkey: Ütopya Yayınları.

Solmuş, T. (2012). *Sinemada Psikoloji: Anormal Davranışlar*. İstanbul, Turkey: Doruk.

Sparks, R. (1996). Masculinity And Heroism In The Hollywood 'blockbuster' The Culture Industry and Contemporary Images of Crime and Law Enforcement. *British Journal of Criminology, 36*(3), 348–360. doi:10.1093/oxfordjournals.bjc.a014099

Spierenburg, P. (2010). *Cinayetin Tarihi: Ortaçağ'dan Günümüze Avrupa'da Bireysel Şiddet* (Y. Yavuz, Trans.). İstanbul, Turkey: İletişim.

Stam, R. (2000). *Film Theory: An Introduction*. Blackwell Publishing.

Stirling, P. (1966). *Turkish Village*. New York, NY: John Wiley & Sons

Storey, J. (2000). *Popüler Kültür Çalışmaları-Kuramlar ve Metotlar*. İstanbul, Turkey: Babil Yayınları.

Stravdires, S. (2010). *Kentsel Heterotopya*. İstanbul, Turkey: Sel Yayıncılık.

Süalp, A. T. Z. (2009). Yabanıl, Dışarlıklı ve Lümpen "Hiçlik" Kutsamaları Seyrelmiş Toplumsallık ve Yükselen Faşizan Hallerin "Post"lar Zamanı. In D. Derman, (Ed.), Türk Film Araştırmalarında Yeni Yönelimler 8: Sinema ve Politika. İstanbul, Turkey: Bağlam.

Suhas, M. (2015). *There's A 'Star Wars' Lightsaber Facebook Filter That You Need In Your Life Right Now*. Retrieved from https://www.bustle.com/articles/129993-theres-a-star-wars-lightsaber-facebook-filter-that-you-need-in-your-life-right-now

Sümer, Z. S. (2009). Tarih İçinde Görünürlükten, Kadınların Tarihine: Amerikan Kadın Romanında Feminist Bilinç Ve Politika. Selçuk Üniversitesi Sosyal Bilimler Enstitüsü (Doktora tezi).

Sweet, E. V. (2013). *Boy Builders and Pink Princesses: Gender, Toys, and Inequality over the Twentieth Century* (Doctoral dissertation). The University of California, Davis, CA.

Tang, S. H., & Hall, V. C. (1995). The overjustification effect: A meta-analysis. *Applied Cognitive Psychology*, *9*(5), 365–404. doi:10.1002/acp.2350090502

Tannen, D. (1990). *You just don't understand: Women and men in conversation*. New York, NY: Ballantine Books.

Taşkaya, M. (2009). *Beden Politikaları ve Reklamda Kadın, 2*. İstanbul, Turkey: Uluslararası Suç ve Ceza Film Festivali.

Tasker, Y. (1993). Masculinity, the body, and the voice in contemporary action cinema. *Screening the male: Exploring masculinities in Hollywood cinema*, 230.

Tepe, F. F. (2017). Turkish mother citizens and their homefront duties: The cold war discourse of the *Türk Kadını* magazine. *Feminist Formations*, *29*(1), 25–52. doi:10.1353/ff.2017.0002

Tepe, F. F., & Bauhn, P. (2017). Two arguments about women's rights in the *Türk Kadını* magazine 1966–1974. *Galatasaray University Journal of Communication*, *27*, 135–152.

Terzi, E., & Koçak, Y. (2014). Hemşehri Dernekleri, Hemşehrilik Bilinci ve Kentlileşme İlişkisi Üzerine Bir Araştırma: İstanbul/Sultangazi'deki Karslı Hemşehri Dernekleri Örneği. *Selçuk Üniversitesi Sosyal Bilimler Enstitüsü Dergisi*, *32*, 137–150.

Texier, C. (1990, April 22). Have women surrendered in MTV's battle of the sexes? *New York Times*.

tgc.org. (2019). Retrieved from https://www.tgc.org.tr/bildirgeler/t%C3%BCrkiye-gazetecilik-hak-ve-sorumluluk-bildirgesi.html

Thon, J.-N. (2016). *Transmedial Narratology and Contemporary Media Culture*. University of Nebraska Press.

Tillion, G. (2006). *Harem ve Kuzenler* (Ş. Tekeli, & N. Sirman, Trans.). İstanbul, Turkey: Metis.

Timisi, N. (2011). Sinemaya feminist müdahale: Laura Mulvey'de psikanalitik seyirciden teknolojik seyirciye. In M. İri (Ed.), *Sinema Araştırmaları: Kuramlar, Kavramlar, Yaklaşımlar* (pp. 157–182). İstanbul, Turkey: Derin Yayınları.

Compilation of References

Topçuoğlu, A., & Eroğlu, S. E. (2013). Sosyal Sermayenin Akrabalık Hemşehrilik ve Güven İle İlişkisi: Konya Sanayi İşletmeleri Örneği. *HAK-İŞ Uluslararası Emek ve Toplum Dergisi*, *2*(3), 124–145.

Topçuoğlu, N. M. (1995). *Basında Reklam ve Tüketim Olgusu*. Konya: Vadi Yayınları.

Toprak, B. (1982). Türk kadını ve din. In N. Abadan-Unat (Ed.), *Türk toplumunda kadın* (2nd ed., pp. 361–374). İstanbul, Turkey: Araştırma, Eğitim, Ekin Yayınları.

Toska, Z. (1998). Cumhuriyet'in kadın ideali: Eşiği aşanlar ve aşamayanlar. In A. B. Hacımirzaoğlu (Ed.), 75 yılda kadınlar ve erkekler (pp. 71–88). İstanbul, Turkey: Tarih Vakfı.

Tuik. Gov. (n.d.). *Turkiye Istatistik Kurumu*. Retrieved from http://www.tuik.gov.tr/PreTablo.do?alt_id=1068

tuik.gov. (2019). Retrieved from http://www.tuik.gov.tr/PreTablo.do?alt_id=1068

Tura, S. M. (2016). *Freud'dan Lacan'a Psikanaliz*. İstanbul, Turkey: Kanat Kitap.

Türkeş, A. Ö. (2009). Milli edebiyattan milliyetçi romanlara. In T. Bora & M. Gültekingil (Eds.), *Modern Türkiye'de siyasi düşünce, cilt 4: Milliyetçilik* (pp. 811–829). İstanbul, Turkey: İletişim Yayınları.

Turkey Journalists' Society. (2019). *Turkey Journalists' Rights and Responsibilities Statement*. Retrieved from https://www.tgc.org.tr/bildirgeler/t%C3%BCrkiye-gazetecilik-hak-ve-sorumluluk-bildirgesi.html

Türkoğlu, N. (2007). *İletişim Bilimlerinden Kültürel Çalışmalara Toplumsal İletişim Tanımlar*. İstanbul, Turkey: Kalemus Yayınları.

Ulusay, N. (2011). Yeni Queer Sinema. Fe Journal: Feminist Critique, 3, 1-15.

Uluyağcı, C. (2001). Sinemada Erkek İmgesi: Farklı Sinemalarda Aynı Bakış. *Kurgu Dergisi*, (18), 29-39.

Ünsal, A. (1996). Genişletilmiş Bir Şiddet Tipolojisi. In Ö. Solok (Ed.), Şiddet. Cogito (pp. 6-7). İstanbul, Turkey: Yapı Kredi.

Urbanski, H. (2017). The Kiss Goodnight from a Galaxy Far, Far Away Experiencing Star Wars as a Fan-Scholar on Disney Property. In S. Guynes, & D. Hassler-Forest (Eds.), Star Wars and the History of Transmedia Storytelling. Amsterdam, The Netherlands: Amsterdam University Press.

Urry, J. (1999). *Mekanları Tüketmek*. İstanbul, Turkey: Ayrıntı Yayınları.

Usta, S., & Bilgi, E. (2017). Hemşehrilik Bilinci ve Kent Konseyleri: Karaman İlinde Bir Araştırma. *Süleyman Demirel Üniversitesi Sosyal Bilimler Enstitüsü Dergisi*, *1*(26), 223–252.

Vatandaş, C. (2011). Toplumsal Cinsiyet ve Cinsiyet Rollerinin Algılanışı [Gender and Perceptions of Sex Roles]. *Istanbul Journal of Sociological Studies,* (35), 29-56. Retrieved from http://dergipark.gov.tr/iusoskon/issue/9517/118909

von Stackelberg, P. (2011). *Creating Transmedia Narratives: The Structure and Design of Stories Told Across Multiple Media* (Unpublished Master's Thesis). School of Information Design and Technology, State University of New York Institute of Technology, Utica, NY.

Warren, K. (1994). *Ecological Feminism*. London, UK: Routledge.

Webster, J. W. (2017). Han Leia Shot First: Transmedia Storytelling and the National Public Radio Dramatization of Star Wars. In S. Guynes, & D. Hassler-Forest (Eds.), Star Wars and the History of Transmedia Storytelling. Amsterdam, The Netherlands: Amsterdam University Press.

Weeks, K. (2013). *Feminist Öznelerin Kuruluşu*. İstanbul, Turkey: Otonom Yayıncılık.

Whitham, G., & Pooke, G. (2018). *Çağdaş Sanatı Anlamak*. İstanbul, Turkey: Hayalperest Yayınları.

Wildgen, W., & Heusden, B. (2009). *Metarepresentation, self-organization and art*. New York, NY: Peter Lang.

Wolf, M. J. P. (2017). Adapting the Death Star into LEGO The Case of LEGO Set #10188. In S. Guynes, & D. Hassler-Forest (Eds.), Star Wars and the History of Transmedia Storytelling. Amsterdam, The Netherlands: Amsterdam University Press.

Wolfgang, M., & Ferracuti, F. (2010). *The Subculture of Violence*. Taylor & Francis E-Library.

Wood, H. (2006). The mediated conversational floor: an interactive approach to audience reception analysis. Media, Culture & Society, 29(1), 75–103. doi:10.1177/0163443706072000

Wood, J. C. (2004). *Violance and Crime in Nineteenth-Century England*. Taylor & Francis E-Library. doi:10.4324/9780203391181

Wood, J. T. (1984). *Who cares: Women, cure, and culture*. Carbondale, IL: Southern Illinois University Press.

Woodman, S. (1991). How super are heros? *Health, 40,* 49, 82.

Yağan Güder, S., Ay, A., Saray, F., & Kılıç, İ. (2017). Okul Öncesi Dönem Çocuklarının İzledikleri Çizgi Filmlerin Toplumsal Cinsiyet Kalıp Yargıları Açısından İncelenmesi: Niloya Örneği [An Examination of Cartoons Watched by Preschool Children in terms of Gender Stereotypes: Case of Niloya]. *Eğitimde Nitel Araştırmalar Dergisi, 5*(2).

Yağiz, A., Demirel, A. S., Karabay, D., Yalçin, G., Egemen, M. S., & Utku, Y. (n.d.). *Yerel Medyanın Dijital Teknolojilere Uyumu: Türkiye'deki Yerel Gazetelerin Dijital Medyayı Kullanımı Üzerine Bir İnceleme*. Retrieved from http://www.academia.edu/9728266/Yerel_Medyan%C4%B1n_Dijital_Teknolojilere_Uyumu_T%C3%BCrkiye_deki_Yerel_Gazetelerin_Dijital_Medyay%C4%B1_Kullan%C4%B1m%C4%B1_%C3%9Czerine_Bir_%C4%B0nceleme

Yakın, O. (2009). 1980 Sonrası Yeni Gerçekçilik Örneği Olarak Düttürü Dünya. *Kebikeç,* (27), 331-350.

Yaşartürk, G. (2012). Domestic Space and Violence in Turkish Cinema: My Violence is Because of My Love. *Fe Dergi, 4*(1), 14–27. doi:10.1501/Fe0001_0000000060

Compilation of References

Yavaş, S. (2018). *Oğuz Atay'ın Roman Ve Öykülerinin Psikanalitik Açıdan İncelenmesi, Adıyaman Üniversitesi Sosyal Bilimler Enstitüsü*. Adıyaman: Yüksek Lisans Tezi.

Yildirim, T. (2019). *Secret of the Mystery of the Hotel Room Solved*. Retrieved from http://www.hurriyet.com.tr/gundem/otel-odasindaki-sir-cinayet-cozuldu-41171221

Yılmaz, A. (2007). Reklamlarda Toplumsal Cinsiyet Kavramı: 1960-1990 Yılları Arası Milliyet Gazetesi Reklamlarına Yönelik Bir İçerik Analizi. *Selçuk Üniversitesi İletişim Fakültesi Dergisi*, 4(4). Retrieved from http://www.acikerisim.selcuk.edu.tr

Young, M. I. (2009). *Yaşanan Bedene Karşı Toplumsal Cinsiyet: Toplumsal Yapı ve Öznellik üzerine Düşünceler: Cogito Düşünce Dergisi*. Yapı Kredi Yayınları.

Yüce, K., & Kazan, Ş. (2006). Edebiyat Bilgi ve Teorileri. İstanbul, Turkey: Arı Matbaacılık.

Yücel, Ö., & Melek Baba, Ö. (2017). Relationship between Levels of Student Alienation and Hemsehrilik Attitudes of University Students: A Study on Kırgız-Turkish Manas University Students, Universal. *The Journal of Educational Research*, 5(7), 1182–1191.

Yüksel, E. (2016). Güneşi Gördüm ve Teslimiyet Filmlerinde Trans Kimliklerin Mekânsal Örgütlenmesi ve Sınırlılıkları. *Fe Journal: Feminist Critique*, 8(2), 138-148.

Yüksel, N. A. (1999). Toplumsal Cinsiyet Olgusu ve Türkiye'deki Toplumsal Cinsiyet Kalıplarının Televizyon Dizilerindeki Yansımaları [Concept of Gender and Reflections of Gender on TV Series in Turkey]. Kurgu Dergisi, 16, 67-81.

Yüksel, S. D. (2010). Sinemada Ulusal Kimliğin Pekiştiricisi Olarak Kadınlar. *Selçuk İletişim Dergisi*, 6(3).

Yüksel, E. (2016). Güneşi Gördüm ve Teslimiyet Filmlerinde Trans Kimliklerin Mekânsal Örgütlenmesi ve Sınırlılıkları. *Feminist Eleştiri*, 7(2), 138–148.

Yuval-Davis, N. (2003). *Cinsiyet ve Millet*. İstanbul, Turkey: İletişim Yayınları.

Zihnioğlu, Y. (2009). Kadın kurtuluşu hareketlerinin siyasal ideolojiler boyunca seyri (1908–2008). In T. Bora & M. Gültekingil (Eds.), *Modern Türkiye'de siyasi düşünce, cilt 9: Dönemler ve zihniyetler* (pp. 805–817). İstanbul, Turkey: İletişim Yayınları.

Zografu, L. (n.d.). *Lokantamızda Prens ve Prensesler Daima Taze ve Bol Masal Sosu ile Sunulur*. Kriton Dinçmen, Scala Yayıncılık.

Zürcher, E. J. (2016). *Modernleşen Türkiye'nin tarihi* (33rd ed.). İstanbul, Turkey: İletişim Yayınları.

About the Contributors

Gülşah Sarı works as an Assistant Professor at the Department of Radio Television and Cinema, in Abant Izzet Baysal University, Turkey. She became a PhD in İstanbul University, Department of Radio Television and Cinema in 2016. She held a master degree in Marmara University, Department of Cinema in 2010. Her recent interests include social media, gender and new communication technologies. She has published several papers in journals including advertising, product placement, transmedia and cinema.

* * *

İkbal Bozkurt Avcı graduated from Radio, Television and Cinema Department at Selçuk University, Konya. She had MSc and PhD degrees from at the same department and university. Currently, she is doing MSc at Inonu University, Department of Philosophy. She is a Research Assistant of Radio, Television and Cinema at Firat University, Elazig. Her academic interest in Turkish and World Cinema, cultural studies, sociology, philosophy, cinematic philosophy.

Derya Çetin graduated from and earned a MSc degree at Radio, Television and Cinema Department at Ege University, İzmir. She had a PhD degree at Ankara University, Department of Radio Television and Cinema. She is an Assistant Professor at Bolu Abant İzzet Baysal University, Department of Radio, Television and Cinema. Her academic interests are Turkish and World Cinema, political economy of film industry, cultural studies, and women's studies.

Mevlüde Deveci graduated from Radio, Television and Cinema Department at Ankara University, Ankara. She had a MSc degree from the same department at Ataturk University. Currently, she is working on a Phd at Marmara University, Department of Radio, Television and Cinema. She is a lecturer at the Department of Audio-Visual Technics and Media Production in Fırat University, Elazığ. Her academic interests are in news, new media technologies, communication sciences.

About the Contributors

Pelin Erdal Aytekin continues her academic career as an Assistant Professor Phd at Aydın Adnan Menderes University Communication Faculty, Department of Journalism, and has been publishing at national and international level for about 10 years. After graduating from Social Anthropology, she specialized in cinema theory at postgraduate level. She focuses and maintains her work in the context of the relationship of these two main disciplines in the perspective of media and communication studies.

Gökhan Gültekin was born in Elazığ in 1985. He graduated from Selçuk University, Faculty of Communication, Radio Television and Cinema Department in 2009. He completed his master's degree in July 2012 and PhD degree in December 2017. Gültekin, who is a research assistant at Cumhuriyet University since May 2012, is one of the authors of İletişim Okumaları (Literatürk, 2013), Gözdeki Kıymık (Metis, 2016), Filmin Sonuna Yolculuk (Beta, 2016), Is it Real? Structuring Reality by Means of Signs (Cambridge Scholars, 2016). Gültekin, whose main field of activity is cinema, has various publications on popular cinema, cinema semiotics, crime films, cinema ideology, cinema-aesthetics, cinema-reality and cinema-philosophy.

Özge Gürsoy Atar graduated from Kemal Atatürk High School in 2003. She works as an Assistant Professor at the Department of Cinema and Television in Beykent University. She completed a Ph.D. at İstanbul University in April 2016. She held a master degree in Marmara University, Department of Radio, Television and Cinema in 2011. Between 2011 and 2015 she worked as internet television planning specialist at the Digiturk. Her research concerns Television, Media Study, New Communication Technologies, New Media, New Television, IPTV, OTT, Media Planning, Digital Culture, Communication İn Digital Culture. She has published several papers in television and new media.

Şebnem Gürsoy Ulusoy graduated from Istanbul University Faculty of Literature, Information and Document Management (2005). She received her MA degree in Marketing Communication and Public Relations from Bahcesehir University (2007) and her PhD degree in Media Studies from Yeditepe University (2016). She started to work at İstanbul Gelişim University in 2017 (She worked as a training coordinator at İstek Foundation, Acıce Schools). She is still working at the School of Applied Sciences in İstanbul Gelişim University. Her main fields of study are interpersonal communication, academic communication, communication disorders and communication limitations.

About the Contributors

Özgür İpek was born on Sept. 8, 1986 in North Cyprus. He works as an Assistant Professor at the Department of Radio Television and Cinema, in Sivas Cumhuriyet Üniversity, Turkey. Özgür İpek became a Ph.D. in İstanbul University, Department of Radio Television and Cinema in 2016. He also held a master degree in Istanbul University, Department of Radio Television and Cinema in 2012. He has published several papers in journals and books including politic cinema, cinema philosophy, Cinema of Iran and subaltern characters in movies.

Arzu Karasaç Gezen graduated from Gazi University Faculty of Communication, Department of Public Relations and Publicity. She received her master's degree from Ankara University, Health Sciences Institute, Health Management Department. In 2013 "Restructuring of Health Services in Turkey presentation in the newspapers of the Health Transformation Perspective Program" on doctoral thesis at Ankara University Institute of Social Sciences graduated from the Public Relations and Publicity Department. He is currently a faculty member at Abant İzzet Baysal University in Bolu. His research interests include health communication, children and media, and organizational communication.

Kelvin Ke Jinde is lecturer in film and media education. He previously taught at Singapore Institute of Technology, Nanyang Academy of Fine Arts, and Lasalle College of the Arts. He is also an independent video artist and filmmaker.

Berceste Gülçin Özdemir completed a Ph.D. at İstanbul University in December 2016. Her research concerns feminist film theory, psychoanalytical film theory, Turkish cinema, independent cinema, digital cinema and characters' representation in film narratives. She is a Dr. Visiting Lecturer at İstanbul University, instructing about television and cinema lessons.

Tansif Rehman has a PhD in European Studies. He has also completed six different Masters in the respective field of Social Sciences, i.e., MA (Economics), MA (International Relations), MA (Philosophy), MA (Political Sc.), MA (Sociology), M.Sc. (Gender & Women Studies). He has also completed 56 Certification/Credit Courses, 11 Miscellaneous Diplomas, eight Government of Pakistan Trainings, four Certification Courses and Diploma (Languages) - Deutsch, English, Italian, and Russian. He is a Commissioned Class-1 Gazetted Officer, currently appointed as the Head of Sociology Department at a respective government institute in Karachi (Pakistan). He is also working on various projects along with working as a Teaching Associate at the Department of Criminology (University of Karachi). He has several publications and more than 18 years of teaching experience, as well as 12 years of research experience.

About the Contributors

Rengim Sine Nazlı, Bolu Abant Izzet Baysal University, Faculty of Communication, Department of Journalism Assistant Prof. Dr. Faculty Member. She is working on new media, critical media theories and journalistic studies.

Fatma Fulya Tepe is an assistant professor at the Faculty of Education, Istanbul Aydın University, Turkey. She graduated with Magna Cum Laude from the Department of American Culture and Literature at Istanbul University. Her Ph.D. is from the Sociology Department of that same university. In her Ph.D. thesis, she studied the division of labour in the domestic life of Istanbul female academics working within the fields of basic sciences and engineering. Dr. Tepe has also published articles relating to gender studies, oral history, and hybridity. In a research project, financed by the Scientific and Technological Research Council of Turkey (Tübitak), she has analysed the discourse of the Türk Kadını magazine (published between 1966 and 1974) from the point of view of state feminism. In 2018, her research was published as a book with the title Milliyetçi Devlet Feminizmi Söylemi Türk Kadını Dergisi (1966–1974) Örneği (Ankara: Gece Kitaplığı). In 2017, her article "Turkish Mother Citizens and Their Homefront Duties", based on the same research, was published in the journal Feminist Formations.

Işıl Tombul graduated Ege University Communication Faculty Radio Television and Cinema Department in 2003. She completed master's degree at Ege University Social Sciences Institute in 2006 and completed PhD. at Ege University Social Sciences Institute in 2011. The author studies on discourse, gender, cinema, digital media.

Dilek Ulusal graduated from Gazi University Communication Faculty Journalism Department in 2003. She graduated from Erciyes University Journalism Department in 2007 with a master degree. She graduated from Gazi University as PhD degree in 2018. She studies on cinema, television, communication studies.

Index

A

action cinema 178-180, 182-184, 186, 190-192
aging action hero 178-179, 181, 184-189, 191-192
Anatolian field 77-78, 86
Anatolian Women 35-39, 41, 44-47, 51, 53-54, 58
archetype 180-184, 188-190, 192, 195

B

biological sex 16, 92-93, 177, 247, 277

C

classical narrative cinema 228, 230, 237-238, 242-243, 247, 298
communication language 68
Communication Research 33
consumption culture 121, 123-126, 130, 136, 139
culture industry 124-126, 139

D

Dutturu Dunya 260-262, 264-265

F

family communication 59-60, 69-70, 75
fandom 197-198, 203, 205-209, 217
female characters 59-60, 67, 86, 90, 92, 96-97, 100-102, 104, 106, 109-113, 115-116, 172, 197, 208-209, 228-230, 235, 237-244, 247-249, 251, 253-257, 282, 302, 305
femininity 2, 5, 7, 11, 16, 18, 39, 44, 67, 91-93, 95, 116, 217-218, 231-232, 239-241, 243, 248-249, 253, 270, 283, 286
feminism 16-21, 33, 48-49, 78, 208-209, 230, 233-235, 240-241, 250, 281, 295, 298, 301
feminist film theory 241, 248-249, 252, 259, 295-297, 301, 303
fetishism 11-12, 16, 295, 300
film analysis 235

G

Gender Bias 155
gender equality 92, 96-97, 99, 109, 115, 117, 120, 208
gender inequality 13, 91, 120, 179
gender representation 2-3, 13, 17, 19, 95, 140-141, 155, 291
gender roles 2-3, 5, 7, 9, 13, 17, 48, 81, 90-91, 95-96, 101, 104, 109, 111, 114, 116-117, 142, 155, 249-250, 252, 260-261, 274, 276, 278, 281
glass ceiling 5

Index

H

Hardbody Film 181, 195
hegemonic masculinity 178, 180, 190, 192, 196, 220-221, 225, 285-286
heroic masculinity 178-179, 191, 196
heroism 35, 39, 41-44, 50-54, 178, 181, 184-186, 189-191, 198
honky tonk 260-269, 272-274

I

ideology 13, 18-19, 40, 51, 54, 61, 77, 79-80, 82, 123, 127-130, 140, 151, 155, 196, 236-237, 242, 248-251, 253, 256, 292, 295-296
Interpretive Social Science Approach 294
Iranian Cinema 248-249, 253-254, 256-257
Iranian society 248, 255-256
Istanbul Ladies (women) 38-39, 51-52, 58

M

main stream cinema 259
masculinity 2, 7, 11, 16, 18, 44, 91-93, 95, 143, 157-158, 160, 162-173, 176, 178-181, 183-185, 187, 190-192, 196, 198, 205, 217-218, 220-221, 223-225, 231-233, 238-239, 248-249, 253, 285-286
Mass culture 31, 127, 139
Maternity Representations 59, 73, 75
mythology (myth) 95, 100, 183, 195, 203-204, 259, 266

N

narration 197, 201, 217, 249, 253, 255
narrative structure 211, 243, 247, 299-301, 305
nationalist poetry 43, 51, 53-54, 58
New Queer cinema 222
New Realistic Cinema 259
New Wave Cinema 259

P

political poetry 36, 52, 58
political weapon 297-298
Prejudice 155
private sphere 21, 60, 228-231, 235-237
public sphere 32, 43, 48, 225, 228-233, 235-240, 243, 283

Q

queer cinema 222-223
Queer Theory 227

R

Republican Women 39, 58

S

Semiotic Film Theory 259
sex roles 3, 91, 94, 96, 113, 120
Sexual Discrimination 120
sexuality 142, 177, 217, 219, 227, 232, 235, 247, 251-252, 279, 282-283, 290
SMS 140-141, 145, 151-152, 155
social gender 2, 17-19, 228-243, 247
social identity 67, 76, 125
social media 59, 63-66, 68, 70, 72-73, 76, 123, 130, 205
Star Wars 197-198, 201-210, 217
stereotypes 10, 30, 90-91, 94, 96, 114, 120, 140-145, 151, 155, 231-232, 251, 281, 292, 296-297
subjectivity 12, 230-231, 233-235, 238-243, 247, 249, 295, 297, 301
Susuz Yaz 275-277, 281-282, 287-290, 292, 294

T

Tanıl Bora 38
transgender 12, 16, 206, 227
Transmedia 197-205, 208-209, 211, 217

337

trope 182, 196
Türk Kadını 35-36, 39-41, 53
Turkish cinema 12, 157, 160-164, 167, 171-173, 218, 223-226, 229, 231, 236, 243, 260, 262, 265, 276, 282, 284, 292
Turkish women 18, 35-39, 41, 44, 47, 50, 52, 54, 66
TV series 5, 9, 59-60, 68, 72, 76, 162

U

urban culture 59, 64, 76, 261

V

Visual Pleasure 12, 252, 290, 297-298, 300-301

W

Westernization 37, 58
White Savior Narrative 196
Woman Programs 34
women's roles 12, 59, 76, 247

Y

Yılanların Öcü 161, 275-276, 281-282, 286-287, 289-292, 294

Z

Zeki Ökten 260, 262, 264
Zenne 224-227

Purchase Print, E-Book, or Print + E-Book

IGI Global's reference books can now be purchased from three unique pricing formats:
Print Only, E-Book Only, or Print + E-Book.
Shipping fees may apply.
www.igi-global.com

Recommended Reference Books

ISBN: 978-1-5225-1955-3
© 2017; 397 pp.
List Price: $205

ISBN: 978-1-5225-8217-5
© 2019; 102 pp.
List Price: $135

ISBN: 978-1-5225-8163-5
© 2019; 393 pp.
List Price: $185

ISBN: 978-1-5225-6061-6
© 2019; 396 pp.
List Price: $265

ISBN: 978-1-5225-7195-7
© 2019; 310 pp.
List Price: $195

ISBN: 978-1-5225-8194-9
© 2019; 328 pp.
List Price: $145

Looking for free content, product updates, news, and special offers?
Join IGI Global's mailing list today and start enjoying exclusive perks sent only to IGI Global members.
Add your name to the list at **www.igi-global.com/newsletters**.

Publisher of Peer-Reviewed, Timely, and Innovative Academic Research

IGI Global
DISSEMINATOR OF KNOWLEDGE

www.igi-global.com   Sign up at www.igi-global.com/newsletters   facebook.com/igiglobal   twitter.com/igiglobal

Ensure Quality Research is Introduced to the Academic Community

Become an IGI Global Reviewer for Authored Book Projects

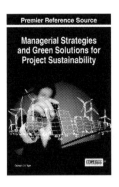

The overall success of an authored book project is dependent on quality and timely reviews.

In this competitive age of scholarly publishing, constructive and timely feedback significantly expedites the turnaround time of manuscripts from submission to acceptance, allowing the publication and discovery of forward-thinking research at a much more expeditious rate. Several IGI Global authored book projects are currently seeking highly-qualified experts in the field to fill vacancies on their respective editorial review boards:

Applications and Inquiries may be sent to:
development@igi-global.com

Applicants must have a doctorate (or an equivalent degree) as well as publishing and reviewing experience. Reviewers are asked to complete the open-ended evaluation questions with as much detail as possible in a timely, collegial, and constructive manner. All reviewers' tenures run for one-year terms on the editorial review boards and are expected to complete at least three reviews per term. Upon successful completion of this term, reviewers can be considered for an additional term.

If you have a colleague that may be interested in this opportunity, we encourage you to share this information with them.

www.igi-global.com

IGI Global Proudly Partners with

eContent Pro International® Publication Services
*Committed to Excellent Service, Affordability, and the Highest Quality
From Manuscript Development to Publication*

Publication Services Provided by eContent Pro International:

Scientific & Scholarly Editing

English Language Copy Editing

Journal Recommendation

Typesetting & Publishing

Figure, Table, Chart & Equation Conversions

Translation

IGI Global Authors Save 25% on eContent Pro International's Services!

Scan the QR Code to Receive Your 25% Discount

The 25% discount is applied directly to your eContent Pro International shopping cart when placing an order through IGI Global's referral link. Use the QR code to access this referral link. eContent Pro International has the right to end or modify any promotion at any time.

Email: customerservice@econtentpro.com

econtentpro.com

www.igi-global.com

Celebrating Over 30 Years of Scholarly Knowledge Creation & Dissemination

InfoSci®-Books

A Database of Over 5,300+ Reference Books Containing Over 100,000+ Chapters Focusing on Emerging Research

GAIN ACCESS TO **THOUSANDS** OF REFERENCE BOOKS AT **A FRACTION** OF THEIR INDIVIDUAL LIST **PRICE**.

InfoSci®-Books Database

The **InfoSci®Books** database is a collection of over 5,300+ IGI Global single and multi-volume reference books, handbooks of research, and encyclopedias, encompassing groundbreaking research from prominent experts worldwide that span over 350+ topics in 11 core subject areas including business, computer science, education, science and engineering, social sciences and more.

Open Access Fee Waiver (Offset Model) Initiative

For any library that invests in IGI Global's InfoSci-Journals and/or InfoSci-Books databases, IGI Global will match the library's investment with a fund of equal value to go toward **subsidizing the OA article processing charges (APCs) for their students, faculty, and staff** at that institution when their work is submitted and accepted under OA into an IGI Global journal.*

INFOSCI® PLATFORM FEATURES

- No DRM
- No Set-Up or Maintenance Fees
- A Guarantee of No More Than a 5% Annual Increase
- Full-Text HTML and PDF Viewing Options
- Downloadable MARC Records
- Unlimited Simultaneous Access
- COUNTER 5 Compliant Reports
- Formatted Citations With Ability to Export to RefWorks and EasyBib
- No Embargo of Content (Research is Available Months in Advance of the Print Release)

*The fund will be offered on an annual basis and expire at the end of the subscription period. The fund would renew as the subscription is renewed for each year thereafter. The open access fees will be waived after the student, faculty, or staff's paper has been vetted and accepted into an IGI Global journal and the fund can only be used toward publishing OA in an IGI Global journal. Libraries in developing countries will have the match on their investment doubled.

To Learn More or To Purchase This Database:
www.igi-global.com/infosci-books
eresources@igi-global.com • Toll Free: 1-866-342-6657 ext. 100 • Phone: 717-533-8845 x100

www.igi-global.com

Publisher of Peer-Reviewed, Timely, and
Innovative Academic Research Since 1988

IGI Global's Transformative Open Access (OA) Model:
How to Turn Your University Library's Database Acquisitions Into a Source of OA Funding

In response to the OA movement and well in advance of Plan S, IGI Global, early last year, unveiled their OA Fee Waiver (Offset Model) Initiative.

Under this initiative, librarians who invest in IGI Global's InfoSci-Books (5,300+ reference books) and/or InfoSci-Journals (185+ scholarly journals) databases will be able to subsidize their patron's OA article processing charges (APC) when their work is submitted and accepted (after the peer review process) into an IGI Global journal.*

How Does it Work?

1. When a library subscribes or perpetually purchases IGI Global's InfoSci-Databases including InfoSci-Books (5,300+ e-books), InfoSci-Journals (185+ e-journals), and/or their discipline/subject-focused subsets, IGI Global will match the library's investment with a fund of equal value to go toward subsidizing the OA article processing charges (APCs) for their patrons.

    Researchers: Be sure to recommend the InfoSci-Books and InfoSci-Journals to take advantage of this initiative.

2. When a student, faculty, or staff member submits a paper and it is accepted (following the peer review) into one of IGI Global's 185+ scholarly journals, the author will have the option to have their paper published under a traditional publishing model or as OA.

3. When the author chooses to have their paper published under OA, IGI Global will notify them of the OA Fee Waiver (Offset Model) Initiative. If the author decides they would like to take advantage of this initiative, IGI Global will deduct the US$ 1,500 APC from the created fund.

4. This fund will be offered on an annual basis and will renew as the subscription is renewed for each year thereafter. IGI Global will manage the fund and award the APC waivers unless the librarian has a preference as to how the funds should be managed.

Hear From the Experts on This Initiative:

"I'm very happy to have been able to make one of my recent research contributions, 'Visualizing the Social Media Conversations of a National Information Technology Professional Association' featured in the *International Journal of Human Capital and Information Technology Professionals*, freely available along with having access to the valuable resources found within IGI Global's InfoSci-Journals database."

– **Prof. Stuart Palmer**,
Deakin University, Australia

For More Information, Visit: www.igi-global.com/publish/contributor-resources/open-access or contact IGI Global's Database Team at eresources@igi-global.com

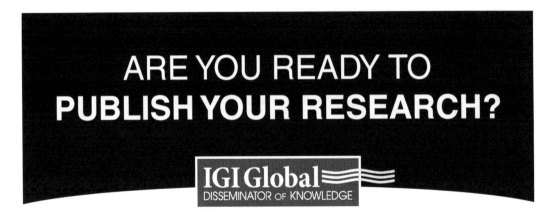

ARE YOU READY TO PUBLISH YOUR RESEARCH?

IGI Global offers book authorship and editorship opportunities across 11 subject areas, including business, computer science, education, science and engineering, social sciences, and more!

Benefits of Publishing with IGI Global:

- Free, one-on-one editorial and promotional support.
- Expedited publishing timelines that can take your book from start to finish in less than one (1) year.
- Choose from a variety of formats including: Edited and Authored References, Handbooks of Research, Encyclopedias, and Research Insights.
- Utilize IGI Global's eEditorial Discovery® submission system in support of conducting the submission and blind review process.

- IGI Global maintains a strict adherence to ethical practices due in part to our full membership with the Committee on Publication Ethics (COPE).
- Indexing potential in prestigious indices such as Scopus®, Web of Science™, PsycINFO®, and ERIC – Education Resources Information Center.
- Ability to connect your ORCID iD to your IGI Global publications.
- Earn royalties on your publication as well as receive complimentary copies and exclusive discounts.

Get Started Today by Contacting the Acquisitions Department at:
acquisition@igi-global.com

InfoSci-OnDemand

Continuously updated with new material on a weekly basis, InfoSci®-OnDemand offers the ability to search through thousands of quality full-text research papers. Users can narrow each search by identifying key topic areas of interest, then display a complete listing of relevant papers, and purchase materials specific to their research needs.

Comprehensive Service
- Over 125,000+ journal articles, book chapters, and case studies.
- All content is downloadable in PDF and HTML format and can be stored locally for future use.

No Subscription Fees
- One time fee of $37.50 per PDF download.

Instant Access
- Receive a download link immediately after order completion!

"It really provides an excellent entry into the research literature of the field. It presents a manageable number of highly relevant sources on topics of interest to a wide range of researchers. The sources are scholarly, but also accessible to 'practitioners'."

– Lisa Stimatz, MLS, University of North Carolina at Chapel Hill, USA

"It is an excellent and well designed database which will facilitate research, publication, and teaching. It is a very useful tool to have."

– George Ditsa, PhD, University of Wollongong, Australia

"I have accessed the database and find it to be a valuable tool to the IT/IS community. I found valuable articles meeting my search criteria 95% of the time."

– Prof. Lynda Louis, Xavier University of Louisiana, USA

Recommended for use by researchers who wish to immediately download PDFs of individual chapters or articles.
www.igi-global.com/e-resources/infosci-ondemand

Printed in the United States
By Bookmasters